Sources Of American Spirituality

Sisters of Mercy

SPIRITUALITY IN AMERICA 1843–1900

Edited by Kathleen Healy, R.S.M.

PAULIST PRESS
New York ◊ Mahwah, N.J.

Library of Congress Cataloging-in-Publication Data

Sisters of Mercy: spirituality in America, 1843–1900/edited by
  Kathleen Healy.
      p.   cm.—(Sources of American spirituality)
    Includes bibliographical references and index.
    ISBN 0-8091-0453-9 (hard)
    1. Sisters of Mercy—United States—History.   2. United States—
  Church history.   I. Healy, Kathleen.   II. Series.
  BX4483.U6S57   1992
  271′.92073—dc20   91-42119
                                                              CIP

Published by Paulist Press
997 Macarthur Boulevard
Mahwah, N.J. 07430

Printed and bound in the United States of America

CONTENTS

The Sister of Mercy

Her face hath caught his shining,
Up in the heights, all in the morning grey.
Beneath her wimple, white as hawthorn in May,
Her clear eyes hold the radiance of the tryst.
How could it be aught else? She visions Christ,
And all her love is twining
Around his crimson wounds and riven heart:
Hers, pierced too, in pity of his smart—
See, on her ebony cross no figure lies—
She is the victim there, in mystic guise!
And not far, enclosure shadowing—
In silent courts where earth had never sway.
Her cloister is the alley of the poor,
She bears a banner
Through a sin-tossed world:
Mercy—God's sweetest attribute—unfurled.

Portland, Oregon
Author Unknown

SERIES INTRODUCTION

The issue of women's role in society is one that has captured the attention of our generation. That attention has extended to the study of our religious lives in the past. Certainly no story of religion in America is complete without reference to the sensibilities and perceptions of women.

What is true of the nation's history as a whole is all the more true of the story of U.S. Catholics during the nineteenth century. It is true largely because of the role that the Sisters of Mercy and their counterparts played. Their presence was felt not only in the schools and hospitals, the shelters and the poorhouses, but also in the everyday life of the Catholics of the time. These women did not live their lives in cloisters. In many cases they were daughters of the very classes of people whom they were serving. They were known to the people and were part of the lives of the young and the infirm. They, more than the theologians sitting in European theologates or Roman curias, helped form the religious sensibilities of those they served. It was they who often first taught children about the sacraments. They who marched them into church to receive those sacraments. They who were there when a loved one died. They who comforted the sick. What was it that they said? What were the ideas that they passed on to thousands whom they helped? How were those ideas shaped by their unique perspectives as women and as Sisters of Mercy?

Those are the questions that we hope to focus on by the presentation of this volume. The answers are to be found in what follows. I can here only add one thought.

It was the Sisters' incarnate presence, their embodying of the ideals of their faith that was a crucial part of their spirituality. That, in one sense, is only indirectly reflected in the texts that we have collected here. These women were not known for their literary skills, although some of them possessed them in abundance. They were not known for the fineness of their learning, although they were in fact very well-educated and prepared for their tasks. It is because of this that we must read their texts as in some sense saying so much more than the narratives themselves relate. The words we have here are symbols of a way of life. Often they are but abbreviations, the full meaning of which can only be learned by looking at the contexts in which they were composed. At times, they are code words as well. What is often not said is as important as what is. The limitations they felt as women, the struggles for legitimacy, the petty hagglings within the communities, the realities of human sinfulness, even among persons so consecrated to unselfish service of others, are all part of these texts. The writers are eloquent in their silence, speaking as it were between the lines of the words gathered here.

The collection in this volume is unique in its breadth and scope. Documents from the whole range of Mercy foundations in the U.S. between 1843 and 1910 are found here. Beyond that we have a variety of genre represented. Convent Annals and historical sketches are offered along with diaries, poetry, letters, reminiscences, and newspaper accounts. The result is in incredibly rich resource waiting to be mined. It is my hope that it will help continue the process of reconstructing the religious landscape of the formative age of U.S. Catholicism.

John Farina

FOREWORD

When John Farina, originator and General Editor of the Paulist Press Series, *Sources of American Spirituality (1850–1900),* suggested that I contribute to the series a collection of spiritual writings of the Sisters of Mercy in the United States during the second half of the nineteenth century, I was delighted to accept. I already had a partial file of Mercy writings, some of which I collected while working on the biography of Frances Warde, published by Seabury Press, New York, in 1973, under the sponsorship of the Federation of Sisters of Mercy of the United States.

Yet I still had many archives to consult in Provinces and Congregations not founded by Frances Warde. Sister Amy Hoey, Executive Director of the Federation of Sisters of Mercy in 1988, when I signed the contract for the present work, *Sisters of Mercy: Spirituality in America (1843–1900),* was most cooperative in helping me. She secured the sponsorship of all the members of the Federation, and continued her own support as well as that of all the members of the Transition Administrative Group of the Sisters of Mercy, 1989–1991.

Sister Doris Gottemoeller, now president of the Institute of Sisters of Mercy of the Americas, established in July, 1991, has warmly welcomed continued sponsorship of my book.

My aim in collecting and editing the present anthology of spiritual writings of Sisters of Mercy in America (1843–1900) was to select those writings which I judged to best represent the spirituality of the Mercy Sisters of that period. Of course I should have liked to include many more writings. But publishing companies have demands concerning numbers of pages! I hope that all Sisters of Mercy as well as others will be happy to read the writings which I believe to represent so beautifully the spirituality of our Sisters from the time of their arrival in the United States until about 1900.

The writings printed in the following collection of documents typify the spirituality of the Sisters of Mercy in America between 1843 and about 1910. They were chosen, with rare exceptions, from the archives of the Sisters of Mercy throughout the United States.

Many of these writings are short because, except for a few Sisters with rare writing accomplishments like Mother Austin Carroll of New Orleans, the Sisters spent most of their time on their combined duties of prayerful contemplation and service of the "poor, sick, and ignorant," the latter expressed in their fourth vow.

After much analysis, the editor decided that division according to literary type was the best and most revealing approach to the Sisters' accounts of prayer and personal experience of spirituality.

Throughout the nine literary types chosen, writings of unequal value to be sure, each account reveals the spirituality of the Sister who wrote it and, even more so, the spirituality of the Sister who lived the experience. When the Sister records her own experience, the Mercy spirituality becomes more vivid and intense.

The editor found it to be a unique experience to gather into one volume so many spiritual testimonies of Sisters living within one half-century. Aside from the spirituality of these Sisters, the dominant theme of the volume, their contributions to American history are revealed in these pages—sometimes rarely known, and sometimes totally unknown to most Americans. The collected writings that follow reveal to a careful reader the spirituality of the Sisters of Mercy as single accounts cannot do. Mercy spirituality *is* identifiable as these pages reveal so clearly.

Mercy spirituality in the Americas develops today (1991) in all its beauty, suited to the time, culture, and country in which it is lived. Perhaps in the future, an anthology of the spiritual writings of the Sisters of Mercy of the Americas (1990–?) will be edited for later readers.

I wish to thank all the Mercy Provinces and Congregations which offered me access so freely to their thoughts and their archives. I thank Paulist Press Managing Editor, Don Brophy, for very generous editing assistance and, of course, John Farina.

And I am grateful for the support of my own community, the Pittsburgh Sisters of Mercy; Tee Nash Herrington, sister of Pittsburgh Sister of Mercy Mary Louise Nash, who executed the illustration for the cover of the book; and Sister Noreen Sheehan, RSM, my indispensable friend and secretary.

Sister Kathleen Healy, R.S.M.
Pittsburgh, Pennsylvania
September 24, 1991

GENERAL INTRODUCTION

OUTLINE

I. Foundation of Mercy Spirituality by Catherine McAuley

II. Irish Historical Influences upon Mercy Spirituality

III. Mercy Spirituality Comes to the United States, 1843:
A New Dimension

IV. Adaptation of Mercy Spirituality to American Influences,
1843–1910

I. Foundation of Mercy Spirituality by Catherine McAuley

When Catherine McAuley established her Institute of Sisters of Mercy in Dublin, Ireland, on December 12, 1831, Archbishop Daniel Murray suggested that work begin at once on a Holy Rule for the Sisters of Mercy, but that until it was completed the Chapter of the Presentation Sisters' Rule on "Union and Charity" would suffice. The office of the Virgin Mary was to be recited daily in English, for Mary was the patron of the Mercy Sisters: Catherine was happy to have her sisters live the Rule of Union and Charity until she had completed the writing of her own Holy Rule.

For Catherine, love of God and one another always remained the precious heritage of the Sisters of Mercy as followers of Christ. The faithful search for mutual charity is a test of the true Sister of Mercy. The deeper meaning of love appears first in community and then among all persons the Sisters serve. The journey to love begins in earnest with the Mercy novice.

The Mercy charism of love of God and human beings is expressed in prayer and service of others. The Sisters desire to pour out this gift of the Holy Spirit upon the people of God. Charity—love for one another and for those whom the Sisters serve—is not a luxury but a necessity for the Sisters of Mercy.

Catherine often reiterated that the Lord reduced all commandments to two: love of God and love of neighbor. He urged his apostles three times at the Last Supper to love one another, and he prayed five times to the Eternal Father to bestow his love upon them. The greatest blessing that God gave to the community was the spirit of loving union, and its model was the love between the Son and his heavenly Father. The charity of the Sisters of Mercy is not an easy practice, but it is essential. The community in which charity lives can overcome all difficulties. Even when mutual charity is difficult, the Sisters are bound to it. "The sun," Catherine once said, "never went down on our anger." The vows are a means to grow in love. The Sister cannot really love unless she loves her Sister as herself. If the Sisters love one another, their love will be so firm that they will never refuse to do or suffer for one another.

The Sister's center of love is God from whom her actions spring as a source. Prayer and forgetfulness of self are essential. Love must be *there,* said Catherine, before it can be exercised. It "covers a multitude of sins and gives witness of Christ to all with whom the Sister associates." To be witnesses to Christ, the Sisters' best service to all women and men is to love one another. To do so they must create community together. Often they must create community in pain, for they are indeed a community of sinners, a pilgrim people. Only in forgiving one another can they move to the eschatological reality promised to us by Christ.

Love, then, was the bedrock of Catherine McAuley's ministry and that of the American founders who followed her. The Sisters proved this statement to be true in their lives. Their love was human and intimate, yet disinterested in its Christ-like embrace of all whom they met. Catherine McAuley's Sisters had a special charism for "young women of good character" because these young girls were greatly in need of their care. So were poor children. The love of the early Sisters of Mercy for those they served did not preclude opposition, hostility, derision, and physical and psychological suffering. The Sisters met the challenges of the status quo, which often meant sickness, over-exertion, exhaustion, or death. The Cross of Christ was a real cross and, like his, a cross of love. The Sisters of Mercy were "founded on Calvary," said Catherine, "there to serve a crucified Christ."

When Catherine wrote her own Holy Rule for the Sisters of Mercy, she based the three vows of poverty, chastity, and obedience upon the love she defined. She stressed the spirituality of the Sisters of Mercy as a union of the contemplative prayer of love with active service of God's people. A few years later she accepted the fourth vow of service of "the poor, sick, and ignorant." The spirituality of the Sister of Mercy can be defined, then, as continual interior contemplative renewal in love combined with active service of the people of God in love.

Mercy spirituality has other dominant characteristics which can be defined. Perhaps the definition requires more than logic. As T.S. Eliot stated of poetry, "it is indefinable but unmistakable." Though the spirit of the Mercy Institute may at times defy logic, we are aware of it when we experience it. The unpublished manuscripts of Sisters who lived and worked with Catherine McAuley in Dublin reveal her spirit which became the life blood of her Institute. All Catherine's teachings were related to the living spirit of the Gospel, and therefore they possess universality. The original manuscripts which reveal her spirit best perhaps, are the *Derry L. MS,* the *Derry S. MS,* and the *Memoirs* of Sister Clare Augustine Moore, all found in the Archives of the Mercy Sisters in Dublin. Manuscripts in the following collection express the same spirit.

Catherine McAuley was brought up during the early years of her life under non-Catholic influence, but her Catholic faith was always strong. Her adoption some years later by a Quaker couple is partially responsible for the fact that she read Scripture daily, and recommended Scripture reading to her Sisters in a period when most religious congregations read pious books rather than Scripture. Thus the spirituality of the Sisters of Mercy can claim a solidity of faith normally unmarred by sentimentality or pious affectation.

The dominant characteristic of Mercy spirituality, as stated above, is continual interior renewal united with active service of God's people. The characteristic differs from that of the great majority of religious congregations for women contemporary with Catherine McAuley. Most congregations remained in their convents and prayed. They did not leave their convents to serve "the poor, sick, and uneducated." Thus Catherine McAuley was called "an illiterate upstart" in Dublin (though she was well educated) and her Sisters were called "walking Sisters" in derision when they left their convents to serve the sick and the poor.

The life of loving contemplation and prayer was stressed by Catherine McAuley as absolutely essential for growth in union with God. She did not see it as an interference with the service of God's people beyond convent walls. She reiterated repeatedly that prayer, both communal and private, and the spiritual and corporal works of Mercy were reciprocal. Mercy spirituality, then, is not that of a complete contemplative nor that of a complete activist. Catherine taught her novices this unified double goal of Mercy essential to the spirit of Mercy.

A second characteristic of Catherine McAuley's Mercy spirituality was a firm belief in the inspiration of the Holy Spirit, revealing the gifts of the Spirit to both the Congregation and individual Sisters. Catherine stressed community spirit, but she also emphasized individual spiritual gifts more strongly than many other religious founders who sometimes followed set patterns of both lifestyle and apostolate. Catherine McAuley's special gift of the Spirit, for example, was the service of the sick poor. Her close companion in Dublin, Frances Warde, received as her special gift instruction of adults in the faith, and her converts were eventually in the hundreds.

A third characteristic of Catherine McAuley's Mercy spirituality may be defined as the vocation of Sisters of Mercy as witnesses to Christ. Catherine believed that the best means of helping one's neighbor is to live a life of holiness oneself. Example influences others to holiness as precept and command do not. Those who teach by word alone do not bear witness to Christ. Though Catherine's calling was indeed unique, she taught her Sisters that to be Christ-like was the way to lead others to Christ.

The fourth characteristic of the teaching of Catherine McAuley on Mercy spirituality is the strong conviction that Sisters of Mercy should serve in love the needs of the people of God in the age and culture in which they find themselves. This characteristic is not fundamental to many other religious founders and their traditions. Some religious congregations have been founded, for example, to teach only children; others, to care for patients with certain illnesses. Catherine McAuley declared, in instructing her Sisters, that the works of Mercy are not limited in their scope. Three particular apostolates were named in the Holy Rule—the service of the poor, sick, and ignorant—because these works were demanded by the people of God in Ireland of the 1830s. Catherine taught her Sisters that they were not limited by these three apostolates. The bounds of Mercy are limited only by the needs of God's people. In fact, three times in the history of the Mercy Institute, appeals were made to Rome to limit the merciful services of the Sisters, and three times Rome supported Catherine's teachings.

Profound confidence in her Sisters and insistence that they too trust one another was a fifth characteristic of Catherine McAuley's spirituality. She trusted very young Sisters to go to new towns and to new countries to found Mercy congregations and to maintain Mercy spirituality within them. This spirit of trust, allowing for freedom and individuality, is even today revealed in the principle of subsidiarity with regard to Mercy community life. The spirit of trust, when lived with complete honesty, produces spiritual freedom and individuality. Wherever "rigidity" has crept into Mercy community living in the past, it must be attributed to Superiors who somehow lost the spirit of Catherine McAuley.

A quality of the Mercy spirituality that can always be stressed in the life of Catherine McAuley and that of her followers is courage, daring, and risk-taking for Christ. Because Catherine believed simply that the spirit of Mercy is a gift given by God, she was willing to take any risk to live it. She manifested complete trust in God alone in carrying out the spiritual and corporal works of Mercy as the objectives of her own life of service. She taught her Sisters that Mercy is God's work; the Sisters were his personal instruments. Therefore, Catherine dared so much for Christ that her Christian witness became a continual source of amazement to others. After only ten years (1831–1841) as a Sister of Mercy, she sacrificed her life for Mercy. She had been available to the people of God where others were not available; she had been involved with God's people in their most profound sufferings; she had suffered unto death.

Catherine McAuley died in 1841 without knowing that her Sisters of Mercy would number 30,000 within a hundred years. She did not know that the Mercy convents in the United States, the first one founded two years after her death, would soon more than double the number of all other Mercy convents in the world. She did not know that within one hundred years it would number 30,000 Sisters, nor that one hundred years after the first American foundation in Pittsburgh, Pennsylvania, by Frances Warde, 861 convents would exist in the United States. Nor did she know that in Ireland, England, Wales, Scotland, New Zealand, South America, Central America, and the West Indies, 648 convents would be serving in Mercy. There must have been something unique in Mercy spirituality which resulted in the Mercy Sisters' growth as the largest English-speaking congregation of women in the world in a comparatively small number of years. This quality was surely a unique union of contemplative prayer with service of "the poor, sick, and ignorant." This unique quality is revealed in suffering unto death in the lives of the Sisters of Mercy as revealed in their Annals over and over again.

Compassionate service, coupled with willingness to risk all for those one serves, produces the suffering servant, whether this suffering results in painful endurance during a lifetime of loving care for others, or suffering unto death, sometimes at a very early age. In the years of their beginnings, the Sisters of Mercy were young in age as well as Mercy spirituality. They would not have used the term "martyrdom" in speaking of their own deaths for those they served as victims of plagues of cholera, typhoid, yellow fever, influenza, and death in war. The martyr has no time to define her suffering.

II. Irish Historical Influences
upon Mercy Spirituality

The Institute of Mercy in Ireland was founded by Catherine McAuley to serve the needs of the people of God in the age and culture in which she lived, a period originating long before the beginning of the Mercy Congregation in 1827 and extending far past Catherine's death in 1841. The greatest afflictions of the people of Ireland to whom Catherine and her Sisters ministered were poverty, sickness, and illiteracy.

Justice as well as Mercy was demanded by the historical age in which Catherine founded her Institute. The seeds of the ministry of justice in early Mercy history are not difficult to trace. The radical quality of the liberation of the children of God sought by Catherine and her companions actually made the Institute of Mercy revolutionary in its founding. While most congregations of women religious of the nineteenth century remained in their cloister to pray, Catherine and her Sisters sought justice for the poor to a degree that startles us if we consider the Irish historical setting of Catherine's prophetic actions. The fourth vow she accepted, "the service of the poor, sick, and ignorant," implies more than it states.

The Mercy vow to serve the *poor* was a direct response to the injustice of the British penal laws in Ireland of the 1820s, which made poverty and ignorance among the masses of Catholics inevitable. These penal laws actually made poverty an Irish institution. No Catholic could achieve a higher position than that of serf to a Protestant master; no Catholic was allowed a decent remuneration for his or her labor; no Catholic could even hope for an office of trust. It was lawful for a Protestant master to take possession of a Catholic's small farm, evicting a family simply on the plea that a Catholic had no right to possession of the property. A proprietor could also deprive a Catholic of his lease if the latter failed to support the Protestant landowner's political stand.

In 1829 the Catholic Emancipation Act was finally forced upon a hostile British Parliament. But because of both continued unjust legal measures and long centuries of wretchedness and suffering, Catherine and her followers found the Irish people in the 1830s and 1840s still in a state of poverty almost unparalleled in the history of the West.

The Mercy vow to serve the *sick* was in turn an inevitable concomitant of ministry to the poor. Masses of the Irish people were subject to malnutrition and tuberculosis, a situation which reached its peak during the so-called "potato famine" of the 1840s. When Irish immigrants sailed for America by the thousands, they were seeking not just a "better living," but relief from poverty and sickness to the point of death. The Mercy Sisters responded to injustice by caring for the sick poor in their little huts in the lanes and alleys of Dublin, carrying with them simple remedies, soups, and soda bread. Frances Warde and her followers, after Catherine's death, responded by following the Irish sick poor to America to administer to them on a new continent.

Finally, the Mercy vow to serve the *ignorant* was a direct response to penal laws which ordinarily forbade even elementary education for the poor. Where poor schools did exist, the religion of the Established Church of England was taught daily. Proselytizing was a common occurrence. No Catholic was permitted to teach in these schools or to open a school of her own. Thus secret "hedge schools" were initiated by Catholics at the same time that the Eucharist was celebrated on isolated hillsides before dawn. The majority of the Irish Catholic people received little or no education. Mercy Sisters responded to these injustices with "free schools" whenever possible after the Emancipation Act of 1829, and with classes at the Mercy House on Baggot Street, Dublin, where young women could both practice their religion and learn a trade to support themselves financially. Within ten years, the ministry of the Sisters of Mercy had spread throughout Ireland.

The attempt to address injustice was thus at the very core of the intent of the fourth Mercy vow. It is a little difficult to make clear to the American mind of the 1990s that Catherine and her Sisters were unique in their practice of the ministry of justice in Ireland of the 1830s and 1840s. For example, if a poor young woman appeared in a disheveled condition at a Dublin house at 2:30 a.m. and begged for help, to refuse her was a normal response. "Go to Kitty McAuley on Baggot Street. She takes anyone," was also a cynical response which embodied the average attitude of a Dubliner toward such a young woman in trouble. The person seeking refuge was considered "undeserving." But Catherine's sense of justice was reflected in her maxim: "It is better to relieve one hundred imposters, if there be such, than to suffer one deserving person to be sent away empty."

Justice and humanity were expressed, moreover, in the manner in which the Sisters served others. "Remember," said Catherine, "there is a great deal less said in the Holy Rule on visiting the sick poor than on the manner of visiting them." When Catherine brought a poor demented woman from a shack on Liffey Street to Coolock House near Dublin, she cared for her tenderly, despite the fact that the woman—with the perversity of madness—resented her benefactor intensely. Similarly, Frances Warde suffered the criticism of polite citizens of Carlow when she sent her Sisters to nurse the town prostitute, Poll, in her final illness. For Frances, to minister to Poll's human needs was a matter of Mercy justice.

As spiritual directors, the early Mercy Sisters revealed that their pursuit of justice began with their own Sisters and then reached out to all people. Spiritual instructions in the convent were often initiated by a reading from Luke's Gospel quoting Isaiah (4:16–22):

> The spirit of the Lord has been given to me,
> for he has anointed me.
> He has sent me to bring the good news to the poor,
> To proclaim liberty to captives and to the blind new sight,
> to set the downtrodden free, to proclaim the Lord's year of favor.

The Sisters were also reminded that when Jesus closed the Book of Isaiah, he was careful to speak of what he had just read to the people in the temple. Similarly, the Sisters should speak to others of the Word of God which they have read. To bring the good news to the poor and to set the downtrodden free is the message of Mercy justice.

Justice was to be practiced first among the Sisters themselves. "A Superior who does not listen to her Sisters," Frances Warde wrote, "is cruel. And a Superior who does not love her Sisters, but only commands, and reproves, is a Mistress of Slaves." These are strong words. Mercy justice and human dignity must begin among the Sisters themselves before they can be just to others.

In speaking of the education of Irish children, Frances Warde always insisted on justice. She forbade physical punishment because, in her own words, it "destroys truth and degrades the person." Honesty is essential in training children. They must be attracted to the truth by love and well-directed praise of the good. Christ was patient with his disciples. He did not expect overnight change in them. The Sister of Mercy cannot demand more than Christ himself demanded.

If we consider briefly the origins of the foundations of Frances Warde in Ireland before she came to America, we become aware that Mercy justice was at the center of the ministries she was to bring to the United States. For example, the great Irish patriot, Daniel O'Connell, who was responsible perhaps more than any other person for the passage of the Irish Emancipation Bill of 1829, was a friend of Catherine and Frances and was closely associated with Mercy communities in the towns of Carlow and Naas. In 1828, three years before the Mercy Institute was founded officially, O'Connell carved for the Christmas dinner of the orphans at the Baggot Street House founded by Catherine.

Frances did not hesitate to associate herself with O'Connell's political movements in seeking justice for the poor. In the summer of 1841, O'Connell went to Carlow, where Frances was Superior, to solicit votes of freeholders for his son, John, in a county election. O'Connell remained in Carlow for a month, giving political speeches to crowded audiences in front of the town hall. After such meetings, he went to St. Leo's Convent to pray, to participate in the Eucharistic celebration, and to plan the real initiation of Irish emancipation.

Frances Warde's foundation in the town of Naas was a response to a call from Father Gerald Doyle, who was incensed at the extreme unjustices to his people. Although Naas had one hundred Catholics to every non-Catholic, children were forced to attend Anglican Church services and were taught the religion of the Church of England. Doyle, a dynamic "patriot priest," threatened to lay the whole affair before the British Parliament. Catholic natives of Naas, moreover, held spectacular demonstrations of their rebellion against the payment of unjust tithes. Doyle was an enthusiastic friend of Catherine and Frances who sympathized with him in his conflicts with local authorities. The Catholic free school at Naas, St. Mary's, was Frances' answer to the flagrant abuse of the right of children to elementary education.

The question of Mercy justice for the oppressed in the town of Wexford becomes clear when we recall the famous Wexford Rebellion of 1798. A fierce and bloody struggle between the Irish patriots of the town, who fought for their human rights, and the British army had raged for four months without resolution. Finally, a promise of pardon by the British led the rebels to surrender their arms. But the British did not honor their promise, and the Irish patriots were almost decimated by the British cavalry at the sordid "Butcheries of Wexford." Frances Warde and her Sisters founded a convent, school and orphanage at Wexford to serve the children and the grandchildren of the "Boys of Wexford" who died in the fruitless strife of '98.

Frances Warde's last foundation in Ireland was in Westport, County Mayo, the poorest county in Ireland in the 1840s. Its poverty was so great that the Irish people always spoke of it as, "Mayo, God help us!" The desire of the Mercy Sisters to redress injustice in Mayo was typical of their service of the poor everywhere. They began the visitation and service of the sick at once. The building available for a free school was in such abominable condition that the Sisters dismissed the children, who applied the first day they arrived, until they could make the school humanly habitable. Westport soon trained innumerable young women, many of whom eventually became Sisters of Mercy in the United States and in England. The Wexford foundation was begun shortly before Catherine McAuley died, and the Westport Convent two years after her death. But Catherine's spirit of Mercy justice was already deeply implanted in the heart of Frances Warde when she went to Naas, Wexford, and Westport.

Frances was to be the first Mercy Sister to sail to America to serve the "poor, sick, and ignorant" in a very different land. The future was indeed unknown. Frances and the six Sisters who accompanied her had no way of knowing that in a comparatively brief historical period of one hundred and fifty years the Institute of Mercy would increase to 25,000 members in 1,500 convents in North and South America, Europe, Asia, Africa, and Australia.

Other great leaders were to follow Frances to America: Mary Agnes O'Connor to New York; Baptist Russell to San Francisco; Patricia Waldron to Philadelphia; Teresa Maher to Cincinnati; Teresa O'Farrell to Arkansas; Mary Agnes Healy and Teresa Perry to Connecticut. Many more names may be added to the American list. But not all the young followers were born in Ireland. Young American women entered the Sisters of Mercy in large numbers. And many not only became great leaders but sacrificed their lives for Mercy.

III. Mercy Spirituality Comes to the United States, 1843: A New Dimension

It is an understatement to say that when Frances Warde and six Mercy Sisters from Ireland came to America in 1843, they entered an entirely different world—a world of cultural upheaval to be sure, a world of complexity and suffering, but a world different in style and range from the Ireland they had left. After crossing the ocean in a sailing vessel, they crossed the mountains of Pennsylvania both by train and by horse and carriage, the latter conveyances suggesting immediate danger if the foot of a horse might slip down the mountain. But the Sisters did arrive safely in Pittsburgh, Pennsylvania, population 25,000, year 1843. Thus the first Mercy foundation in the United States was not in New York or San Francisco; it was in a midwestern town in which they soon learned the spiritual and social dimensions of a new land inhabited by settlers of two or three generations. The Sisters were somewhat overwhelmed by the immense numbers of immigrants they had come to serve. Mercy spirituality in the United States, they soon learned, would extend, as Catherine McAuley had said, to all types of peoples with all needs.

The Sisters had already learned the value of adjustment to new situations in Ireland. Now they revealed their gifts for meeting the needs of God's people "in a new age and culture in which they found themselves." The demand for union and liberty in ante-bellum America had a different form from the demand for basic freedoms in the Ireland the Mercy Sisters had left. And the stirring of religious movements in America revealed a complexity never experienced by the Irish immigrants who had practiced their unquestioned faith in secret under the iron hand of Britain.

The mission that waited the seven Sisters from Carlow in Pittsburgh was the great task of Mercy service of the sick, the orphans, the deprived, and the uneducated among hundreds of immigrants to Western Pennsylvania. Before her death, Frances Warde, leader of the Sisters, was to establish the Sisters of Mercy in Illinois, Rhode Island, New Hampshire, Nebraska, Vermont, Maine, New Jersey, and Philadelphia. But the beginning was now.

15

On December 21, 1843 the Sisters opened their first Convent of Mercy in America, in a rented, four-story brick building on Penn Street, Pittsburgh. The convent was called St. Mary's, and soon a young woman named Eliza Tiernan applied to become the first American Sister of Mercy.

The Sisters marveled that the whole of Ireland could be placed within the State of Pennsylvania alone with hundreds of miles to spare. The very Indian names—Allegheny, Monongahela, Mississippi—had a strange ring to the ears of the young Irish settlers.

Pittsburgh in the winter of 1843 was cold and muddy and smoky. It was already the "Iron City," with coal and coke destined to be two important factors in its development. The city's destiny lay in industry and commerce. The demand for labor was great. The expansion of Pittsburgh throughout the 1840s was almost unbelievable. Within nine months in 1845, as many as 25,000 houses were built in the city and its suburbs. The Baltimore and Ohio Railroad was soon to be extended through Virginia and Pennsylvania to the Ohio River. In the early 1840s the development of Pittsburgh, as of similar industrial cities, was unparalleled in American history.

In a letter to Ireland, Sister Elizabeth Strange wrote from Pittsburgh that, while there were few millionaires in Pittsburgh, there were few people in "*real* poverty." She meant, of course, that dire poverty of the Irish towns of Naas, Wexford, and Westport. Food was cheap in Pittsburgh. Flour was two dollars a barrel, and wheat was forty-five cents a bushel. Yet side by side with amazing industrial expansion developed ugliness and misery. Housing facilities for poor immigrants did not expand proportionately with the population, and slums multiplied. "The Steel Metropolis of the World" depended for its growth upon exploited laborers who were just beginning the fight for just wages and humane working conditions. The Mercy Sisters arrived in Pittsburgh precisely when the city was on the verge of unprecedented growth. They became a significant part of its religious, cultural, and social expansion.

They remembered Catherine McAuley's teaching on Mercy Spirituality: the Sisters of Mercy minister to the needs of *all* God's people through both the spiritual and the corporal works of Mercy. They prefer the service of the "poor, sick, and ignorant," but all people in need command their services. At the same time they are contemplative women, united with their God as they serve others. These Mercy Sisters soon became a significant part of the religious, cultural, and social expansion of the city they served.

To be sure, trouble arose. The people of Pittsburgh in the 1840s were not dominantly Catholic except for its poorer immigrants. The works of the Sisters of Mercy became extensive in both the city of Pittsburgh, its sister city, Allegheny, and the suburbs of both cities. Frances Warde visited the poor house and the inmates of the penitentiary. The managers of the jail became alarmed, however, when numerous inmates expressed a desire to become Catholics after meeting Frances. An old statute forbidding visits of "gentle-women who come for religious purposes" was put into effect. For many years the Sisters of Mercy were indeed denied admittance to the Pittsburgh penitentiary.

A large section of the population of the city was literally floating. Boats and steamers moved continually up and down the Allegheny, the Monongahela, and the Ohio rivers. Catholics who came from small settlements called at St. Mary's for religious instruction by the Sisters and preparation for the Sacraments. Some of them led lives completely circumscribed by the steamboat on the river and the stagecoach on land. More and more people came to St. Mary's. "The Sisters are like the first Christians, for all have but one heart and soul," declared Joseph T. Dean, curate at St. Paul's Cathedral. Mercy spirituality was indeed being felt at the first American Mercy foundation. Sunday school drew large numbers. Baptisms were frequent. Soon many young women of Pittsburgh were attracted to the religious life of the Sisters of Mercy.

A boarding school called St. Xavier's was opened outside Pittsburgh to "provide bread and butter for the Sisters" through tuition. The curriculum was outstanding. Soon St. Paul's Cathedral School in Pittsburgh was taken over by the Sisters. A beautiful orphanage was built by the diocese in 1867, and before the turn of the century the Sisters of Mercy cared for over 1,200 orphans. School after school was opened, and Mercy spirituality had a broad birth in Pittsburgh. *All* the spiritual and corporal works of Mercy seemed to come under Mercy jurisdiction.

In 1846 Frances Warde had the daring to take Margaret O'Brien as Superior and five other young Sisters to establish a new foundation of Sisters of Mercy in the windy wasteland of Chicago. The extreme suffering and exposure experienced by these young women in serving the people offers silent testimony in the deaths of the five youthful pioneers during their first six years in Chicago. Within twelve years Margaret O'Brien herself was to die in caring for the sick of the city in the horrible cholera plague of 1848 during which three young Sisters of Mercy died within twenty-four hours. Frances Warde herself almost lost her life from hardships and exposure on the return journey alone from Chicago to Pittsburgh across the Western plains. The Chicago foundation of the Sisters of Mercy, built on extreme pain, was destined to become one of the largest Institutes of Mercy in the world.

Suffering unto death, however, still awaited the young Mercy congregation in Pittsburgh. In 1846 the Sisters of Mercy opened the first Mercy Hospital in the world in Pittsburgh. The need for a hospital was great because of recurrent epidemics of cholera, smallpox, and typhoid, when many citizens fled the city rather than serve the suffering. On December 1, 1846 the *Pittsburgh Commercial Journal* gave notice that a hospital would soon be opened under the auspices of the Sisters of Mercy to "persons of every class, condition, and religious persuasion," and that assistance would be offered "to the poor and destitute to the utmost limit of the means of the institution." The building used was the convent and school of the Sisters of Mercy on Penn Street. For sixteen months over two hundred patients received care. Sick soldiers returning broken down in health from the battlefronts of the Mexican War made up a large number of the early patients.

Then came the crucial year of test for the Mercy spirituality of Frances Warde and her Sisters in their first hospital. In January 1848 a sick seaman was admitted to the hospital. His illness was diagnosed as typhoid fever. The men's ward was used as isolation quarters. Some eighteen more cases were admitted from the river boats. Many citizens fled the city. From January until April, the available doctors and all the Sisters struggled with the disease. When spring came, an amazing fifteen of the nineteen patients were restored to health.

The Sisters, who exhausted themselves in caring for the sick, did not fare so well. Sister Anne Rigney, a novice, died February 11, 1848. Sister Catherine Lawler, still a postulant, died March 3, and Sister Magdalen Reinbolt, another novice, died March 5. As a crowning sorrow, Sister Xavier Tiernan, Director of Novices and first American Sister of Mercy, died March 9. All of the small staff of Sisters, with the exception of Sister Isidore Fisher, the administrator, were wiped out. The sad story of sacrifice spread not only in Pittsburgh but throughout the country and even beyond the seas. The response of the public was reverential admiration. The holocaust killed all bigotry against the Sisters of Mercy among Pittsburgh residents. The four Sisters were buried in a new little cemetery on the grounds of a new Mercy Hospital under construction. The hospital day book indicates that funerals of many patients took place directly from the Mercy Hospital. The Sisters not only cared for the sick; they buried the dead. Frances Warde's trust in God did not waver. She recalled the Book of Job which she loved: "The Lord gave and the Lord has taken away. Blessed be the will of God."

Mission after mission in Pittsburgh was planned by the Mercy Sisters. Their early sufferings were no deterrent. Our Lady of Mercy Academy, St. Xavier's Academy, and numerous free schools followed one another in rapid succession. During the Civil War the Sisters administered and nursed at both the Western Pennsylvania Military Hospital and Stanton Military Hospital in Washington, D.C.

Frances Warde herself moved from Pittsburgh to Providence, Rhode Island, and then to Manchester, New Hampshire. Indeed, she established approximately two-thirds of the Mercy missions that followed throughout the United States. In 1966, when Pittsburgh celebrated the one hundred and fiftieth anniversary of its charter as a city, Frances Warde was named one of the ten outstanding women in its history. Today she is even closer in spirit to the Sisters of Mercy than she was one hundred and fifty years ago.

It would be a mistake to assume that Mercy spirituality had its chief early development in Pittsburgh. Obviously this statement is not true. The numerous Mercy founders in America mentioned earlier and their Sisters each lived their separate Mercy histories throughout the United States. Each lived in actuality the definition of Mercy spirituality taught so gently by Catherine McAuley. Somehow these early Sisters became "living definitions" of Mercy spirituality. They lived the united contemplation and service that a Sister of Mercy actually strove to exemplify. They were not always "perfect," but the *marks* of Mercy spirituality appeared in their lives, not to be erased. They could do no more than die for their Mercy vows. And they did die for their promises, Sisters of Mercy in all areas of America between 1843 and 1900. The next section of this Introduction will explore Mercy spirituality in America in a broader physical landscape.

IV. Adaptation of Mercy Spirituality to American Influences, 1843–1900

The Sisters of Mercy came to America as the Great American Romantic Movement blossomed. They had little direct connection with the Movement as such, except in the case of the influence of a few individuals. They had come to teach and care for Irish and European immigrants.

Most of the Sisters who came to America were well educated. And the young American women who joined the Congregation were often capable teachers. The Sisters knew the works of Bryant, Poe, Longfellow, Holmes, and Lowell. And they had read Emerson, Thoreau, and George Ripley.

The age in which the Sisters came to the United States was called Romantic and Transcendental because of the search for meaning in the universe pursued by American scholars. The Sisters themselves were not searching out a meaning in creation. They believed they had already found the answers to their major spiritual questions. They desired to offer the principles of Catholicism to American immigrants, chiefly those who suffered at the hands of religious bigots, and to teach them a decent way of living, particularly those who suffered because of their poverty. Thus the Sisters began their American missions by sharing personally in the poverty and hardships of those they served. They did not hesitate to offer their own lives freely in the service of the poor and suffering: the hungry, the victims of the Civil War and of race prejudice, those suffering from cholera, yellow fever, malaria, typhoid fever and, later, influenza. Often they died in the service of the suffering when ordinary citizens ran away for fear of infection.

The Sisters of Mercy in the United States were indeed aware of the Transcendental Movement, especially when it touched those persons who became their friends. Transcendentalism was part and parcel of the age in which they lived. Liberty of thought—whether religious or political—was not a new goal for them; they had brought the right to freedom of thought with them from Ireland. They cherished it, next to the Catholic faith, as a goal they had left Ireland to achieve.

The Oxford Movement and John Henry Newman were near to their hearts as well as their minds. Isaac Hecker, founder of the Paulists, once preached a retreat to the Sisters of Mercy in St. Francis Convent in Brooklyn, New York. The Sister who wrote his retreat notes, and left them in the convent heritage room, demonstrated that Hecker understood Mercy spirituality, perhaps with a touch of rigidity. Most retreat masters spoke with a certain rigor in offering retreats in post-bellum days. In off-hours, Hecker spoke to the Sisters of Transcendentalism and of Brook Farm. These movements were of much interest to the Sisters.

The Romantic Mood and the effects of the Oxford Movement in the United States indeed taught the Sisters of Mercy how to deal amicably with those persons who did not share their own faith. Thus their Congregation was chosen to teach in the university town of Princeton, New Jersey, chiefly because they knew how to relate socially and intellectually with non-Catholics who often discussed Catholicism.

The Catholic Movement among scholars represented by men like Orestes Brownson and Isaac Hecker was fascinating to the Mercy Sisters. For them its best known exponent was James Kent Stone, former Episcopalian and later Paulist and Passionist. He was a protégé of Mother Frances Warde, who educated his daughters at Mount St. Mary's Academy in New Hampshire. Stone suffered intensely all the pain and conflict that both the Catholic hierarchy of New York City and American Protestant bigotry could inflict upon one man who dared to become a Catholic convert and priest. Even some of Frances Warde's own daughters could not understand as she did the suffering bordering despair reserved for Kent Stone in nineteenth century America. The agony of the priest and the Sister provides a moving chapter in American church history. The Mercy spirituality of Frances Warde helped Kent Stone to endure.

Perhaps the best comparison that can be made between Sisters of Mercy and the New England Romantics of the late nineteenth century is that of the intensity with which the Romantics and the Sisters each pursued their spiritual goals. The intensity of the Romantics is found in their writings, whether they be spiritual seekers like Emerson or prophets of Catholicism (as well as seekers) like Isaac Hecker. Orestes Brownson was a friend of the Mercy Sisters who both appreciated their accomplishments for Christ and wrote of their achievements, as will be seen in the following collection of writings.

It was easier for New England spiritual seekers to relate to the Sisters of Mercy because Catherine McAuley had taught them that they were to pursue their goals of caring for God's people in the particular age and culture in which they found themselves. *All* the works of Mercy, spiritual and corporal, were the work of the Sisters. In the United States they served needs of American people which were not always precisely the needs of the Irish people on the other side of the Atlantic. Thus the Sisters soon gained a reputation of adaptability to need wherever they happened to serve.

The Mercy Sisters seldom participated in political struggle, but they served with equal energy the Northerner and the Southerner, the faithful and the bigot, the black and the white. All God's children sought and received their help, and the Sisters taught the Gospel message when it was welcomed, but served with equal vigor those who rejected the teachings of Christ. Thus their converts were in the thousands. Again, they fought for both their own democratic rights and those of the people they served. The Propaganda Fide Archives and the Archives of the Irish College in Rome today hold innumerable letters from both Ireland and America in defense of the rights of the Sisters themselves as well as of the people to whom they ministered.

Perhaps the Sisters revealed their intensity of faith best in their willingness to die almost at a moment's notice in the service of the poor, sick, and uneducated. They offered their lives over and over again in the service of soldiers of both North and South during the Civil War.

These women had little time to keep records of their unique experiences, much less diaries. Therefore the selections of writings which reveal their spirituality do not always do justice to their lives of contemplation and service. Certain accounts are sadly brief. Many of the Sisters' significant experiences were never recorded. The martyr has little time to write her autobiography.

At times a Sister's spiritual experience of prayer and service was so deeply felt that she attempted to write a brief account for her contemporaries and followers in order to reveal how Mercy life was lived in her own time. The reader, however, sometimes has to "fill in" the account from his or her religious and historical knowledge.

Probably only one woman, Mother Teresa Austin Carroll, who served in New Orleans and Alabama, wrote to Sisters of Mercy throughout the United States to request brief accounts of their lived spiritual experiences. She succeeded in recording these experiences which were published by P. O'Shea, New York City, in four volumes, dated 1881, 1883, 1885, and 1888, under the title, *Leaves from the Annals of the Sisters of Mercy.*

Other Sisters of Mercy, who spread throughout the United States in less than a century, wrote various annals as best they could—usually briefly and succinctly. Often the most significant services and sacrifices they offered required all of their energy, so that accounts of these events were written later by Sisters who often had immediate knowledge of these experiences.

The Sisters were deeply aware of the influences upon immigrant Catholics and the effects of the teachings of men like John Carroll (respected for both their education and their social positions) upon Americans. As the immigrant Church became more dominant and the century expanded, the Sisters felt more "at home." The milieu was one they could appreciate. It was, indeed, at least partly what they had hoped to experience in the New World. The religious struggles of the immigrant churches of post-bellum America were only partially a "reenactment" of the Irish struggles they had known at an early age—for democracy prevailed in America. Democracy lessened the bitterness of religious persecution in America of the nineteenth century.

At times the Sisters were persecuted by bigoted Protestants, as in the attack upon the convent of Frances Warde in Providence, Rhode Island, but even frightening events in America could not compare with the three hundred years of persecution suffered by the ancestors and families of these same Sisters in Ireland. The Sisters did not engage in religious debate with non-Catholics in the United States. But when they were persecuted, they demonstrated unusual strength. It was not easy to suffer even the smaller offenses of being attacked verbally on the streets of New England, or of suffering youngsters to mark their religious habits with insults in chalk as they walked the streets of the towns where they served. The Sisters were at times an embattled minority whose dress revealed their beliefs.

It is well to remember that the Sisters of Mercy differed from many other religious congregations of women in America. They appeared as "somewhat of a juridical anomaly among religious congregations." They represented an active, modern spirit combined with a contemplative spirit. That the new wine sometimes burst the old wineskins is not a surprise. The juridical form of a religious congregation will always be subordinate to its ascetical and spiritual foundations. Catherine McAuley had breathed her spirituality into the Sisters of Mercy long before she gave thought to the "legal" aspects of her foundation.

The range of services to which these Sisters devoted themselves in education and in the relief of suffering require to be named. The Sisters cared for the poor, sick, and uneducated. They taught school, catechized, and nursed the sick. They conducted orphan asylums, homes for the aged, residences for working girls, homes for women. They superintended day nurseries and summer camps; they taught Christian Doctrine vacation and catechetical schools. They opened refuges for Magdalens, convalescent homes, secretarial schools, social service centers. They cared for the sick in their homes and for prisoners in their cells. They conducted maternity hospitals and leprosaria. In the United States they developed and enlarged a complete system of feminine education—grammar schools by the hundreds, over two hundred high schools, and eventually more colleges for women than any other congregation of women religious. They taught thousands of black children and Indians. In short, they were different from congregations of women religious founded *only* to pray in their convents or to teach, perhaps, only grade school children. All of the works of the Sisters of Mercy were combined with the contemplative spirit of prayer to make their Mercy spirituality unique.

The Sisters of Mercy served in the Civil and Spanish-American Wars. In epidemics of cholera in Nashville and Chicago, smallpox in Cincinnati, yellow fever in Natchez, and influenza in Philadelphia and other large cities they also served. In floods and earthquakes in San Francisco, Sacramento, and Chicago, the Sisters were among the first volunteers.

A listing of the services of the Sisters offers, to some extent, the range of Mercy spirituality. "I would rather be cold and hungry," said Catherine McAuley, "than that the poor in Kingstown or elsewhere should be deprived of any consolation in our power to afford." To love and serve the poor was to help them in soul and body. This hallmark of Catherine's spirituality overflowed to her associates. "If Christ were standing before me now, what would he do?" echoed the American Mercy founder, Frances Warde.

Demands upon the Sisters of Mercy never lessened. Mother Baptist Russell in San Francisco; Mary Agnes O'Connor in New York; Teresa Maher in Cincinnati; Margaret O'Brien in Chicago—all had letters from bishops on their desks at all times begging the Sisters to open new missions in their dioceses. Both corporate and individual apostolates grew in numbers as requests multiplied.

The offering of the Sister of Mercy found completion in the vows, but the evangelical counsels never implied a false separation from so-called "lay Christians." In fact, the first mark of a religious vocation, according to the Sisters of Mercy, was the following: "A true religious is a true Christian." Religious life offered greater facility for the observance of the essential duties of Christianity. The vows were the way in which the Sister of Mercy chose to be a merciful Christian. Prayer and contemplation for the Sister of Mercy found balance in the fourth vow of service. Christ-like goals, not always perfectly achieved, were always sought. Their origin was in community life. Faith reached even the foolhardy. Hope reached all. Failure was never anticipated. Christians of all types joined the Sisters of Mercy to serve others, especially when calamity demanded compassionate service. Often the service of the Sisters was as *voluntary* as the service of "lay" ministers to the needy. Superiors did not "demand" sacrifice of life in war and in killing epidemics.

The Sisters worked with "lay people" in many missions, North, South, East, and West. They served in New England and upstate New York, seeking out poor, sick Indians on forgotten reservations. They ransomed slaves in Civil War days. In caring for wounded soldiers, they were given the right to pass over battle lines without using passwords. The army recognized the Sisters when they saw them in tattered clothes, wearing rabbit skins for shoes. At one point, after the battle of Shiloh, a few Sisters served several hundred men in one small tent camp. Numerous examples appear in the following pages to demonstrate that for the Sisters of Mercy, the *poor* meant those who fought in battle with nothing to eat and no bed in which to sleep; people who lived in shacks and hovels; illiterate people, people who had never heard of Christ. "Poor" encompassed physical illness, mental breakdown, prejudice, racism. Love of God and service of his people were two sides of the same coin.

"Long range planning" in the second half of the nineteenth century was seldom present when the poor were being served. The needs of God's people were obvious, not complex. The people suffered from what we today call "social sin," but the answers to their needs were simple. The sick, the poor, the suffering required food, clothing, rooms in which to live, schools, orphanages, night schools, training in trades. Often the answers were clear, but difficult to carry out.

Specific examples of Mercy services, as found in the following pages, reveal that any type of suffering called for help. Mercy was needed everywhere. The Sisters never spoke of "foreign missions." So far as service was concerned, Liverpool, New York, and Australia were in need of compassionate help as was South America.

The Sisters actually courted risks in order to be available to serve the poor. They trusted in Christ alone. "Union and charity" was their motto. Indeed, they were sometimes *suspicious* of auspicious beginnings in their ministries. Yet they attracted the wealthy as well as the poor. They broke down Yankee prejudices and even trained the "stern New England character" to understand the faith and the work of the immigrant Irish nun.

The Sister of Mercy, whether Irish or American, was always associated with devotion to the Virgin Mary, a devotion not always appreciated by American non-Catholics who believed that Mary received greater honor from Catholics than she deserved. The first follower of Christ, the Sisters considered Mary the model of perfect response to Jesus Christ. They looked to her for help, guidance, and protection in *all* their undertakings. They recited her "Little Office" daily and publicly proclaimed her as the patron of their Congregation. They sought through public communal devotions to honor her and to seek her help in all their apostolates. They looked to her with confidence and trust as a model of openness to the Holy Spirit. On Mary's Feast Day of Mercy, September 24, they dedicated themselves to her service. It was no accident that so many "Academies of Our Lady of Mercy" appeared across America that when the name of such a school was mentioned, the answer was, "Which one?" Non-Catholics in great numbers attended these schools because of the quality of the education offered. Many converts to the Catholic Church were the result. The Sisters of Mercy acknowledged Mary in the words of her Son: "Blessed are those who hear the Word of God and keep it."

The Sisters of Mercy, because they dared to combine contemplative prayer with active service of others, were sometimes condemned in early America. Controversy between the prophetic and the unprophetic have always produced crises. Reading the Sisters' account of their own experiences, one wonders sometimes how they survived their extraordinary lives. The truth is, they did not always survive, as we shall see in the accounts in the following collection of writings. Also, we may judge the question of survival by visiting the burial grounds of Sisters of Mercy all over the United States and counting the numbers of young women religious who died in their early twenties in the service of all who needed them. The writer has not come across even one account of a Sister of Mercy who refused to serve the sick and dying when she herself was put in danger of death.

The above type of sacrifice was a by-product of Mercy life. Contemplation and prayer always united with willing service. The American Sisters of Mercy, like Catherine McAuley, read Scripture daily all their lives in an era in which many women religious were more apt to read their *Holy Rule* than the Bible. In the convent in which Frances Warde died in Manchester, New Hampshire, the last Bible of the American Founder lies open in the heritage room. It was published in very large print because Frances was almost blind in her last years. More important, the pages of this Bible are well worn from use. To read the Bible, Frances taught, "is absolutely essential because a true religious ought not to acknowledge any master but Jesus Christ and him crucified." When asked how some Sisters accomplished so much for Christ, Frances said: "It is astounding how much time was at the command of the saints, and how little seems to be at the disposal of the generality of Christians."

The Mercy spirit of freedom in America resulted in a refusal "to make too many small congregational laws." Certain practices of some congregations were outside the bounds of Mercy spirituality. One finds, for example, a negative attitude with regard to certain customs: dislike for needless multiplication of vocal prayers in community; dislike for ceremonies such as kneeling before Superiors; preference for baptismal names over new saints' names among Sisters; dislike for the title "Reverend Mother"; dislike for certain approaches to the Chapter of Faults; dislike for displaying the crucifix on the religious habit; dislike for obtrusive qualities in the outdoor dress of the Sisters. Most of these preferences can be traced back to Catherine McAuley, and most are carried out as common practices among American Sisters today. The rejected customs were often "products of their time" difficult to overlook because of Catholic religious society.

In America the Mercy Sisters stressed freedom in their convents. Their houses were person-centered in the sense that they stressed family affection and spirit. News, joys, and sorrows were shared by letter with new foundations. Reading the letters of the Sisters, one has the impression of friends communicating, not of legalities carried out, nor of a tight government system. Personal relationships were important. "Mother" as a title was preferred to "Reverend Mother."

The Sisters believed that the convents should mutually sustain one another. Differences were settled by consultation, as in the controversy over whether the Sisters should teach middle class girls as well as the poor. In all controversy, the principle of "union and charity above all" was the guide to action. Moral union was preferred to commanding authority.

The Christian challenge and the Mercy challenge was to live as Christ lived for others. Jesus discovered for all of us what it means to be human. He was radically one for others. When the Sister of Mercy became one for others, she discovered, community happened as a primary indispensable product. In other words, community was a by-product of attempting to live as Christ lived. An early Sister of Mercy, reminded of the Acts of the Apostles, called the early Mercy way of living "Primitive Christianity." The Sisters had all things in common. They prayed together, they celebrated the Eucharist together, taught the faith, cared for all in need—especially young women. Family spirit grew from community life, without detriment to freedom and collegiality.

Compassion for others sometimes backfired. Mary Anne O'Connor, the sister of Bishop Michael O'Connor of Pittsburgh, was accepted back into religious life a third time after failing twice in the days when a first dismissal was usually considered final. Her Superior had no regrets: she preferred to err on the side of compassion. "My heart went out to her," she said simply, "and I could not refuse her."

As the Mercy Sisters moved from North to South, or from East to West, in America, they were always at the cutting edge of the development of Catholicism from Maine to California. It was the nature of these women to live at the frontiers of Christian evolution, to suffer as the people they served suffered.

A concrete example will illustrate the kind of daring these Sisters regarded as the apostolic mission to which they were called. In June 1879 Frances Warde sent a group of Sisters from Manchester, New Hampshire to the Indian Reservations in Maine—to Pleasant Point, near Perry, on Passamaquoddy Bay. She chose these Sisters, two of them—Clare Leeson and Martha O'Brien—quite young, and the third, de Chantal Leeson, in her seventy-fifth year. The Sisters traveled from Eastport, Maine, across Passamaquoddy Bay by canoe in torrential rains. Weary, tired, and drenched, they found no fire in the dreary, damp hut that was to be their Convent of Mercy. A few musty crackers were in a dirty box. One dirty bed comprised the furniture. The two young Sisters gave the bed to the older woman and slept on the dirt floor covered with filthy animal skins, while the wind blew through the cracks in the wood. The next day, the visiting pastor from Eastport gave the Sisters ten dollars to buy food. They sent a boy to purchase bread and milk, and he stole half their money. They are still there today. Taking risks was ordinary existence for them.

Following immigrants North, South, East and West in the United States, Sisters of Mercy were pioneers in one of the greatest episodes in American Church history in the 1840s, 1850s, and 1860s. They traveled in every way available—from stagecoach to Conestoga wagon—establishing schools, homes, orphanages, hospitals, where none existed. Comfortable living did not exist for them. They were truly "founded on Calvary, there to serve a crucified Christ." Often youth and inexperience appeared to be assets rather than deterrents to ministry. If the young sacrificed their lives, it was not before they planted enduring centers of Mercy.

As in the case of the Irish Sisters of Mercy years before them, one may ask of the American Sisters: What was the motivation behind all the suffering, compassion, risk-taking—in short, unlimited mercy of the Sisters? The motivation is found in the fourth vow: the search for *justice* for the "poor, sick and ignorant." The fourth vow centers in the Christian moral obligation to seek for justice.

The American Sisters sought for justice for themselves as well as for others when truth demanded it. In Providence, Rhode Island they defended themselves against "Know-Nothings" who attempted to put them out of their convent and set it on fire. They fought successfully against prejudice in Manchester, New Hampshire that had led to the closing of public schools. When the second Bishop of Chicago attempted to deprive the Sisters of their motherhouse property, young Agatha O'Brien defended the Sisters' rights successfully! When Bishop James Healy of Portland, Maine attempted to interfere with congregational elections and internal affairs of the Sisters, they protested to the Pope with success. In Jersey City, when the pastor of St. Patrick's Parish put the Sisters out of their convent, they challenged him publicly and received the support of the parish—and of New Jersey historians. In a similar situation in Philadelphia, the people of Assumption Parish supported the Sisters against an unjust pastor and offered them a home as a convent and a new school to administer. Eventually the Philadelphia Sisters became one of the largest Mercy congregations in the country.

To be sure, the strongest missions of the Sisters of Mercy for justice were not in protection of their own rights, but in the service of the poor, sick, and uneducated. When the Mercys celebrated one hundred and fifty years of Mercy in 1981, a national article could speak of "the independent stances and thrilling action for justice" which Mercys had demonstrated in America since 1843. Justice was a keystone of Mercy action wherever the Sisters served.

Justice *within* the Mercy communities in America represented the radical quality of freedom of the children of God. The Sisters saw human dignity as a goal of their religious vocation. This requirement had to be expressed in Mercy communities as social bodies. Redress of injustice was a mission of Mercy which identified the seeds of justice first among the Sisters themselves. In other words, Mercy justice began with the Sisters and then went out to all whom they served.

When the Sisters first arrived from Ireland to America, they had been shocked by slavery. Bishop James Healy's father had owned slaves in the South; his mother was a mulatto slave girl; yet he was the Bishop who served the Sisters in Manchester, New Hampshire. In the South *before* the Civil War and during it, the Sisters ransomed blacks. They served the Indians on reservations in the Northeast when no one else served them. They considered the fight against bigotry in New England a matter of justice, even though WASPS attacked them on the streets and called them "emissaries of Rome." The Sisters helped to pave the way for successful anti-bigotry crusades in New England.

Even as far West as Little Rock, Arkansas, in 1857, Sister Paula Lombard was shocked to learn that a black man was offered to the Sisters for sale as a slave. Ironically, Little Rock became one hundred years later the site of a powerful struggle for black freedom. It is well to remember that slavery was an accepted American institution until the mid-1860s, and that Indians were shunted to poverty on distant reservations long after the Civil War. Wherever slavery of any type appeared where the Sisters of Mercy served, they opposed it strenuously.

The ministry of Mercy arises from the cry of human beings for justice. Mercy, responding to the cry, must serve justice. The question faced by all who truly seek justice is not only one of individual justice but of what might be called planetary morality. A decisive change in the direction of moral theology on the societal level was needed not only in 1843–1910, but is needed perhaps more so in the 1990s.

The Mercy Sisters in America assumed a free, decisive, prophetic voice in contending for the poor and suffering who were unable to fight for their own liberation. They were prophetic because they understood the meaning of Gospel justice. They found prophetic answers. They knew their mission was boundless and unlimited. In Mercy, time and eternity meet.

The Sisters were deeply aware, then, of their vocation as Christian witnesses. They knew that the most effectual means of rendering themselves useful to their neighbor was to give an example of holiness. The way to holiness is shorter by life examples than by rules. St. Augustine said, "We can hardly be moved to do what is right unless we see others do it." Precisely here is one of the great values of religious life in community. When Catherine McAuley first opened her Mercy House on September 24, 1827, she did not at that time contemplate the founding of a religious community. She *did* have the desire to live for others in the love of Christ, both among her co-workers and among the broader community of the poor, sick, and ignorant. The Congregation was thus a beautiful product of the love of God for all. Prophetic witness was the core of compassionate Mercy. Witness through service was more essential than simple exhortation. God offered the Sisters the service of the poor as pure gift: "the cup of cold water, compassion for the poor with no hope of return from anyone except God."

The Sisters in prophetic witness bonded with Christ-like apostles who chose to work side by side with them in Mercy. Priests, doctors, "lay persons" who followed the same goals as the Sisters were welcome as companions in Mercy mission. The Sisters were said to reveal "a sixth sense" in identifying persons who shared their ideal of service by incorporating them with Mercy ministry.

The Sisters' companions in service often shared their poverty. Indeed "poverty was a common mark of Mercy foundations." In Pittsburgh the Sisters opened a public laundry to secure the money to provide food; in Chicago they lived first in a "shanty" of sixteen by forty feet, "a sieve in summer and a shell in winter"; in Loretto, Pennsylvania they had to borrow wood for fuel, to bring water from an outside pump, and to bake bread in an iron pot; in Philadelphia they moved mattresses every morning to convert bedrooms into classrooms; in all their missions—Buffalo, Rochester, Omaha, Yreka—they shared the poverty of those they served. Their account books reveal such items as "eight cents given to a poor man."

The *special preference* of the Sisters was the service of poor women.

"No work can be more productive of good to society or more conducive to the happiness of the poor than the careful instruction of women." But the Mercy mission was broad. The Sisters came to America at a crucial point in the development of American cities and the American Church. Bishops all over the United States begged for their services to the poor because of their reputation for perseverance, no matter what the demands made upon them. They were asked to serve the immoral, the wayward, the demented.

Subjected to cold, poverty, and hunger together with those they served, the Sisters themselves succumbed to tuberculosis, poor nutrition, and exhaustion, or they died as they cared for victims of plagues of cholera and yellow fever. Somehow their numbers were always replenished. When young women were found engaged in day-long manual labor in American cities, the Sisters opened night schools after their own day-long labors. When no buildings were available for schools, the Sisters established schools in church basements. When helpless orphans were brought to their door, orphanages originated on the spot. The special charisms of service were experienced freely.

The Sisters of Mercy, attempting to love and serve God and his children with simplicity and singlemindedness, did not feel unrequited in their labors of love. In St. Luke they read of the apostles on the way to Emmaus, talking of all that had happened during the crucifixion of Christ. The apostles met Christ on the way. The Sisters were taught that they take Christ with them when they visit the sick people they serve. If the apostles met Christ on the way, so do Sisters who serve the sick and the poor. They receive more than they give. "They themselves are enriched immeasurably by spending time and energy among God's needy." Thus spoke Catherine McAuley. The Mercy mission spread all over America. As Catherine would have said, "It is God's work."

One could cite hundreds of missions opened across America by Mercy Sisters for students of all ages. Convent schools were opened to secure bread and butter for the Sisters. Or a piano was found so that the Sisters could offer music lessons in the convent so as to purchase food.

The teaching of the Sisters was indeed endless. They instructed poor immigrants in the steerage of their sailing vessel on the way from Ireland to America in 1843; traveling from New Hampshire to a new foundation in Omaha, they had to stop overnight in St. Joseph, Missouri, and there they cared for the sick, hungry, weary immigrants on their way West; in Bangor, Maine they opened dark basement schools under St. John's Church in order to teach poor children; when their pastor in Manchester, New Hampshire brought a little seven year old girl to their convent and asked if there was room for her, the Sisters opened an orphanage; in

Northern California they served the people during the terror of the Vigilantes in 1856, instructed prisoners in San Quentin Prison, and opened one of the first homes and schools for unwed mothers in the West; when railroad construction began in New Jersey in the 1870s, the Sisters followed the immigrant railroad laborers to Bordentown and instructed workers in the New Jersey barge canals; in Burlington, Vermont they opened an orphanage and school, and an asylum for the mentally disturbed; in Northern New York State they taught on the St. Regis Indian Reservation and conducted night classes for lumbermen working in the forests; in Oswego they rode handlebars on the railroads to nearby towns in order to teach Christian doctrine; in Manchester, New Hampshire they asked parishioners to contribute "a dime a brick" to build a school. In short, there were no limits to Mercy in education. The Sisters were teaching always, formally or informally.

I.

MERCY SPIRITUALITY IN THE WRITINGS OF EARLY AMERICAN SISTERS

OUTLINE

Introduction

Frances Warde: From Book of Private Prayers

Frances Warde: From Lecture on the Use of Time

Mother Austin Carroll: The Character of Frances Warde

Sister Paul Xavier Warde: The Spirituality of Frances Warde

Frances Warde: Spiritual Maxims

Frances Warde: Favorite Scripture Passages

"The Sisters of Mercy" in *The Pittsburgh Catholic,* July 6, 1844

Sister Mary Philip Neri Bowen: Maxims

Mother M. Gertrude Cosgrave: Maxims

Mother Mary Frances Monholland: Maxims

Mercy Author Unknown: Tradition Lives Always: On Racism

Sister Mary Angela Lawler: On Community Friendship

Mother Patricia Waldron: An Offering of Our Friends to God

Mercy Author Unknown: On Mother Regis Wade and Friendship

Sister Mary Augustine McKenna: Promise To Help Homeless Children, New York

Mother Mary of Mercy Carroll, New Orleans: On Light Received Through Suffering

Sister Mary Juliana Purcell: On Religious as Instructors of Youth

Mother Mary Patrick McCallion: The Spirit of Mother Catherine McAuley and Her First Sisters

An Appreciation of Mother Genevieve Granger: A Holy Woman

Mother M. Joseph Devereux, New York: Death by Accident

Sister M. Xavier McDermott: Death by Yellow Fever in Louisiana

Mother M. Austin Carroll: On Slavery, St. Martin, West Indies

Mother Baptist Kane, Translator: *Meditations*

Mother M. de Sales Reddan: Death of a Saint

Instructions for Postulants, Mississippi, 1850: On Sainthood

Sisters of Mercy: From *A Catechism of Scripture History,* for Children

Mother M. Baptist Russell: Prayer for Faith

Prayers for Dedication of College of Mount Saint Mary, Plainfield, New Jersey, 1908

Prayers for the Sick: Brooklyn, New York, 1879

The Prayer of the Sisters of Mercy of New Jersey

INTRODUCTION

Mercy spirituality in America between 1843 and 1910 is revealed in the prayer life of the Sisters of Mercy and in their fourth vow: the service of the poor, the sick, and the ignorant. While apostolic labor expressed in the line, "Her cloister is the alley of the poor," strikes the observer most immediately, the more one becomes acquainted with the early American Sisters of Mercy, the more one becomes cognizant that contemplation and service are reciprocal in the life of the Sisters. Or perhaps better said, contemplation and service are one: they are never separated either in theory or in action.

This unity is well expressed in the prayers and writings of the later nineteenth century Mercy Sisters revealed in the following selections throughout this book. Most of them are brief, as the Sisters had little time for writing; their actual vows of both community prayer and service of the poor, sick, and unlearned are amazing to the reader of the 1990s. Christian service of society today, if not in actuality, then in its manifestations, has changed. To read the writings of the early American Sisters—some simple and profound, some complex and profound—is an exercise not in nostalgia but in profound reverence, sympathy, and gratitude. The challenge to the reader on the verge of the twenty-first century is to not be deceived by seeming simplicity, but to enter into the profundity of predecessors whose lives were centered in God in a manner that defined commitment as both totally permanent and totally accepting of suffering.

The will of God was not theological theory. God's action in the lives of the Sisters who wrote the following thoughts on spirituality was absolutely real. Their faith was not open to question. Whatever their joys or sufferings, the meaning of these experiences was centered in spiritual belief. The price demanded for faith, as revealed frequently in later sections of this book, was frequently life itself. And whether the Sister who sacrificed her life was twenty-one or eighty-one became almost irrelevant. To serve those in need to the utmost was the ultimate response to the vows of religion. And this ultimate response was frequently either demanded or sought. God was central in the day-to-day life of the Sister of Mercy of the second half of the nineteenth century.

*   *   *

FRANCES WARDE: FROM BOOK OF PRIVATE PRAYERS

Suscipe

O God, into Your hands I commend my spirit. To You I abandon my hopes and fears, my desires and repugnances, my temporal and eternal prospects. To You I commit the wants of my body; to You I commit the more precious interests of my immortal spirit. . . . Though my faults are many, my miseries great, my spiritual poverty extreme, my hope in You surpasses all. It is superior to my weakness, greater than my difficulties, stronger than death. Though temptation should assail me, I will hope in You. Though I should sink beneath my weakness, I will hope in You still. Though I should break my resolutions, I will look to You confidently for grace to keep them at last. . . . I trust in You for You are my Father, my God. . . . I am Your loving child who put my trust in You, and so trusting shall not be confounded.

A Morning Oblation of Myself to My Celestial Mother the Ever Blessed Virgin

Beloved Jesus, Mary, Joseph, and good Angels, I humbly and gratefully thank you for my preservation of the past night, and I beg of you to accept the offering I make of myself to you this day with all that I am and have, that through you I may not lose any opportunity of promoting the glory of my good God. And I beg by your intercession that he will be pleased to accept this desire in gratitude for the great blessings he has graciously conferred on me, which grateful feeling together with the most perfect humility I beg, I implore of you to obtain for me. For your blessed protection I beg to offer myself, my dearest and only Mother, to you in whom after my adorable Creator I have the greatest confidence, and on whose holy protection and maternal care I have the strongest claims—not only that your Divine Son left you to us as our Mother, but being deprived of my dear earthly Mother—I do, with my own free will, with my heart and soul humbly and earnestly beg to take you for my Mother, and entreat you to take me as your child with all that I am and have. You are the most merciful and kindest of Mothers—you are pleased to style yourself. . . . [Continuation of prayer is missing in notebook.]

Morning Offering

. . . My God, I offer you all the duties of this day, and implore your supporting, enlivening, and animating grace in order to serve you this day with humility, fervor, affection, and cheerfulness, and in the true spirit of mortification and penance. I ask these graces for this day in particular, desiring to spend it as if it were to be the last of my mortal life. I beg the same favors for Reverend Mother and for every Sister in this Institute. I beg also the grace of opposing my evil inclinations, humors, and temper with vigor and watchfulness, but sweetly and charitably, and of returning to you affectionately when I fall. Grant, Lord, that every exertion I make in your service may be made with a pure intention of pleasing you alone and with a great desire of promoting your glory, and that I may scrupulously avoid the praise and esteem of creatures. . . . I have one favor more to ask of you, O my God, which is that you give me such a conviction of my own nothingness that I may feel neither surprised nor hurt when I receive any real or imaginary slights from creatures . . . frequently calling to mind that unless we suffer with you, we shall not be glorified with you. . . .

Prayer Before Holy Communion

Lord, I am not worthy to receive you on account of my sins, not worthy, on account of the little service I render you, of the little love I bear you. Speak only one word and my soul shall be healed. You can, dear Jesus, with one word supply everything that is wanting in me. Do it, then, dearest Jesus, my Lord. I firmly believe the truths the Holy Catholic Church believes and teaches, and particularly that I am now going to receive the true body and blood, soul and divinity of my Lord and Saviour Jesus Christ under the form of bread, whole and entire, as it is in heaven, the same that has been of the Virgin Mary, and that suffered under Pontius Pilate, and was crucified. I believe it more than if I saw it with my own eyes because *you* have revealed it, who art truth itself. And in this faith I will live and die with your holy grace. Amen.[1]

FRANCES WARDE: FROM LECTURE ON THE USE OF TIME

How did Frances Warde accomplish so much, how did she live continually in such amazing fulfillment in Christ? A spiritual lecture she often read to the Sisters at Manchester, quoted later by Sister M. Catherine Garety, gives a hint of an answer:

It is astonishing how much time was at the command of saints, and how little seems to be at the disposal of the generality of Christians!

How eminently did the saints fulfill the duties of their lives —union with God, devotion to the different offices their lives called for—and still they did not fail to find time for the charity for which only *the few* seem to find time.

Frances was indeed a woman united with God. Through her union with him, her time seemed a kind of eternal timelessness. Her love and service of others transcended time. She was able to do more than is humanly possible.

Every moment of her life seemed to be filled with her apostolate to such an extent as to appear almost miraculous.[2]

MOTHER AUSTIN CARROLL: THE CHARACTER OF FRANCES WARDE

Persons brought into close contact with Mother Warde, especially in her later years, seeing only her marvellous success and the honors that fell thick and fast about her, were sometimes tempted to think that her life had been all sunshine. In point of fact, however, no originator of great enterprises ever experienced more thwarting, more contradictions, more ingratitude, more persecution, even from those to whom she naturally looked for assistance and encouragement, than did this distinguished and extraordinary woman. And the fact that, during her worst experiences of the vanity, the folly, the narrowness, the jealousies of some with whom she had close relations, she looked on poor human nature more in sorrow than in anger, is perhaps the best eulogy of her noble heart.[3]

SISTER PAUL XAVIER WARDE: THE SPIRITUALITY OF FRANCES WARDE

Public testimony to Frances Warde's holiness is only a recognition of human awareness of her union with Christ and all men in love and service. Like Catherine McAuley, her earthly ideal, Frances did not confide to others—with the possible exception of William McDonald—the depth of her life with Christ in God. Hints of her inner life exist in the meager number of her written words which remain today. It is certain that she transcended great suffering through the joy of her union with Christ. Her grandniece, Sister Paul Xavier Warde, recalled a rare statement of Frances concerning her spiritual gifts. Sister Mary Agnes wrote:

We are not surprised to learn that a long and serious illness followed her arrival in Pittsburgh from Chicago, for her bodily strength did not equal her great will. In speaking of this most trying journey afterward, Mother Warde seemed to have forgotten the sufferings in the memory of her religious privileges at Toledo, "blessed then as I was with more consolation from the good God than I deserved."[4]

FRANCES WARDE: SPIRITUAL MAXIMS

A true religious ought not to acknowledge any master but Jesus Christ, and him crucified.

Above all, novices should be taught to be good Christians, for often professed sisters as well as novices know their Institute and Constitutions, and know little of the Gospel of Jesus Christ.

The first mark of a good vocation is a sincere desire of leading a Christian life, because a true religious is no other than a true Christian, a true member of Jesus Christ.

To conduct religious [women] in the way of peace and promote their advancement in virtue requires a science quite different from that of the most learned and pious men.

Since it is so difficult to find an accomplished Superior, how much more difficult to meet one who is perfect.

The Superior [who lacks discretion] will use rigor when gentleness is most necessary, will pardon when she should correct, and wound those very persons whom it is her duty to cure.

To govern well, one must be indulgent and severe, liberal and saving, gentle and determined, simple and wise.

Regulations should be uniform, but for the particular direction of souls, great diversity is necessary.

A Superior truly humble cannot fail to govern well; distrusting herself, she will place her entire confidence in God.

Not to endeavor to gain the heart, to be content with commanding and reproving, is not to be a Superior but a Mistress of slaves.

The true model of a Superior is the good Shepherd.

Oh! If I could relate all the mischief which is done by those who find fault without distinction, without considering that reproofs should be remedies!

Faults of weakness must be corrected with great gentleness.

Enforce with authority what is a matter of obligation, but content yourself with advising what is only a matter of counsel, exhorting to the practice of it in terms of friendship.

It would be cruel [for a Superior] not to listen to her Sisters. . . .

Assuredly Adam did wrong and his fault was known to the Almighty, but God listened to the offender.

Our divine Lord did not make his disciples perfect at once, but allowed them to acquire perfection gradually.

Close to God, all is peace and contentment in him. . . . I put myself without reserve in God's hands. (*Journal*)

The more questions are asked, the more doubts are avoided. . . . Many do not enter the road of prayer because they are not humble enough to make inquiries. . . . One question proposed with simplicity is often the occasion of many instructions.

I very much desire that nothing but perfect union and charity should exist amongst us.

Esteem highly the happiness of being the servant of the servants of God.

How full of joys and deep sorrows my life has been, none can tell.

An Emperor is accounted by the world to be a great personage, and Jesus is only esteemed as a poor, mean, obscure artisan. . . . Jesus employs himself in humble labor, and the worldly man is served by others.

The innocent Jesus presents himself before Pilate to be interrogated about crimes he never committed, and shall I think it hard . . . to examine myself concerning faults of which I am guilty?

In communicating himself spiritually to the poor, our Lord influences us with an ardent desire to receive him in reality . . . and rewards us with a more perfect knowledge of himself.

We should consider a good spiritual book as a letter sent from heaven, a faithful counselor of our souls, a mirror in which we can see things as they really are. . . .

Recreation contributes much to give a new vigor to the spirit. We speak of things which relax the mind and tend to our spiritual advancement.

Be not of the number of those self-sufficient persons who imagine that attention to small devotions betrays weakness of mind.

We should receive all things in whatsoever manner they may happen as coming from the hand of God who sends them with tender love for our greater good.

Let all be lost, provided God be not lost.

Let nothing dwell in our hearts which might trouble our peace or cause sadness and indignation. Take great care lest any resentment steal into your heart.

The sight of the poor should fill us with tender compassion. . . . We should embrace with joy the opportunity of instructing them in the knowledge of God and the way of salvation.

Instructing the poor should be most carefully embraced by all as being most pleasing to Almighty God and his Virgin Mother.

One single Communion is sufficient to transform a sinner into a saint.

In Holy Communion the soul acquires a knowledge of her God and truly tastes the sweetness of his divine presence.

What can the Father refuse us, having given us his beloved Son?

Those who are faithful in small observances are usually faithful . . . in those which are greater.

Retreats have been the means of sanctifying many.

We may receive it as a certain maxim that to live free from temptation is utterly impossible.

That ship alone can reach safety which in time of calm prepares for a storm.

Never judge anyone, but endeavor to excuse faults and have a good opinion of others.

Do nothing through human respect, but do all things purely to please God.

We may compare the just suffering temptation to the metal of which a ciborium is made. It is melted in the crucible, cast into a mold, beaten with a hammer, again applied to fire for gilding, and after that it becomes a precious depository of the consecrated body and blood of Christ.

Rejoice in feeling want, for this is perfect imitation of Christ who, being rich and powerful, became poor for love of us, suffering hunger and thirst, heat and cold, weariness and want.

We should find our hearts so penetrated with the love of God that it may appear that our actions are much less performed by ourselves than by the love which reigns in us.

Contemplate Christ at prayer clothed with his sacred humanity. . . . Place yourself in spirit by his side . . . and beseech him to teach you to pray.[5]

FRANCES WARDE: FAVORITE SCRIPTURE PASSAGES

St. Paul, 1 Cor 13:4–13	Mother McAuley: Familiar Instructions
"Charity is patient:	"Mercy receives the ungrateful again and again, and is never weary of pardoning them.
"Charity is kind:	"Let us show love without remissness.

"Charity envieth not:

"Let us rejoice when good is done, no matter by whom it may be accomplished.

"Charity dealeth not perversely:

"Common sense is the most necessary quality for a teacher. Common sense is the most uncommon of all things.

"Charity is not puffed up:

"Never let us dwell on the good we have done, but rather on what we might have done had we been more faithful to God's grace.

"Charity is not provoked to anger:

"We cannot feel the same always, but we should endeavor to control our countenance.

"Charity thinketh no evil:

"We can never be happy until we are convinced that we are treated by everybody better than we deserve.

"Charity beareth all things:

"Without the cross, the real crown will not come.

"Charity hopeth all things:

"Put your whole confidence in God. He will never see you want for means to do his work.

"Charity endureth all things:

"It is a special favor of God to be made teachers destined to train little ones in his knowledge and love.

"Now there remaineth faith, hope, and charity, these three, but the greatest of these is Charity."

"Remember, if there are a hundred regulations to be observed, the most important is Charity."[6]

"THE SISTERS OF MERCY" IN *THE PITTSBURGH CATHOLIC*
JULY 6, 1844

It may be justly expected from us to give some account of "The Order of Our Lady of Mercy," as the only house belonging to it in the United

States is the one in this city. The object which the members aim at is indicated in a great measure by the name. It is the performance of "corporal and spiritual works of mercy." Though it may be said that they aim at all, as occasion may require, they devote themselves particularly to the visiting of the sick and poor, and affording aid and consolation to the afflicted, to the instruction of the ignorant, and the protection of distressed women of good character. The institute aims at uniting with the practice of those active duties a high degree of the perfection of the contemplative life.

To enable the Sisters to attain as much as possible the perfection of their state, the exercises which their rule enjoins are beautifully varied; the duties of the active and contemplative life are blended together in such a manner that the fervor and recollection of the one are carried through the performance of the exercises of the other, supporting each other mutually and imparting to all that spirit of Christian fervor and active love, which is so amiable an illustration of the sublime maxims of the Gospel.

At one hour the Sister is engaged in holy meditation, contemplating the riches of God's Mercy and Goodness, or assisting at the holy sacrifice of the Altar, laying deep the root of that spirit of charity which shall animate her during the toils of the day; at the next, she wends her way to the house of sorrow, and bends over the bed of misery to speak words of consolation to the afflicted or impart succour to those who are pressed down by poverty. She returns home at the appointed hour to join in the canticle of praise, and sing the glories of the Father of all whose Providence "reacheth from end to end mightily, and ordereth all things sweetly."

She will then meet, perhaps, some female who knew but little of the wonderful ways of God, but she speaks to her of his judgments and righteousness, and raises her mind, and prepares her heart, for the exalted destination to which God invites her. Here she is found wiping off the tear that trickles down the burning cheek of the dying patient, and there endeavoring to soften the exasperated feelings of the child of sorrow, who knows nothing of the dispensation of love whence she could derive consolation. Again, she will return to nourish her own soul in prayer, and examine her own conscience in the presence of her Maker, that she may ascertain whether any human frailty has insinuated itself in the exercise of her various duties, and then undertake to correct the fault which silent meditation before the crucifix will surely reveal and suggest the most certain means of amending.

Day succeeds day in the performance of these similar avocations. The wisdom of the Church has provided her a succession of holy duties, and alternate exercises by which she is enabled to contend against the weariness which might attend uniformity, to enter every day into herself more deeply, and explore more and more that endless labyrinth of the human heart, to unravel its windings, detect and correct its faults, enkindle in it the flame of divine love, and fit the soul for the fruition of that God whose great attributes are Mercy and Love. Conforming to the spirit of her holy institute she will be sure to drink deep of the spirit of the Gospel, and spread abroad amongst many its holy fragrance, and thus prepare herself, and lead others to meet that God who came down from heaven but to enkindle the flame of divine love.

Such is the object, and such is the life of the Sister of Mercy. An order of men with the same name was founded in the thirteenth century. Its principal object was the redemption of Christian captives from bondage; in attaining this, the members bound themselves to sacrifice their liberty and their lives. The modern order aims at the performance of the corporal and spiritual works of mercy animated by a similar spirit, though the circumstances of our times happily do not present the danger to life or liberty in the same appalling form.

"The Order of the Sisters of Mercy" was founded in Ireland in 1827 by Mrs. McAuley—In its object and in its constitution it evidently met a demand of the age. Numbers of ladies of the highest rank in life joined in the noble undertaking. They have now several houses in Ireland and some hundreds of members. Houses of the order have been formed also in London, Birmingham, Liverpool, Sunderland and other places in England, most of them on a magnificent scale; Sisters have gone to Nova Scotia and Newfoundland; the house in this city is the only one as yet in the United States; it was founded in the beginning of the present year.

"Houses of Mercy" for the reception of distressed females of good character are attached to most of the Convents in Europe. They are received there, and instructed in some handiwork that will afford them means of subsistence as well as in the exercise of their religious duties, and then provided with suitable situations where they can learn an honorable independence. Schools are also attached to most of the houses, instruction is given to grown females; but those duties are never allowed to exclude that attention to the sick and poor which has always been a prominent duty of the order, or that diligence in the strict performance of the choral duty and other public and private exercises of piety at home, which are the source whence the spirit and usefulness of the order is derived. They have endeavored always to retain more of the spirit of the contemplative life in the discharge of their various duties than most of the other operative orders.

Let us hope that God will impart the same blessing to the good work here, which he has done elsewhere, making the institution grow in numbers and increase in the spirit of the Gospel, and spread amongst many the sweet odour of Christian virtue. What more glorious object can be wished for, than to see these institutions which breathe forth the sweet balm of piety multiply and increase, giving glory to God on High, and becoming the means of communicating to men on earth evangelical peace.[7]

SISTER MARY PHILIP NERI BOWEN: MAXIMS

One thing we must aim at in ordering our lives is seeing Christ in every person and every thing.

The sense of the presence of God which we shall perhaps never fully attain should, nevertheless, be desired and striven for. As Jesus Christ came to reveal God to us, so the effort to see Christ in our surroundings is a more successful way than any other of keeping God before our eyes.

What is meant by seeing Christ in creatures? It means that whatever happens, we are to disregard the apparent cause or agent, and to say with devotion: "This is all His Holy Will! This is His love!"[8]

MOTHER M. GERTRUDE COSGRAVE: MAXIMS

She who has attained to the possession of spiritual things can never be deprived of her source of happiness.

Soar upward on the wings of aspiration; be fearless, and believe in the loftiest possibilities.

Mind is the infallible weaver of destiny; and the web woven upon the loom of life is character.

Dream lofty dreams, and as you dream so shall you become.

Whatever your task may be, concentrate your whole mind upon it.

Under the circumstances, do that which you believe to be right.

Follow under all circumstances the highest promptings within you.

Make pure your heart and you will make your life rich, sweet, and beautiful.

Be as a flower content to be, to grow in sweetness day by day.

If you would perfect yourself in knowledge, perfect yourself in love.

She who controls herself, controls her life, her circumstances, her destiny.

Without self-knowledge there can be no abiding peace of mind.

The children of the Kingdom are known by their lives.

Know this to be true, that circumstances can only affect you in so far as you allow them to do so.[9]

MOTHER MARY FRANCES MONHOLLAND: MAXIMS

In Chicago during the first decade of convent life, several Sisters died, some of whom were efficient and accomplished teachers, whose places could not easily be filled, as vocations for the West were few and far between at that early period. The scant accommodations the convent afforded, the piercing frosts intensified by the lake breezes, the long distances to be traversed through snow-drifts to the schools on the north and west sides of the city, told heavily on the Sisters' health. There were not members enough for the work.

To relieve Mother Agatha O'Brien's anxiety, Mother Mary Frances Monholland did the work of many, never complained of labor, and was a pillar of support to the disheartened Sisters. In the midst of the gloom, she spoke hopefully, amusing them with her quaint sayings:

"Put your shoulder to the wheel, and the work is done."

"Don't fret about your future, you will sleep half of it away."

"This is a winter view of things, the summer has to come."[10]

MERCY AUTHOR UNKNOWN:
TRADITION LIVES ALWAYS: ON RACISM

An institution owes its personality to its traditions. Without these, it remains merely a building, a structure of brick and stone. Mercy Hospital, Manistee, is blessed in its traditions. Planned and loved by the saintly mother Alphonsus, it yet breathes her spirit of gracious hospitality, of dedication to God's glory, through the service of the neighbor. Mercy Hospital is an institution that will live. It has a soul.

What matter if the flesh be white or black or brown? The dying Saviour wore for all the thorny crown.[11]

SISTER MARY ANGELA LAWLER:
ON COMMUNITY FRIENDSHIP

Mother Mary Agatha was a woman whose great heart went out to the poor, the sick, and the suffering. To those who stumbled and fell she stretched out a strong, kindly hand. This same spirit she instilled in her Sisters.

Years after Mother Mary Agatha was dead, Sister Mary Angela Lawler, who had been in the novitiate with her, said,

Mother Agatha was the uplifting spirit. She would say to me, "We must bear all and work while we are young and strong, and when we grow old, dear Sister, you and I, and [when] our hospital has been blessed and our labors may be given into other hands, then we will walk in the garden and talk of old times and laugh at the hardships of today."

But Sister Mary Angela added sadly,

I am old and the hospital has been blessed, but I walk in the garden alone. Mother Agatha was taken from us eleven years ago; yet her example and precept are always with us. She was gentle, brave, and kind. She encouraged us to work and to economize in every way. . . . We were happy while we worked and God has blessed our efforts.[12]

MOTHER PATRICIA WALDRON:
AN OFFERING OF OUR FRIENDS TO GOD

There is something, O my God, which costs me yet more than all; it is the sacrifice of my friends, and behold, Lord, I freely make it, though my heart bleeds as I pronounce the words. Accept it then graciously, and in exchange for me, be Thou, O Lord, their friend. From the present moment, think of them the more as I shall endeavor to give them up for the love of Thee. . . . Oh, may they love Thee and begin to know by experience how happy a thing it is, to forget everything else in order to remember Thee.

Thou who hast created me, have mercy on me. Thou who hast formed me, who hast made my body with its humors, affections, temperament, constitution. Thou who knowest the current in which my humors run, who knowest the heat or sluggishness of my blood. Thou who knowest my strength and my weakness. Thou who knowest my every act, and Thou who hast made my soul, who hast given me my natural character, who hast given me such tenderness and hast left me such weakness, have mercy on me. Thou knowest all, Thou knowest the inward struggle, the constant defeat, the bitter failures. These are all I have to offer Thee.

O Jesus, hidden God, I cry to Thee, O Jesus, hidden light, I turn to Thee, O Jesus, hidden love, I run to Thee. With all the strength I have I worship Thee. With all the love I have, I cling to Thee. With all my soul I long to be with Thee, and fear no more to fail or fall from Thee. . . . Free me, O dearest Lord, from all but Thee, and break all chains that keep me back from Thee.[13]

MERCY AUTHOR UNKNOWN:
ON MOTHER REGIS WADE AND FRIENDSHIP

In giving reproof, Mother Regis was never loud or harsh. Those who received correction from her could not help feeling that she was a mother performing a painful duty who gained the hearts of the Sisters by the sweetness and strength in which correction was given. Memories of those days still linger around the hearts of the Sisters who were fortunate enough to be trained under this good mother. In friendship she was loyal and faithful. Never in our life have we seen such devoted friendship as that which existed between Mother M. Regis and Mother M. Austin, as it had indeed been an old and tried friendship formed in the cradle of their religious lives, dating back to the Manchester Novitiate. It lasted through sunshine and shadow, and at the close of life was found fresh, having never caused a furrow on the brow or a wound in the heart. Each was to the other something more than friend. They were in reality sisters and loved each other as if they had been bound by family ties, so unchanging was their friendship to the last.[14]

SISTER MARY AUGUSTINE MCKENNA:
PROMISE TO HELP HOMELESS CHILDREN, NEW YORK

"In the name of our Lord and Saviour, Jesus Christ, and under the protection of His Immaculate Mother, Mary, ever Virgin, I, *Sister Mary Augustine,* for the love of His Sacred Heart, do resolve, but not vow, to suffer all the blame, shame, and humiliation, toil, trial, and trouble, that it may be God's will to permit, in order to establish a home for homeless children. I protest that, in all that concerns it, I rely solely on the assistance of God and the guidance of the Holy Spirit, especially in what will be required by this resolution; and further, that I will not do anything in relation to it except in obedience."

The above document, dated first Friday, November, 1869, was kept at *the back of her vows,* and was placed in Sister Mary Augustine's coffin the first Friday of August, 1873, and buried with her. Plenty of blame, shame, and humiliation recompensed her generosity. But on her death-bed she could thank God for her answered prayer. *Over eleven hundred children* were sheltered in her convents, and she had been the chief instrument in that great work.[15]

MOTHER MARY OF MERCY CARROLL, NEW ORLEANS:
ON LIGHT RECEIVED THROUGH SUFFERING

One of the many good things that come to us from the Cross is that it keeps our poor hearts detached from this world, makes us feel that we are exiles and pilgrims, and teaches us to look forward with longing to the time when we shall exchange it for our eternal home. Oh life is very short! What folly, then, to waste any of its precious hours on trifles.

How I pray that I may see things as the saints see them—as they saw them when they were here. I often think that what changed most of them from being sinners, or mere ordinary Christians, into heroic souls, was a flood of light which came down on them from above, revealing to them the vanity, the falsehood, the unreality, of the things of earth—how everything, but the great God, is only smoke, vapor, or, as St. Teresa says, a dream which will be nothing when we awake. Truly may we say, with another great saint: "My God, and my All!" for, outside of our Father in heaven, there is absolutely nothing worth possessing or coveting.[16]

SISTER MARY JULIANA PURCELL:
ON RELIGIOUS AS INSTRUCTORS OF YOUTH

1. When a young person enters a convent, one motive, to save her soul, is supreme in her over all others. Yet by the fact of crossing the threshold of a religious house, she assumes grave responsibilities towards the church in particular, and society in general. Religious Institutes are not founded merely to provide retreats for persons piously desirous of withdrawing from the world that they may reach their last end the more easily. The church of God, to a great extent, wisely entrusts to Religious who are peculiarly fitted by their profession and manner of life to undertake it, the training and culture of children, that precious portion of her flock. Hence too much importance cannot be attached to your vocation as a member of a teaching order, since the opportunities it furnishes of promoting God's glory and the salvation of souls are almost unlimited.

2. You must be careful not to degenerate into a mere teacher of secular branches; that would be to sacrifice the end to the means. Your faith should be so ardent as to keep ever before your mind that it is with

the souls of the children you are especially charged. In other schools, they
can get secular learning. But while you shed the light of science on their
understandings, you should place the principles of religion in their hearts.
In ninety out of a hundred cases, all the religious training a child gets
comes from you. The greater number of children will by circumstances be
deprived of the blessing of frequent instructions and salutary admonitions: in later life they will be so engaged in worldly cares as not to find
time for instruction where it is given; or if they have the will and the time
to go in search of it, it cannot be had.

How many of the children who attend your schools have vicious or
careless parents and associates, whose influence and example all but destroy the salutary effects of the instructions imparted? But you must labor
all the more zealously because of the dangers to which the children entrusted to you may one day be exposed. Be sure that the impressions you
make on their young hearts will not easily be effaced, though they may be
forgotten or disregarded for a time. How necessary it is, therefore, that you
should labor with untiring zeal and charity in the faithful discharge of
your duties, in the Sunday school, in the classroom, in the orphanage, on
the visitation, in public institutions, wherever, in fine, you can find children to instruct or souls to be guided and trained in the knowledge and
love of Jesus Christ, and grounded in the doctrines of our holy Faith.

3. Your success in the great work of teaching and instructing will be
in proportion to your efforts to fit yourself for your duties. Every child
under your care is like a block of marble out of which you are required to
carve a figure. Now, if you lack the skill, knowledge, and ability requisite
for such a task, you will fail; or the image you produce will be devoid of all
beauty and symmetry. The secret of success in teaching lies in your appreciation of your vocation. You must regard each little one as the temple of
the Holy Ghost, the shrine of God's image; and hence you should have for
each child the greatest respect. If you wish your labors to bear fruit, be
yourself all that you ought to be to the little ones of Jesus Christ; let Him
be your model; copy His meekness, patience, sweetness, and zeal. Let
your whole life, manner, and conduct be a living illustration of the doctrines and virtues you inculcate. For, if a child observe in you the imper-
fections and frailties she is accustomed to see in other persons, it will be
impossible for her to be influenced for good by your words, for you do not
practice what you teach. "Our lives should be conformable to our words,
and our works to the holiness of our profession."

It would be well to examine yourself closely regarding the manner in
which you habitually acquit yourself of your duties in the schools and
other places where you have to do with children. You should make strong
resolutions to correct whatever has been amiss, and beg of God through

the intercession of the Queen of Heaven to help you in future to perform your duty perfectly.[17]

MOTHER MARY PATRICK MCCALLION: THE SPIRIT OF CATHERINE MCAULEY AND HER FIRST SISTERS

The prevailing characteristics of her letters [Catherine McAuley] are *good sense, solid piety,* intense love and compassion for the suffering and ignorant, gratitude for the smallest acts of kindliness done to her or hers, with holy and tender friendship for those united to her by spiritual kinship. Dashed off as they were in moments snatched from most absorbing occupations—some written in the stillness of night, some at the bed of a dying Sister, some in the solitude of retreat, some in the mirthful recreation hour, they are clear, forcible and to the purpose. The calm, dignified foundress seems lost in the weak woman oppressed. They show her to have been thoroughly unselfish, to have possessed great patience, even joy under suffering which belongs only to the higher paths of the spiritual life. The least troubles of her children have her warm, ready sympathy even when her own heart seems breaking. She first grieves with them and then directs their thoughts to the motives of consolation which faith proposes.

She was one of those holy, high-minded women who inspire others, including men, with their lofty enthusiasm, and such persons lift their friends above the meanness and littleness of poor unaided nature and share with them their own ardor and simplicity. In the direction of her children, Catherine showed strength and tenderness—duty, the duty of the hour must be done and well done; and crosses which Christ sends them must be received with cordial acquiesence to the divine.

Considerateness for others formed a marked feature of her character. She was able to enter into the spirit of a joke, but quite powerless to carry it on if it would cause anyone the least uneasiness.

I think what pleased or most took our fancy in Mother Catherine was the absence of a manner which said, "I am the Foundress."

I never saw any remarkable woman who was more free than Mother Catherine from everything that could suggest the idea of what the world calls a "clever woman." She was a true mother and a lady. She regarded herself as a humble instrument in the hand of God, who was making use of her in a work not of her own doing.

Weighing everything according to God's standard, she never forgot that "the Institute is founded on Calvary," and therefore she exercised the virtue of the crucified in an eminent degree.

She considered God alone in all things and all things in God.

When a Sister spoke to her of some trouble of mind, she closed the interview by saying, pointing to the picture of Our Lord crowned with thorns, that if we looked more to our suffering Lord, our trials would seem very light and consolation would soon come to our hearts.

Jesus was silent—this was the subject of her daily meditation. . . . It schooled her into reserve as to the gifts bestowed upon her that she might be able to say, "My secret to myself." Once only did these superabundant favors throw her off her guard; she who preferred Calvary to Thabor once complained that the sun shone too brightly—too brightly for an exile.

The heaven-inspired trait of rejoicing in the success of others had a charm in her eyes which endeared its possessors very much to her heart.

Catherine McAuley had great confidence in and reliance on the Providence of God in everything she undertook.

Catherine to her Sisters:

"Partings from home and friends to enter religion are sweet sorrows, but partings in religion are bitter sorrows."

"My legacy to the Institute is charity."

"You should show joy in your countenance—the joy of serving your master. They who are animated with the spirit of their vocation are the happiest people in the world."

"Bless and love the fatherly hand that wounds you. He will come again, both hands laden with blessings."[18]

AN APPRECIATION OF MOTHER GENEVIEVE GRANGER:
A HOLY WOMAN

The power of discerning *truth* in doubtful matters was remarkable in Mother Genevieve, and she not only recognized it in herself, but she had the faculty of making it clear to others. How many times in all her years as Superior she was called upon to scatter the mist of doubt in the minds of young and old, and when she had finished her exposition of the truth, how clear it all seemed!

A certain Sister says, "Mother Genevieve told me after she became Superior that her greatest trial was a tendency to sadness." Yet who would have suspected it? No matter who applied to her for advice or assistance, she was always cheerful and sympathetic, never referring to her own trials, and always endeavoring to lighten the burden of others, to cheer the dejected, to encourage the faltering. . . . She would frequently say, "How good God is! We have given Him only what is His by right. . . . We are simply paying our debt. . . ."

When fault was found with anyone in her presence, she would remark, "Well, now let us find some good in her; all have more good than at first sight it may seem. . . . When we are clear-sighted to the faults of others," she would say, "it is a sign we are neglecting our own. Charity is the bond of perfection—first God, then our neighbor; seeing God in each one and loving all in Him and for Him. We cannot fail in conversation if we carry this out, for we will be most careful not to hurt the feelings of another. Coldness or resentment should find no place in the heart of a servant of God. . . ."

"St. Teresa says the reason God loves humility so dearly is because He is the Supreme Truth, and humility is truth.". . . In conversation with Mother Genevieve, one could not help feel greater reverence for God and less esteem for self. . . .

Asked on one occasion if diplomacy of language did not mean insincerity, she replied, "No! but it does mean grace in conversation and effectiveness in argument, for St. Francis de Sales taught that it is a holy dissimulation and may be cultivated with excellent results."

She was of the opinion that none of us are fond of persons who are ready at all times and under all conditions to criticize and say bluntly, "You are wrong!" Their self-assertiveness and superiority of manner render them ungracious. The same thought can be expressed in a kindly manner. . . . To be told you are making a mistake at once puts you on the defensive; to ask if you have not made a mistake leaves you in a receptive mood, open to discussion. . . .

Mother Genevieve feared nothing so much as injustice to anyone, even a child. She never sided with a pupil against a teacher, as she knew that would lessen authority, but if she thought the punishment too severe she lost no time in reasoning with the teacher.

Her spirit of recollection was admirable, and while at prayer she seemed so absorbed that no one cared to interrupt her. . . .

If a good woman in any state of life is one of the glories of creation, Mother Genevieve said, surely the religious woman cannot be in the background. She quoted the ancient philosopher, "A little thing gives perfection, but perfection is not a little thing. . . . No amount of proficiency in languages, arts, and sciences is of any value without virtues that tend to make these wise and good.". . .

"Sometimes in our lives we will meet with something hard to bear," she said, "but whatever we do, if it is not done to please God, it is of no

account for eternity. If the motive is good, it will be great in His sight. . . .
He knows how weak we are and is always ready to forgive if we ask
pardon. . . . God is so generous He will let nothing done for Him go
unrewarded."

Mother Genevieve was sometimes asked to explain the Mercy Rule
to the assembled Community. Her interpretation was always logical and
thoroughly spiritual. . . . She knew full well that the road to Heaven is by
way of the cross—so she believed and so she taught others. To use her own
words, "We cannot go to Heaven in a rocking chair.". . .

It requires self-control not to display the authority which is ours by
right. Over thirty years of governing a large Community, Mother Genevieve was never dictatorial. Rather, she seemed to ask a favor when she
wanted anything done. Yet Providence allowed her to have trials of all
kinds. She often seemed to be the butt of others, especially Superiors, one
of whom acknowledged in after years how she had impulsively, and without sufficient reason, humbled Mother Genevieve before the whole Community in a serious way. If remonstrated with for taking so much punishment without in the least excusing herself, Mother Genevieve would
reply, "It is all right. It's the will of God for me." Her patience was nothing
short of marvelous. . . .

Lines from a Sister's Notebook on the
Death of Mother Genevieve Granger

One morning I showed Mother Genevieve a clipping from the Chicago newspaper, telling that there was to be a Requiem Mass at the Cathedral for the repose of the souls of two boys we knew, who had been hanged
on the twenty-second of the month. . . .

A week later, at evening recreation, I said, "Mother Genevieve, I had
no zeal today at the jail." She looked surprised, but when I told her we did
not neglect anything, she seemed pleased and said, "Of course it was hard,
Sister, about those poor boys. . . ."

She loved every one of us and appreciated every effort on our part. . . .
She would say to each of us, "Sister, keep your holy rule and it will keep
you." Charity was the virtue dearest to her heart. . . .

On one occasion it came to her knowledge that some cloistered nuns,
who had recently arrived in Chicago, were sadly in need of the necessaries
of life. Although we were in very straitened circumstances, even in danger
of losing the Academy by reason of a heavy mortgage, she had her grocer
send a wagon-load of provisions of all kinds to the immediate relief of the
nuns. By her direction, the poor were never sent away without food, and
sometimes her last dollar went into the pocket of a beggar. When Mother

Bursar would remonstrate with her about what she thought to be impru-
dence, she always smiled and said, "God will provide." She became
known as the "Little Mother of the Poor."

It is almost a week since Mother Genevieve's face lit up in smiles
when I went to her. Less than three hours before she became unconscious,
I saw her dear eyes for the last time. . . .[19]

MOTHER M. JOSEPH DEVEREUX, NEW YORK:
DEATH BY ACCIDENT

"Our recent heavy affliction in the loss of our beloved and saintly
Mother Joseph is so heartrending that I have been unable until now to
attempt to write you the harrowing details. And yet I want you to know
everything, that you may do justice in the *Annals* to as holy a life as was
ever led by any of the saints.

"Our dear sister was sixty years of age on the third of May last, yet
was appointed many months ago to one of the humblest duties in Balmville (that of refectorian, which in the present instance involves a great
deal of labor and the many inconveniences of a country house): she labored in this duty with the alacrity of sixteen and the hearty good-will of a
novice, and in the faithful discharge of her duty met a martyr's death.

"A boy was appointed to bring hot water to the refectory, after each
meal, from the kitchen, which is a floor below. On the fatal day in question, St. Joseph's day, the poor child drew a pail of boiling water from the
boiler at the kitchen range and, when halfway up-stairs, set down the pail
and ran back for soap which he had forgotten. Meanwhile, Mother Joseph
came holding with both her hands a large plate of butter to be put away in
the ice-box, for which purpose she had to descend this same staircase.
Always quick in her movements, she plunged one foot straight into the
cruel water, stumbled and fell, the butter making boiling oil of the water
which poured over her, scalding her most fearfully, back, feet, and limbs.

"Imagine her after this (of course the accident happened in a few
seconds, though it takes so long to tell) walking back upstairs to the refectory where the two sisters engaged in helping her were still at work. To the
question, 'Mother, dear, what happened to you?' she said, 'I met with a
little accident, and shall go to my cell and change my clothes while you
finish here.' She walked up two flights of stairs to her cell, and the two
Sisters dropped everything and followed her. As they removed her clothing, the skin came off in flakes from all the wounded places, and her
untold agony began. The doctor said, the moment he saw her, that the

accident was fatal, although he could not convince the Sisters that Mother Joseph would die. He said the worst sign was that she was so stunned from the shock as not to realize her condition, and that her going up-stairs as she did was a miracle. She was not unconscious, however, and the moment the terrible torture began she insisted on getting out of bed, knelt down at the bedside, and said in a loud, clear, ringing voice, that thrilled through every heart: 'My good God, Thy will be done.' This was her incessant prayer until she expired on Friday evening at half-past six o'clock saying: 'My Jesus, mercy.'

"The doctors, one Catholic, the other Protestant, were equally amazed and edified at her heroic endurance. The latter said: 'She has suffered a thousand years in one night,' yet never a murmur. Nothing but prayer and the most touching aspirations; her moaning through that terrible night was heard all through the house, and filled every heart with agony. The Sisters fixed a complete bed of raw cotton saturated with sweet-oil, and when she was placed on it she said: 'Oh! my dears, this is heaven.'

"With all her active spirit and ardent love of the poor, she was a true contemplative, united to God amid the most harassing cares and duties. God permitted that she should be misunderstood in great measure by the new superiors of the previous ten years, but her humility was so sincere that she really believed herself to be of no account. She used to say she regretted that the time allotted for sleep was so long; it kept her so many hours away from the Blessed Sacrament, and during the day her visits were countless—brief when her time was limited.

"Long years ago she made a compact with herself 'never to think of anything disagreeable,' and the 'disagreeables' were crowded upon her from every side in every possible way. What, then, were her words but echoes of the golden charity with which her heart was filled?"[20]

SISTER M. XAVIER MCDERMOTT:
DEATH BY YELLOW FEVER IN LOUISIANA

On November 5, Sister M. Xavier McDermott, whom the Sisters among themselves used to style "the saint of their band," scrubbed her cell and arranged its poor furniture with unusual care. She then put her accounts in perfect order, saying: "I must spare my dear Sisters trouble." On Sunday, she heard Mass and received Holy Communion for the last time in the chapel she loved so well. About eleven, she was sent to bed, but the Sisters could not believe her really ill, and smiled when she said yellow fever was hanging about her. They knew she was weak from overwork, but, to their intense grief, her presentiment proved a prophecy.

She spoke beautifully of the rewards God will surely give to all who love Him and persevere in His service. The enthusiastic manner in which she now spoke surprised all, for she had always been most undemonstrative. Her life had been, in many ways, a life of suffering and, consequently, her last words had the greater weight. "My dear Sisters," said she, "never falter in the divine service. No matter what you have to endure, continue to love and serve our dear Lord, under the mantle of our Lady of Mercy. All I have suffered from childhood bears not the smallest proportion to the joy that now fills my heart. I would gladly live my life over again, and suffer a thousand times more to give greater glory to God, and win a little of the happiness I now enjoy. Never until you lie on your death-bed will you understand the grandeur of your vocation, and the peace and joy that will bless your closing hours if you strive earnestly to live up to your rules and become good Sisters of Mercy."[21]

MOTHER AUSTIN CARROLL:
ON SLAVERY, ST. MARTIN, WEST INDIES

In every way Père Jan was utterly fearless. On his first coming to St. Martin, his great devotion to the colored race was not relished by some of his aristocratic parishioners. He told the writer that on several occasions men stood up in the church and drove their slaves from the Communion rail. They had evidently intimidated some of his predecessors. But Père Jan soon showed these people that the poorest slave was as much to him as the highest magnate: it was only the immortal soul he cared for in any one. People thought that the slave should not kneel at the same railing as they, but Père Jan was no respecter of persons.

He had come to St. Martin in a rather disturbed epoch, ten years before the breaking out of the war in 1861. The Union regiments had been charged with wreaking awful vengeance on this town and every other haunt of the wild and vengeful "Cadien." The Acadians, regarding the war as a fight against their ancient enemies, the English (in their so-called descendants, the Yankees), fought furiously, and their battle-cries, like those of the Indians, struck terror into the hearts of their opponents. By what could be gathered on the spot, St. Martin was not a paradise for the slave. Père Jan did all he could to mitigate the misery of those whose masters seemed inclined to forget the teachings of humanity, not to speak of Christianity. The Sisters of Mercy on their arrival opened schools for colored children. Slaves, as a rule, were not unkindly treated; they were too important as the wealth-producers of the country. But there were instances in which the influence of Père Jan was useful, and he never feared to exercise it on behalf of the lowly and unfortunate. The war swept away slavery.

The writer endorses the sentiment of the only man of Irish birth in St. Martin, a poor shoemaker, who had his own views of right and wrong and the courage of his convictions: "I always thought that human beings, black or white, should not be exposed for sale like cattle, and that no man should be a slave to another."[22]

MOTHER BAPTIST KANE, TRANSLATOR: MEDITATIONS

"Meditations on the Sufferings, Life and Death of Our Lord Jesus Christ, translated from the French by a Sister of Mercy," is the title of a new work to be published by Robert Clarke & Co. We have received the first number of this valuable book and we recommend it to the patronage of the public. It is the intention of the Sisters of Mercy of Cincinnati to build a church on their lot on Third Street, and by the sale of this work they hope to realize a large part of the funds necessary for its completion. This church is much needed by the people below Third Street, and we hope that the Sisters will be generously aided in this spiritual and corporal work of mercy.

While the *Meditations* probably enjoyed a good sale, particularly among the religious communities that drew heavily for their spirituality on the Ignatian Exercises (and most of them did), no building fund, then or now, can be realized on royalties alone. Fairs were faster, if not so edifying, and so on Christmas Eve a fair of three weeks' stand was opened in Chocnower's Hall on the other side of Third and Central. Around three thousand dollars were raised, but, "as dearth of money was generally felt, [we] did not reach expectations," the annalist admits. Sometime later an exhibit of Munich statuary with representations of the birth of Christ and other Christian mysteries, and scenery to add to the effect, was displayed in the sodality chapel.[23]

MOTHER M. DE SALES REDDEN: DEATH OF A SAINT
BY HUGH P. GALLAGHER

A prejudice has long prevailed in the world that Christian piety is a kind of selfishness which concentrates man's feelings upon himself—a barrenness and insensibility of heart which, under the pretext of loving God alone, separates man from his fellow-creatures and makes him indifferent to all that concerns them—a kind of senseless enthusiasm, which by removing him, in thought, to Heaven, makes him a useless member of society on earth; and that the childish subjection to trivial observances in religion but checks the soul in its heavenward ascent and unfits it for things great or worthy of immortality.

Divine Providence seems to have intended an utter refutation of an error so unjust and injurious to religion, in raising up such examples as Mother de Sales, and giving to an astonished world many women, with no science but the Gospel, no philosophy but pure charity, and whose greatest resource is their zeal; who have conceived and accomplished enterprises for which the contributions of thousands and the wealth of kings would be inadequate.

From the inexhaustible spring of her charity, this lady has provided, to an almost incredible extent, for every want—relieved every misery—and arrested the course of public disasters. Who can be a stranger to the interest that such a life inspires? Souls who sympathize with the miseries of their fellow-creatures—who lament their inability to dry their tears—learn from her life, by what secrets charity and mercy multiply their resources and work their miracles! Widows, orphans, aged—the miserable of every class—bless the memory of her whose immortal solicitude will continue to relieve generations to come, and support them by the hands of those she has given them as mothers and as servants.

And you, O men of the world, cast your prejudices this day aside, judge from facts, and tell me, is not this perfect child of the Gospel a most perfect benefactor of mankind? Who has struggled more devotedly or more successfully than she against man's two greatest plagues—guilt and misery? Volumes might be filled with the account of her immense labors, but their record has been kept in Heaven, where alone she wished them known, and where only they can be recompensed. Christians, ponder well the sublime lesson of her life, and the appalling warning its close furnishes. "Watch ye, for ye know not at what hour the Lord cometh. . . ." R.I.P. Amen.[24]

INSTRUCTIONS FOR POSTULANTS, MISSISSIPPI, 1850:
ON SAINTHOOD

Saints are not made in a day, nature will feel, and it is therefore especially necessary to bring before our minds the model given us by our

Blessed Lord in His life of trial and suffering while on earth. The path He trod was the path of Mercy, but though it produced the fruits of eternal life for His followers, it brought forth nothing but thorns for Him. The very earnestness and zeal of the multitude would have tried the patience of anyone but Him; they allowed Him no time for refreshment or repose; and yet He would not allow them to be sent away fasting. He had compassion on them and worked a miracle rather than allow them to suffer. And when the disciples wished to dismiss the women whose love made them importunate to attract His notice to their children, He could not permit it, but called and blessed the little ones and captivated the hearts of the parents by saying "that of such is the kingdom of heaven." He has given and will continue to give the grace necessary to accomplish all that is required for each of us.

At first view it would seem as if the exercise of the spirit of Mercy could not demand anything painful. To comfort the afflicted, to console the sorrowful, to relieve the suffering are agreeable even to nature, and when to this is added the support of grace, and the encouraging promise held forth by our holy faith, we feel inclined to believe that the task can never be other than a delightful picture; but if we look a little deeper we will find that to be ever ready at the call of obedience, amid all the vicissitudes of mind and body to which poor human nature is subject, requires a degree of virtue founded only on the practice of continual self-denial. For tender and soothing as mercy ever is toward those on whom it lavishes its affectionate cares, it often exacts from those who exercise it hard labor and painful self-denial. To be sent to console the sick when the harassed and weary spirit itself stands in need of support and sympathy; to be appointed to visit the prison, the hospital, or to engage in the constant labor of the school and to feel that our bodily weakness is not such as to justify our claiming an exemption, and yet sufficient to insure our suffering keenly from the fatigue attendant on the duty—these tasks are not easy. . . . For this life, both for soul and body, placing confidence in God, say with David, "I am needy and poor, but our Lord taketh care of me."

St. Augustine says that the more the heart is withdrawn from earthly things the easier will be its access to God, and the soul thus truly disengaged can unite itself to God with the utmost perfect love, saying as the prophet did, "What have I in Heaven, and besides Thee what do I desire on earth? O my God, Thou art the God of my heart and my portion forever." Understand well what this poverty is: it is to be poor in spirit. It does not consist in wearing poor clothes. You might do this and still covet praise or preferment. You must be dead to these things. You must do what the world would term unacceptable, if an unkind or mortifying word is said or something is done toward you that in the world would be considered an affront, and to resent it would be deemed quite justifiable. . . .[25]

FROM A CATECHISM OF SCRIPTURE HISTORY,
Compiled by the Sisters of Mercy for the Use of Children Attending Their Schools.
First American Edition, Baltimore, 1854

Samples of Questions

Chapter XLII, pp. 282–283.

Question:

Did St. Mary Magdalen remain at the sepulcher after St. Peter and St. John returned home?

Answer:

She did. While she was still weeping, she stooped down, and looking into the sepulcher saw two angels in white, sitting one at the head and one at the foot where the body of our Lord had been laid. They said to her: "Woman, why weepest thou?" She replied: "Because they have taken away my Lord, and I know not where they have laid him." Then turning back, she saw our Lord himself standing but did not know him; he said to her, "Woman, why weepest thou?" She, thinking it was the gardener, said, "Sir, if thou hast taken him hence, tell me where thou hast laid him, and I will take him away." Jesus said to her, "Mary." She immediately recognized him and in a transport of joy, turning, said "Rabboni."

Question: Did our Lord appear to the other holy
                               women who had accompanied St. Mary
                               Magdalen on her first visit to the
                               sepulcher?

Answer: He did. When they were returning from
                               the sepulcher with haste to relate to the
                               disciples the happy tidings
                               communicated to them by the angel, our
                               Lord met them and addressed them:
                               "All hail." They took hold of his feet
                               and adored him. He bid them fear
                               nothing, and to tell his brethren they
                               should seen him in Galilee.

Question: Did the Apostles believe the reports of
                               St. Mary Magdalen and the other
                               women when they asserted that they had
                               seen our Lord and repeated what he had
                               said to them?

Answer: No. They considered what the women
                               said only as idle tales.[26]

MOTHER M. BAPTIST RUSSELL: PRAYER FOR FAITH

Mother Baptist Russell frequently said the following:

My God, I thank You for pardoning me so often. Give me grace
to be faithful to You, hereafter. I do not ask for fervor nor delight
in Your service, but only the grace of fidelity to You in all things;
this is all I ask, all I desire.

Here is another very practical note:

We know this to be true, humility is not a solitary virtue, but
includes many. For are not the really humble also meek, gentle,
laborious, patient, docile, obedient, cheerful? In short, do they
not possess every virtue? And why not? Does not the Scripture
assure us, "God giveth His grace to the humble?"[27]

PRAYERS FOR DEDICATION OF COLLEGE OF MOUNT SAINT MARY, PLAINFIELD, NEW JERSEY, 1908

Final Three Prayers:
Let us pray—
Visit, we beseech Thee, O Lord, this habitation, and drive far from it all the snares of the enemy. May Thy holy angels dwell herein and preserve in peace all those who live, teach and study herein, and may Thy blessing be upon them forever. Bless, O Lord, this house and may there dwell here health, holiness, humility, kindness, meekness, mildness, and the fullness of Thy law, obedience and thanksgiving to God the Father, the Son, and the Holy Ghost. And may this blessing remain upon all who dwell, teach and study herein; may the sevenfold grace of the Holy Ghost descend. Through Christ our Lord—Amen.

Let us pray—
O Lord, who, all present in every place of Thy domination, alone worketh therein, hear our prayer, and be its protector, and let no malice of the adverse spirit avail against it, but by the virtue of the holy cross and by the operation of the Holy Ghost may pure service be here rendered to Thee, and devout freedom dwell here. Through Christ our Lord—Amen.

Let us pray—
Aid us, O Lord, our God, and defend with Thy perpetual help those who trust in the protection of the holy cross. Through Christ our Lord—Amen.

College of Mount Saint Mary, Commencement, 1919
Baccalaureate Sermon in St. Joseph's Church, North Plainfield by John W. Norris, J.C.D., rector of St. Peter's Church, New Brunswick. Theme was "The Dignity of Womanhood as Depicted in the Book of Wisdom."

Commencement Address by Dr. James J. Walsh, Fordham University.
"Dr. Walsh congratulated the young women in having had their training at Mount Saint Mary where the main business of the professors was not to learn things for them, but to have them learn themselves. . . . St. Mary's will in the comparatively near future be looked upon as an institution of learning where young women can get at once a thorough college education and training in the great principles that underlie right living . . . and will make them a great help for the problems of reconstruction which we must all face if the benefits following war are not to be lost. We made the world safe for democracy, but now we have got to make democracy safe for the world. . . ."[28]

PRAYERS FOR THE SICK: BROOKLYN, NEW YORK, 1879

On The Visitation of the Sick

Mercy, the principal path pointed out by Jesus Christ to those who are desirous of following Him, has in all ages of the Church excited the faithful in a particular manner to instruct and comfort the sick and dying poor, as in them they regarded the person of our Divine Master, who has said, "Amen I say to you, as long as you did it to one of the least brethren, you did it to me." The many miraculous cures performed by our Saviour and the power of healing granted to the Apostles evince His great tenderness for the sick. Let those whom Jesus Christ has graciously permitted to assist Him in the persons of his suffering poor, have their hearts animated with gratitude and love, and placing all their confidence in Him, ever keep His unwearied patience and humility present to their minds; endeavoring to imitate Him more perfectly every day in self-denial, patience, and entire resignation.

Thus shall they gain a crown of glory and the great title of children of the Most High, which is assuredly promised to the merciful.

Prayer Before Visiting the Sick

O God the Holy Ghost, author of life and sanctity, deign to inspire and sanctify every thought, word and action while I walk in the path of Mercy which Jesus trod on earth. Grant that I may bring comfort to the sorrowful and peace to the troubled heart. May all my words and actions be so conformable to my divine Model that I may not have to reproach myself with a cause of the slightest disedification, but that I may deserve truly to find my Saviour in the poor I serve for His sake. Amen.

Prayer at the Beginning of Sickness

To Thy infinite goodness, dear Jesus, we recommend this Thy Servant, whom Thou hast been pleased to visit with illness; take her into Thy care and be her physician; give a blessing to the remedies that shall be used; we leave her entirely in Thy hands and hope that, as Thou hast comforted the afflicted in giving health to the sick, so Thou wilt be pleased to strengthen and enable her to bear like a Christian whatever portion of the Cross Thou hast appointed for her; give her patience in this sickness, and sanctify it by Thy grace, that she may receive it as coming from Thy hands: and if it be pleasing to Thy holy will, restore her again to health. Help her, O Lord Jesus, direct and comfort her under this trial, for as

Thou art just, so Thou art merciful. Show her then Thy mercy, for the sake and in the name of Jesus Christ, our Saviour and Redeemer. Amen.

To Our Blessed Lady, Queen of Martyrs

Remember, O most gracious Virgin Mary, that it has never been heard of in any age, that those who implored thy powerful protection, or sought thy mediation, were ever abandoned by thee. Animated then with holy confidence, we cast ourselves at thy feet and beseech thee, O Mother of God, to adopt this sufferer for thy child and take upon thyself the care of her salvation. Let it not be said, Mother of Mercy, that she has perished at thy feet, where no one ever found but grace and salvation. Amen.

An Earnest Petition for All Graces

O Father of Mercies and God of all comfort, in whose hands are life and death, look upon Thy suffering child, give her strength and patience, perfect her in the virtues of faith, hope, and charity. Take from her heart all painful anxiety for health, fill it with lively confidence, let its only desire be that Thy will be done. She unites her sufferings to those of her Saviour, and hopes firmly for pardon and eternal life. Grant her whatever graces she needs, a happy death, and a glorious eternity.

To Mary

O Mary! thou who desires so much to see Jesus loved, if thou lovest this thy suffering servant, this is the favor she now begs of thee to obtain for her: a great love for Jesus crucified. Thou obtainest from Thy Son whatever thou pleasest. Pray then for her, and console her, O Mother of Mercy. Obtain for her also a great love for thee, who of all creatures are the most loving of God. And through that grief which thou suffered on Calvary, when you beheld Jesus expired upon the Cross, obtain for her a happy death. Amen.

For the Dying

Jesus Christ was crucified and died for you. Be ready then to die for Him, that you may enjoy Him in the kingdom of heaven, which He promised to those who trust in Him. (Here present a crucifix.) Embrace Christ with tender affection and with firm confidence that thou wilt soon see Him in heaven whom you behold on the cross.

Divine Redeemer, she beholds You and embraces You with all the affection of her soul. She depends on Your merits. She hopes to sing eternal praises to You, Holy Trinity: Father, Son, and Holy Ghost. She will now say what perhaps she may not be able to say at her last moments. O Father of Mercy, into Your hands she commends her soul for time and eternity. She willingly takes leave of the world and all it contains, for nothing can satisfy her but Thee.

O Holy Mary, who assisted at the death of thy beloved Son, obtain for your servant the grace of a happy death. O glorious St. Joseph, who died in the arms of Jesus and Mary, assist her in her last hour. Amen.

To the Blessed Virgin for a Happy Death

O Queen of Martyrs, who witnessed the agony of your dying Son, look with compassion on your servant when she enters the agonies of death. We know that you are the great comforter of dying Christians, you are their powerful advocate and secure refuge. Obtain for her the grace to be of the happy number who choose you as their dear Mother. Mother of Mercy, who has never been known to forsake anyone who trusted in thee, do not forsake her when she appears before God. Implore for her all the graces necessary for her, that she may provide for herself a solid foundation for confidence in the mercy of God at the hour of her death. Amen.

For the Dying Aged

O God of Mercy, look down on this your servant in the fullness of her years, who acknowledges that from the cradle to this hour you have been to her a loving Father. The young and the strong perished at her right hand, the plague destroyed those at her left, but she was defended by Your good will, and she lives to glorify Thee. Now that she is old and feeble, be still her staff and support. Weak and weary of her pilgrimage, she turns to you for consolation and repose. How long she is yet to live, you alone know. Be it according to Your will. She remembers Your mercies, and she longs to behold you. Therefore, we implore You, Father and Creator of all, who has bestowed so many favors on Your servant, grant her the grace of a holy death and joyful eternity. Amen.

Prayer for a Happy Death

O my Lord and Saviour, support me in my last hour in the strong arms of Thy sacraments, and by the fresh fragrance of Thy consolation. Let the absolving words be said over me, and let Thy own Body be my food, and Thy Blood my sprinkling, and let Mary breathe on me, and Thy glorious saints and my own dear patron smile on me, that in them all and through them all, I may die as I desire to live, in Thy faith, in Thy Church, and in Thy love. Amen.[29]

THE PRAYER OF THE SISTERS OF MERCY
OF NEW JERSEY

Father, You will "that all may be one"; help us to witness that one-ness forever in a true community of love. Teach us gentleness of heart, for "happy are the gentle; they shall have the earth for their heritage." Make the earth our heritage, and as true apostles let us prepare it for the coming kingdom of Your love.

Grant to our Congregation new members in whom the scripture will be fulfilled: "You will shine in the world like bright stars, because you are offering it the Word of Life." Let all of us offer the Word to mankind as Mary did, through our work, our prayers, and our life.

Grant to our Sisters who suffer, consolation and strength of soul; to our Sisters who have gone before us in death, the happiness which "eye has not seen, nor ear heard"; to all who have helped us in any way, eternal reward; to all who have hurt us in any way, the happiness of Your love. Help us to live so that we may say, as Mother McAuley did of the first Sisters of Mercy, "the sun never went down on our anger."

Bless our families and friends, those who work with us and those for whom we work. Bless all Your world, and grant that we may be a part of that blessing.

May we be forever thankful that You chose us "before the world was made . . . chose us in Christ, to be holy and spotless, and to live through love." In the Spirit of Love, may we share our life here and hereafter. Amen.[30]

Notes

1. Frances Warde, *Book of Private Prayers,* Convent of Mercy, Carlow, June 16, 1837. Given to Kathleen Healy, RSM, Pittsburgh, by Mother Joseph Boyle, St. Mary's Convent, Naas, March 16, 1969.
2. Sister M. Catherine Garety, *Mother Xavier Warde,* Boston, 1902, pp. 227–28. See also: Sister Mary Xavier Toohey, *Memories of Mercy,* Unpublished Manuscript, 1931. Archives, Portland, Maine.
3. Carroll, *Annals, IV,* pp. 260–61.
4. Sister Paul Xavier Warde, "A Chapter of Incidents," *Mount St. Mary's Record,* Manchester, II (January 1894), pp. 15–17.

5. Frances Warde, *Spiritual Maxims,* Convent of Mercy, Carlow, February 2, 1839. Copies are in Mercy Archives, Convent of Mercy, Pittsburgh, Pennsylvania, and Silver Spring, Maryland.

6. Frances Warde, Favorite Scripture Passages. Quoted in Janet McMaster, "The Christlike Personality of Catherine McAuley," *Mount Saint Mary Journal,* Burlington, Vermont, April 1947, p. 5.

7. "The Sisters of Mercy," *The Pittsburgh Catholic,* July 6, 1844, p. 133. This newspaper article, "The Sisters of Mercy," is the earliest American publication on the Sisters of Mercy, defining who they are.

   The Pittsburgh Catholic, the oldest continuing Catholic newspaper published in the United States, was founded by Bishop Michael O'Connor of Pittsburgh in 1843. The article referred to has no name of the author indicated, but it is impossible that it could have been written with its keenly knowledgeable approach to the Sisters of Mercy without consultation of Frances Warde and her sisters, and of Bishop O'Connor as well.

   Emphasis is on (1) the variety of apostolic works of Mercy carried on by the Sisters of Mercy and (2) reciprocal contemplative and active life of the Sisters as obviously accepted by the first seven Sisters of Mercy in the United States.

   Concomitantly with the article published in *The Pittsburgh Catholic,* it is well to mention a statement made by Father John McErlean, "first postulator of Mother McAuley's cause," who prepared extensive materials for a life of Catherine McAuley which were turned over to Father Roland Burke Savage, S.J., author of *Catherine McAuley: The First Sister of Mercy,* Dublin: M.H. Gill and Son Ltd., 1950. Father McErlean, commenting on *Extracts from Instructions of the Venerated Foundress, Catherine McAuley,* Manuscript of Sister M. Magdalen de Pazzi, 115 pp., stated:

   > These extracts are drawn up so as to form a commentary on the *Rules and Constitutions* [of the Sisters of Mercy]. The Foundress is quoted down to p. 53, and the first part of the work reminds me of her style. The second half has nothing very characteristic. (Dublin Archives).

   On *page 19* of these *Extracts,* Sister Magdalen de Pazzi's manuscript states the following:

   > Some persons, unacquainted with the spirit of the Institute, imagine that we should confine ourselves to the Works of Mercy named in the *Rule,* but this is a great error and quite

contrary to the intention of the Holy Foundress. All the Works of Mercy belong to the Order, but as it seldom happens that one community could take so many duties upon themselves without overburdening the Sisters, *three* are specified as being peculiarly characteristic of the Institute. . . .

The above paragraph corroborates the teaching of Frances Warde who frequently referred to Catherine McAuley as her source for teaching that *all* works of Mercy are practiced by the Sisters of Mercy. Frances also taught the principle of reciprocal contemplation and service in the life of the Sister of Mercy.

It should be added here that Sister Mary Sullivan, RSM, Rochester, New York, completed a study called "Catherine McAuley's Scholarly and Literary Debt to Alonso Rodriguez: The 'Spirit of the Institute' Parallels, "*Recusant History, XX* (May 10, 1990), pp. 81–105, in which Sister Sullivan demonstrated that the manuscript called "The Spirit of the Institute" or the "Bermondsey Manuscript" copied, altered, omitted, and added to the following work of Rodriguez: *The Practice of Perfection and Christian Virtues,* "First Treatise: The End of The Society of Jesus." An available translation of Rodriguez is *The Practice of Perfection in Christian Virtues,* translated from the original Spanish by Joseph Rickaby, S.J., Chicago, Loyola University Press, 1929. Rodriguez's treatise, like the "Spirit of the Institute," once attributed to Catherine McAuley, stresses the necessity of reciprocal contemplation and active service in practicing the life of Mercy.

Our conclusion from the above three sources is that all include the following major objectives which have come under discussion at various times in the United States since 1843:

(1) The Sister of Mercy incorporates reciprocal contemplation and service of others in her life of Mercy.

(2) All the spiritual and corporal works of Mercy are practiced by Sisters of Mercy.

Finally, we also discover in the above mentioned *Extracts from Instructions of the Venerated Foundress, Catherine McAuley,* Dublin, p. 17, the following words:

We should animate our faith . . . when required to practice what we feel particularly difficult in the observance of our *Rule.* . . . We should also respect the practices, observances, and customs which are traditions of the Order, and flow from the same source; one may be considered the written, the other the unwritten law for us. . . . The Sisters are admonished to avoid making comparisons between the regulations of one religious order and those of another. The Almighty has different designs for each. . . . How many souls have been saved through means of the members of the several [Mercy] convents that have been established in a few years. . . . Our perfection consists in keeping the *medium* between these two states [contemplative and active] without passing into either extreme. . . .

8. Mother M. Philip Neri Bowen, who served in both Pittsburgh and Mount Washington, Maryland, was a gifted writer whose articles were published in leading American periodicals. Because she never signed her articles, most of them are unknown.

9. Mother M. Gertrude Cosgrave was Co-Founder of the Cresson Sisters of Mercy. Archives, Cresson.

10. *Life of Mary Monholland,* by a Member of the Order of Mercy, Chicago, J.S. Hyland and Company, 1894, pp. 32–33.

11. Mercy Author Unknown. Preserved by Sister M. Joseph Miller, Manistee, Michigan, 1912.

12. Sister Mary Lucille McGee and Sister Marjorie Allen, *The Quality of Mercy,* Lincoln Press, Royal Oaks, Michigan, 1980. Mother Mary Agatha entered the Convent of Mercy in Davenport, Iowa in 1870.

13. From an old, worn, hand-printed page found among Mother Patricia's (died 1916) possessions. Archives, Philadelphia.

14. Author Unknown. Archives, North Plainfield, New Jersey, n.d. Mother Regis Wade was Superior of the Trenton Foundation, later united with Bordentown.

15. Quoted in Mother Austin Carroll, *Annals of the Sisters of Mercy, III,* 1888, p. 209.

16. *Ibid.,* IV, 1895, p. 487.

17. From *Meditations for a Three Days' Retreat,* P. O'Shea, Publisher, New York, 1880, pp. 50–53. Archives, New Orleans.

18. Mother Mary Patrick McCallion. Small black book of Private Prayer, 1919. Archives, North Plainfield, New Jersey. Article seems to have been copied from writing of a Sister who knew Catherine McAuley.

19. Sisters of Mercy, *Reminiscences of Seventy Years (1846–1916),* Fred J. Ringley Co., Chicago, 1916, pp. 185–213.

20. Mother Austin Carroll, *Annals, III,* 1888, pp. 199–202.

21. *Ibid., IV,* 1895, pp. 400–01.

22. *Ibid., IV,* 1895, pp. 438–39.

23. From Mary Ellen Evans, *The Spirit Is Mercy,* Newman Press, Westminster, Maryland, 1959, p. 106.

24. From Sermon by Rev. H.P. Gallagher, in Mother Baptist Russell, Copy of *Original Script Annals,* Vol. I, Archives, San Francisco.

25. Book of Handwritten Instructions for Postulants, Novices, and Young Professed, Mississippi, Approx. 1850. Archives, St. Louis.

26. Sisters of Mercy, *A Catechism of Scripture History,* John Murphy and Company, Baltimore, 1854. Published also in London and Pittsburgh. Archives, Detroit.

27. Mother Russell, *The Life of Mother Mary Baptist Russell,* New York, Apostleship of Prayer, 1901, p. 128.

28. Dedication Ceremony, College of Mount Saint Mary, Plainfield, New Jersey, October 18, 1908.

29. Prayers for the Sick: Book in Long Hand. Dedication: To My Dear Little Sister, April 27, 1879. Heritage Room, Mercy Motherhouse, Brooklyn, New York.

30. Published in Sisters of Mercy, *Mercy,* New Jersey (1873–1973).

II.

AMERICAN MERCY CONVENT ANNALS

73

New Orleans, Mobile, Saint Martinsville
New Orleans—Joys of Early Days; House of Mercy and Training of
Women; Foundations Throughout the South; Schools in Mobile; Yellow
Fever Epidemic in New Orleans; Perils of Travel: A Diary; A Different
Christmas

New York City
Dramatic Foundation—New York; House of Mercy; Sainthood and
Suffering of New York Founder

Pittsburgh
Founding of the First American Mission—Pittsburgh; Schools; Poor
House; Penitentiary; Bigotry; Typhoid Fever Epidemic in Pittsburgh;
Fire at St. Xavier Academy

Bordentown, Princeton, Plainfield
Romance and Suffering in Bordentown, Mount St. Mary's, Georgian
Court

Providence, Hartford, New Haven
Pioneer Days; Attacks and Insults; Surprising Growth

**San Francisco, Sacramento, Yreka, Rio Vista, Red Bluff, Grass Valley,
San Diego**
Exciting Beginnings in San Francisco, 1854; Early Missions in San
Francisco; Magdalen Asylum; Service in San Quentin; Floods in
Sacramento; Great San Francisco Earthquake, 1865; Smallpox
Epidemic in San Francisco; Sacrifices of the Sisters, Suffering and
Service in Yreka, Rio Vista, and Red Bluff; Grass Valley, California;
Southern California: San Diego

Scranton
One Hundred Years in the Province of Scranton: Four Major Origins

South Carolina
The "New" Sisters of Mercy in South Carolina

INTRODUCTION

Convent Annals of the American Sisters of Mercy, reproduced here in comparatively short selections, reveal both simple and startling experiences in the daily lives of the Sisters. Many of the annals quoted came directly from the Archives of Mercy Convents. Also, many of these Convent Annals were researched and written by Mother Austin Carroll, who had both a talent for writing and an amazing sense of the importance of history, which led her to write to innumerable convents throughout the United States and Ireland to collect by correspondence historical information concerning Mercy missions. The American Sisters of Mercy owe a great debt to Austin Carroll.

In the following chapter, an attempt has been made to select both ordinary and unusual experiences recorded by the Sisters of Mercy. Wars; catastrophes; fires; plagues of yellow fever, cholera and typhoid; attacks by bigots—all these were an essential part of the lives of the American Sisters of Mercy in the second half of the nineteenth century. Yet these experiences were apparently endured with a calmness and faith acceptance which the Sisters regarded simply as part of everyday life. Calls to serve the sick, war victims, and the dying were never refused. Service in schools, hospitals, homes for homeless women, night schools, and orphanages arose wherever Mercy Sisters appeared.

No matter whether old or young, the Sisters of Mercy were always ready to sacrifice their lives to save lives. A tour of Mercy cemeteries throughout the United States is a revealing and startling experience. Sisters in their teens and early twenties continually sacrificed their lives to serve others. These ultimate sacrifices were regarded as "normal" for the Sister living her fourth vow of service.

While Mercy Annals reveal concretely the spirituality of sacrifice, the Sisters themselves, through reciprocal contemplation and service, marked an essential unity in their lives. A statement in *The Pittsburgh Catholic* of 1844 gives pause to the reader of 1990: "The Sisters of Mercy have endeavored to retain more of the spirit of the contemplative life in the discharge of their various duties than most of the other orders." The contemplative-active life of Catherine McAuley, originating in her actual living and in her love for and study of Holy Scripture, led to a contemplative-active spirit among her Sisters of the late nineteenth century.

*   *   *

BALMVILLE ON THE HUDSON AND ALBANY, NEW YORK

A Remarkable Development

The New York Mercy Community, founded from Dublin in 1846, established convents which became Motherhouses in St. Louis, Brooklyn, and Worcester, Massachusetts. "Local houses" were opened in many areas, including Greenbush, New York; Balmville, New York; and far-away Eureka, California. The well known Albany Motherhouse eventually developed from Greenbush.

Balmville on the Hudson, however, offers a fascinating background story. The lady who once owned the property at Balmville which eventually fell to the Sisters of Mercy had been an Anglican nun in England. By reading the works of the nineteenth century Catholic apologist, Father Fredick W. Faber, she became convinced that the truth was not to be found in Protestantism. She was advised by her Superior to leave her Anglican Community at once. A stranger in London, she soon knocked at the door of the Fathers of the Oratory. Advised that she was already a Roman Catholic at heart, she was introduced to the nuns of the Assumption. Under their instruction, she was received into the Catholic Church and became a Sister of the Assumption. To regulate her affairs before taking vows, she visited New York to dispose of her late father's property in Balmville. Visiting the Sisters of Mercy, she informed them that she would like to see her old home converted into a convent. The beautiful spot soon became the Convent of Mercy at Balmville.

Though one hears little of Balmville today, what strikes the reader of Mercy history is that it provides only one example among many Mercy properties throughout the world which became sites for convents in striking ways.[1]

Magnificent Salve Regina College in Newport, Rhode Island, was also established by the Sisters of Mercy in a most unusual manner. When Frances Warde passed through Philadelphia on her way to Pittsburgh back in 1843, she had met Emily Harper, granddaughter of the great patriot, Charles Carroll. The two became close friends and remained so for the rest of their lives.

The Harpers had a summer residence in Newport, Rhode Island, and wished to establish a Convent School there. The Newport Convent, St. Mary's of the Isle, became the most outstanding school in Newport. Later when the heir of one of the wealthiest families in Newport desired to relinquish a famous mansion by the sea, he offered it to the Mercy Sisters. Legend—true or false—says that he did so in a spirit of revenge which centered around a family quarrel! In an astonishing way, the Providence Sisters of Mercy, with a mansion as its source, built what is one of the most beautiful colleges in the United States.

Perhaps the most remarkable story of all in the context of amazing beginnings is that of beautiful Georgian Court College, New Jersey, established on the property of a mansion that once belonged to millionaire George Jay Gould. The entire Georgian Court estate suggested the luxury of a Roman Emperor, but it was also a witness to tragedy and suicide. By "sheer luck" or the grace of God, the New Jersey Sisters of Mercy purchased it for a minimal sum.

One must, however, include the addendum that the great majority of Mercy institutions had their birth in the poverty which the Sisters of Mercy shared with those whom they served. The complete story of Georgian Court would require a book in itself. As Arthur Brisbane wrote in the *New York Evening Journal* under the heading, "A Rich Man's Extravaganza":

> Nothing really well done in this world is wasted. . . . A girls' college in a palace! It was built for a few, but it is used by many. What is called the luxury of the rich becomes in due time a source of education and great public benefit. . . .

BALTIMORE

Meaning of Mercy Vocation

During the first three years of its existence (1855–58), the Baltimore sisterhood increased slowly, but surely. Some entered the Poppleton Street convent only to leave in a few months. Mother Catherine Wynne had a rare talent for discerning spirits. She was not afraid to tell postulants, apparently very promising, that they were not suited to her Institute. Like other saintly superiors, she often said that one member dead to self and perfectly devoted to God could achieve more for His glory in the salvation of souls than a hundred devoted to selfish aims. She realized that she was called by God to train souls in the religious life, the awful duty of all superiors. To the accomplishment of this work she bent all the resources of her grand character, and to it she devoted the sincere affection of a loving heart.

Among the nobler spirits of the Order, few accomplished so great a work in so short a time, and with such poor resources as Mother Catherine Wynne. She was sent to found a religious community in one of the largest cities in the country, with but three companions, and scarcely any temporal means. In about six years, death came upon her, but she had sunk the foundations of her spiritual house so deep that its strength might, by the divine mercy, bid defiance to future storms. She felt that the truest riches, and the most solid support she could bequeathe to her Order, would be souls thoroughly grounded in the virtues of the religious life. For this she worked, and in this she succeeded. Her spiritual children were devoted to her. A strict disciplinarian, she could loosen the string when necessary lest the bond might break. She had the talent of one who rules, the tact to discern the differences in the souls she was called to govern, and the wisdom to give each the duties most fitted to her capabilities and needs. . . .

Service in Military Hospitals

The last public duty of importance Mother Catherine Wynne performed was to change the "Old Infirmary" into a Military Hospital, upon the opening of hostilities between the Northern and the Southern States. The Administrator of the Washington Infirmary gave it to the military authorities, but insisted that the Sisters remain. Government officials were assured control, but Sister M. Colette O'Connor continued in charge, while other Sisters were sent from the Baltimore Convent to help in the work. Hundreds of sick and wounded of both armies received from the Sisters those ministrations so needed in the hour of agony. The spiritual good achieved is known only to God. Numerous soldiers received the last rites of the Church. . . .

In 1861, after the death of Mother Catherine Wynne, the Baltimore Sisters received the startling information that the "Old Infirmary" or Washington Hospital had been burned to ashes, the Sisters serving there barely escaping with their lives in their efforts to save the patients. The sick found a temporary refuge in the City Hall. . . .

The following morning, a few nursing Sisters set out to see Washington authorities, carrying only such necessaries as they could gather up. They obtained temporary possession of the "Old Armory Hall," where Sisters and patients soon assembled. They were joined by Catholic girls who had served with the "Old Infirmary" as domestics, and who refused to leave the nuns. The War Department now took possession of three senatorial residences near the Capitol and transformed them into a military hospital, known as the Douglas, from the name of the honorable gentleman who resided in the largest of the mansions thus utilized. The Sisters visited and nursed the sick and wounded at the Douglas every day. . . .

Spiritual Decisions in War Time

The great Civil War now raged fiercely. Numbers of mangled bodies were borne daily and nightly from the field of battle to the Capital and the neighboring cities. The Sisters of Mercy everywhere devoted themselves as far as possible to these suffering members of Christ. At the Douglas, good was effected on an immense scale. The Sisters were fully sustained by the medical faculty, all of whom proved sincere friends; and the orderlies who assisted them in the wards were most childlike and devoted "boys," as they termed themselves. The patients were childlike in their demonstrations of gratitude and affection, and anyone whose behavior implied the slightest disrespect to a Sister of Mercy would have fared as one who had in these exciting times been guilty of political treason.

Sister M. Colette O'Connor remained in charge, and it is doubtful if it were ever the fortunate lot of a Superior to inspire the public officials with whom she had to deal with more perfect confidence in her word, or deeper respect for her person. When called upon to decide anything serious, she would say: "I will give you my reply in a few minutes. . . ." She would then go before the Blessed Sacrament and, having asked the divine aid, give her answer. Once when a Dr. Thompson rang for her at an unusual hour to say that a battle had just been fought, and numbers of wounded were expected every moment—could she accommodate them? she gave an affirmative reply, but only after praying a few moments for light before the Blessed Sacrament. More patients came than she expected. Yet at the greatest inconvenience to herself and the Sisters, she insisted that every one should be received, though the doctor in charge thought it impossible. "Sister M. Colette," said he, "never breaks her word."

Sisters in Vicksburg: School and War

From Baltimore to Vicksburg was a long and dreary journey in 1859. The Sisters left on the morning of October 9 and reached Vicksburg on the evening of the twelfth. For three days they were guests of Mr. Antonio Genella. On October 15, the feast of St. Teresa, they took possession of a large brick dwelling which they soon transformed into a convent. This house had been bought for a school, the Congregation helping to pay for it. Here the Sisters opened a school on October 22. The project was very successful. Sixty children came the first day, and the number continued to increase. All went on prosperously till the gunboats came: the school was broken up, and the convent became a hospital for the sick and wounded who had been lying about the city without sufficient care. The bombardment of Vicksburg was going on, and the Sisters were requested to take charge of the sick. . . .

The Sisters nursed the sick and wounded successively at Mississippi Springs, Oxford, Jackson, and Shelby Springs, moving ahead as the "enemy" approached. This period was one of intense labor for the Sisters, and of terrible hardships for the soldiers. For the Sisters, the necessaries of life would have been luxuries, and as the war progressed, their clothing became such that their nearest friends could not have recognized them. Their laborious lives were varied by many odd incidents, and they were consoled by many conversions. About a year before the close of the war, Bishop William Henry Elder wished them to return to Vicksburg, as the Commanding General had invited them. Four returned, leaving the rest with the disabled soldiers. With considerable difficulty, the four Sisters got leave from the Confederate General to withdraw. After reaching Vicksburg, they were kept out of their property by the Federal authorities. Their convent had become the headquarters of General Henry Warner Slocum, and they were obliged to accept a second time the hospitality of their friend, Mr. Genella. Mr. Edwin M. Stanton, Secretary of War, at the urgent request of his friend, Father Michael O'Connor, S.J., formerly Bishop of Pittsburgh, restored their property. . . .

Conversions During Civil War

The Sisters of Mercy conducted hospitals for the sick soldiers in many parts of the country, and conversions multiplied wherever they nursed these patients, though they never spoke of religious controversy. The men had an odd way of putting things, but, as they said, they always "got there." One wounded man murmured: "One fold and one shepherd —true words—I'll get in—it all came on me like a lightning flash—Here I am, Sister—your way's the right way—let me have the Sacraments. . . ."

Another said: "Sister, I'm ready for you now. It's just as if the Almighty threw something at me, and when it struck me, I felt that your religion was the true one."

A rather rough genius asked the Sister who was dressing his wounds to read him some "comforting Scripture." She read from St. John: "And other sheep I have that are not of this fold; them also I must bring, and they shall hear my voice, and there shall be one fold and one shepherd." "Stop there, Sister," he shouted, "That's strong—call the priest."

Service at City Hospital in Baltimore

In 1874 the Baltimore Sisters were asked to take charge of the City Hospital, on South Calvert Street, the most miserably arranged and poorly furnished public institution in the city. It was in charge of young, talented physicians from the South who, owing to the reverses of the war, came to practice their professional duties in Baltimore. A college of physicians and surgeons was attached to the Hospital, the faculty received from the Mayor a contract for the reception of the "casualty cases" of the city, and the destitute sick were not sent to the poor-house. The wards were under the management of a matron and a corps of male and female nurses, and here, in the very heart of the Monumental City, was an aggregation of human wretchedness seldom witnessed even in public almshouses. In small, ill-ventilated wards, lay some sixty men, women, and children, in the worst stages of disease, or so mangled by some terrible accident as to be scarcely recognized as human beings.

Patients of every description were huddled together. An attempted suicide case lay, perhaps, next to a pious mother or father whom want, and, not seldom, the neglect of unnatural children, had cast on the public charity. They had not even the hope that their earthly remains would receive decent burial, since they might be claimed after death for the dissecting-table. The nurses were inexperienced in treating the agonies endured by the unfortunate sufferers.

Several times in the past the Sisters had called at the City Hospital in compliance with the request of some poor Catholic patient. On one of these occasions a priest who had just administered the Last Sacraments without the cleanliness requisite for the performance of the sacred rites exclaimed: "Sisters, if you had charge of this place, how much might be accomplished for the salvation of souls."

At last Mother Alphonsus was asked to assume the entire management. She hesitated. It seemed to be dooming the Sisters to certain death to place them within these walls. On the other hand, much might be achieved for the glory of God, and could a Sister of Mercy sacrifice her life to greater advantage than that of special servant of the destitute sick? All the Sisters agreed that it would be a blessed work. On November 11, 1874, the anniversary of the holy death of the Foundress of the Order, six Sisters took up their abode within the noisome walls of the City Hospital. The joy of the poor patients was indescribable. Tears of gratitude streamed down faces, as words of loving sympathy were spoken in their ears, and efforts made to render their miserable beds more comfortable.

The filth and destitution had been simply horrible. The Sisters had literally to dig up the dirt from the floors. The food had been served in dishes which, from meal to meal, had not been washed. Upon many beds there were no sheets, and only very soiled coverlets. . . .

In one of the wards was a Frenchman in daily expectation of death from consumption of the throat, which caused him excruciating pain. To the distress of his nurses, he uttered no prayers; fearful curses crossed his mouth, and he could not control his hatred of religion sufficiently to treat the Sisters with ordinary politeness. His fellow-sufferers were shocked at his recklessness. The Sisters prayed. The man was a renegade Catholic. When a Sister suggested that he should see a priest, he said: "Were I sure I should die today and go to hell, I would not see a Catholic priest." And when the chaplain spoke to him kindly, he repeated the same words. His curses and blasphemies grew worse. But the Sisters united in prayer. Then one morning as a Sister approached his bed, he half raised himself, and said: "I am dying. O Sister, for God's sake, get me a priest." . . .[2]

BELIZE (BRITISH HONDURAS)

Suffering During Yellow Fever Plague

In September 1886, yellow fever broke out in Belize (British Honduras). There had been isolated cases earlier, but no notice was taken of them. Governor Goldsworthy called September 6, and asked the Sisters to visit the suspicious cases; as they had nursed yellow fever in New Orleans, they could diagnose correctly for him. His anxiety was great. Unhappily, the Sisters were not able to allay his fear by denying the existence of the disease, though they gave him much comfort by nursing, and by showing others how yellow fever should be nursed.

On September 15, Father Cassian Gillet, who was only a few months over from England, was taken sick with the fever, and in a few days despaired of; but God heard the prayers of his brothers, the Sisters, and the people, and he began to improve slowly. Despite the watchfulness of the Sisters who nursed him day and night, he had a relapse, but he grew better by degrees, and said Mass on October 17. Now one of the pupils, a lad of 14, who had made his first Communion at the convent, was attacked by the fever. He craved the attendance of the priest and the Sisters, but his non-Catholic guardians refused his request, and sent for Father di Pietro only when the child was dead.

The townspeople often wondered that there was never any sickness at the convent. But the trial came after four years' immunity. On May 28, 1887, Virginia Martinez, one of the boarders, became ill. Dr. May, finding the case grave, called in another physician for consultation. The child asked for the Sacraments and she watched for the tinkling of the bell that told of the coming of the Blessed Sacrament, and when all knelt, the doctor, though not a Catholic, knelt with them. She received her Lord, and remained in quiet thanksgiving for a long time. On Whitsunday, the Holy Ghost came for the child. Her companions were inconsolable. And the Sisters grieved, not for the loss of the favored soul, but for the poor parents who did not know of their bereavement. The mode of burial was not to the liking of the survivors, but it was according to the law. The doctors ordered a coffin from the gaol; it came by boat to the Sisters' wharf, no paint, no varnish, plain boards. The body of the child was lifted by the four corners of the sheet, and dropped into the coffin. The lid was nailed down. The Sisters insisted on covering the coffin with black merino. The men took it on their shoulders to the little row-boat at the wharf, in which they placed it, putting the child's mattress on top. The Sisters, who followed the body to the boat, besought the men to remove the mattress, and to show all proper respect to the remains, which they promised to do. Father di Pietro went to the graveyard by land and gave the body Christian burial.

The Sisters found these arrangements so sad that they left the children in the school so that they might not see such a burial. This, however, is the manner of burying all who die of this contagious disease. Officials fumigated the buildings, and the Sisters were ordered to move from the infected house at once. The military hospital at St. George's Cay was placed at their disposal, and they were banished May 30. On June 4, they returned. On June 11, Sister Anita, a lay-sister, became ill. Next day, the doctor prescribed for her, but she grew rapidly worse. A second physician was called, and her condition was fluctuating; on the third day, at noon, a change appeared, and she received the Last Sacraments. She said she did not fear death. The Sisters playfully told her she could not get off so easily; she had more work to do for God. "It may be," said she, "but I do not think I shall get well. I am ready to die, if it be God's will." She died in a few days.[3]

BUFFALO, HAZLETON

House of Mercy, Buffalo

From all eternity, God, in His goodness, had ordained February 11, 1858 as a great day in the calendar of time. On that day His Immaculate Mother chose, through the instrumentality of a poverty-stricken child, to give us Lourdes, a mecca of hope for countless sufferers in mind and body. On that same day, through the instrumentality of a bishop, she chose to bring to Buffalo four Sisters of Mercy dedicated to the service of the poor, the sick, and the ignorant.

On the following Sunday, the Bishop offered the Holy Sacrifice of the Mass at St. Bridget's, after which he introduced the new pastor and the Sisters of Mercy to the congregation. There were many in the church that day who had known the Sisters of Mercy at home in Ireland (the "walking Sisters," they called them) and who, that morning, offered a fervent prayer of thanksgiving that Sisters had come to labor among them.

The Sisters went courageously to work to find out the needs of the parish; the sick who were to be visited and consoled; the children who were to be instructed; the destitute who were to be helped. No doubt they organized classes as soon as possible. *The Catholic Almanac, 1857–1858* lists:

> St. Joseph's Academy, Our Lady of Mercy, Buffalo, Sister Mary Regis Madden, principal and supervisor, 30 pupils, grade school, 200.

Home for Homeless Girls

One of the first projects of Mother M. Philomena (appointed from Pittsburgh to Buffalo) was the opening of a home for homeless girls. A bazaar opened at Dudley's Hall, September 18, 1861 and continued for a week. The notice states that a local band was on hand to enliven the occasion with good music. There were a number of tables exhibiting various types of needlework. "The object," as stated in the newspaper,

> is noble and enterprising, to establish a House of Mercy or a home for homeless girls who may be out of employment or broken in health. It is to be an asylum for defenseless immigrant girls, often a prey to unprincipled avaricious agents. The protection and maternal care of all such young females as well as the education of female youth constitutes the daily labors of the Sister of Mercy whose order is famed, not only in this country, but throughout Europe. Many are the monuments erected in the name of charity in this city during the last twelve years through the untiring and self-sacrificing zeal of Bishop John Timon, but a home for homeless girls is dear to his heart.

Announcement was made on July 13, 1863, "The cornerstone of the House of Mercy intended as a home for girls will be laid Sunday, July 19, 1863." The imposing ceremony took place as scheduled. It was witnessed by members of various Irish and German Catholic societies who marched from their respective halls to the place of consecration. These with the immense congregation of both sexes made an imposing assemblage.

Times were hard throughout the nation, and the Sisters suffered many privations—poor clothing, scant fare, lack of many necessities. We are told that on feast days a special treat was ginger snaps, and on very special feasts there was molasses to go with the ginger snaps. There was much work to be done and only a few to do it, but these few had the will to dare anything for Christ and His poor. Clad in long black cloaks, with black bonnets covered by gauze veils, the Sisters were familiar objects as they moved about, carrying brown baskets filled with comforts for the poor. Many a time a little portion was saved from their own scanty meal. Often one Sister on a visitation cared for the sick person, while her Sister companion helped tidy the house and feed the children, thus comforting the suffering family. In many cases, the Sisters had to provide clothing for half-clad children. Today we speak of this help as "social service work." No social service work in our day could begin to compare with what was done by these early religious! These services endeared the Sisters to the people and brought blessings down upon the community.

The Sisters made light of their own privations. An early member tells us that on Saturday nights they were sent in small bands to the back part of the mud-floored basement to polish their shoes. A few would take turns in stamping their feet to keep the rats away while the others plied the blacking brushes. Their pastor shared with them the little he had. Common foods were scarce. Yet, with the little they had, they deprived themselves of sugar for a whole year in order that they might have money enough to buy a new carpet for the sanctuary at Easter. Trifles, perhaps, but trifles make perfection, and these Sisters were truly great in their love of God.

On Good Friday, 1865, the whole nation was stunned by the news that the beloved president, Abraham Lincoln, had been assassinated. Buffalo shared the nation's grief. Stores were closed; schools were suspended. Flags flew at half-mast. Every window bore some sign of grief, from an elaborate display to a single black ribbon. Enroute to Springfield, Illinois, by train, the body remained in Buffalo overnight at St. James' Hall. It is estimated that over 100,000 men, women, and children viewed the remains throughout the twenty-four hours that the body lay in state. Bishop Timon arranged that prayers be offered for the departed President at the Masses on the following Sunday.

On January 14, 1868, the Sisters were bereaved at the death of their beloved Mother M. Philomena Devlin. Surely Mother Philomena was one of God's chosen. It required a good deal of courage for her to come on alone from Pittsburgh in 1860 to become Superior of a group of Sisters about whom she knew absolutely nothing, except that they were Sisters of Mercy. She established the little pioneer group on solid rock and, although she did not make a number of foundations, her Sisters became living examples of Christ-like charity in their own little portion of the vineyard. If one is to judge Mother M. Philomena from the works of her daughters among the poor of St. Bridget's, we know that when she appeared before her God that January 14, she heard, "Come, ye blessed of my Father, and enjoy the Kingdom that was prepared for you."

Hazleton Schools

The first break in St. Bridget's little community came in September, 1874. Father O'Hara of St. Gabriel's Parish in Hazleton, Pennsylvania applied to Mother M. Joseph Browne to give him Sisters. Mother M. Joseph sent five Sisters.

The first Monday in October, 1874, the Hazleton school opened with 350 children registered. A night school was also opened for men and boys employed in the mines during the day. Married men with families came to learn "to read, to write, to cipher." The little community prospered from the beginning despite keen poverty and hardship. Non-Catholic citizens preferred to send their children to this school because of the opportunity for moral development. Later, Hazleton was united with the Wilkes-Barre community.

Not too much information is available concerning the activities in the Buffalo St. Bridget's school during these early years. In 1876 the following report was made by the priest accompanying the Most Reverend Bishop to the school for visitations:

> The bishop visited the schools (academy and girls' and boys' grade school) attached to the convent of St. Bridget's, which I am happy to say are in a flourishing condition. I cannot conclude this brief note without bearing cheerful testimony to the efficiency of our Catholic schools under the management of the Sisters of Mercy. The Sisters here are of highly cultivated minds; they are constant in their efforts to instill into the intellects and hearts of their charges the seeds of Christian culture, which never fail to bear plenteous fruit in their season.

Injustice

At this time seventeen Sisters were engaged in teaching at St. Bridget's. In 1875 the parish paid a salary to these seventeen of a little more than a total of seven hundred dollars, or forty-two dollars per teacher per year. The article mentioning the above continues, "there are no better teachers in the world and no better school" in our city than St. Bridget's. Furthermore, the Sisters are not like Oliver Twist continually "asking for more." But that's no reason why they should not at least be paid enough to keep body and soul together![4]

CHICAGO

Mission of Mercy Hospital, Chicago

In his address on the occasion of the laying of the corner-stone of a new Mercy Hospital, Chicago, its history was epitomized by a well-known physician. The hospital was opened after the cholera of 1849 had scourged the citizens.

"Its growth has been steady and uniform, until we now lay the foundation of a magnificent structure which will remain for years an ornament to the city, a perpetual monument to the liberality and charity of its founders, and an asylum for the suffering and afflicted of many generations. During its past history, without the aid of public appropriations or private endowment, and constantly embarrassed by the temporary structure it has occupied, the hospital has accommodated and kindly treated more than six thousand human beings suffering from serious diseases, at least one-fourth of whom were cared for gratuitously. Its doors have been open alike to every class and creed.

"It has received the professional services, always gratuitous, of the most eminent members of the medical profession.

"In regard to the ability and faithfulness of the Sisters of Mercy in the management of the hospital, I can speak in terms of the fullest commendation. Having visited it professionally from its incipient organization to the present hour, I must say that in cleanliness, good order, kindly attention, and Christian liberality I have not seen its equal in any other public hospital in the country. . . . When the self-sacrificing Sisters of Mercy shall have finished and furnished every room, from basement to attic, with themselves in readiness to care for the sick, and the board of physicians and surgeons to aid them, there will yet lack only one thing to render its usefulness complete."

The doctor thus endeavored to excite the rich among his hearers to found at least *twenty free beds for the poor*. This number would accommodate on an average one hundred and fifty patients a year.

"To clothe the naked, to feed the hungry, to help the sick, are among the highest and holiest injunctions of the Divine Author of Christianity. . . . There can be but one sentiment in regard to the universally binding character of these admonitions. They are as broad in their scope as the brotherhood of man, and as binding as the divine impress can make them. . . . On the great day of judgment the questions will come: Did ye visit the prisoner? Did ye clothe the naked? Did ye feed the hungry? Did ye minister to the sick? Christianity demands not merely negative virtues but positive acts of human kindness."[5]

Saint Xavier, Chicago, and Civil War

Certain pleasant occurrences actually did take place in war time, the recital of which served to enliven the convent recreations for years after the Civil War. One of the band who had been on "the war-path" lived until September, 1915; almost oblivious to every other subject, Sister Mary Elzear always brightened up when asked if she remembered the war. She smiled particularly when she heard General John Charles Fremont's name, and exclaimed, "He was a perfect gentleman."

The latter part of 1864 was an eventful time in Chicago. Companies of Federal troops with squads of Confederate prisoners often passed the convent en route to Camp Douglas, situated in a southern suburb of the city. This camp was in charge of Colonel Sweet, of Wisconsin, and it was said the poor southern prisoners might be more humanly treated; it was also said that there was a great dearth of food in camp. The undercurrent of feeling in the city was strong; an indignation meeting was held, and a committee of investigation was appointed. When they appeared before Colonel Sweet, he refused them admission. Then these humane gentlemen called on Mother Mary Francis, and asked her to visit the Camp so that its needs might be supplied. Of course she consented, and with a companion, she undertook this duty herself. The sentry refused admittance. She then drove to the mayor's office. He courteously received the Sisters and gave them a note to Colonel Sweet, telling him it would silence unfavorable reports if he admitted the two Sisters to the Camp. They drove back to the latter place and sent the note to the Colonel who allowed the Sisters to visit the prisoners and care for their needs.[6]

The Great Chicago Fire (1871)

About ten o'clock Saturday night, October 7, 1871, a fire broke out on Clinton Street, Chicago, which, owing to a strong south wind and the poor state of the buildings, was brought under control with great difficulty. On Saturday, about nine o'clock p.m., while the Sisters were at prayers, a second fire broke out six blocks west of the first, in a cow-stable. The whole world has heard of Mrs. O'Leary's cow, and the kerosene-lamp which that restive animal kicked over when her mistress was milking her on that peaceful Sabbath evening; and of the fatal consequences of that murderous fluid which laid a city in ashes. True, the stable of the O'Leary household was burned, and the fate of the historic cow is a mystery. But Mrs. O'Leary herself, in mortal terror of being arrested as an incendiary, barricaded the doors and windows of her domicile, and lay on the top story until Chicago enterprise—alert even on that awful night—discovered her. She then solemnly and stoutly denied all knowledge of the catastrophe on her own part, and on the part of her calumniated cow. And, indeed, the first fireman on the spot partly exonerated this much maligned pair, for, after the closest investigation, he declared that he could not ascertain the barn or the stable in which the fire had originated, nor could the watchmen who held their lonely vigils on the city towers.

What is to our purpose is that the Sisters were disturbed at night-prayers by smothered noises at a distance, which were no small distraction to them. Mother M. Vincent, who was giving out the Litany of the Saints, laid down her book and left the chapel. She had scarcely done so when the court-house bell rang out a general alarm.

From a great distance the Sisters saw advancing toward them a trail of fire, increasing in width and volume every moment. Sometimes it crossed the great business blocks diagonally, driven by a furious southwesterly wind, and irresistible in its progress. It dashed embers and firebrands in every direction, and the wooden buildings in its path were annihilated in minutes. Some of the Sisters said they thought the whole city would be destroyed, and sent for carriages to convey the inmates of the two Mercy houses to the hospital. The smaller children were sent off first, then the larger; then the inmates of the House of Mercy and most of the Sisters. No one thought at this time that the flames would come as far as the convent. At midnight Father Gavin, assistant at St. Mary's, came to remove the Blessed Sacrament. He advised the Sisters to leave, saying he felt sure the whole place would be consumed before morning.

How could the Sisters that remained after midnight go through such streets? It seemed certain death to venture out of their convent home. There was fire north, south, and west of them; the only place free from flames was Lake Michigan. Yet they could not believe that their home, the fruit of so many prayers and tears, was doomed.

Some gentlemen, relatives and friends, now crowded into the convent to help them save anything that could be easily removed.

One hundred thousand people, or about one-third of the inhabitants of Chicago, were rendered homeless that night; 2,124 acres of the most thickly settled portion of the city were a waste; 17,450 buildings were destroyed. But the charity evoked was in proportion to the calamity. In a few days bread, clothing, and all the necessaries of life poured into the stricken city. And the contributions in money, sent literally from the whole world, were little short of three million dollars. Money and goods together reached nearly seven million dollars. It was not for long that human beings were huddled together in the parks and on the prairies; all that charity and benevolence could do for them was speedily done.

For some cause or other, possibly a change in the wind, the old convent did not fall as soon as many other buildings treble its size. It was still standing at nine A.M. on Monday. But at half-past nine not a vestige of it remained. When the Sisters went to view the ruins the only thing that retained any form was the marble statue of Our Lady of Mercy that stood in an oratory over the front door on a beautiful marble altar. It had fallen outward on the stoop; the head and hands were broken. They took it home, had the head fastened on, and kept it as a relic of the happy early days. It may still be seen in a glass house in the garden of the new convent. In the library is a still older relic—a picture of the crucifixion, brought from Europe in Bishop William Quarter's time. It was the first altar-piece in St. Mary's Church, and occupied the same position in the Mercy Convent at the time of the fire. Some months after, two Sisters saw it in the basement of the present St. Mary's. No one knew how it had come there, but it was restored to the community to the great delight of all, especially the older members.

The dearest recollections and associations clung about the old convent. In 1851 Mother M. Agatha gives a pleasant picture of the good done there. Speaking of a visit to Bishop Henni and other prelates, she says: "I suppose they saw we were doing the best we could. Although everything here is plain and humble, still it is almost incredible the good that is being done for our holy religion. You can scarcely imagine the amount of labor which our Sisters go through; yet all, thank God, is perfect peace, perfect unity: And oh! dear Sister, is not that preferable to all other things? We have now charge of three Sunday schools, St. Mary's (Cathedral), St. Patrick's, and the Holy Name. These are all about two miles apart, yet we have to walk. We have also two free schools well filled, two asylums containing eighty-six orphans, the hospital, and the select school. From this you can imagine all that has to be done. We have to struggle to make ends meet, but yet we have all that is necessary and what more should religious desire?"

Suffering and Success

The Chicago foundation was tried by every ordeal—poverty and riches, friends and lack of friends, prosperity and adversity, plague, war, fire—and, sustained by the Almighty, came out of every peril unscathed. Nothing could be more humble than its beginnings, in 1846, in a poor hut on the bleak prairie. "Unless the seed die, it remaineth alone." Of the valiant women who came there through perils by land and sea, only one survives to tell the tale [1888]. Nothing can well be more splendid than the success of the Chicago foundation today—success achieved through the cross.[7]

CINCINNATI

Guide for Religious Life

. . . At this time (1858) Rev. Mother M. Teresa Maher, Founder of the Cincinnati Congregation, had brought with her, from St. Joseph's, Kinsale, Ireland, a manuscript copy of the Exposition of the Rule and Constitution of the Order, entitled, "*Guide for the Religious called Sisters of Mercy.*" It embodies in its clear, concise, and simple pages, the Spirit and Mission of the Sisters of Mercy, and has received the approval of high ecclesiastical authority. The "Guide" is the work of Mother Francis Bridgeman, of St. Joseph's, Kinsale, who made her Novitiate under the Reverend Foundress, Mother Catherine McAuley, from whose lips Mother Francis imbibed the beautiful Spirit of the Order and Its Rule, which is stamped on every page of her admirable work. A supply of printed copies of the Guide was shortly thereafter received and copies were bought by different Houses of the Order in the United States and elsewhere.[8]

Campaign for Funds in Cincinnati

On Sunday evening of this date, November 6, 1865, in aid of the Night Refuge of the Sisters of Mercy, a talk was given in the "Margaret Hall" by Professor Andres. The proceeds amounted to $600.00. In order to collect funds for the Night Refuge, the Sisters published the following circular:

Convent of the Order of Mercy, Cincinnati

The Sisters of Mercy who have arrived in Cincinnati are known to be solemnly devoted to the education of females, to the visitation of the sick, and to the care and protection of distressed, unemployed women of exemplary character. They feel as yet their sphere of action is considerably limited for want of necessary means and a sufficiently large establishment. They are desirous, with the blessing of God and with the aid of a good and benevolent people, to extend to this populous city all the advantages contemplated by this Institute.

The scene of sorrow among the sick, which the Sisters witness in their visits of Mercy, are most painful and affecting, and can be relieved only by the combined charity of all those who are willing to share, according to their means, in the sweet burden of assisting their fellow creatures in the trying hour of sickness, particularly when aggravated by distress. The Sisters have fitted up a House of Refuge contiguous to their Convent for the benefit of a few distressed females who, by their temporary accommodation, may be rescued from extreme destitution, and who for a few days or weeks may have lodging and support and also instruction in their business and in the duties of their state in life, until under Providence suitable situations may be provided for them.

The Sisters now appeal to the benevolent public and, unwilling to burden any of those whose hand has been so frequently extended of late to help other establishments, solicit the small sum of *two cents per week.* This contribution will hurt none, while it can effect much good if all generously comply with the small demand. Collectors will be appointed by the Sisters to call regularly on those willing to aid. The charities of the Sisters are confined to no particular sect. To prevent imposition, a book will be given to each collector with a printed form in front signed by the Mother Superior of the Convent. "Amen, I say to you, as long as you did it to one of these my least brethren, you did it to me." Matt. XXV, 40.

Ladies requiring servants can be supplied at the convent of the Sisters of Mercy every day from one till two o'clock, Saturday and Sunday excepted.[9]

Sodalities

Members of the *Sodality for Women* of Cincinnati assemble every Sunday afternoon before Vespers, in the Sodality Chapel, for instruction in their religious duties and for devotional exercises. By the Act of Consecration they place themselves under the protection of the Mother of God, and by studying to imitate her admirable example endeavor to advance in virtue and piety. They go to Confession and Holy Communion once a month and on principal festivals of Our Lord and His Blessed Mother, spend, besides the ordinary morning and evening services, a quarter of an hour every day in mental prayer or spiritual reading, visit the sick members and assist them to prepare for the sacraments, and when anyone is called to a better life, they recite the Office of the Dead, and hear Mass for her soul for eight successive days.

The *second Sodality* opened was one for *Young Girls,* in April, 1859. Then with the beginning of a new school year in September, the Holy Angels' and Divine Infant Sodalities were begun for the older and younger children respectively. Within the two years that followed, there came into being four more sodalities: St. Joseph's Association for relief of the poor, sick, and dying; the Confraternity of the Blessed Sacrament to offer adoration and reparation to the Blessed Sacrament; St. Anne's Society for parents of children attending school; and another group mentioned only as "a circle of young ladies" who met weekly at the convent to receive religious instructions and for encouragement of piety and the edification of the neighbor.[10]

Floods in Hamilton, 1913

After Dayton, the next place that received the terrible stroke of the flood was Hamilton, Ohio. In this place our Community was doubly interested as our beautiful Mercy Hospital was in water up to the second story.

The Sisters say that at about 11 o'clock on the morning of March ———, a rushing roar of water was heard, but before anyone could reach the spot, the terrible velocity with which the water came pulled the large Hospital door from its hinges and raised it from its place, thus flooding the lowest floor of the Hospital before notice could be given.

The Sisters had already removed from the store rooms a great quantity of the materials used in the dressing of the wounds of the sick, an act that was really providential. In fact, as soon as all were appraised of the rush of the water, each person who was able set to work and carried all perishable articles as well as beds. Someone made the remark that she could not imagine how she was able to carry some article of furniture by herself as it was very heavy, but no doubt the thought of the suffering sick gave strength to her arms.

The Hospital was in a terrible condition, particularly in the basement and on the first floor. The mud and debris were piled high, and it took weeks to clean these floors.

As in Dayton, the whole city suffered, and it is recorded that the Hamilton flood destruction was really greater than Dayton's. It would be utterly impossible to restore the losses or build up the city for years.

The Sisters suffered great hardships since water and fire, the two essentials, were very meagre. There was plenty of water outside, but it could not be used! Yet, as far as is known, not one patient died. Of course, this result was owing to the sacrifice made by the Sisters who day and night made strenuous efforts to procure food and drink for the poor sick patients.

The Archbishop (of Cincinnati) paid a very friendly and sympathetic visit and gave his blessing to all in the Hospital. He remarked that it was wonderful how the Sisters and patients lived through the terrible disaster, but he was pleased to see such self-sacrifice manifested by all the religious. It may be well to mention that when the water was rising rapidly and no assistance could be received from the Chaplain, the Sisters thought well to remove the Lord from the Tabernacle, fearing the place would be flooded before the next day. What a beautiful and spiritual procession that must have been. . . . Cincinnati also was plunged in water, but, Deo Gratias, the destruction could not in any manner be compared to that of the cities of Dayton and Hamilton. . . .[11]

Influenza Epidemic

In response to a personal appeal from Father Regis Barrett, O.S.B. for Sisters to help nurse the victims of a serious *epidemic of influenza* in the mining regions of Kentucky, in the late fall of 1918, sixteen Cincinnati Sisters were selected from the volunteers. After hasty preparations and instructions, the group left the Convent of Mercy, Freeman Avenue, November 4, 1918. They arrived at Lexington, Kentucky the same day. A group of Catholic Red Cross workers met the Sisters and divided them into two groups, taking eight to St. Catherine's Academy and the remaining eight to St. Joseph's Hospital. Here the Sisters of Charity of Nazareth gave them gracious hospitality. On Tuesday, November 5, Major McMullen assigned the group at St. Catherine's to their destinations.

The work was truly one of Mercy, for the fear of the contagion kept ordinarily charitable people away from the homes of the afflicted ones. Frequently the Sisters had to prepare the bodies for burial, as well as care for the sick, assist the dying, and console the bereaved.

Despite the handicaps and inconveniences, and long journeys in mule carts, the Sisters were able to relieve thirty or forty families each day. The lack of sanitation in the mining villages greatly hindered the work of allaying the disease. The Sisters remained at their posts until November 20, when the severity of the epidemic passed and the local agencies were sufficiently established to take over the care of the stricken.

Although several of the Sisters were later attacked by influenza, only one, Sister Mary Raphael O'Connor, contracted the disease while on duty at Van Lear. After a little more than a week, Sister was stricken and had to be brought home. Although every possible care was given to her, she succumbed to the disease and died on November 20, the day on which her companions were leaving their field of labor.

Many of the scenes of the disease are indelibly imprinted on the minds of the Sisters who worked in the primitive conditions in the mining camps. To understand the conditions, one must recall the temporary type of dwelling, built off the ground—the space between frequently serving in lieu of chicken coop or barn—and the one room where the family, often eight or ten or more in number, lived.

Among the Red Cross workers and townspeople to whom the Sisters are especially indebted for their courtesy and hospitality are the Sisters of Charity of Nazareth.[12]

Educational Training in Cincinnati

Mother McAuley required that her religious should devote themselves in a special manner to the training of women and girls. She left nothing undone to educate the young Sisters for the efficient discharge of this task. The Foundress thought that the most important factor in any school is the teacher, and the qualifications most desired in the teacher are a whole-souled devotion and moral integrity. Without these, the leader cannot hope to impart the essential moral lessons to the pupil, for one is powerless to communicate character, goodness, or spirituality unless one possesses them herself.

Absorbed in their many duties, the Sisters of Mercy did not neglect the important work of education. The Infant Boys' School, begun in the basement of St. Thomas Church, was probably discontinued after the community's transfer to Fourth Street, but in the new location another school was set up. No date can be found for its beginning, but in all likelihood it was September, 1860. By 1863 the Fourth Street school was functioning with proficiency that elicited the following remarks from the *Cincinnati Telegraph:*

> A more thorough or more practical inquest of its kind we have seldom witnessed than that to which the pupils of this institution were subjected on Wednesday last. In reading, spelling, parsing, geography, arithmetic, enunciation, catechism, the elements of natural history, etc., the test by interrogators was searching in the highest degree, eliciting explanations which, for promptness and correctness, left nothing to be desired.[13]

LITTLE ROCK, ARKANSAS, AND HELENA, MONTANA

Attacks by Know-Nothings in Arkansas

As a rule, the Sisters had little to suffer from bigotry in Arkansas. In those remote days they were looked upon as the most precious boon which Providence could bestow on the rising country. People blessed God on account of them and the bishop for bringing them. They thought it a great thing to find for their children in the backwoods of Arkansas teachers of the highest order—ladies who could instruct them in every accomplishment, and at the same time imbue their minds with every religious and moral virtue, and while bestowing mental culture keep their hearts free from evil in the period of youth. Few States at that early period, 1851, possessed such schools, and the rareness of this blessing made the people value it the more.

During the Know-Nothing movement, it is true, the religious suffered and were frequently in danger of their very lives. The creatures who engaged in this odd species of attack were constantly prowling about the shanty known as the convent, uttering fearful blasphemies against everything sacred in the eyes of its inmates. They had sworn the destruction of this poor house, which a strong man could almost knock down with his shoulder. The friends of the community, Protestant as well as Catholic, earnestly besought the Sisters to seek safety in flight, and provision was made in more places than one for their security. But they preferred to stand their ground, and stay at the foot of the altar, should God call for sacrifice.

Suffering in Civil War in Little Rock, Fort Smith

During the Civil War the Sisters in Little Rock, Arkansas, opened a hospital for Confederate soldiers. They owned a good brick house opposite the convent, into which they received at least twenty-five ailing men. Two or three died every day, but their bunks were speedily filled with others. When General Price, after his defeat in Missouri, retreated to Little Rock, men were dying on all sides from cold, sickness, and exposure. The Sisters were indefatigable in serving these poor men. The Little Rock Garrison was composed largely of Texans, many of whom on their beds of sickness embraced the faith. Where St. Andrew's Cathedral now stands was a coffin factory, which at one period of great mortality turned out forty coffins a day for the deceased warriors. For a while there was almost a famine. Ladies had to dress in furniture cotton, shoes were fifty dollars a pair, a spool of thread cost four or five dollars. Food itself was at famine rates. Clothing such as the Sisters usually wore could scarcely be got at any price.

For nearly two years no one in the convent tasted tea or coffee. Once, when Father O'Reilly was coming from Fort Smith to Little Rock, the Sisters of the Fort, who had some way or other procured a little tea, sent some in a stocking by their good friend for Reverend Mother's feast-day celebration. Want of sufficient food and clean clothing was partially the cause of the high death rate. Ladies, Protestant as well as Catholic, kindly aided the Sisters in their ministrations of mercy. To prevent the remarks likely to be made should the local clergy attend the hospital, the Sisters called on the Chaplain of the "Pelican Rangers," a Louisiana regiment, to give the Sacraments to the dying soldiers whom they had induced to prepare for eternity. The Confederate officers who were personal friends of the Sisters gave them a guard of seven men to protect the convent at night.

Priests and religious were closely watched by both parties, and any bias, or supposed bias, towards either was carefully noted. It was well known that the Sisters of Mercy were equally kind to Federals and Confederates, but the Union men sometimes suspected them of a slight leaning towards "the enemy."

General Price was three days taking his troops and wounded out of the vicinity. The incoming Federals and the vanquished Confederates passed on either side of the convent grounds. As the last detachment left, shells and bombs were discharged from the gunboats at the wharf in the hope of destroying the receding troops of the Confederate army. These destructive missiles passed harmlessly over the convent, but shattered many of the tombstones in the city cemetery, at some distance.

General Steele gave the Sisters a guard, which never left the grounds for seventeen months. (General Steele entered Little Rock on September 24, the Feast of Our Lady of Mercy, as celebrated that year. The inmates of St. Mary's never forgot.) "The enemy" was now at the Rock. Being hungry, they took the citizens' provisions, not forgetting to appropriate hay and corn from the convent granary. In ignorance of the nature of the institution, the Northern troops bivouacked on the grounds and helped themselves to whatever was movable. The Federal authorities, however, treated the Sisters with great respect. At daybreak the Sisters could see the Union soldiers looking through the windows of the first floor and school-rooms, and hear them say: "What place is this?" One cow was walking out where the intruders had broken the fence. A Sister said: "There must be Catholic Irishmen among these Northern soldiers. If they see the religious habit, they will respect it." Taking a child as a companion, she went towards them. A soldier advanced to meet her. "Will you be kind enough, my friend," said she, "to turn our cow back into the enclosure?" "Certainly, Madam," said he, in soft accents that suggested the banks of the Suir. "Can I do anything else for you?" From that moment the Sisters and the new brigade were the best of friends. And if the soldiers did make free with their hay and oats before they knew to whom the premises belonged, they made ample restitution. For when the Sisters had no longer means to get food for their large family, the Federals supplied them from the commissariat.

Proclamation of Freedom for Blacks in Helena

Helena is not without its memories. The Sisters who nursed the dying can see in spirit the gory field, and hear the clash of arms and the din of battle. They thank Heaven for the relief they were able to afford the sick and wounded, irrespective of nation, color, or religion. It was in the barn of their convent that General Steele, in the name of his government, proclaimed the negroes free. The saturnalia which followed that auspicious event will never be forgotten by the terrified inmates of the convent. Those newly made free roamed through the town armed with knives and clubs, drunk with liquor. There were few or no white men at home; the conflict had shifted its quarters. The women barred their doors and barricaded their windows. When the enthusiasm had spent itself, the women had again to thank God that they were unmolested.

Sometimes the Sisters had to go in skiffs to visit the sick. Occasionally, when the river overleaped the levees, there were sixteen feet of water in the streets. More than once the General, who lived next door to the Sisters, had his dispatches brought to his house in a small steamer. The convent, reached by a flight of thirty-three steps, was high above the water, but the floods caused great suffering in many ways. Bishop Fitzgerald paid his first visit to the Helena convent in 1867 in a boat which was moored to the banister of the convent until he came out.

Teaching Old and Young in Arkansas

The Arkansas religious gave themselves to God in early youth, and He Himself blessed old age in those who had attained it, and sustained the young in their labor for Him. They have seen strange vicissitudes while they themselves remained steadfast. They have borne the burden of the day and the heat, while others have faltered and dropped out of the ranks. Trials of every species have assailed them, but, as we have seen, not even war at their doors could injure them. We shall leave them in their fair homes by river, spring, grove, and mountains, in their setting of greenery, praying that their future may be worthy of their past. They have borne nobly and well the yoke of the Lord, and taught others to bear it. For if there be one work of mercy more than another in which this Sisterhood has excelled, it is in teaching the young and the old to serve God, to serve Him who is to reign. Magnificent will be their reward from their Father who is in heaven. "For they that instruct many unto justice shall shine like stars for all eternity."[14]

NEW ORLEANS, MOBILE, ST. MARTINSVILLE

New Orleans—Joys of Early Days

There was, and still is, in the rear of the first residence of the Mercy Sisterhood in New Orleans, a small house, consisting of four rooms, partially furnished, which was used as the beginning of a House of Mercy in 1869. . . . The Sisters were not a month in Louisiana when they had schools, visitation of the sick and public instructions, and a House of Mercy in operation, though the community numbered only six.

Everything looked bright in these early days, marked by so much true friendliness and affection, and blessed by so many incidents calculated to draw out one's better qualities. This delightful period was like an oasis in the desert of life: as for crosses, they had none. Even the weather was propitious; as the summer wore on, they found the heat far less oppressive than the heat they had endured in Northern cities. One and all affirmed that never, since the days of the Holy Foundress, had Sisters of Mercy been more happily situated. Their virtues were magnified, their shortcomings overlooked. Father Meredith, who went in July to give a retreat in a distant convent, wrote back: "The Sisters here seem very nice, but they have not the sweet simplicity of our New Orleans Sisters. I know of none like our own." When the Rector gave the first retreat, he said he had only to console, animate, and encourage; there was nothing serious enough for correction. The Sisters seemed to increase in favor with God and man as they increased in age.

House of Mercy and Training of Women

Within the first decade of its existence, the House of Mercy sheltered over a thousand poor but good women, most of whom were provided with situations. Father Duffy took immense interest in the opening of this establishment. But it never evoked the sympathy that might be expected. People will help orphans, the sick, the lame, the blind, even the sinful; but to aid healthy young women who, they say, should be out working, is not to be thought of; they fail to see that to make capable workers, women must be properly trained. Anything done by the Sisters in this way must be done almost by stealth; and circumstances seem to require that the House of Mercy should be rather a resting-place for the over-worked than a training-school for workers. The very persons who complain that nothing is to be got but "unskilled labor" deem it unjust to keep workers in training, and proclaim that they can get all the training needed in their respective situations.

Foundations Throughout the South

The services of the Sisters of Mercy were requested in many places as they increased in numbers. St. Patrick's school for boys and girls fell under their care in 1873, Archbishop Perche having asked them as a personal favor to assume the charge. Some four years later, they were relinquished, as the buildings had to be sold in consequence of the pecuniary difficulties of the diocese. In March 1875, the Sisters opened their first branch house in Biloxi, at the request of Bishop Elder and the pastor of that town. In September, 1876, they opened St. Alphonsus' Orphan Asylum, corner of Washington and St. Patrick streets. In September, 1877, at the request of Bishop Quinlan, they planted a branch in Pensacola and, in January, 1878, in the neighboring village of Warrington. In March 1881, they founded a convent at St. Martinsville, and in January, 1883, another at Belize, British Honduras. In August, 1884, the Jesuit Fathers having asked for Sisters for Mobile the previous year, a colony was sent to the Gulf City. St. Michael's, New Orleans, Jeanerette on the Teche, and Selma, in Alabama, followed. Selma was founded September 8, 1891, at the request of Right Rev. Bishop O'Sullivan.

Schools in Mobile

Sister Margaret Mary of Mobile took the greatest interest in the schools. "The Bishop and our pastor deem them second to none in Mobile," she writes. "Please pray for the success of the examinations; six of our pupils are working for diplomas. If they succeed they will be the first to receive such an honor in St. Joseph's Institution. . . . Time flies with wonderful rapidity; death is quickly catching up with us all; the thought of many graces wasted, time perhaps lost, naturally inspires fear. Every day I appreciate more and more the goodness of our loving Saviour towards me. So far as I can judge, God can never bestow a greater favor on any one than a religious vocation. Such peace and happiness as I have enjoyed during the five years I have been in the convent, I never imagined could be experienced in this world. . . . Good parents, devoted teachers prepared the way for the graces in store for me."

Yellow Fever Epidemic in New Orleans

The Sisters spent their days among the stricken. In the evening some went in a barouche to the worst districts, carrying with them everything necessary to treat the disease, especially in its earlier stages. For the doctors could not reach them all; and the Sisters, from long experience, knew what to do. In this way many lives were saved. Within the convent there were twenty-four cases and three deaths. In the Orphanage no case originated, but several children were brought in from dead or dying parents, in a dying condition. Even of these, only one died. This was deemed extraordinary, for the mortality among children was so large as to strike with fear the old fashioned people who believed in that pathetic and poetic phrase, "When the doves fly aloft, look out for storms." And many recalled the awful words of the prophet: "Because thou hast forgotten Me, I will bereave thee of thy children."

Southern cities have a bright look in the long summer, with their soft skies and luxuriant vegetation. But in the sad months of the epidemic of 1878, a pall seemed to overshadow the fair Crescent City. Stores were almost bereft of customers, streets deserted; no crowds, no loud talking, no driving about for pleasure, under the shadow of the pestilence. The angel of death was abroad. Cavalcades of death turned the corners from all directions; at first, the funerals were large; later, the mourners were few, and followed the silent march of the dead like shadowy spectres. No bells rung, no trains coming in, no music in the streets, no requiem services over "the loved, but not the lost," in the stately churches, everywhere the gloom of the grave.

Under one aspect, yellow fever proved a blessing, though in a horrible guise. It knit together the sundered peoples of the North and the South, as the soul of Jonathan was knit to the soul of David. It effaced many bitter recollections between the blue and the gray, by inspiring a splendid generosity in the victors and a noble gratitude in the vanquished. To the Church it did the work of an evangelist by painting Christ to men, and of an apostle, in bringing men to Christ. To many a prodigal it was a last grace. It awakened a sense of dependence on the Supreme Being who wounds only to heal, chastising us in mercy and love, because he is our Father. Seldom was there a greater revival of prayer. Crowds thronged the churches at the early Masses, and the Holy Table was surrounded with trusting souls. Eager worshippers besieged the Tabernacle, beseeching the hidden God to show mercy to all whom they felt to be near and dear.[15]

Perils of Travel: A Diary

Ash Wednesday. Went to early Mass in the pretty little Church of New Iberia and had the happiness of receiving Holy Communion.

At 9:30 we set out for St. Martinsville. We had a strong Jersey Wagon, a fine pair of horses and a colored driver. Owing to the dreadful condition of the roads, he had a round-about direction which lengthened the distance from eleven to fifteen miles.

The plantations along the road . . . were alive with men and women hoeing, cleaning, and planting. The bad weather and severe winter will make the crop rather late next season.

In a lonely part of the road our horses took fright at some old clothes and bags fluttering in the wind from an oak tree by the road side. Only for the Mercy of God who gave the driver a cool head, courage, and strong arm, we would not have escaped with whole bones. After ten minutes, the driver succeeded in getting the animals under control and then made a detour so that the fluttering of rags could not be seen. At another place we were obliged to get out of the carriage and walk the length of a square, holding on by the fence rails, to keep from falling in the ditch. Then we had to make a big jump which was anything but graceful.

The wind was high and we had to keep our veils fastened, else they would be torn to shreds by the pointed wire fence. Without any more adventures except coming across carcasses of cows, mules, calves, pigs which had perished from cold and which made our horses shy, we reached St. Martinsville about 1:00 p.m. . . . .[16]

A Different Christmas

Christmas. "Priest told the Sisters he would give them Communion at the Church at $5\frac{1}{2}$ a.m., so we started off in the rain, with lantern and umbrellas. To our great surprise, we found the Church locked. Sisters M. Carmelita and Paula went to the priest's house to get the keys. They came back followed by Father Lafarge. We received Holy Communion. Then after thanksgiving, hoped to have time to eat our breakfast, but the Mass bell rang and off we had to run. We remained for the three Masses which were said by Father Lafarge, S.J. . . . We received two fine cakes and a dish of turkey and an oyster pie!!![17]

NEW YORK CITY

Dramatic Foundation—New York

Towards the close of 1845 Bishop John J. Hughes, New York City, applied in person to the parent-house of the Institute, Dublin, for some Sisters of Mercy for his episcopal City. The superior expressed her willingness to accede to his request, but could not spare a single experienced member to take charge of the foundation. So many establishments had been made by an Order not yet fourteen years old that Mother M. Cecilia Marmion might say, as did the holy foundress some years previously, not that "hands and feet are plentiful enough," for she needed more of these useful members, but that "the heads were all gone." The bishop, determined not to leave without what he had come for, pressed the question. "Well, my lord," said Mother M. Cecilia, "there is a Sister of ours in London. If she will undertake the business, we will see what can be done."

Bishop Hughes determined to speak for himself, and posted to London. He found Bishop Griffiths more ready to take Sisters than to give them. Nothing daunted, he waited on Mother M. Agnes O'Connor. It was a case of mutual admiration. He felt he was in the presence of a woman who could carry out his views, and she saw that her life-work lay on the other side of the Atlantic. A letter from Dublin proposed to her to take charge of the Sisters preparing to go to New York. She replied: "Here I am: send me."

House of Mercy

The object of the New York institution was to endeavor to relieve every phase of human misery which aid or sympathy could reach. The

Sisters protected and educated young girls of good character, but destitute and friendless. The consequences of the disastrous famine that desolated Ireland, 1846–47, had driven thousands of her children to these hospitable shores. The young girls among them attended the House of Mercy, New York, daily at stated hours, until suitable situations were found for them. Food and pecuniary aid were given to those out of employment, and they were provided with decent lodgings. It soon appeared that the chief work of the New York Sisterhood during this crisis ought to be this branch of their institution known as the House of Mercy.

In May, 1848, the Sisters moved to a spacious convent, at the corner of Houston and Mulberry Streets, recently vacated by the Sisters of the Sacred Heart. Part of it was appropriated to the young women. And the Sisters had the happiness of being able to protect, relieve, and instruct those who were the special objects of their Institute; for it will be remembered that to protect poor women of good character was a main object of Catherine McAuley. Bishop John J. Hughes took the greatest interest in this project, and had collections taken up for it in all the churches of New York, Brooklyn, and Jersey City. A House of Mercy was immediately begun. It was incorporated by Act of Legislation, April 12, 1848.

Sainthood and Suffering of New York Founder

"As winter approached, our founder, Mother M. Agnes O'Connor became unable to go up and down stairs. We fixed her comfortably in the small parlor which had formed part of the first chapel, and was at the door of the new one. Here she was in close proximity to the Blessed Sacrament, while being also in the midst of her Sisters.

"Till December the physician held out hopes of her recovery. On the morning of the 18th, feeling unusually depressed, she said: 'I do not think it is possible for me to live longer in this state; may God's will be done.' Every remedy prescribed failed to produce the desired effect, and the most sanguine saw that God was calling the beloved Sister to Himself, and saw fit to leave their earnest prayers unanswered. The last sacraments were administered. The Sisters were in grief, and when the priest was about to begin the anointing, Mother Agnes gave them a very grave look, and then said to the priest, with great effort: 'Excuse me, father; I must ask you to delay a little.' Then turning to us she said: 'Sisters, have you forgotten your rules and customs? Where are your candles and church-cloaks?' We were so overwhelmed with sorrow that no one had thought of them. When the tapers were lit and the church-cloaks on, Mother Agnes, with a smile, bowed to us and motioned the Father to proceed. Every hour increased her suffering. About midnight, Dr. O'Reilly took leave of her with deep feeling. She said a few words expressive of her gratitude to him. The Sisters surrounded her bed, reciting the litanies with voices broken with tears, pressing the crucifix to her lips after she had become insensible to exterior things.

"God seemed to have accepted the excruciating anguish she endured during her long illness, and spared her the pain that usually accompanies the last moments. Hers were so gentle, so peaceful, that the anxious eyes of her devoted Sisters, who watched every expression of her dear face and counted every breathing, could scarcely distinguish the moment when her soul left her body at about one a.m. The Sisters then closed the eyes of the first and best beloved superior and foundress of St. Catherine's Convent of Mercy, New York."[18]

PITTSBURGH

Founding of the First American Mission—Pittsburgh

A beautiful spirit of charity prevailed among the early members of the Sisters of Mercy, which has not diminished in their successors. "There never was," writes one, "a more united community." Always ready to help, serve, and oblige one another, it might be said of them, as of the first Christians, they had but one heart and soul. The first American reception ceremony took place in Penn Street chapel, Pittsburgh, the bishop officiating, February 22, 1844. Miss Margaret O'Brien, future superior of Chicago, received the white veil. . . . It was remarked as a pleasant coincidence that the first clothing took place on a day of such joyful import to America. Those who selected it did not know it was Washington's birthday, but, when they heard it, took it as a good omen of their success in America.

The first public ceremony was the profession of Sister M. Aloysius Strange and the reception of Frances Xavier Tiernan, first American Sister of Mercy. The bishop, desirous that his people should have a clear understanding as to what the life of a Sister of Mercy involved, offered to preach on the occasion. As Miss Tiernan's family was extensively known throughout Western Pennsylvania, the Catholics and non-Catholics of that region were largely represented. To make the reception as impressive as possible, Mother Warde had arranged that the blessing of the candle and its reception by the novice-elect should take place before High Mass in the Cathedral.

After the Gospel the bishop explained the religious state in general and the Mercy Order in particular. He dwelt especially on the probation through which candidates must pass previous to making vows, and their perfect freedom of choice during that stage of the religious life, compulsory seclusion, which many believe the Church authorizes, being quite contrary to Mercy spirit. His auditors would see at the ceremonies of to-day that the free will of the contracting parties was necessary to the validity of the contract. He sketched the duties of a Sister of Mercy to the poor, sick, and ignorant, showing the great advantage of such a society to the community, and the blessings it must bring wherever it is established. At the Communion the professed-elect read and signed her vows. The audience, listening and looking on with the deepest interest, understood that this was the final consecration. The Te Deum was chanted in Gregorian style by the clergy and students with fine effect.

But when Miss Tiernan, the grand centre of attraction, came forward to be interrogated according to the ceremonial, the interest was intense. As she retired to change her dress, the strongest emotion was observed, which, when she returned in the habit of a Sister of Mercy, found vent in tears of joy, sorrow, or sympathy. The close came at last. The *Ecce Quam Bonum* was sung in choral style; all seemed to feel the truth of the words, though few knew their meaning. All in the vast assemblage knew—some for the first time, some better than they had known before—what it is to be a Sister of Mercy, and many said: "It is a blessed life, here and hereafter."

On the return to the convent, Mother Warde, assisted by her willing daughters, offered the hospitality of their humble home to a large number of guests. Sister M. Xavier Tiernan was "the cynosure of all eyes," and the joy that lit up her countenance eloquently testified that she already felt how good and pleasant it is to dwell in the house of the Lord. Her evident happiness dissipated the grief of her parents, brothers, and sister, who were now convinced that the cloister was to be her home.

Schools

In September, 1844, the Sisters of Mercy opened their first school in the United States. The provisional convent was poorly adapted for educational purposes. The classes were taught in a long basement, with large windows at each end, arranged as a school, or, as the vernacular said, "fixed so." Bad as the accommodations were, the school was soon filled with bright, happy children from five to sixteen years old, to whom the Sisters gave unremitting attention. The basement, with its bright, studious scholars, was perhaps as happy a spot as could be found in the Smoky City.

The happy children of that remote period had just what they needed.

They learned to read, write, and speak well—accomplishments not over-common to-day. They could "cast accounts," and had a fair knowledge of history, geography, and poetry. Their taste for reading was directed and cultivated, and the love of good books was instilled into their minds. Catechism was well studied, and they were thoroughly instructed in their duties to God, their neighbor, and themselves. To parents and superiors they were taught to be obedient, loving, and respectful, to spare them trouble, and to be as self-helpful as possible. They were shown how to take part in the darning, mending, and general sewing of their families; and polite, orderly habits were inculcated by word, and still more by example. They were taught by noble women, and visited frequently by a bishop "to know what was a liberal education. . . ." The school had a common-sense aspect—an air of avoiding fooleries and preparing little people for the stern duties likely to devolve on them in after-life.

The ever increasing number of the pupils compelled the Sisters to change their back parlor into a class-room for the third division, the first and second classes quite filling the basement. After two years and a half in Penn Street they removed to a more commodious dwelling in April, 1846.

Poor House

Every week the Sisters visited the poor-house in Allegheny, about a half-hour's walk from the convent. It was poor in every sense of the word —an old wooden rookery, large, but not sufficiently so for its twenty or thirty occupants, men, women, and children. Cleanliness was almost unknown in this ill-ventilated, miserable home; the inmates had a woe-begone expression most distressing to see. The visits of the Sisters cheered them, and they looked forward to them with evident delight. The Sisters tried to console them in their privations, lessen as much as possible their sufferings, and induce them to take a right view of their situation. The poor inmates listened eagerly to the words of comfort and advice. When a Catholic inmate was ill, the priest came to the institution, which was entirely under non-Catholic control, all the officials being Protestants.

Penitentiary

The Sisters also visited the Penitentiary, a fine stone structure, then in the country, but the city has long since stretched to where it stands. The gentleman who superintended it, Major Beckham, and his wife and daughters, were most friendly to the Sisters. Yet later, when it became known that some non-Catholic inmates were eager to become Catholics, the manager invoked the existence of an ancient by-law forbidding the visits of gentlewomen who came for religious purposes. The clergy who occasionally looked in upon the convicts, and a functionary, called the "Moral Instructor," who distributed tracts in their cells, were deemed sufficient for their spiritual regeneration and religious consolation.

That they could no longer visit the prisoners as before caused great regret to the Sisters, especially to Mother Warde, who had always gone herself to the prison, to the great comfort of its inmates. She was deeply interested in their welfare, and they regarded her and her companions with affectionate veneration. All her life she had great zeal for converts, and a special grace for drawing them to the Church. True, she could keep her zeal within bounds, and was not wont to interfere with any one when uninvited. But she knew, too, that she ruptured no law of her adopted country by giving, in her own wonderfully eloquent style, to everyone that asked her, a reason for the faith that was in her. Still, the managers were alarmed on seeing that almost all their charges wanted to become Catholics, though what harm such a course was likely to do to the poor creatures was never explained. Would it not rather have been a blessing had the Sisters succeeded, when so many had failed, in teaching the convicts the theory and practice of the ethics involved in the Ten Commandments? And such was the only doctrine these fervent Sisters had taught them.

Bigotry

Rarely has bigotry of this species been encountered by the Sisters of Mercy. Prison officials are happy to see the prisoners converted or in any way influenced for good. Often they have affirmed that so conducive to good discipline are the visits of the Sisters that wherever they visit, the labors of the keepers are perceptibly lightened. As to the good done the prisoners in their forlorn, desolate condition by the visits of friends who come, in the Name of the Lord, to sympathize with them, console and encourage them, one must have been a prisoner, abandoned by friends and almost by hope, to appreciate it fully.

Typhoid Fever Epidemic in Pittsburgh

The deadly type of typhus known as ship-fever appeared in Pittsburgh early in 1848, and continued to rage through spring and summer. Night and day the Sisters served the unfortunate sufferers, and *five choir Sisters and three lay Sisters died,* martyrs of charity. It was deemed a special blessing that Mother M. Xavier Tiernan, whose whole energies were devoted to the stricken, escaped its ravages. Night after night she sat watching with patient attention to gain the dying to God, and wonderful success blessed her heroic devotion and that of her Sisters. Frequently the effects of prayer were visibly manifested in the conversion of sinners.

But Mother Xavier Tiernan's incessant attendance on the poor victims in a close ward, however, exhausted her rather delicate constitution. She was attacked by a virulent erysipelas, from which she had not strength to rally. Mother Warde, being seriously ill, was denied the sad consolation of assisting her dying Sister, who several times asked: "Where is Reverend Mother? Why is she absent?" And hearing she was ill, "Do not disturb her," said she, "but get her prayerbook and read the last prayers for me." Calm, beautiful, and holy was the death of this lovely and beloved Sister, first American Postulant, on March 9, 1847.

The loss of so many of her children, and the anguish and fatigue of this awful period, completely shattered Mother Warde's health. Dr. William Addison declared she would die if not removed immediately from the convent house of death. Indeed, serious fears were entertained for the rest of the community. The bishop took them all to his own house near the cathedral, himself and the cathedral clergy receiving hospitality meanwhile among the members of the congregation.

In 1848 a large Mercy Hospital was built on Stevenson Street, which has often been considerably enlarged, and is one of the best conducted in the country.

Fire at St. Xavier Academy

A friendly priest wrote as follows to Dr. James O'Connor, brother of Bishop Michael O'Connor:

"You are already acquainted with the particulars of the sad calamity which has fallen St. Xavier's, Latrobe, which will be felt by no one more deeply than yourself. It seems, indeed, an inscrutable Providence which would permit such an institution, the child of so many prayers and labors for the glory of God, to perish when it seemed best fitted to realize the holy designs of its founders. I have not visited the scene, but it is quite enough to see the woe-begone faces of the Sisters to know how great is their loss. Mother Superior returned this morning, looking the picture of distress. They have determined to rebuild at once, and meanwhile keep their pupils at Loretto, or the guest-house.

"But where are they to get means to rebuild and furnish the Academy? They have lost everything, for the insurance of twenty thousand dollars will hardly cover their indebtedness. They make an appeal this week in the *Pittsburgh Catholic* for assistance.... I know of no more urgent and deserving claim on the charity of those whom God has blessed with abundant means.... I first acquired it from you."

The Sisters' letters to the bishop and his brother give details of this awful calamity: "The fire was first seen by one of the pupils, who told Sister Dominica. She went with Sister Scholastica to the attic of the middle building, near the cupola. The fire spread with dreadful rapidity. The organ commenced playing, or rather sounding above all the noise, until the roof fell in. Sister Ligouri was in the children's dormitory when a blazing pine fell on the bed next to her. She threw the mattress out of the window. This was the first she knew of the fire. Soon the roof of this part of the building fell down into the old chapel. Had the fire broken out at night, many lives would have been lost. . . . ."

"It seems as if the heavens opened and all the rain in them poured out," wrote Mother Isidore. "I have been sitting up all night, and am perfectly wretched in mind and body," wrote the Mother-Superior. "There is too much excitement yet to know what will be done. Father Abbot of St. Benedict's and all the Benedictines from the monastery were over; they saved all that was saved." "We went next day to see the ruins," wrote another, "and truly you could hardly imagine the scene of desolation." Three small fires arose in different parts of the chapel; now and then the wind would bring down a brick or two, and the sound of our feet on the snow, the whistling of the wind, the peopling of the place with the loved and blest made one feel sober enough. Yet from the depths of my heart I thank God that another sorrow is over. How many more are in reserve for me before I die?"

"In the cars and at the station all were offering their sympathy. I remained at Loretto a week, during the most piercingly cold weather I ever experienced. Thirty-one children are with us at the guest-house. We suffer many inconveniences, of which no one complains, for we are united and happy, made more dear to one another by our common sorrow."[19]

BORDENTOWN, PRINCETON, PLAINFIELD

Romance and Suffering in Bordentown, Mount St. Mary's, Georgian Court

Bordentown, New Jersey, was almost 200 years old when Mercy Sisters came there in 1873. It was the center of activity between New York and Philadelphia. Located just below Trenton where the Delaware River crooks its elbow to gather more sunsets, it was a cross roads settlement where stage coach, railroad, and canal barge met. Washington, Lafayette, Franklin, Paine, and Clara Barton were on its community roster. Joseph

Bonaparte, brother of Napoleon and ex-King of Naples and of Spain, bought an estate on the River Bluff which he called Point Breeze. The first Catholic Church was established there in 1842.

On September 24, 1873, Frances Warde led six Sisters to "the Convent" at Second Avenue and Bank Street. The building commanded a breath-taking view of the Delaware. St. Mary's Parochial School and St. Joseph's Academy prospered in Bordentown. The Convent became an independent foundation in 1877. Summers were beautiful, winters were bitter. The Convent was poorly heated. The kitchen stove provided heat; a pump in the kitchen provided the total water supply; candles provided light. The evening she arrived, Mother Warde asked the pastor when gas would be provided. "That," he replied, "is coming up the street, but it hasn't gotten this far yet." The gas arrived thirteen years later.

In 1881 the Mercy Convent in Princeton, New Jersey, was united with the Bordentown Convent. And the schools of the Sisters of Mercy opened their magnificent center at Mount St. Mary's in Plainfield, New Jersey. Mount St. Mary's College and Academy in the Watchung Hills was dedicated in 1908. The Gould Estate in Lakewood, New Jersey, became Georgian Court College in 1924. The change from gas light in Bordentown (1886) to a magnificent college at Mount St. Mary's (1908) required only twenty-two years. Arthur Brisbane was right. The Lord's ways with the Sisters of Mercy in New Jersey were amazing.[20]

PROVIDENCE, HARTFORD, NEW HAVEN

Pioneer Days

The establishment of the Sisters of Mercy in Hartford, Connecticut shortly after Bishop Bernard O'Reilly's consecration has been characterized as "one of the most fruitful services rendered by that distinguished prelate to his diocese." The foundation was made in the spring of the year 1853 from the Mother House in Providence, Rhode Island, itself but an infant in point of size and years. The same ardent zeal that prompted Mother McAuley to offer herself for the mission to Nova Scotia, to assist poor emigrants and their children of whose sufferings she had heard, burned in the heart of her eldest and best loved spiritual daughter, Mother Xavier Warde, Superior of the Providence Order.

Since Providence was the cradle of the Sisters of Mercy in this area of the United States, it may not be irrelevant to relate here some of the incidents connected with their inauspicious advent to that city, as put down in the Annals of the Sisters of Mercy.

Attacks and Insults

Arriving at Providence from Pittsburgh, the Sisters were received stealthily because of the permanence of bigots. They reached the city, March 12, 1851, the feast of the Translation of the Remains of St. Francis Xavier, the party comprising Mother Xavier Warde, and Sisters Camillus O'Neill, Mary Joanna Fogarty, and Mary Josephine and Paula Lombard. Indeed, had these women been guilty of some dreadful crime, more pains could not have been taken to isolate them. No sooner had the Sisters taken possession of their poor little cottage on Weybosset Street than the mob gathered, broke all the windows, and hooted at the inmates. The inveterate hatred of the benighted people among whom the Sisters' lot was cast never slumbered. Whenever they appeared on the streets, their lives were in danger. To have their clothing soiled with mud or marked with chalked crosses was no uncommon experience.

On an appointed evening, the Providence Know-Nothings came several hundred strong, reinforced by fellow conspirators from Boston, Salem, and other places. All were fully armed and they brought with them some kegs of powder to be used to demolish the convent. As was afterwards learned, the bishop's house and various churches and schools were to share the same fate. . . . The governor and mayor had been appealed to in vain. In this emergency the Catholics of Providence, mostly stalwart Irishmen, made their way toward the convent and stationed themselves in no inconspicuous way in and about the grounds. The Bishop moved around among his people and spoke a few words to the rioters, telling them bluntly that the Sisters would not leave the convent even for an hour and that he would defend them even with his heart's blood if necessary. A Protestant gentleman, a Mr. Stead, addressed the crowd, warning them to abandon their unlawful designs and disperse. The mob kept up a continuous hooting, but not a shot was fired or any actual violence attempted, and after parleying among themselves they concluded not to molest the convent.

About two years later, May 12, 1853, four members of the Providence community, Sister Paula Lombard, Superior, Sister M. Teresa Murray, Sister M. Baptist Coleman and Sister M. Lucy Lyons, arrived in Hartford under more propitious circumstances. On the following day, May 13, Sister M. Camillus Byrne, a godchild of Mother McAuley, and four associates opened a convent at New Haven.

To provide for the arrival of the Sisters of Mercy in Hartford, the Rev. John Brady, the devoted pastor of St. Patrick's Church, had arranged a small two-storied brick house on Allyn Street for their accommodations. True to their vocation, the zealous religious lost no time in entering upon their duties in the classroom, for within a week after their coming they began teaching in the basement of St. Patrick's Church.

"They had nearly two hundred girls who were separated from the boys by a partition running lengthwise through the long room. The boys were taught by a 'master' and were never as numerous as the girls." Here the Sisters did a great work.

From the beginning the Sisters received orphans in the convent, and before the first year was over they were so crowded in their little house that the pastor was obliged to purchase a more spacious building on Trumbull Street. Here they moved the following spring and opened an academy for girls.

Surprising Growth

For twenty years after 1853, there were only two convents of Mercy in Hartford and they were mission houses depending on the Mother House in Providence. In 1872 a great impetus was given to the work of the Sisters in Connecticut by the division of the diocese. Hartford now became the episcopal see for Connecticut alone, and Providence remained the residence of the Bishop of Rhode Island. At the division, the Sisters of Mercy had the privilege of choosing between the two dioceses. The majority of them remained just where they happened to be located at the time. The separation was sad. Some left their natural sisters or near relatives on the opposite side. In many cases fond ties were broken.[21]

SAN FRANCISCO, SACRAMENTO, YREKA, RIO VISTA,
RED BLUFF, GRASS VALLEY, SAN DIEGO

Exciting Beginnings in San Francisco, 1854

The voyage up the Pacific was more like a pleasure trip. The sea was perfectly calm, the air balmy. There was not a case of sea-sickness on board. Before any of the other passengers had emerged from their staterooms every morning, the Sisters were on deck and had their morning prayers, office, and meditation finished. As they neared their destination, it was calculated that they would, with God's blessing, reach the city of San Francisco on the morning of December 8, the feast of the Immaculate Conception and the day of its definition. All joyfully prepared to receive Holy Communion in thanksgiving on that day. On December 7 they began to catch glimpses of the coast range, and the excitement produced by the hope of soon landing in the gold region was intense. About midnight the vessel got into San Francisco Bay, but the religious remained on board till five next morning. There was little sleep to be had that night. The passengers were in groups on deck and in the cabin.

On leaving the ship the Sisters drove directly to St. Patrick's Church on Market Street, and reached it just as the good old pastor, Father Maginn, was turning to salute the congregation before the last Gospel. With hands and eyes raised towards heaven he blessed his flock of twelve or fifteen persons, all of whom he had assembled that morning to celebrate the feast.

There were then three churches in San Francisco—St. Francis, on Vallejo Street; St. Patrick's, on Market Street; and the old adobe church at the Mission Dolores, then a suburb, but now an integral part of the city. St. Patrick's and St. Francis' Churches were of the poorest description. The brick Cathedral was opened, but in an unfinished state, some weeks after the arrival of the Sisters of Mercy.

The Sisters of Mercy were hospitably received by the Sisters of Charity, whose house adjoined St. Patrick's Church. The archbishop and his vicar-general came later in the day to welcome them. On leaving, his grace promised to say Mass for them on Tuesday, December 12. The Sisters, thinking he knew nothing of their history, wondered why he had selected a day so memorable to them, it being the anniversary of the foundation of their Order. They afterwards learned that their anniversary is the greatest of the Mexican feasts of the Blessed Virgin, Our Lady of Guadaloupe. On January 2 they moved to a small, neat house on Valley Street, which contained six rooms and a kitchen, all small, and had been selected on account of its proximity to the county hospital, where the Sisters had a good field for their labor, until they could decide as to their future course.

The Presentation nuns had opened a school, and were now engaged in teaching. Consequently, a school was not for the present a pressing necessity. The first visitation of the sick was made January 4. The Sisters were called in to see a dead woman, as it was supposed. But while they knelt to offer a prayer for the poor creature, they noticed signs of life. Immediately they sent for a priest, meanwhile employing the usual means of restoring life. The woman revived and was conveyed to the county hospital, where she lingered for several months.

A house next to the convent was rented for a House of Mercy, and this branch of the Institute was opened in a very simple way. Yet it enabled the Sisters to do a considerable amount of good. In the beginning it was filled with children sent to San Francisco to await news of parents in distant gold mining camps. Communication being difficult, it generally took a long time to notify parents of the arrival of their children. Steamers came once a month; later, twice a month. No matter what hour of the night the steamer arrived, the newsboys went their rounds, shouting out in full capitals: "Arrival of the NORTHERN STAR!" "Here's your Boston PILOT! New Orleans PICAYUNE! New York HERALD!" Often the Sisters were aroused from their sleep by these cries, "and then," writes one of the few survivors of these early days, "our hearts would jump, hoping there was a letter from our loved home, and many times we were doomed to disappointment." Every day two or four Sisters spent many hours in the county hospital, where they had the happiness of relieving and consoling numerous wretched people, bringing negligent Catholics to the sacraments, and a goodly number of non-Catholics to the faith.

Early Missions in San Francisco

When the Sisters of Mercy settled in San Francisco in 1854, it used to be said that the little city had but one direction in which to grow, that is, through the Old Mission, and out on the road to San José. No one imagined that grandees would climb the sand elevations, as they have conspicuously done on the almost perpendicular Nob Hill. The site of the first convent, Rincon Hill, is solid rock, and was once the fashionable part of the city. The finest residences were erected on its slopes and perched on its summit. The second street spoiled the neighborhood for their purpose. The fact that the authorities would not be satisfied with a moderate grade, and required all the streets to slope towards the water, for a while deterred the Sisters from finishing their buildings.

The convent site is still very beautiful, and commands a fine view of the harbor. The Sisters secured eight acres for a Widow's Home. The solid hills about the city still remain, but the sand hills have been cut down to fill the swamps, now called "made ground." When Bishop Alemany came to San Francisco in 1850, a ship was anchored in Montgomery Street, now in the heart of the city. Being a peninsula, the city has no suburb on three sides. Hence land was more valuable than in other cities, and it was difficult to get a large piece of land within city limits, or at a reasonable distance.

Meanwhile the Sisters were looking for a more spacious house than the one they occupied. The city authorities were then building a new hospital, to which the patients were to be removed in October. The old brick county hospital was put up for sale. Its location was then quite central—Stockton Street, between Valley and Broadway. The Sisters decided to purchase it, which they did in July for thirteen thousand dollars. This sum they borrowed on interest, and the city became their tenant. At this period the care of the sick was let out by contract. Very soon cholera made its appearance. It was introduced into the city from the shipping, and immense was the terror it excited. The Sisters had already served some months in the temporary cholera hospitals in Clonmel and Kinsale in 1849; one had nursed cholera in 1832. They were familiar with all the phases of this dreaded disease and the best remedies. Now they were in their element. Day and night they worked among the stricken, and by their skill and devotedness, under God, they saved hundreds of lives. But as they conceived this to be only their duty, they never dreamt that their heroism would draw upon them the admiration that followed. . . .

The hospital grounds, meanwhile, though not extensive, were very beautiful. All the flora of California were there, and the banks and braes were radiant with the flowers of the island-home of so many of the sick and their kindly nurses—crocuses, primroses, wall-flowers, blue bells, gilly-flowers, hyacinth. Schools were developed with an attendance of over five hundred, and a House of Mercy for young women out of situation, besides an Old Ladies' Home, in which the ancient beneficiaries were not disciplined like children, but had their own cozy rooms, and could do pretty much as they pleased. The Sisters instructed and prepared for the Sacraments the boys of St. Brendan's parish, and indeed, at almost all hours, people came to the convent for instructions.

The Magdalen Asylum, Potrero Avenue, which opened in 1856, stood in the midst of five acres of land, highly cultivated. . . .

Magdalen Asylum

A room in the new Magdalen Asylum was assigned to a Miss Taylor, and every evening as the Sisters went to Matins, one of them took her out on a little balcony to walk. This was all the airing she could get. Though the Sisters strained every nerve to sweeten the rigors of her penitential life, for eight months she went through a terrible conflict, and was often on the point of throwing up all in despair and returning to her old life of luxury. But as soon as she applied her mind in good earnest to the study of religion, she felt she had something real to cling to for support. Accustomed to a life of indolence, in the beginning she would let the sisters make her bed, sweep her room, and render her every menial service while she rocked listlessly in a chair. But before a year had elapsed, Amanda was an altered being. By degrees she became a model of industry and devotedness. The first who joined her was a very young girl, the care of whom was a godsend to the lonely creature. Then came another and another, till the

Sisters had to allot a whole suite of apartments for their accommodation and erect a balcony for their sole use. Such was the foundation of one of the finest and best conducted Magdalen Asylums in the world. Within a short period, the San Francisco Sisterhood had all the works of mercy in successful operation. . . .

Service in San Quentin

In the public institutions, open to them at all times, the Sisters of Mercy were treated with marked courtesy by the officials. In the State Prison, San Quentin, on San Francisco Bay, there were usually over 1,400 inmates; in the jail, over 200; in the city and county hospitals, over 400.

The State Prison of California was situated at San Quentin, a lovely spot in the mountains, across the bay, some twenty-four miles from San Francisco. In this institution the Sisters found one thousand four hundred men and thirty-five women, of every tribe and tongue and people and nation, and even, as a prisoner remarked, "some of the unclassified of the human species." Excepting the Chinese, the inmates were mostly American by birth, and could read and write.

The Sisters visited the House of Refuge and the Industrial Schools. They traveled free in the street-cars. The first line had Dr. Bowie, J.A. McGlynn, and other kind friends among the directors. These gentlemen declared that the street-railroads should always be free to Sisters of Mercy, a precedent followed by each succeeding line, and there are now over thirty. When a certain line withdrew the permission, the people showed their displeasure by boycotting it. After a few weeks, the directors restored the privilege. Many societies are under the direction of the Sisters. The Children of Mary, who were especially numerous, made their monthly communion in the convent chapel, and met every Sunday in their assembly-room. They looked quite picturesque in their blue cashmere cloaks and white veils. In various parts of the city and State, the Sisters conducted large Sunday-schools and taught boys as well as girls. . . .

Floods in Sacramento

When the Sisters of Mercy established a convent in Sacramento, in October, 1857, they lived in a house previously occupied by the pastor. The basement became the school. They began with 120 children. Disastrous floods occurred December 9, 1862. Thousands were deprived of shelter, and all who could rushed to San Francisco. The Sisters threw open their convent to the sufferers, and it was soon filled. The city authorities supplied bedding, and all classes of food and clothing. Never had St. Mary's such busy times as while it was occupied by the Sacramento sufferers. The penitents did good service in altering clothes to suit the needy, and in other ways.

On December 9, 1861, the weather was clear and bright, and the schools opened with a good attendance. About ten o'clock, a man rushed in for his daughter, saying there would be a flood. Another fellow, and another arrived until the school was thinned, and the Sisters dismissed all, though they saw no cause for apprehension. They looked from the balcony in the direction indicated by the men, but the landscape showed nothing unusual. One Sister jocosely remarked: "If the flood really comes, we can go see our new house in San Francisco."

Twenty minutes later the Sister on the watch perceived the water rolling over the roads on the northeast, so rapidly that before noon the waves were flowing roughly under the convent walls. The Sisters began to remove their stores from the cellar, but the whole lower story was soon under water. They had their pianos raised, hoping to save them, but so quickly did the water rise that the idea of saving anything was abandoned. Every moment they expected the priest to remove the Blessed Sacrament. They arranged a temporary altar in the attic. But no priest appeared. The Sacristan carried the tabernacle upstairs, the Sisters preceding her with bells and wax-lights.

The one-story houses in the neighborhood were covered before the water reached the convent. The Sisters gave a room to a family consisting of father, mother, and two children. The poor mother spent hours on the balcony, gazing vacantly on the surging waters, and bewailing the loss of her hard-earned home. Her eight cows were floundering about, seeking terra-firma. More than once they jumped on the floating sidewalk only to get a fresh plunge. A large dog carried a pup in its mouth and placed it in a tree, and swam back, evidently to secure another. The convent dog had a dry bed on a table in the school-room. As the Sisters had only a tiny grate, dinner was put on after breakfast. Wonderful to relate, the Sisters were never without Mass; a Chinese priest rowed in a skiff to the upper floor every morning, and celebrated the Holy Sacrifice for them.

The Sisters went daily in a large boat to the Pavilion, an immense building thrown open to the poor. Naturally, there was a great deal of sickness, and many deaths occurred. Families that had upper lofts withdrew to them; those who had not, took possession of deserted houses; the Sisters had ample scope for their zeal. As late as May, half the city was still under water. To minister to the sick and the dying, the Sisters had to turn their prow towards windows on the second and third floors, and mount planks to enter. All the streets of Sacramento are lined with trees, and rowing between their tops in spring, when they are in full bloom, was like moving through a bizarre scene. Never has the writer seen any city so thoroughly filled with trees, vines, and flowers, as Sacramento. The houses are mostly handsome fancy cottages, light and airy in structure. To see them rising out of the smooth water was as charming a sight as could be imagined, if one could only forget all the misery the picturesque roofs and gables sheltered.

The convent never wholly recovered from the effects of these awful floods. Instead of being the highest portion of the city, it is now the lowest, as the land around was raised from ten to twenty feet. The church had a good basement and was ascended by a flight of steps. But the basement had disappeared, and the church is now entered by descending several steps. People who know what grading means in some western cities— where mountains are brought low and valleys filled up—will understand the trials and difficulties of the Sisters in the lonely city of Sacramento, where they are still the only Religious.

Great San Francisco Earthquake, 1865

It would seem as if the Sisters of Mercy were to have experiences of every possible kind in the beautiful city by the Golden Gate. On Sunday, October 8, 1865, towards noon, a violent shock of earthquake arose. Two lesser shocks followed.

A Sister, who, with the others, felt them, gives some idea of the alarm created: "We were at dinner when we felt our benches and the floor shake under us. You never can mistake an earthquake, however slight it may be. So we immediately blessed ourselves, and each made her offering, which was scarcely over when the whole house shook like a monster dog getting up from sleep. In an instant all were kneeling, and I said a few prayers aloud. My voice was not very steady, for there is something horrible about an earthquake. While it was passing, the thought flashed across my mind: 'What a world of trouble I should be spared, here, at least, if it launches us all into eternity.' With us, it was over in a few seconds, but in other places it was felt for fifteen minutes. Our weakest patients got over it without much alarm. All the clocks stopped, but there was not the least damage done.

"In the city, however, the injury and alarm were great. A large brick building, almost complete, was thrown down, and had it not providentially been Sunday, many poor workmen would undoubtedly have been in the ruins. Quantities of delft and glass were destroyed. Several houses split open, and some sank a few feet. The few accidents that did occur were caused by want of presence of mind in the parties themselves. One gentleman jumped out a window and broke his leg; a like fate awaited a lady who rushed downstairs. In the confusion of getting out of the Synagogue, two or three arms were broken. No accident occurred in the Catholic churches, though the alarm was great among priests and laity. A young priest who had never before experienced anything of the kind, made his exit in double-quick time, but returned when the terror was over, and finished Mass. No one was more timid than the saintly Archbishop. He, too, fled, but the majority of the people neither moved nor spoke. Father Heneberry, a missioner, was preaching at St. Francis, and in the midst of a sermon on the judgments of God he had just put to his audience the question: "Are you prepared, should God summon you this moment?" The first shock stopped him; the second sent him speedily to the foot of the altar.

"The people fled from their homes, and hundreds threw themselves on their knees in the open streets. At the third shock, Monday, 11 a.m., a child jumped from the second-story of a public school, and would doubtless have been killed had not a man who was passing caught her in his arms. Several shocks in distant parts of the city the Sisters did not feel, probably because they were on solid ground, in fact on a mass of rock, and their house is one of the most substantial in the city. The crackling of timbers and falling of plaster added to the terror in the Cathedral and other churches; with the Sisters there was not a sound, save the low, rumbling noise that usually accompanies an earthquake. At the Asylum, the inmates were in the chapel singing Vespers, as they do every Sunday and holiday. All behaved well, though much frightened. When the shock was over, one cried out: 'O Sister, open the doors and let us off.'

"Later, the hundreds of inmates in the Sisters' Institutions were terrified by another earthquake. At a quarter to eight, during Mass, came a violent shock, lasting forty-two seconds. Shocks took place before the Consecration, but the priest did not even turn around. When a few of the congregation cried aloud for mercy, he quieted them by a wave of his hand and went on with the Holy Sacrifice. Having no idea of the damage done in the city, two Sisters went to visit some dying men and women. They were surprised to find all business suspended, crowds in the middle of the streets, and the sidewalks strewn with glass, and other debris. Many homes were rendered uninhabitable, especially in the 'made ground.' Four poor creatures were killed by falling houses, and the injured, many of whom were brought to the Sisters' Hospital, were very numerous. At 10:30 a.m. another severe shock was felt, followed by many lighter ones, which kept the timid in alarm, day and night. For weeks after, hundreds slept in the public squares. There was a general rush from the grand hotels which, being on the beach, and more showy than solid, suffered considerably. The U.S. Marine Hospital, and several other public buildings were made uninhabitable. . . ."

Smallpox Epidemic in San Francisco

The Sisters left the Pest-House, where they cared for the smallpox patients, on May 27, 1869. They were detained a week by the lingering death of Homer Judkins, the last of eighty-two persons received into the Church during the epidemic. Out of these, fifteen recovered; the others went to meet their God. There remained at the Pest-House at their departure eighteen patients, all convalescent. A few days later, the Sisters had to return and nurse the whole crew, officers and men, of a French man-of-war, who were stricken with smallpox in the harbor. All recovered, and the Sisters remained until the last patient was discharged.

Sacrifices of the Sisters

In 1889, the holy remains of thirty Sisters of Mercy sanctified the convent cemetery in San Francisco. The mortality has been larger than in any other Order on the Pacific Slope, but the herculean labors of these holy women in cholera and smallpox epidemics, and, indeed, at all times, accounts for this difference. When the Sisters purchased the Asylum property, the streets crossing it had been closed by the Legislature. The public officials have been invariably kind to the Sisters, and have thrown open to them all public institutions. Six Sisters go every Sunday to instruct the Catholic inmates of the Male Industrial School. The female department is in their own hands and occupies a wing of the Asylum. The Sisters of Mercy have not been gold-seekers or gold-finders: the golden fleece never descended on them in the Golden Gate. For forty-one years, they have been barely able to sustain their vast charities and are not now wholly free from debt. As has been well said, the world beholds these women, with no science but the gospel, no philosophy but charity, no resources but zeal, conceiving and accomplishing enterprises for which the wealth of kings would be hardly adequate. From the inexhaustible spring of charity, they have provided, to an almost incredible degree, for every want, relieved every misery, and served in every public disaster.

They have certainly deserved well of Church and State, but, in their case, virtue is left to be its own reward. They struggle on in inconvenient quarters in St. Mary's Hospital. Others in the same field might have reaped sheaves of gold. But one doubts if any could have done more for Christ and His outcast, suffering members.[22]

Suffering and Service in Yreka, Rio Vista, and Red Bluff

The second Mercy Foundation on the Pacific Coast was Yreka, the most Northern town in the State, on the Oregon border. We have not the remotest idea of the hardships on that long cold journey of the Sisters to Yreka in a lumbering stage coach, the only means of traveling the 170 miles between the nearest railroad town—Tehama—and Yreka, the county seat of mountainous Siskiyou.

Late in 1870 Bishop Eugene O'Connell, of Marysville, applied to Mother Frances Warde in Manchester, New Hampshire, for Sisters to open a boarding and day school in far-off Yreka, a one-time prosperous mining town in the northern limits of the Diocese. Mother Warde was not very eager for the Sisters to go because of "the great distance, the inclement weather, and the burden of debt the Sisters would be expected to assume."

Yet, six Sisters agreed to go. They arrived in Yreka late on the evening of February 2, 1871. They were cold, tired, and weary after the long stage coach ride over mountains and valleys, snow and ice, through streams where there were no bridges. Furniture awaiting them was one bed, an old piano that had done duty in various camps ever since wagon roads had taken the place of mountain trails over which passengers, freight, mail, and express were transported on mule back. A gloomy beginning!

Yreka contained about 1200 people. It was the remnants of a once prosperous mining town. The mines were worked out, and former inhabitants had sought other fields of adventure. The Sisters opened classes in March, 1871. In the schools, efficient teaching was done, including drawing, painting, needlework, and music.

Few Catholics, sparse population, declining property, and the burden of debt led to the inevitable. Four Sisters finally left Yreka and settled in Rio Vista, California, Archdiocese of San Francisco, an opening suggested by Mother Baptist Russell of San Francisco. The remaining Sisters in

Yreka moved to Red Bluff, about 200 miles from Yreka. In December, 1881, the last Yreka Sisters said goodbye to "many privations, labors, and crosses," on the eleventh anniversary of their arrival. The last words in the Yreka Annals were: "Who can tell what good had been done during the eleven years spent in the mountains of Siskiyou County, where children who in those days would not have had an opportunity of being instructed, were prepared for the Sacraments?"

On December 3, 1881, when the only train that came to the northern part of the Sacramento Valley rolled into Red Bluff at 4:00 a.m., four Sisters alighted at the station. A new convent and school was being built. Furniture was brought from Yreka. In March, 1882, the school was opened. The school had many talented graduates. Students ranked high in the County examinations, the only method of obtaining teachers' certificates.

Between 1912 and 1944, the following developments succeeded one another: a new convent, a hospital, a new school building, a second new convent, and a new residence hall. The Sisters of northern California finally prospered after hard days in Yreka, Rio Vista, and Red Bluff.[23]

Grass Valley, California

The Vicariate of Marysville was the original See of the first Episcopate in Northern California, with the Right Reverend Eugene O'Connell as its first Vicar apostolic. After the Sisters' visit to Grass Valley, Mother Baptist Russell wrote to Bishop O'Connell informing him that the Archbishop was willing for the Sisters of San Francisco to undertake a new mission at Marysville and that she was prepared to send a few Sisters for the work.

The Sisters did not take up their work in Grass Valley until June, 1863. The San Francisco community was not large, and there was much work to be done; the long delay in making the new foundation indicates how difficult it was for Mother Russell to spare even the few who would start the new convent. Too, this was just after the disastrous floods in Sacramento, and the community there had suffered many set-backs. Sacramento was, as yet, a branch of St. Mary's in San Francisco, and Sisters had to be sent back and forth to keep the works of both places running smoothly.

Finally, on August 20, 1863, the little band of pioneer Sisters for the Grass Valley mission reached the mountain town.

St. Vincent's Orphanage was commenced in March, 1865. In May of that year, the cornerstone of the new convent was laid. In April of 1866 the first orphans, a family of four destitute children from Sierra County, claimed refuge. They were followed in a few days by another family of four, poverty-stricken in the extreme, from Shasta County. Within two months, thirty motherless, homeless little ones were in the care of the Sisters. A large debt on the orphanage and lack of means to furnish the house made it almost impossible for the Sisters to carry on the work; meanwhile pressing requests to take more children were coming in daily. When, after unremitting struggles and hard work, the orphanage was practically free from debt, Mother Morgan received a letter from Bishop O'Connell informing her that he and his Council had decided to convert the orphanage into a home for boys only, and to send the girls to the Sisters of Charity who were then in Virginia City.

The plan would have separated brothers and sisters and caused many heart-aches among the children. Mother Morgan proposed to the Bishop that he buy a piece of property on Pleasant Street and open a boy's orphan asylum there. She informed the Bishop that she and her Sisters could take care of such an institution.

St. Patrick's Orphanage succeeded the one on Pleasant Street. Here, set back in the woods, the old frame building was home to as many as a hundred boys at a time. This home for boys and St. Vincent's for girls served until 1930 when the frame buildings were condemned, and both groups were moved to the new, modern brick building in Sacramento.

Early in the history of the orphanage in Grass Valley, the Sisters opened Mt. Saint Mary's Academy to help defray the expenses of the orphanages. This school proved to be one of Northern California's leading resident schools. Many graduates went from Mt. Saint Mary's into excellent positions, not only in Grass Valley and the surrounding area, but throughout California.

During the formative years from 1857 to 1886, while the Sisters were so much a part of the religious and cultural life of Sacramento and Grass Valley, the leadership of Mother Russell of San Francisco was paramount in the work carried on. A proof of the respect and admiration of the people of this city and all Northern California is found in the fact that in 1915, the year of the memorable Panama-Exposition in San Francisco, the SACRAMENTO UNION published a volume entitled MAKERS OF NORTHERN CALIFORNIA as its contribution to the historic event. This included full-page photographs and brief biographical sketches of nearly a hundred men selected as outstanding in the story of the State, but those of only two women. One of these was Mother Baptist Russell, listed as "Pioneer Mother Superior in Northern California."[24]

Southern California, San Diego: From Durango to Salinas to San Diego, to Tucson

Mother M. Michael Cummings was born on a farm at Madisonville, Illinois, on the 8th of July, 1853. She was the youngest of seven children.

Fond of books and out-door life, she became, nevertheless, deeply impressed with the truths of religion and listened to the call to religion. Secretly longing to give herself up to the care of the poor and the sick, she was permitted at the age of 17 to enter the convent of the Sisters of Mercy on Thirty-third and Morgan Streets, St. Louis. There she was formed to the religious life by the much beloved Mother de Pazzi Bentley, who as a novice in the Mother House, Baggot Street, Dublin, Ireland, volunteered for the New York foundation and was there professed . . .

In the fulfillment of her vows, under the wise motherly supervision of Mother de Pazzi, Sister Mary Michael nursed the sick in the hospital, visited the poor and needy, and was especially devoted to consoling the abandoned and lonely prisoners in the city jails. In 1882, Bishop Macheboeuf of Denver, Colorado, begged Mother de Pazzi for some of her Sisters in the service of charity. Sister M. Michael volunteered to go to this new field of labor with Mother M. Baptist Meyers as superior. Bishop Macheboeuf, on February 18, 1882, named Sister M. Michael assistant to the Superior at Durango, Colorado. There she remained five years till she was named Superior of a new hospital at Ouray, in the same state. The labors in the Rocky Mountains were soul-taxing, arduous beyond conception. The privations of those days can hardly be made conceivable to us now-a-days, surrounded as we are by modern conveniences and comfort. As assistant and superior, Sister Michael won the esteem and love of her Sisters and of all who came in contact with her.

When after eight years of this service, she was asked by Bishop Matz to go to the assistance of Mother Bonaventure of Salinas, California, she readily consented. After a very short time, Mother Bonaventure and the Sisters with her concluded that Salinas was not able to support a religious community. At this juncture, Mother M. Baptist Russell of San Francisco suggested that they open a mission in San Diego, as she had been requested by Bishop Moran of Los Angeles to send some of her Sisters there. The Archbishop of San Francisco for some reason or other did not approve of establishing a branch house outside of his diocese, although intensely desired by Mother Russell. The latter accordingly advised Sisters Michael and Alphonsus to place themselves under the jurisdiction and direction of Bishop Moran and open a house wherever he desired.

The Bishop received the two Sisters with manifestations of paternal interest May 29, 1890, and sending them to San Diego with his blessing expressed the hope "that God would prosper and multiply the little mustard seed."

The Sisters had no means of their own. How were they to build a hospital and establish a home for themselves? The task was an unusually arduous one, the more so as the city was then suffering from a depression in business, and the difficulties encountered by the Sisters were greater than they had anticipated. Both the Bishop and Fr. Ubach, their venerable pastor of San Diego, suggested the purchasing of a site on the mesa, north of the city, now University Avenue, and later the very place where after some years St. Joseph's Hospital was erected, but the two destitute Sisters were constrained to seek property of less expense. For the present, they believed it advisable to content themselves with renting the upper stories of the Grand Central Block, situated in the heart of the business district of the city, at the corner of Sixth and H Streets. Even this was accomplished only after surmounting many difficulties, and encountering opposition and vexations that could well have broken the spirit of the little community. At this juncture Mother Michael received letters from the Superiors at St. Louis, urging her to come "home." Had it not been for the responsibilities already assumed, she would have "shaken the dust from her feet" and returned to the old mother-house, where she would have found rest for her mind and body. However, throwing all her care upon the Lord, she bore up under the strain, and comforted herself with the thought that if God wished the work to prosper, He would send help in time. That help did come.

The first San Diego house of the Order of Mercy was to be founded and grounded on the cross. Nevertheless, after the first bursts of intolerance and misapprehension had passed away, those not of the faith as well as those within the church looked upon the enterprise with favor. The newly founded community soon found work in abundance. Those nursed back to health by the Sisters' watchful solicitude sounded the praises of the kind and competent nurses far and wide. Truly, humiliation was the community's badge, poverty its watchword, the cross its refuge and final victory.

The Sisters were not long in discovering that better hospital accommodations were required than their temporary quarters provided. The foundation of the new center building and first unit of the hospital was laid on an eminence near where the road, now called Sixth Street, begins to descend into the historic Mission Valley. The location was less than a league from the crumbling ruins of the first Christian Church on the western coast. Mother Michael in later years often remarked that every time she had commenced a new building or unit, she had not a cent in her hands for its construction. Somehow or other, the frame of the center building of St. Joseph's Hospital arose and in 1891 the work was finished and blessed.

That same year Mother Michael set aside a few rooms for the aged. These people multiplied on her hands, so that she felt constrained to erect a building of twelve rooms for the old people on the hospital grounds. In 1920, when she had added several cottages to it for the aged guests, she supplied them all as well as the convent with steam heat. Many observed the talent Mother Michael developed in the erection of new structures, and in the renovation and remodeling of old buildings. The instructions she gave builders were remarkably detailed and full; nothing escaped her notice. She prepared in advance for every eventuality and carefully superintended the works as they progressed.

In 1903 and 1904, Mother Michael ventured to construct the large eastern wing of St. Joseph's Hospital. As all buildings heretofore were begun without funds on hand, so this wing was no exception. To many observers it seemed perfect folly. Some remarked that the Sisters must have taken leave of their senses and that the building would not be occupied for the next 300 years. Notwithstanding such prognostication, the building was fully occupied before the end of three years.

That same year a training school for nurses was established under the superintendence of a Miss Sullivan, a bright active woman, a graduate of Mercy Hospital, Pittsburgh, and a post-graduate of St. Vincent's Hospital, New York City.

For years Mother Michael was preoccupied with one concern about the future. Where would she secure postulants to fill the ranks of the aged Sisters and to satisfy the multiplied demands made by patients and doctors? Was it not extremely desirous that houses in various cities and dioceses be amalagamated? How was it to be accomplished? That was the subject of many years' fervent prayers. At last, after many meetings, on the 5th of April, 1921, the Sisters of Los Angeles and San Diego voted in favor of amalgamation with the Sisters of Mercy in Arizona. This union was ratified by the Holy See. Later, on the second day of July of the same year, the most blessed union of all the Sisters of Mercy in San Francisco and in the dioceses of Los Angeles and Tucson was effected. When a telegram from San Francisco was received in San Diego, announcing that the votes of the Sisters there favored the proposition of general amalgamation, there was a feeling of great joy throughout the community, but no heart swelled with more gratitude than that of Mother Michael. Now she felt she could pronounce her "Nunc Dimittis" . . .

On the Golden Jubilee of Mother Michael, the main exercise of the gathering was a beautiful classic address by Father Paul Dillon. He spoke of her, in part, in simple, beautiful words:

> I live for those who love me,
> For those who know me true,
> For the heaven that shines above me
> And awaits my spirit too,
> For the cause that needs assistance,
> For God's poor that lack subsistence,
> For His Kingdom in the distance,
> And the good that I can do.[25]

SCRANTON

ONE HUNDRED YEARS IN THE PROVINCE OF SCRANTON: FOUR MAJOR ORIGINS

When one studies the spirituality, the history, the special origins of Mercy provinces and congregations throughout the United States, one becomes more and more amazed at God's plans for the Sisters of Mercy founded by Catherine McAuley. Unlike the origins of many religious communities, the Sisters of Mercy present bewildering perplexities and surprises in their development that only the grace of God can make understandable!

There are many, many reasons why I am deeply happy to be invited to celebrate your centenary with you. Relationships between the Provinces of Scranton and Pittsburgh are closer than I would have realized if I did not have the happy privilege of exploring the origins of the Sisters of Mercy. The Province of Scranton, of course, is not co-extensive with the Diocese of Scranton, and today we are particularly interested in the Sisters of Mercy in the Diocese.

However, let me mention just briefly the four major origins of the Sisters of Mercy in the Scranton Province because I am particularly proud of the close relationships of so many Provinces and Congregations of Mercy throughout the United States.

1. In 1848, only five years after the first Sisters of Mercy arrived from Carlow, Ireland, the first community of Mercy Sisters in what is now the Altoona-Johnstown Diocese went from Pittsburgh to Loretto. In 1879, this same community became independent from Pittsburgh and moved its motherhouse to Cresson. When Altoona Diocese was established in 1901, the Cresson community became a part of it. And in 1929, the

Cresson Sisters joined the Sisters of the Union to become a part of the Province of Scranton.

2. In 1869, the Sisters of Mercy in Chicago, the first congregation, founded from Pittsburgh by Frances Warde in 1846, sent a foundation to Harrisburg. When the Union was established, the Harrisburg Sisters also became a part of the Province of Scranton.

3. In 1857, Frances Warde, who left Pittsburgh for Providence, Rhode Island, in 1851, founded the Rochester, New York, Congregation. The following year, Rochester sent a foundation to Buffalo. However, the original founders returned to Rochester, and Pittsburgh Sisters of Mercy, at the request of the Rochester Superior and Bishop John Timon, took over the Buffalo foundation in 1861. Then, in 1874, the Buffalo Sisters made a foundation in Hazleton, Pennsylvania (Mother Theresa Cantillon), the *first* convent of Mercy in the Diocese of Scranton, which had been established six years before (1868) under Bishop William O'Hara.

4. It is well that the centenary of the Sisters of Mercy in the Scranton Diocese is celebrated in 1875 rather than 1874! In 1875, the Pittsburgh Sisters of Mercy sent a foundation under Mother Regina Cosgrave to Wilkes-Barre in the Scranton Diocese. Three years later (1878) the Wilkes-Barre community became an independent mother-house, and in 1899 Hazleton was united with the Wilkes-Barre community. So that, when the Union was established in 1929, all four communities that I have just discussed provided the sources of your present Province which had direct or indirect origins in Pittsburgh and Frances Warde: Cresson through Loretto; Harrisburg through Chicago; Hazleton through Rochester and Buffalo; and Wilkes-Barre directly from Pittsburgh. So you see, historically we are all one.

I might add that the same year that Wilkes-Barre became an independent community, 1878, Mother Regina Cosgrave, who was Superior in Wilkes-Barre, was elected Mother Superior of the Pittsburgh Sisters. That year was one of decision, when some Sisters chose to go back to Pittsburgh, others to remain in Wilkes-Barre.

The first postulant from the Scranton Diocese was trained in Pittsburgh and sent as a novice to Towanda. In fact, five Wilkes-Barre novices were trained in Pittsburgh, and received in Wilkes-Barre. In the Dallas Archives, the first postulant is called "the first seed of the Diocese of Scranton." That Diocese itself was originally a part of the Diocese of Philadelphia, and so was Pittsburgh, for in 1809 the Diocese of Philadelphia included all of Pennsylvania, Delaware, and part of New Jersey. So you see, our Diocesan origins and our Mercy origins are all united. It seems especially appropriate, therefore, that in your centenary year, Mother Concilia is the General Superior of the Union and Mother Silver-

ius, Executive Director of the Federation. We couldn't have planned a
better year for celebration for Scranton if we tried![26]

SOUTH CAROLINA
THE "NEW" SISTERS OF MERCY IN SOUTH CAROLINA

Bishop John England of Charleston, South Carolina, one of the greatest American prelates of the nineteenth century, visited Dublin and Carlow in search of Sisters of Mercy for his diocese in 1841, and nothing came
of it. Later, Columbus, Georgia had the only Sisters of Mercy who
claimed Catherine McAuley as their Mother-Founder. In some years,
they branched out into Macon, Georgia.

But there were other zealous Sisters who had the name of "Sisters of
Mercy" and who were established in various parts of Georgia. Originally
they were founded by Bishop England of Charleston after his failure to
secure Mercy Sisters from Ireland. Bishop England himself trained his
new Sisters of Mercy in the duties of the religious life. In 1845, a colony of
Sisters was sent to Savannah and later to Augusta, Georgia. In 1850,
however, the State of Georgia was detached from the See of Charleston
and formed into the Diocese of Savannah. The "New" Sisters of Mercy
established houses in other parts of Georgia and served the poor, sick, and
ignorant wherever they were found. Many women who entered their convents thought that the Dublin Sisters of Mercy were their origin, and
finally some dissatisfaction resulted from the fact that these Sisters were
neither approved nor confirmed by the Holy See.

When Rome was petitioned for approval of these Mercy congregations, the official reply was that Sisters of the same name and similar
objects were already approved and confirmed, and that new confirmation
would be superfluous because the "new" Sisters could be affiliated with
the already approved Congregation.

In 1891, the Superior of the "McAuley" Sisters of Mercy in the neighboring diocese of Mobile was asked by the Holy See and by Bishop
Thomas A. Becker to undertake this good work.

The Mobile Superior [Mother Teresa Austin Carroll] with ecclesiastical approbation, went to Savannah in 1892 to instruct the "New" Sisters
of Mercy, and seventy Sisters in that diocese received the veil and the
habit of the original Sisters of Mercy, having been instructed in their
Rules and Customs. Like the Macon and Columbus communities, they
became one of the Savannah houses.

These "New" Sisters of the original Congregation of Mercy educated
thousands in the State of Georgia; offered heroic devotion to the sick in

the cholera and typhoid epidemics that desolated cities in Georgia; and nursed the soldiers of North and South in the sixties.

In the words of Mother Austin Carroll, "these Georgia Sisters enlightened the ignorant and ameliorated the sufferings of the destitute and sick in every district blessed by their presence."

They offered a beautiful example of what we call "amalgamation" in the present century.[27]

Notes

1. Mother M. Teresa Austin Carroll, *Annals, III,* 1888, pp. 167–69.
2. *Ibid., IV,* 1895, pp. 72, 87–88, 82–83, 90–91, 76–78, 83, 110–115.
3. *Ibid.,* pp. 449–51.
4. Sister M. Gerald Pierce, *Annals of Sisters of Mercy,* 1858–1958, Archives, Buffalo, New York.
5. Carroll, *op. cit., III,* 1888, pp. 260–261.
6. Sisters of Mercy *Annals,* 1864, p. 71. Archives, Chicago.
7. Carroll, *op. cit., III,* 1888, pp. 302–304, 309, 312.
8. *Annals,* Sisters of Mercy, 1865, p. 55. Archives, Cincinnati.
9. *Ibid.,* p. 58, Circular for Collection of Funds for Night Refuge.
10. Sister Mary Charlotte Wammes, *The Sisters of Mercy in the Archdiocese of Cincinnati,* 1858–1944, Catholic University of America, 1944, p. 23.
11. *Annals,* 1880–1916, 1913. Archives, Cincinnati.
12. *Ibid.,* 1918.
13. Sister Mary Grace, *History of the Educational Work of the Sisters of Mercy in the Diocese of Cincinnati,* 1941, p. 38.
14. Carroll, *op. cit., IV,* pp. 336–37, 368–70, 378–79, 383–84.
15. Carroll, *op. cit., IV,* pp. 393–94, 405–06, 408, 462, 470–74.
16. *Annals,* St. Martinsville, Louisiana, 1880, pp. 2–3. Mercy Archives, New Orleans.
17. *Ibid.,* December 25, 1881.
18. Carroll *op. cit., III,* pp. 77–80.
19. Carroll, *op. cit., III,* pp. 82–87, 122–24, 136–38.
20. Sister Mary Ignatius Hogan, *Chronicles of Early Mission Days* (1873–1898). Revised by Sister Marie La Salle O'Hara (1945–1946). Archives, Sisters of Mercy, Plainfield, New Jersey.
21. *Pioneer Days* in Providence, Hartford, New Haven. Archives, Hartford, Connecticut. Author not named.
22. Carroll, *op. cit., III,* pp. 476–78. 480–488. *IV,* pp. 29–30, 31–34, 35–36, 47–49, 59–61.
23. *Red Bluff Annals,* Sisters of Mercy, Red Bluff, California.

24. Sister M. Evangelist Morgan, *Mercy, Generation to Generation,* San Francisco, Fearon Publishers, 1957, Chapter V, pp. 87–157, 225.
25. Memoirs of Mother Mary Michael Cummings of San Diego, California. Compiled from Various Sources by H.C. No dates, pp. 3–25. Archives, Burlingame.
26. From Talk Given at Celebration of Centenary of Scranton, September 20, 1975.
27. Carroll, *Annals, IV,* 1895, pp. 352–55.

III.

HISTORICAL SKETCHES OF MERCY MISSIONS

Plainfield, New Jersey; Red Bank, New Jersey:
Frances Warde in Bordentown, 1873, Development of Congregation in New Jersey; Service in Influenza Epidemic: Deaths and Death-Bed Conversions; Schools Reopened; Development in Bordentown and North Plainfield

New York:
Civil War; Sanatorium Gabriels, New York

Oklahoma:
Indian Territory Missions

Idaho and Utah:
Pioneering Sisters in Idaho and Utah

Philadelphia:
Arrival in Philadelphia; Classroom and Hospital; Influenza Epidemic

Portland, Maine:
Historic Account of Mercy Hospital in Portland, Maine; Education at All Levels in Portland

Portland, Oregon:
Home for Business Women with Contemporary Theme

Providence:
New Convent in Providence; Bigotry in Providence

Rochester:
Travel in Care of Sick; Service in Flu Epidemic

St. Louis:
Foundation; Civil War; Pension School; Soup House; Prisoners; Orphanage; Night Refuge

Tennessee:
Unusual Foundation in Tennessee; Spirit of Mercy in Nashville

Mississippi:
Civil War and Vicksburg

Yreka-Rio Vista-Red Bluff:
Unique Foundations and Hardships in California; Struggles and Transfers

INTRODUCTION

A first thought about "Historical Sketches" might be: What are the possible relationships to spirituality? Yet Mercy historical accounts are astounding revelations of the spiritual lives of Mercy Sisters of the late nineteenth century. Because of the amazing records left by the Sisters, and because of our attempt to cover various geographical areas of the United States in our selections, the sketches chosen have had to be short but revealing. In the long run, it was thought best to use an alphabetical arrangement of geographical areas because of the complexities of dates and experiences.

Repetition sometimes appears—not in the sketches themselves, but in the experiences related differently by early writers. For example the Civil War itself, the great westward movement, earthquakes in San Francisco, the Great Fire of Chicago, yellow fever, cholera, typhoid, influenza are all endemic to late nineteenth century America. The fascination of the varied accounts of these events lies in the spirituality revealed by the Sisters of Mercy responding to these challenging episodes.

Pioneering experiences in Oklahoma, Arkansas, Michigan and other Western states; provision of services for everybody in need—prisoners, orphans, the homeless, the hungry; actual "wild" experiences in the Civil War when survival was the crucial question; hospitals opened everywhere "on a shoestring." These services were the meaning of the Fourth Vow of the Sisters of Mercy.

Sketches are chosen occasionally for their humor or their human notes—for example, the story of the little girl in Yreka, California, who wrote weekly letters to a father who never responded to her. Or the account of the widowed mother and her six daughters—all seven Sisters of Mercy in Manchester, New Hampshire.

A very few tributes and appreciations by later writers are included because they express the spirituality of the Sisters of Mercy in the late nineteenth century with a magnificent honesty which the Sisters themselves seldom employed. What we learn of the Sisters' spirituality in accounts written by themselves is beautifully indirect—as spirituality always is.

*　　　*　　　*

135

MERCY SISTERS IN ALABAMA

Service of Sisters in Shelby Springs in Civil War

The last stop for the Sisters of Mercy of Alabama in their progress of service to the sick and wounded of the Civil War was Shelby Springs, sixty miles northeast of Selma. The decision to locate a hospital there had probably been made by the Confederate surgeon general, Samuel Preston Moore, whose duty it was to direct the distribution of sick and wounded across departmental or administrative boundaries. The Shelby Springs site, with its mineral waters and hotel, had been turned into a recruitment and training center by the Confederates when the war began. Then, in July of 1863, the Confederates decided to convert the former spa into a hospital, one operated principally as a retreat and convalescent home for soldiers who would stay until they were well enough to return to duty or were given leave.

By this stage in the conflict, the Confederate War Office had begun to eliminate many of the small, inefficient infirmaries that had dotted the South. The move now was toward larger general hospitals that were not restricted to troops from particular units.

The main facilities at Shelby Springs consisted of a large ballroom and a long line of cottages, which the sisters discovered were "opened to every wind of heaven." And everywhere, as Sister Ignatius put it, dirt was in "melancholy ascendancy." Although the nuns were subsisting on only half rations because their supplies were low, they quickly transformed the large ballroom into a surgical ward and the cabins into private hospital quarters. To supplement their supplies, they occasionally traded with a "sharp old hoosier woman" who provided goods and produce in exchange for what little money the nuns had left—plus the pattern the sisters used to make their capes.

When the hospital was completed, patients were brought in by rail, which ran a few hundred yards from the grounds. After March, 1864, when the hospital was officially designated a general hospital, the facility became known simply as General Hospital, Shelby Springs.

Despite the best efforts of the medical staff, many of the patients died. If a soldier survived the initial hazards of the battlefield, his likelihood of dying from an infectious disease was great. Three times as many Confederate soldiers, in fact, died from diseases as were killed in battle. Long months of campaigning, exposure to the elements, poor diet, and medical ignorance about simple hygiene and infection all took their toll on Confederate and Union soldiers alike. The most common diseases were malaria, pneumonia, and dysentery.

While the Shelby Springs hospital was a safer and more comfortable haven for the sick and wounded than were many hospitals of the time, both staff and patients faced formidable hardships. As the months went by, the need for clothing for the staff grew critical. The nuns managed to patch their own black habits together with white thread, but Father Leray's clothing proved more of a problem. Eventually the sisters made him a pair of trousers out of an old shawl, and a shirt out of a brown dress belonging to one of the postulants.

The helpful priest saw to it that religious services were continued. He provided for regular confessions, held mass, and made altar wine out of grapes which he squeezed into a tub. Many patients, however, viewed the Catholics on the staff with suspicion and distrust, and some patients were so adamant in their hostility toward Catholics that they refused treatment from the nuns.

The sisters found such strongly held religious prejudices difficult, but not impossible, to overcome. One nun, who had been turned away twice by a soldier whose wound she had attempted to dress, returned for a third time and warned the patient of the rougher treatment he would receive from the doctor. The man burst into tears and asked her to forgive him for "he had been taught to believe badly of sisters."

Sister Ignatius, writing in her journal, is cautious and philosophical in commenting on the effect of religious discussions on the patients. The war and the devastation it wrought, she writes, was every person's overriding concern: "We had the consolation of the return of some to the Faith, who had been negligent, and the baptism of others, sick and dying, but the demoralizing effect[s] of the war were great." At least one "good old soldier," a patient at Shelby Springs, was equally resigned to the devastation of the war. "Them that this war don't bring down," he said, "ain't bringable."

In March 1865, General James H. Wilson made his infamous raid through Alabama, burning and sacking major Confederate iron works and strategic sites along Alabama's industrial corridor. From his temporary headquarters in Montevallo, Wilson sent out details to destroy selected targets, including the town of Shelby, only a few miles east of Shelby Springs. Union troops undoubtedly passed near the hospital, but they made no attempt to destroy it.

Wilson's raid was the North's grand finale in Alabama. A week later Lee surrendered at Appomattox. After the port of Galveston yielded June 2, 1865, the worst war on American soil came to an end.

The same month, Father Leray and the remaining sisters returned to Vicksburg via Mobile and New Orleans. Undoubtedly they were greeted by a warm reception from Mother de Sales and the other nuns. Three years had passed since they began their heroic mission through the war-ravaged South, and never once during that time did they receive any financial compensation for their services, such as a salary from the Confederate government. The dedicated work of the Sisters of Mercy in the South as well as in the North captured, however, the attention of Jefferson Davis and Abraham Lincoln, both of whom left glowing tributes to the Order.[1]

CEDAR RAPIDS, IOWA

The Sisters of Mercy and Mound Farm

In 1906, the Sisters of Mercy of Cedar Rapids became associated with Mound Farm, "the cream of Cedar Rapids real estate, the finest farming land, the best situated and the most attractive country residence in Iowa." Since 1875, St. Joseph's Academy had been the sisters' motherhouse and novitiate, a boarding school for girls, and a parochial day school. By 1906, it had become too crowded to accommodate further growth, and the sisters began to search for a new home.

Uninhabited for nearly a decade since its foreclosure, the buildings at Mound Farm had served as grain storage and as a refuge for occasional hunters. Some thought had been given to establishing a cemetery on the land, and Coe College officials had looked at it as a possible site for that institution's expansion. Mother Mary Gertrude McCullough and her council, with a farsightedness vindicated in future decades, on March 12, 1906, elected to lease the Mound Farm property for five years, and in April began remodeling the mansion to accommodate a boarding school to open in December.

The REPUBLICAN DAILY, March 31, 1906, acknowledged the transaction and hoped "that by the time the lease expires the school will have developed enough to warrant the purchase of the property." It described the land as:

> an ideally healthful and sanitary site for a school. . . . It is said to be possible to see into all seven of the counties which surround Linn: Benton, Buchanan, Delaware, Jones, Cedar, Johnson, and Iowa. It is just far enough removed from the city to be secluded and restful, and yet near enough to share all the city's advantages. . . . The building will be placed in first class order, and will be ready for occupancy by next September at the latest.

Whatever the distant view, the more immediate glance showed a long-deserted house in need of much repair. The only good floor was in the dining room; grain had to be cleared from the ballroom, loose plaster and broken windows repaired, and the roof mended. Partitions were installed, the walls repapered, and the whole house scrubbed—all work done by the sisters, including Mother Mary Gertrude, and a few hired workmen—to put the house in "first class order."

In a talk prepared for the opening of the sisters' centennial celebration, July 21, 1974, Sister Mary Xavier Reilly told of those early days (1906):

"The word went round that we were to have a new home at the city, a farm of considerable size, and—wonder of wonders—a mansion. True, God had not promised us a mansion, but He had promised us a hundred-fold and we accepted it humbly. At least, that's what we thought we were doing. All that summer of 1906, alluring wisps of news came floating back from the sisters who were already dwelling in the mansion: word of the sunken garden, the carriage house, good enough for people to live in, the horses (by this time we had acquired a team, the Belle and Toy of our early history), the glorious sunrises and sunsets—and not one word about the rats. To those of us still sweltering in the heat and crowding of old St. Joseph's the welcome message came from a promised land. A very young sister wrote:

'Members of my profession band were told after the ceremony on August 6, we were to have a week at the new home—a rest it would be.'

'So on the late afternoon of our profession day, we walked to First Avenue to board the street car that banged and clanged its way out to Sixteenth Street, where we began the long up-hill trek to our mansion. Were there no cabs? Of course there were, but with cabs came fares. Only that morning we had made a vow of poverty, and here was just a chance to make good.

'The road was long, the day warm, and we were carrying our rather extensive luggage. But the first sight of our new home, the glimpse of the red brick mansion through the massive trees, made up for everything. The few sisters and girls there greeted us warmly. Supper, prayers, recreation on the veranda, a trip around part of the house, and we were assigned to spacious bedrooms.

'Now all evening an uneasiness had been growing on me. That trip to see the house, the conservatory, the ballroom, the servants' quarters—the great gloom was setting over everything. It was all just right for one of Poe's most horrendous stories. Well, the house settled down for the night, but it was only the pause before the storm. Scampering of light feet, fighting, squeaking. Where? Everywhere! You see, before our purchase of the Greene place, this mansion had been used as a granary, furnishing an idyllic haven for the rats. Now they were being evicted. Relentlessly, the sisters and one lone ferret were fighting them, slowly but surely decimating their ranks. These horrors of the night must have been the 'last hurrah' of a vanishing tribe. So went our first night and most of those that followed.

'The first morning? Mass: breakfast, then Sister Mercedes, acting superior, ticked us off on her fingers to various jobs of house cleaning. It was wonderful, though, to see the beautiful wood and marble come out from their coats of dust and dirt. And there's nothing like house-cleaning to keep up a spirit of camaraderie!'

"As Mother Mary Lawrence Hallagan later remarked:

'Our beginning was not influential, nor was it powerful, but it was a good beginning—a beginning that followed the way of poverty, humility, charity, and forbearance in the service of the poor, the care of the sick, and the education of youth. It was the way pointed out by our saintly foundress, *a way that leads to the very heart of God.*' "[2]

CHICAGO

Pittsburgh to Chicago, 1846

Bishop William Quarter cordially welcomed the weary Sisters of Mercy from Pittsburgh to the Chicago Foundation, and took them to St. Mary's Cathedral, a very unpretentious building on the corner of Wabash Avenue and Madison Street. There they laid down their burden at the Master's feet and heartily thanked Him for their safe arrival. Then came the housing of the little band. Bishop Quarter vacated his own home, which was only a poor little one-story, frame building; yet it was a palace compared with that to which he retired on this occasion. The one he left for the sisters was described by them as a sieve in summer and a shell in winter, but his fatherly kindness compensated them; this humble prelate said Mass for them daily as long as he lived.

In a short time the sisters opened a school in the old frame church, in the rear of the Cathedral. Unable to give the material aid he wished, the Bishop advised Mother Mary Agatha to write to the Society for the Propagation of the Faith in Lyons for pecuniary assistance. In reply the Society sent $4,000 and three large oil paintings, copies of old masters—one, "The Agony in the Garden"; another, "Mater Dolorosa"; the third, the "Holy Family," not quite so large as the others. They were saved from the fire in 1871 and are still in possession of the sisters, who look on them as great relics of early days.

Mother Xavier Warde, who had accompanied the missionaries to Chicago, remained to see them settled; and then she left by stage, Dec. 27, for distant Pittsburgh. She had appointed Mother Agatha O'Brien as Superior. The Chicago Mission, which nearly cost Mother Warde her life, was blessed by God, as it thrived through many tribulations.

On the same day on which Mother Warde left Chicago, Miss Mary Monholland arrived from New York to enter the new Chicago community. A strong character of much experience and older than the others, she was of great assistance in financial affairs. In time she became the fourth superior at St. Xavier's. Her journey to Chicago was made by boats on the Great Lakes. On Lake Michigan a storm arose and the travelers were very much alarmed. The vessel was driven toward the Milwaukee shore, but could not reach it. At last an immense wave swept over the deck carrying many passengers with it into the seething waters, Mary Monholland among the rest. The people of Milwaukee worked bravely to save the unfortunate travelers. W. B. Ogden, afterward Chicago's first Mayor, witnessed the catastrophe and saved some of the drowning passengers. Seeing Mary Monholland struggling in the water, he succeeded in seizing her and raising her on his shoulders and brought her to land.

Asiatic Cholera, 1854

The year 1854 can never be forgotten by the Mercy Sisterhood in Chicago. Asiatic cholera ravaged the city throughout the entire summer. Fourteen hundred and twenty-four persons succumbed to the fearful plague. Burials—not always of the dead—were to be seen day and night.

The sisters laid aside all other duties to visit and care for the sick, especially among the poor, and Mother Mary Agatha took her turn as faithfully as the others. On July 7 she went to visit the Mercy Hospital, which was overcrowded with poor suffering humanity. Among the number Sister Mary Veronica, one of the community, was very ill, and Mother

Agatha wished to see her. It was a warm day; she was exhausted after her long walk, and over-heated. On her return she asked for a drink of water. In a short time she was seized with such violent symptoms that she had scarcely strength enough to reach the Infirmary. The morning of the eighth of July she died amid the tears and prayers of her devoted sisters.

Two others were soon in a dying condition from the cholera, Sisters Mary Bernardine and Louis—and on the next day it was a sad sight to see two sisters carried out of the convent. The sisters had died within twenty-four hours in the service of the cholera patients. On the eleventh, Sister Mary Veronica also died of the same epidemic at the hospital.

The news of Mother Mary Agatha's death caused universal grief throughout the city, as she was known and loved by all. How her spiritual daughters felt her loss could never be described.

Asiatic Cholera, 1873—Second Epidemic

On August 16, 1873, Rev. Mother Genevieve of Chicago received a letter from the Diocesan Chancellor's office, stating that some physicians had sent a committee to the Bishop, to represent the deplorable condition of poor sufferers who were attacked by the cholera, to plead for sisters to visit them and if possible to remain and nurse them. She read this letter to Sister Mary Alphonsus Butler, who immediately offered to go, and asked for Sister Mary Jane Duggan to accompany her. Mother Genevieve said, "This must be optional; I cannot appoint any sister to risk her life, but you may ask the one you choose, and if she is willing to undertake the labor, I consent." Sister Mary Jane was only too glad to be chosen to undertake the labor of helping the cholera sufferers.

It was a very warm day when these two sisters started out with only a vague description of the location where the scourge had its headquarters. "Somewhere south of the city," the letter stated. They entered many houses between the hospital and Fifty-seventh Street, but found no sufferers. Though very tired, one of them said, "Let us go west a couple of blocks. . . ." This couple of blocks extended from Cottage Grove to State Street.

Just as they reached the latter, a gentleman accosted them asking if they were Sisters of Mercy. He said he was Dr. Simon, and he was a member of the Committee that applied for the service of the sisters; that aid was needed for the souls as well as for the bodies of the stricken people. The old Smallpox Hospital was then located on a prairie on Wentworth Avenue between Thirty-seventh and Thirty-eighth Streets. There some of those sought by the sisters had been placed, and the doctor was anxious that the sisters should visit several houses in that neighborhood and advise the people to bring the cholera patients to the hospital so they might have better care, and also prevent the spread of the disease. The sisters promised to do so next day, also to ask permission to stay every day in the hospital, and to try to send a detail at night.

On August 17, 1873, the sisters went to the duty assigned them. It is impossible to give an accurate account of the terrible state of the hospital and its patients. An old weather-beaten frame shanty, unpainted, unclean, and bereft of all furniture, except beds in which men and women were suffering most excruciating torture, without any human being to give aid or comfort. There was no separation of the sexes; all were in one large room; and, to make matters worse, the women had no proper clothing. The first thing to be done was to find a separate place for the sick women; and a sister asked Dr. Simon what could be done about this. He said: "Do what you think best, but here is the only room that has a window." However, the man and his wife who had the care of this plague spot helped to fix a couple of rooms; and to provide ventilation, holes were made in the wall of each room.

The first day's nursing produced some amelioration of the sad condition. When the homeward journey was taken, people called the sisters into several houses to see the sick; the greater part of these had big feather beds, although the weather was extremely warm at the time. However poor the hospital accommodation was, surely it was better than could be found in the miserable places which these people called home.

One morning at about eight o'clock, the sisters arrived at the post of duty, to find but two living of the dozen whom they had under their care the previous day. One young woman had just arrived; she had been ill for about ten days; she first had cholera, and then typhoid fever. Some two or three mustard plasters were fastened in her flesh. To remove these was a terrible ordeal for both the patient and the sister. This woman cursed and struck the patient nurse, who was trying to relieve her. She said the sisters were paid for all they did by the city. How she conceived this untruth it is impossible to say, for even carfare was never asked for, nor offered. Certainly the reward was expected, but not an earthly one!

A male nurse, an English Episcopalian, was very kind to the patients; the two sisters and this man (excepting the night nurse supplied by the sisters) were all the help to be found in this wretched place. The janitor carried the dead away and went for the food supply, which his wife cooked. How anyone could eat in such a place is a mystery which the sisters could not solve. They brought lunch and went outside to the prairie to eat it, but the experiences of the morning removed all desire for food; they left the lunches for some poor tramp to relieve his hunger. At last, the second cholera plague saw its end in Chicago.[3]

DETROIT

Detroit Province Formed

Following the announcement of the creation of the Mercy Province of Detroit on July 8, 1940, all the sisters belonging to the new province prepared to leave for new destinations. The exact time for the canonical creation of the Province of Detroit was mid-day August 16, 1940. While the community of Edgecliff, Cincinnati, was at noon prayers in the chapel, Mother Mary Carmelita Manning and her Assistant, Mother Mary Raymund O'Leary, quietly went to the auditorium door where a car and a driver were waiting for them to begin the journey to Michigan. A new car replaced the one being taken. More than that, the debt on the recently erected provincialate and college building in Cincinnati was to be liquidated by the newly erected Province of Detroit.

The seeding of the new province is graphically recounted by Mother Mary Carmelita Manning, the great raconteuse, herself:

> We were told to just take our trunks and go to Detroit and rent a house. We were leaving a beautiful new Provincial House and College, which we had built and had the pleasure of living in for only one year and a half. After all of our struggles over nine years to get a home in Cincinnati that we could call our Provincial House, naturally the parting was not easy, as we had grown to love each sister we were to leave behind. But we had the happy thought that we had about six hundred sisters in the Detroit Province whom we also loved.

> Renting in Detroit was prohibitive because of the high cost of rent for a home that would be adequate to accommodate the newly appointed councilors. St. Joseph Mercy Hospital in Ann Arbor had just finished a new wing, at the moment unused. Since this was my first mission after profession, I felt we would be welcome to take over the top floor of the new wing and temporarily establish our provincial headquarters there. So God and Our Lady of Mercy filled our hearts with joy, knowing that we were not just to live from our trunks.

> After the first Council meeting, Mother Mary Raymund and I started out to search for a site in Detroit on which to build the new provincial house, novitiate, and college. The second day we were driving around, we saw an old sign on a big tree saying "For

Sale" and giving a telephone number. We went to the nearest gas station and called the number, asking if the property was still for sale. The weak voice of an old gentleman answered and said, "Oh, yes, but buy it quickly or I will lose it for taxes."

We returned to Ann Arbor feeling that God had blessed our day's effort. We called our Detroit attorney to get a real estate agent to get an option on the property, a site of forty acres. He did this and we signed the deed a few days later at a bargain for property in a fine residential area.

An architect was employed to draw plans for our new home within the price Mother General said we could spend. When the bid was returned, it was eight hundred dollars less than the allotment, so we broke ground in November, 1940.

The winter months were severe for building and we were faced with restrictions because of World War II. Ready mixed cement was only available after 4:30 p.m. when trucks finished the day's hauling for war construction. But each day seemed to bless the undertaking. On July 16, 1941 Mother Mary Raymund and I ate our dinner on the Feast of Our Lady of Mount Carmel in the new building. Our table was an orange crate and our dinner was sandwiches and coffee sent to us by the sisters at Mt. Carmel Mercy Hospital. We spent our first night in the new Provincial House. The building was far from finished, but we were notified that the furniture was being delivered and someone had to be there to sign and check for it.

The novices were to be transferred from Dubuque August 18, 1941. Mother Mary Raymund's Silver Jubilee was to take place on August 15, and the General Chapter was to convene in Washington on August 28. Mercy College was to open for registration on September 8. The calendar was rapidly diminishing working days. . . .

After we were settled, we decided to landscape the campus. We got a bulldozer and had a lake made, then built a rose arbor and a belvedere. We wanted a grotto, but when we got a price on it, we thought we couldn't afford it. One of the sisters, Sister Mary Esther Heuss, heard about it and said, "I will get you the grotto." I said that the bid without the altar was $15,000. She said, "I am coming to Detroit to see a friend who is ill and I will tell him about it and you will get your grotto." After her visit to her friend, she sent me a check from him and every week I would get checks from people I had never heard of. Finally, we had the $15,000. Then I wrote to sister to tell her I couldn't receive any more for the grotto, but I still didn't have the altar. A few days later, I got a letter from a Judge in Dubuque saying that a man had died and left money for our altar.[4]

The War Between the States

St. Thomas Aquinas defines mercy as "heartfelt sympathy for another's distress, impelling us to help if we can. . . . Mercy takes its name from *misericordia,* denoting a compassionate person's heart for another's unhappiness."

What human beings term adversity, God terms opportunity. The Sisters of Mercy chose His translation and served on the battlefield, on American soil where brother fought brother in the war that began in 1861.

The War Department files in Washington, D.C., record the names of the Sisters of Mercy from New York, Pittsburgh, Chicago, Baltimore, Vicksburg, and Cincinnati who nursed in this conflict. Their names were also indelibly engraved on the hearts of thousands of soldiers in blue and in gray.

When the government summons went out through Edwin Stanton, Secretary of War, the Sisters of Mercy were among those who responded to the needs of the times. Trained in Mercy Hospitals, the sisters came ready to serve.

Many of the "men" in war were mere boys, and the sisters could recall, as could those who served at Scutari and Balaclava, many a story like the one of the sixteen year old boy who, burying his face in his pillow, moaned as a sister carefully sponged his shattered shoulder. Finally he groaned, "Who is doing that?" "A Sister of Mercy," came the answer. "No," he whispered. "No one but my mother could do that. . . ."

One night in the Stanton Hospital in Washington a tall, gaunt man entered the building, greeted the sisters with great courtesy and moved along the many rows of cots, shaking hands and chatting a moment with the soldiers from the North and from the South. When the sisters came together for night prayers, Mother Mary Rose Hostetter asked the sisters to pray often and frequently for their visitor of that evening—Abraham Lincoln. Later he was to write:

Of all the forms of charity and benevolence seen in the crowded wards of the hospitals, those of the Catholic Sisters were among the most efficient. I never knew whence they came or what was the name of the Order. More lovely than anything I have ever seen in art, so long devoted to illustrations of love, mercy, and charity, are the pictures that remain of these sisters going on their rounds of mercy among the suffering and dying. Gentle and womanly. . . .

A tribute from the military staff of Stanton Hospital stated:

These Sisters of Mercy were not afraid of toil, self-denial, or hardship, so that they could glorify God and relieve the anguish of mind and body of the Federal soldiers in the Stanton, or of its sick and dejected prisoners of war.

The tribute of Cardinal O'Connell to the sisters who nursed in the army hospitals was:

Some of these holy women, worn out with prolonged hardships, paid with their lives for their heroic devotion. They, as well as the soldiers fallen in the fight, gave all to the Republic.

As in the Crimea where two Sisters of Mercy died and were given military funerals, so in the War Between the States sisters died in service —two of the Chicago community and four from Baltimore. Mother Mary Collette O'Connor of Baltimore died on July 16, 1864, at Stanton Hospital, and her remains were escorted to Baltimore and buried with full military honors. Many other sisters, exhausted by their unremitting duty, day and night, never regained their strength.

The New York Sisters of Mercy who nursed at Hammond General Hospital, Beaufort, North Carolina, and later at Stanley House, Newberne, North Carolina, were a puzzle to the entire staff as well as to the patients. Upon their arrival the sisters found the five hundred room Hammond Hospital, a former luxury hotel, not only denuded of ornament, but stripped of even essentials. When a sister requested water to bathe a patient, an attendant brought it and stood watching her care for the man. As she straightened up, the attendant asked, "Is he a relation of yours, Ma'am?" To his astonishment the sister replied, "Sir, I never saw him before, but we are here to care for everyone."

Mother Mary Madeleine Tobin found herself faced with the problem of lack of necessary supplies that would have been familiar to the veterans of the Crimea. When the medical staff told her that there was nothing to

do but wait, Mother Mary Madeleine declared that she would do something else. She sent off a complete requisition list to the War Department
with the statement that this request would be honored or she and her
Sisters would return to New York. Shortly a ship was seen pulling up to
the dilapidated wharf at Beaufort, and medical supplies, linens, kitchen
utensils, lamps, kerosene, brooms, scrub brushes, pails, and foodstuffs
were unloaded. From then on, the "North ladies," as the Sisters were
called, were in command.

When Mother Mary Madeleine, who had been serving as general
superintendent, was obliged to return to St. Catherine Convent where she
was Reverend Mother, the chief of the medical staff asked who was to take
her place. "Sister Mary Augustine McKenna," she replied. "The cook?"
he asked, outraged. "Is that the way you do business?" "Yes," Mother
Mary Madeleine answered. "Every Sister must be prepared to discharge
any duty entrusted to her." The irony was that Sister Mary Augustine was
one of the best educated women in the community.

Today the Red Cross nurses and the armed service nurses are honored with well-deserved praise for their work on the battlefields. In the
1860's there was no great humane organization like Clara Barton's Red
Cross and there were no women in military service. It was the Catholic
Sisterhoods with hundreds of volunteers who stepped into the breach.

The war over, they returned to their convents, not forgetting their
promises to many a dying soldier. They devotedly concerned themselves
with the welfare of war widows and orphaned children.

In the nation's capital at the junction of Rhode Island and Connecticut Avenues stands an impressive monument to the memory of the Sister-
nurses from twenty different communities who served in the War Between the States. It sums up the work of these heroic women:

> They comforted the dying, nursed the wounded, carried hope to
> the imprisoned, gave in God's Name a drink of water to the
> thirsty.[5]

The well-known Rev. S. Parkes Cadman, speaking before a YMCA
meeting in Brooklyn, New York, September 21, 1915, declared:

> The Sisters of Mercy are heroines of the cross. Would to God
> that our women everywhere shared their sacrificial spirit. Ask
> any veteran of the Civil War and he will tell you of their value. If
> we had fewer *tangoers* and more Sisters of Mercy, the world
> would be better.[6]

Account of Camp Life in Michigan

In the year 1893 the Sisters left for C and D Camps to solicit funds to enable us to get a new furnace for the men's ward of the hospital. From Cadillac, Michigan, we went to a Catholic family whose father was a foreman at one of the camps. A team of horses and two-seated sleigh were given us with a one-arm driver to travel thirty-five miles. When we entered a side camp, our rig was broken, and upon asking to stay long enough to fix it, and also to ask the campmen for a donation, we were told it would not be worthwhile. So we continued a little farther until we came to the main camp of one hundred men. We were warmly welcomed, for they had not seen a woman for a year, and they said it was worth five dollars to see one. The men were all in the shanty preparing for the next day's hard work, drying their socks and mackinaws around a huge stove in the center of the shanty. At first entering it was not very pleasant for us, but such a life of hardship did not mean much to them. One of us took one side of the shanty, and the foreman talked with my companion on the other, as we continued to present our cause and state our reason for begging in this way. Some of the boys were trying to sew up the holes in their socks and clothing; others were lying on their bunks and writing. One would have to be quite tired to rest on boards covered with a little hay and a horse blanket. One poor boy was asked how old he was—only twenty-one. And does your mother know where you are?—No, but I will write to her because I cannot endure it any longer.

The boys were very generous that evening. Then the foreman took us to his office, a small building large enough to keep books and a few shelves where mittens, mackinaws, and felt shoes were kept to accommodate the men, and two bunks were given to us to rest 'till morning. He went out and we were left alone. Locking the door, we examined the bunk—which would it be, the top or the bottom? We chose the top as it would give us more air and, as the pigs were sleeping under the floor, we would be farther from them. . . .[7]

MANCHESTER, NEW HAMPSHIRE

Mother and Six Daughters as Sisters of Mercy in Manchester and Portland

Sister Mary Francis Xavier Leeson was closely identified with the beginnings of Saint Joseph's schools for girls in Manchester, New Hampshire. The first classes for boys of the parish were held in the dressing rooms of what is now the city Manual Training School on Lowell Street. The main rooms of this building were used by public school children. The late Sister Mary Josephine Wheeler and her sister auxiliaries had charge of the Catholic boys. And bright lads they were! Full of fun and harmless mischief, they studied and advanced rapidly in the important subjects taught them by the sisters, for they knew their school days must be soon interrupted by work in the factories. They had few of the advantages of children of today; yet it was wonderful how much knowledge they acquired. Most of them grew up to be thrifty, upright citizens, filling positions creditably in nearly every walk of life.

The next school was in an old-fashioned dwelling house which stood where Saint Joseph's High School now stands.

The children sat in little wooden chairs with pockets at the sides for their books and slates. Stoves heated the schoolrooms, and in the pantry attached to the "kitchen schoolrooms" was a pump which supplied "spring" water when the children needed a drink during the long sessions of three hours in the forenoon and three hours in the afternoon. The pupils were advanced as rapidly as possible. When they reached the fifth and sixth grades, the girls were promoted to the new school for girls which occupied the building opposite the Convent on Union Street, later the House of Saint Martha.

God blessed these primitive beginnings and year by year better accommodations were provided. Soon the pastor of Saint Joseph's had the rooms attached to the south east corner of the church rebuilt for a girls' school. On the lower floor was the original chapel, twenty-four feet by fifty feet; on the second floor was a large hall used for Sunday school classes and for meetings of the different societies. The building was transformed into good classrooms, heated by wood stoves, and the girls were removed from the Lowell Street school which was left to the boys. Later, the new brick building on Lowell Street, now known as "Saint Joseph's High," was constructed for the ambitious, intelligent lads, who had faced the privations of pioneer education. Sturdy and matter-of-fact they were, and they fully appreciated the fine new school and the advantages provided for them. With their early rugged training, they had acquired character and strength of will which served them well in after life.

The new girls' school was prosperous; the long day passed all too quickly when pupils were hungry for learning. Sister Francis and her assistants were enthusiastic in their work. Earnest girls vied with each other in coming early in the morning to start the wood fires in freezing winter weather. In the church on Sunday afternoons, and at four o'clock during May, Sister Francis had sodality processions, meetings of the Angel Guardian Society for the very young pupils, the Office for the Children of Mary, and other devotional gatherings for purposes of instruction and prayer.

From Saint Joseph's school, Sister M. Francis was sent to Portland, Maine, as local superior to succeed Mother M. Gonzaga. There were parish schools, an academy and an orphanage to be attended by the sisters. The supervision of the Portland convent and schools was no light task for any one. There was also much visitation of the sick, and instruction classes and sodalities in the evening and on Sunday afternoons. Sister Francis was a young nun to assume the responsibility of this charge, but the work prospered. Bishop David William Bacon was "Father and friend" to the community. With Longfellow, Mother Francis could say in later years what Mother M. Gonzaga had said before her, for these two first superiors of Portland were always enthusiastic in their loving interest for their early mission and its many works of mercy. Too, there was a captivating charm about the old town and the poet's lines were quoted many a time:

> Often I think of the beautiful town
>   That is seated by the sea.
> Often in thought, I go up and down
>   The pleasant streets of that dear old town.
> And my youth comes back to me."

About the time that Sister M. Francis was in Portland, her mother, Mrs. James Leeson, came from Dublin and entered the novitiate at Manchester under Mother M. Xavier Warde. Only the youngest member of the family, except those in religion, was living. This daughter accompanied her mother to America, and Mrs. Leeson placed her as a pupil at Mount Saint Mary's Academy. Her name, Eleanor Elizabeth Leeson, may be found in the old registers of that institution. A few years after her mother became a Sister of Mercy with the religious name of Sister Mary de Chantal, Eleanor entered the novitiate and was professed as Sister Mary Camilla. The noble mother who gave her six daughters to God as Sisters of Mercy entered the same order with her daughters and lived the life of a fervent religious for several years. She was a brilliant conversationalist—it was a treat to listen to her entertaining talks.

At the time of her death, one of the older sisters wrote the following paragraphs concerning Sister M. de Chantal, mother of six Sisters of Mercy:

She was young with many of the greatest characters of the nineteenth century, for Pope Leo XIII, Cardinal Newman, Cardinal

Manning, and Mr. Gladstone in Europe, and others of heroic, brilliant fame in our own country were children when she was a child. It is a precious boon to have great contemporaries; it is a more valuable one to be born in the midst of great events. This boon was hers, for it was in the vicinity of the date of her birth that Napoleon Bonaparte was being forced to learn that "God is not always on the side of the strongest battalions." Also, about that time, Lord Castlereagh and the Duke of Wellington were preparing to assist at the Congress of Vienna to give justice to nearly all European countries except their own native land, Ireland.

Before the end of her girlhood, the Duke of Wellington was conquered on a greater Waterloo than that where he triumphed over Napoleon Bonaparte. Too, Sister de Chantal saw Daniel O'Connell stand Wellington's victor with "Catholic Emancipation" in his bloodless hand. When over seventy years had left their chill on her heart, it was still warm, when those days were recalled. What then must have been the fire which burned in her soul for her country when she was a girl of seventeen and heard the matchless words of O'Connell himself!

Was it not the fact of her living in the atmosphere of such mighty events at the beginning of her life which preserved her from the narrowness of mind so often to be regretted in man and woman? It was easily perceived that she had no care for trifles, and that she dwelt in the midst of useful thoughts. Yet it was evident that her woman's sphere was wide enough for the exercise of the desires and the energies of the highest type of woman.

During the last fifteen or sixteen years of her life, she threw all the forces of her gifted mind and generous heart into the work of becoming a prayerful, edifying religious. Her useful, eventful career closed December 28, 1893, in her convent home, Mount Saint Mary's, Manchester.[8]

Celebration of Mercy Golden Jubilee in Manchester, 1893

In 1893, Mother M. Beatrice and the Manchester Sisters of Mercy thanked God for the foundation of the Sisters of Mercy in the United States in Pittsburgh in 1843. Their "thank you" was said in the chapel of

Mount Saint Mary where Bishop Bradley pontificated at a Solemn Mass of Thanksgiving.

Bishop Denis Bradley's words at the conclusion of the Golden Jubilee Mass are too telling and sacred to be overlooked in our reminiscences. For you who have followed the Manchester Sisters of Mercy since 1858, we repeat them:

> My dear sisters: You have called us here today to join with you in commemorating the fiftieth anniversary of the establishment of your Institute in the United States. You do well to stop at this milestone which marks an important point in your journeyings in the discharge of your duties as religious. It is wise to pause from time to time in our labors and to look back over the past and consider what we have done, and how we have done what we have had to do. By so doing, if we discover that all things have been well done, we are encouraged to greater labors for the future; if we have not done well, we shall discover what we must do to make our labors more acceptable.
>
> And what have the Sisters of Mercy done in these United States during the past half century, and how have they done what they had to do? Fifty years ago, at the time of their introduction into the United States by the learned and zealous Bishop Michael O'Connor, of Pittsburgh, they numbered seven; today, within the limits of this republic, they number 2,800. Fifty years ago they were found in one diocese; today they are found in every archdiocese of the country, even the most remote —Santa Fe and Oregon. In addition to the fifteen archdioceses in which they have foundations, they are also found in thirty-eight dioceses, fifty-three in all in the United States.
>
> And how has that been done which they have had to do? God alone knows, God alone rewards; but if it were left to our human eyes to judge, we should say unhesitatingly that the work has been well done. This will appear evident when we consider the character of the work which the Sister of Mercy is called upon to discharge. There is nothing in it that is agreeable to the demands of human nature, and much, yes, almost everything, that is repugnant to human nature. That the work has been well done is also evidenced by the rapid and extensive spreading of the Order throughout the United States.

No gala event at the Motherhouse ever eliminated the young ladies of Mount Saint Mary Academy. In Our Lady of Mercy Hall, on the afternoon of December 21, 1893, they enacted a beautiful drama entitled "A Vision of Angels," written and directed by Mother Xavier Warde's grand-niece, Sister M. Paul Xavier, whose talents we first met in 1879 when she came as a child boarder to the Mount. One of the audience afterwards said of the production, "A poet, a musician, and an artist put their souls into it." But we know that it was but one soul with a three-fold gift that directed and pervaded all, and that soul did not belong, as the signature under the printed copy of the pageant suggests, to "Marguerite," but to Sister M. Paul Xavier.[9]

MICHIGAN AND MINNESOTA TO KANSAS

Unusual Foundations from Big Rapids, Michigan and Morris, Minnesota, 1886; Kansas City, 1893

The spirit of Mother Catherine McAuley was brought to Kansas in the mid 1880's. By mere chance two Sisters of Mercy, Sister Mary Teresa Dolan of the Big Rapids, Michigan, Community and Sister Mary Francis Murphy of the Morris, Minnesota, Community, enroute to Los Angeles, had a stop-over at Fort Scott, Kansas, for the convenience of assisting at Mass on Sunday, November 15, 1885.

They called upon the pastor of St. Mary Queen of Angels church, Rev. Francis J. Wattron, and asked him to direct them to some Catholic family for hospitality over Sunday. Father Wattron assured them that there was plenty of room at the rectory and invited them to stay as his guests. This kind offer was gladly accepted by the tired travelers who were grateful to be located so close to the church.

Sister Mary Teresa had served as Reverend Mother in Big Rapids for the unexpired term of Mother Mary Thecla O'Brien from August 25, 1883 to August 15, 1885. She was serving as Mother Assistant when she asked to be relieved of her duties temporarily because her physician had advised that a change to a drier climate would be beneficial to her health. She had suffered a rather severe attack of pneumonia the winter before and had been left with a persistent bronchial cough. Although reluctant to take this advice, she had found the usual remedies of no avail and finally decided to make a temporary change to a convent of the Sisters of Mercy in California, a foundation from Kinsale, the house from which her friend, Mother Mary Joseph Lynch, had come.

By the time the sisters reached Kansas, they were well-worn by fatigue and perhaps regretted having started on the journey. Train service in the early 1880's did not have the comforts of faster travel of later days.

Mother Mary Teresa had a confidential talk with Father Wattron and explained the purpose of the western trip. While he listened sympathetically, he was not of the opinion that Los Angeles with its long rainy season was the best place for her to recuperate. Kansas, he said, had more sunny days and a drier climate. Father Wattron told the sisters that a convent of Mercy established in Kansas would be a godsend to the first diocese in the state. The diocese of Leavenworth was only eight years old and, except for the Sisters of Loretto in St. Paul and the Sisters of Charity in Leavenworth, there were no religious to help with the work of the new parishes coming into existence.

It was no wonder that the Sisters of Mercy were welcomed by the lonely parish priest who had tried in vain to locate sisters to teach the children of his parish. While the sisters had no intention of remaining or offering their services, the story of the missionary work so badly needed in Kansas was very interesting and appealed to them. Great need for the works of mercy begged for consideration.

In their room that evening the sisters talked long and late into the night. The result of their deliberations was the cancellation of the trip to California. The next day they were still good listeners. They learned of the many ways in which, if they were to remain, they could be a great help to the over-burdened pastor by practicing the works of mercy: visiting the sick, instructing the children. However, this question would have to be decided by their superiors; so, changing their plans, they decided to return home and present the matter.

The bishop assured the sisters of his approval and blessing. He would gladly welcome a foundation of the Sisters of Mercy in his diocese. With this encouragement the sisters returned to their motherhouses in Big Rapids, Michigan and in Morris, Minnesota. In Michigan the petition for an establishment in Fort Scott was given some consideration, but there were no sisters to spare or funds to equip a new mission. However, the community, reluctantly it seems, decided to give it a trial. Sister Mary Teresa Dolan offered her services and a novice, Sister Mary Dolores Drew, also volunteered to go. She had asked for missionary work and this would give her some experience before making her vows. In Minnesota, Sister Mary Francis Murphy was also making the same request of her community.

Father Wattron had written that a furnished house and maintenance would be provided for the sisters by the parish. There would be little that he could offer for salaries except the voluntary offerings of the faithful. Trusting in Providence, the sisters replied that they would come and that Sister Mary Teresa and Sister Mary Dolores would be ready to leave Big Rapids at his call and that Sister Mary Francis would join them from Minnesota.

In Fort Scott the men of the parish, aided by the women, in January, 1886, began refurbishing the old church building, formerly a Civil War barracks. Although Father Wattron had planned for a school and this was the work that had been discussed with the sisters, the doctors in Fort Scott insisted upon a hospital. Father Wattron not unwillingly yielded to their demands. When the three sisters arrived in April, 1886, the hospital was "ready." It was cramped and inconvenient, and consequently the number of patients that could be admitted was severely limited, but in addition to nursing in the hospital the sisters visited and tended the sick in their own homes.

Mother Mary Teresa, who had had charge of the novices while serving as Mother Superior in Big Rapids, had brought manuscript copies of the novices' directory, guide, and meditations from Big Rapids. She undertook to complete the training in religious life of the one novice. Sister Mary Dolores Drew made her religious profession on July 16, 1887, and immediately became Mother Assistant. From 1890 to 1893 she was Mother Superior. The first local postulant, a wealthy young widow, Elizabeth Nulty Knapp, entered on April 28, 1888. She was received as Sister Mary Josephine and some twenty years later became the first Kansan Mother Superior. Because of her invaluable aid to the struggling community, she has fittingly been called the preserver of the Sisters of Mercy in Kansas.

A community growing, albeit slowly, and the rapidly increasing number of patients demanded a more commodious building. The sisters acquired land and erected a four-story brick hospital to which the patients were transferred in 1880. St. Mary School opened in the remodeled former hospital.

In 1893 the sisters were asked to take charge of a hospital for railroad employees in Kansas City and Sister Mary Josephine Knapp, superior, with two sisters left Fort Scott to open this hospital. This first branch from Big Rapids had begun to put out its shoots.[10]

MISSISSIPPI:
VICKSBURG, MERIDIAN, AND JACKSON

A Harrowing Experience

We hope it will not be irreverent to compare Sister Mary Vincent Browne, a simple Sister of Mercy, to the great Saint Teresa, mystic and doctor in the church of God, but by many of her characteristics, especially her keen sense of humor and her inexhaustible fund of common sense, we have often been forcibly reminded of passages in the life of this great saint. Few religious are called upon to lead such a life of constant activity, so full of rapidly succeeding difficulties in their labors for the church.

Martha Browne was the youngest member of a devoted Catholic family. So robust was the Browne type of Christianity that little Martha when only an infant was carried sixty miles in a sleigh to be baptized. These were Christians who had learned to take more care of the soul than of the body, so that we cannot marvel that in this home circle bloomed four religious vocations. After the death of her mother, Martha followed the example of her sisters, Fannie and Mary, whose early departure from the paternal roof was still a sad but holy memory. Under the name of Sister Mary Vincent she made her profession with Sister M. Ignatius Summer in Baltimore. She had hitherto enjoyed robust health, and in the beginning of her religious career was employed in the visitation of the sick. In this essential duty of a Sister of Mercy she was initiated by Sister M. Camillus, the godchild of Mother McAuley, who is often referred to in the life of the venerable foundress. The lessons transmitted from the fountain head could not fail to impress her to whom "Noblesse Oblige" of religious vocation was an abiding principle. These lessons were taught faithfully to the young religious of the first foundation in the sunny South in Vicksburg.

When the school at Vicksburg opened, Sister Mary Vincent was chosen to teach the boys. No one could have more readily won boyish allegiance than she; her approval was the highest reward at which they aimed. Many of her larger boys were obliged to leave school never to return on account of war conditions, but they carried into a turbulent world lessons of manliness and high purpose inspired by this faithful religious.

During the trying days that grew out of the vicissitudes of Civil War and the wanderings of the sisters from hospital to hospital, it was Sister Vincent's diplomacy that negotiated and carried out the plans of Superiors. In all of the hospitals that were served by the sisters during their three years of exile, she was what would have been termed today the superintendent of nurses. Her personality was an amiable combination of mirth and seriousness. In her ministrations to the sick and wounded she was a mother, and the letters which reached her from childless mothers and widows to whom the sisters had sent messages of the death of loved ones, were teeming with expressions of gratitude. Sometimes a letter would come from a soldier himself who had experienced her care in the hour of pain.

It was always Sister Vincent who was left in charge of the little band of sisters when Mother de Sales was obliged to leave her spiritual children for any purpose. After the long stay at Shelby Springs, when the surrender of Vicksburg made it safe for Mother de Sales to claim the convent property, it was Sister Vincent who guided the little flock and bore with wonderful heroism the long days and weeks of uncertainty while waiting for news, at the same time cheering the young sisters under her charge and making a joke of their many privations.

The writer recalls one instance of Sister Vincent's resourcefulness under great difficulty. In the epidemic of 1878 she was appointed to lead a band of sisters to Meridian, where they were to open a convent and from whence they were to try to get into Jackson. Meantime Meridian was beginning to get very much excited over the fever situation. Sister M. Vincent and Sister M. Alphonsus Hoey were to go to Jackson, and Sisters M. Camillus, M. Bernard, and M. Stanislaus were appointed to Meridian. As the bursar was preparing the lunch basket for the journey, which took nine hours instead of the ordinary five, Sister M. Vincent laughingly said, "Fix enough for a week, for I think we will have to sit on the railroad track tonight to eat our supper." Her injunction was obeyed. In the meantime, between the farewells and departure from Vicksburg, the excitement and terror of the Meridianites had reached its height. A mass meeting of the citizens had resolved to establish a "shot gun quarantine." This decision was wired to the conductor on the A. & V., and he was forbidden to allow any passengers to leave the car for that city; in fact, they had to go through at a great speed and stop only a few moments at Meridian.

The sisters, all unconscious of the trial before them, were sitting in the coach waiting for the conductor to come to take their tickets. He had passed and repassed and had given them only scowling looks. As the train reached Bovina, a little station ten miles from Vicksburg, it stopped and the sisters' trunks were violently thrown off the train. The conductor approached the sisters and said, "Your trunks are off the train; you must get off too; I cannot take you sisters to Meridian." Sister M. Vincent remained calm and said, "We have our tickets; we paid our fare to Meridian." The conductor became excited and said, "I have orders not to take you to Meridian." Sister M. Vincent answered, "How far can we go before we reach Meridian?" The conductor handed her a time table. By this time the attention of all the passengers had been attracted to the sisters, but Sister Vincent quietly glanced at the list of stations and smiling, said, "I'll get off at Chunky; it has a comfortable sound." This seemed to satisfy the conductor, who left the sisters in peace for the rest of the journey.

The young sisters who were accompanying sister were far from being reassured, for they had a dim recollection of Chunky, by the Chunky River, and it seemed a very lonely spot consisting of a few homes and a fishing shed. By way of excusing the excited conductor, Sister M. Vincent said, "You know, sisters, we have been in retreat; the fever has spread very rapidly in Vicksburg, and this poor man is panic-stricken because he thinks we will bring the fever to Meridian where he lives." As the train neared the destination, the sisters gathered their belongings for a final departure, and the baggage man who had taken off the trunks at Bovina now stood ready to throw them off for good. As the train drew near the lonely spot it slowed sufficiently for the sisters to alight. Here again they received a kindness for Sister Vincent's sake; one of her old boys was a volunteer flagman and he waited long enough to light a substantial torch which burned brightly after the train and the twinkling light had disappeared, leaving the woods to darkness and the desolate nuns. There was a long silence in which the sisters, sitting on their trunks in a lonely woods at 11:30 p.m., were trying to get their bearings. Who can know the fervent prayers of Sister Vincent at this trying situation?

Father Vally was equal to even this occasion, for while the City Fathers were drawing up quarantine laws of stringent necessity, he went to two of his devoted friends, Mr. A. McMillan and Mr. James Griffin, asking them to engage the services of Mr. John Semmes, who lived four miles to the west of Meridian. So busy were the loyal Catholics that soon all things were in readiness to meet the sisters at any point along the A. & V. Messrs. McMillan and Griffin drove the wagon that would carry the sisters' baggage, and Mr. Semmes and his friend from Washington, D.C., Mr. Joe Bowmar, drove the other wagon. These knights to the rescue were ordered not to bring the sisters on the main road, so they zigzagged through the woods for the entire thirteen miles.

Returning to the nuns sitting on their trunks at Chunky, we find them cheered by a light luncheon on which Sister Vincent had insisted. "Let us say our beads together," she said, "that our Lady of Mercy will help little Father Vally to see a way out of this difficulty." Not long after the rosary was recited, while our brave Sister Vincent was striving by pleasant conversation to divert the sisters from their forlorn situation, a distinct rumbling of wheels was heard and the grateful sound soon convinced the sisters that help was at hand. Then they, too, began to speak in a loud tone so as to make known their whereabouts to the gallant rescuers.

Presently a voice out of the brush and undergrowth whispered audibly, "Are the sisters there?" And presently one wagon and then another emerged from the thicket, and by the dim light of a lantern carried by Mr. Bowmar they recognized their friends who had come so far to get them. It did not take long to fill the wagons with trunks and nuns, and soon they were on their way to "Noisy Hill," where everything had been prepared to receive them until they would be allowed to enter Meridian.

In the moment of relief, better imagined than described, the sisters uttered fervent prayers that God would forever bless the heroic man who risked taking into his home and family persons coming from a plague-stricken city.

Father Vally did not know yet how his plans had succeeded, so he rode out to "Noisy Hill" early next morning, carrying with him various articles that would make the sisters more comfortable. The meeting was a joyful one, and Father and the sisters congratulated each other on having succeeded in reaching the parish where they could work for the good of the congregation in case the fever should reach Meridian. One of the City Fathers reported Father Vally's visit to the authorities, and as soon as he returned to Meridian he was arrested and given twenty minutes to leave town.[11]

NEBRASKA

Hospital, Orphanage, and Schools in Omaha (1864–1910)

Mother Ignatius Lynch of Omaha always willingly cooperated in worthwhile civic enterprises. For example, the city of Omaha was stirred by the sufferings caused by the great Chicago fire of October 9, 1871. A collection was immediately started under the sponsorship of the WEEKLY HERALD. The Sisters of Mercy, regretting they could spare no more, promptly sent a check for $50 to the HERALD office, to which the HERALD replied:

> To the Sisters of Mercy: On behalf of the Chicago sufferers and our Omaha Relief Committee, I have the honor to gratefully acknowledge your contribution of $50 to this great calamity. The munificence of this donation, coming from those whose lives are devoted to works of charity and beneficence and who are known to be poorly able to give it, will add fresh lustre to your noble deeds, and will be warmly appreciated by all classes and creeds.
>
> In justice to that gentleman, it is proper to state that Mr. Edward Creighton happened to be present when your contribution was received. He immediately handed us $50 for the sisters which is herewith transmitted.

The large portion of charity cases made the problem of upkeep of Mercy Hospital in Omaha a serious one. This difficulty the press aptly presented:

There is not within our midst an institution more deserving of the patronage of our citizens than Mercy Hospital. The sisters are overwhelmed with applications for admission, while their resources, just now, are so meagre that it is a problem of no mean proportions to make both ends meet. But a very small number of their patients pay their way, and it is positively necessary that those who do shall support the dozens of those who are unable to recompense the sisters for their care and labor. Notwithstanding their slender resources, the sisters cheerfully assume every new burden, and do their very best in every case. There are now dozens of people walking our streets who owe their recovery from disease to this institution. Only when it becomes impossible for the sisters to perform the duties so voluntarily assumed for the want of means, do they appeal to the public. In order to enable them to meet the extraordinary demands upon their charity, we would suggest the propriety of an organized effort in their behalf. The hospital is full of patients who must receive care and nourishment, and means must be forthcoming to carry on the good work. The question is, "Shall Mercy Hospital be without the necessary adjuncts to carry on the Samaritan labor?"

George M. Miller, editor of the WEEKLY HERALD (1874), retained a professional interest in Mercy Hospital. On the afternoon of June 18, 1874, he called at the hospital for Sister Mary Joseph Jennings, the superior, and asked that he might go through the institution. The account of his experiences appeared as a feature newspaper article the following day:

The building is situated among large trees on a prominence overlooking the entire city, and cooled by the pure fresh breezes from the river; no lovelier nor cooler spot for the sick could be selected.

But take into consideration the way in which Mercy Hospital is kept. Consider the scrupulously clean beds and apartments that could not offend the most fastidious, the easy chairs and large library to interest the convalescent, and above all the gentle watchfulness of the sisters, and the place becomes a Gilead.

There is something grand and impressive in a woman foreswearing the gaieties of the world and devoting her life to the benefit of mankind, asking for no return, hoping for no reward but the gracious acknowledgment of her Father. . . . Many is the poor fellow homeless, friendless, and penniless, that has felt the comforts of the hospital and has blessed the sisters in his soul. . . .

So let them continue their work of good, and if their names are not sounded through the world, if their beautiful faith and quiet piety are never appreciated, if they are unknown, save by the friendless, nevertheless there are fervent prayers rising from thankful hearts, and in heaven by and by they will have their reward.

From the very beginning Mercy Hospital lived up to its name, accepting without question rich and poor, Catholic and non-Catholic. The ticket of entry was sickness and misery which the sisters might mitigate. The average number of patients per week was about thirty-five. Of sisters, there were five. One has to recognize the fact that in those days there were no nurses' training schools to aid in the care of the patients.

Typical of the work accomplished is the report for 1874:

Year	1874
Patients	122
Deaths	16
Discharged	94
Still at Hospital	12
Charity patients	50%

The high proportion of charity patients may have been in part a reflection of the troublous days in the state as a whole, made desolate by the ravages of the grasshoppers over an area of two hundred twenty-five miles in width extending from South Dakota through Nebraska and Kansas. Within the afflicted area some 100,000 were destitute.

Quite independent of the sisters' planning, their orphanage work in Omaha commenced, an unsung labor of sacrifice and charity totally unrecorded in diocesan annals. Numerous dependent children have been nurtured by them in body and soul, shielded from the temptations that might have wrested from youth the heritage of catholicity.

The enterprise was a private one, supported by the sisters and their own exertions. Occasional donations bolstered the slim treasury. The smallness of the group prevented the atmosphere inseparable from larger institutions. Neither regimentation nor routine prevailed. Constant vigilance was necessary, but it was practiced in an unobtrusive and sympathetic manner.

Work on a new orphanage progressed rapidly. Generous-minded citizens manifested an admirable disposition to help and encourage the work. At the Convent of Mercy on Castelar Street were sixty some children, thirteen of them tiny babes in the nursery. The rejoicing was general when the orphanage was pronounced ready for occupancy in August, 1891.

One evening as two of the sisters were locking up for the night, they heard the cry of a baby on the steps. They took the tiny shivering creature into the warm house and called the police, who asked them to care for the child. Bewildered, they called a kindly neighbor who directed them in the care of the baby who rapidly gained in weight.

Woven into the warp and woof of Nebraska's development is the influence of the Sisters of Mercy who settled in Omaha three years before the dignity of statehood was conferred on the energetic territory. Their influence, hidden and measureless, extended into the homes of the poor, the sick, the destitute, and the rich. Occasional opposition came from an otherwise hearty and friendly community; occasional mistakes were made by the Congregation itself though, by and large, service was given without stint. Mercy schools—parochial, private, and college—have trained an army of loyal Nebraska youths. Mercy hospitals have meted to the needy and the wealthy an unquestioned service. For thousands of forsaken children, St. James's Orphanage has been a refuge and a home. This pioneer Congregation has left few records, has received little recognition. Poor in the beginning, it fortunately has remained so during successive decades. Of the persevering and loyal cooperation of early bishops and priests, enough cannot be said; they, with the sisters, accepted without complaint hunger and deprivation, even as the poorest pioneer. Together in hardship they laid better than they realized the foundations of the Catholic Church on Nebraska soil.[12]

NEW JERSEY, BORDENTOWN, RED BANK

Frances Warde in Bordentown, 1873

"In 1843, Mother Frances Xavier Warde, then Superior of the Convent of Mercy at Carlow, with a few staunch followers, entered the United States and established the first Convent of the Order in Pittsburgh.

"With heroic courage and indefatigable zeal, she endured long and painful journeys [and] overcame almost unsurmountable obstacles. Nor did she give up until she had founded many convents.

"Though Manchester claimed the devotion of her declining years, her heart was big enough to embrace all, passionately devoted to her spiritual children yet ever ready to give, when duty called.

". . . Rev. Patrick Leonard, then pastor of St. Mary's, Bordentown, early in 1873 petitioned Mother Warde for a colony of her sisters to help him in the work of this growing arduous mission.

"Mother Warde personally conducted the little community of five sisters to their home on the 'Hill Top.'

"With stout hearts—ever keeping in mind the words of the sainted Foundress—'To suffer with God's poor' and that other maxim so wonderfully worked out in the life of Mother Warde herself, 'The cross of Christ be always with us,' Mother Mary Joseph and her assistant, Mother Mary Raymond, accepted the conditions in which obedience placed them.

"And then was founded the first Convent of Mercy in what is now the Trenton Diocese, on the Feast of Our Lady of Mercy, September 24, 1873."[13]

Development of Congregation in New Jersey

Those sisters who formed the nucleus of the Mercy Congregation in New Jersey were Mother Mary Joseph O'Donohoe and Mother Mary Raymond Donahue. These sisters left the Motherhouse of the Sisters of Mercy at Manchester, New Hampshire on September 22, 1873, arriving at the scene of their future labors on the Feast of Our Lady of Mercy. Their future house was a two-story brick building. Some time before the sisters arrived in Bordentown, Mother Frances Warde, American Founder of the Sisters of Mercy, visited there, and secured this building for the establishment of the mission. It was formally opened by her with Mother Mary Joseph O'Donohoe in charge of the convent and school. The newcomers knew no one. They felt alone with God, entering upon a new life. We recall an amusing incident which occurred on the evening of the sisters' arrival. Father Leonard, having furnished the sisters' house with all he thought necessary or desirable, suddenly remembered that he had not put mirrors in their sleeping apartments, and desiring to remedy the oversight, he told the sexton to take one from the rectory for the time being and that others would be supplied later. The faithful sexton appeared on the doorstep of the sisters' house that evening with a pier-glass dangling from his shoulders. The sister who opened the door suddenly saw herself in the mirror. And indeed, no one enjoyed the comic incident more heartily than Frances Warde who told the story of the looking-glass at the community recreation on her return to Manchester.

Providence seemed to smile upon the mission in Bordentown and destine it for greater things. For over twelve years the sisters remained and taught school there, living, as someone expressed it, "in a little world of their own," never complaining of their surroundings or the wants or inconveniences of their class-rooms, though they were not in a most desirable condition. By this time their old building had become a crumbling structure, held together by the force of ingenuity. The walls were damp and the chilling blasts of winter came through the innumerable chinks of the time-worn floors; and no one seemed to realize that there was cold air continually felt from the broken panes of glass or worn-out casements of the antiquated windows. A fine, massive and up-to-date public school stood close by, but the Catholic pupils passed it by as indifferently as if it were not in sight, never comparing its comforts and advantages with the wants and irritants of their own old structure on "THE HILL TOP," proving by this that it was not the school building that made the scholars or contributed largely to their future well-being.

Regulations were few and easily observed; obedience was the ruling power, and excellent work in the advanced grades was the result. In the boys' senior class the gentlemen of the land could not be dealt with or spoken to more courteously, and it was marvelous to realize what an elevating effect this harmless policy had on these rough diamonds, who, in time, became gradually refined. Many a man of them since those good old days has said and written:

> I owe all that's best in me to the years
> I spent at the old school on "THE HILL TOP."

In addition to education, the visitation of the sick and the poor was always an object of tenderest consideration to Mother Mary Joseph O'Donohoe as well as to Mother Mary Regis Wade, who never failed to impress upon the young sisters' minds the privilege afforded them in the relief of God's poor. It was Mother Mary Regis' expressed wish to the sisters that they should never visit the sick poor without bringing to them provisions, clothing, or money.

The sisters had many difficulties with which to contend in these pioneer days when Catholics were pushed into the shade by bigots who believed they had not even the right to walk on the sidewalks for which they were well taxed regardless of religion. To pick one incident out of many, one day in 1885, two sisters were on their way to visit a sick person, unluckily at the hour that the local public school was being dismissed. Some of the boys ran ahead of them, shouting; "Look at the Virgin Marys! Look at the bibs!"

During the Superiorship of Mother Mary Regis Wade, the community received a gift of about twelve acres of land, located on Crosswicks Street, a little outside the town. Mother Regis undertook the erection of

Saint Joseph's Convent on this ground, it becoming the Motherhouse of the Sisters of Mercy. This building resembled in appearance a small monastery of the Middle Ages. It also served as Saint Joseph's Academy.

The Sisters loved old Red Bank, New Jersey, not too far from Bordentown, and no one enjoyed its peaceful surroundings more than Mother Mary Regis who on her missionary visits would remain several days absorbed in its quiet restfulness. At the time of which we write, bigotry was very much on the ascendancy not only in Red Bank but in many other towns in New Jersey, and the sisters had often experienced its bitterness. Directly opposite the convent some of these people had their homes. Their hatred for Catholics and the Catholic religion was so intense that it was impossible for them to conceal their feelings, unwisely acknowledging that "they would rather see his satanic majesty come to settle among them than Catholic sisters."

When the bigots were tired of denouncing the sisters as their neighbors, and after keeping a very close eye on their actions, they finally acknowledged that "they seemed to be good people who did their own work, minded their own business, and did not interfere with their neighbors. . . ." Later, these same people became staunch friends of the sisters, and more than one family became converts.

The parochial school in Red Bank was opened on September 15 with an attendance of thirty-three pupils, and in less than three months the "register" had a daily average of two hundred. As months passed, the number of pupils gradually increased.[14]

Service in Influenza Epidemic: Deaths and Death-Bed Conversions

Influenza, soon painfully familiar to all as "the flu," rode the gaunt Apocalyptic horse of pestilence across the world in 1918, galloping over nation after nation, finally cutting an ugly path of death through the stricken heart of America. To the daughters of Catherine McAuley, the fateful year 1918 brought its challenge, as it did to the rest of the world. Yet somehow, transmitted by the magic of "Fiat voluntas Tua," the challenge lost its starkness and became a plea: "Bring light to the valley! Let death's shadow shrink before divine mercy. Be lamps carrying the Christ-light!"

The dread contagion seemed to strike certain areas with particular intensity. In New Jersey, the cities of Camden and Trenton, the town of Phillipsburg, and the Amboys became sad centers of pestilence. Schools were closed; churches were barred by order of the authorities; gloom filled the atmosphere. The doctors and nurses of the cities and outlying districts worked with professional skill and personal heroism, but the tide of death continued to mount higher and higher. White coats shrugged on weary shoulders as the medical profession tried every known drug, and watched the inevitable failure. Nothing could stop the course of the flu!

The appeal of mayors and health commissioners came from all parts of the diocese. It was in substance a simple plea: "Send us sisters!" The bishop, in turn, called the Superiors of the Congregation of Mercy and placed the petition in their hands. He made but one provision: "No sister shall be assigned to this dangerous task; only those who volunteer are to go."

The most common procedure, modified here and there by local conditions, was this: two or three sisters remained in the convent, constantly preparing broth and soup by the gallons for the afflicted, who could retain nothing else, as well as nourishing meals for the children of the stricken families. Meanwhile the rest of the community was divided into two groups, one helping the feverish patients by day, the other working in the dark, despairing nights. City cars called for the sisters at seven in the morning and returned them, after their twelve-hour labors, at seven that night. Out into the gathering dusk would proceed the evening group, prepared for the long vigil awaiting them. Young sisters who had never seen death walked with gravity from one sick bed to another, feeding, bathing, and consoling the victims of this modern plague.

Particularly tragic were the deaths of young mothers for whom the doctors could do so little. Often their first kiss of greeting to the newborn was their last until eternity. The sisters proved once again the tremendous truth of the axiom: the nun is also a mother, in spirit, to the entire world. Like real mothers the nuns baptized those children likely to die; fed and cared for rosy-cheeked little ones who would live on, motherless; and dried the tears of the slightly older children who would ask so pitifully: "Has Mama gone away to stay?"

As the pestilence spread, many industrial areas closed down factory production, and converted the buildings into emergency hospitals. In busy Camden, for instance, these make-shift wards held hundreds of patients, who looked up through pain-glazed eyes at the nuns—nuns whose natural fear of the deadly contagion was obliterated, for all practical purposes, by charity. In the hilly regions wreathing Phillipsburg, the spectre stealthily stalked its prey. The people for the most part were immigrants, whose hearts had once been lifted to the glad promise made by Liberty:

> Send these, the homeless, tempest-tossed to me;
> I lift the lamp beside the golden door!

The golden door had opened to mountains throbbing with labor and

life. Now these new Americans huddled together, frightened and belliger-
ent. To these sufferers the nuns were attracted by a strong magnet—their
need, their almost despairing need. The sick in the make-shift wards were
pitiful, but those in the gray, somber hills were worse.

Into the hills the nuns went, down seemingly deserted byways, past
rickety huts and sturdy farms in search of the dying. The people of the
country-side followed two diametrically opposite patterns. Some fled the
approach of death, leaving the sick almost deserted. Others crowded
about the sufferers, finding ironic comfort in death's proximity.

Sister Mary Eugene Sheridan kept night watch over a Lambertville
family, the Brooks, all seven of whom died. The mortally-ill mother never
lost consciousness as one by one her little boys and girls closed their eyes
in a last, long sleep. Finally the hand of the baby, curling and uncurling its
infant fingers, moved slower and slower—and was still at last. Sister Mary
Eugene carried the fragile form away, but Mrs. Brooks had already seen
the end of all she cared for in this world. She closed her eyes to wait for
eternity—and six little faces!

The sisters stationed at Bordentown assumed charge of an emergency
hospital hastily contrived at the nearby town of Florence. Sister Mary
Bonaventure Hughes took matters into her strong and capable hands. The
patients, for the most part unfamiliar with Catholicism in general and
nuns in particular, were confused when they addressed her. "Sister"
sounded too familiar, and Bonaventure was a first name; they compro-
mised on "Mother Hughes." And mother she was in more than name to
the lonely and the poor.

The various Protestant ministers who aided in the hospital work were
deeply impressed by the sisters. One of the clergymen watched Sister
Mary Dorothea Ford compose with her hands the features of a dead man.
Within a few minutes he noticed her again, playing a cheerful medley of
songs for the convalescents, on an old upright piano. Shaking his head in
wonder, the minister delivered this accolade: "I've heard of the Red Cross
nurses, but these are Gold Cross nurses!"

Schools Reopened; Development in Bordentown

Within eight weeks the world began to return to its normal life.
Neighbors began to discuss the weather, taxes, prices, young people nowa-
days, the latest fashions—all the blessedly commonplace details that had
seemed too trivial during the tense weeks just past. The sisters knew that
the worst was over when they began to find on their rounds surviving
patients grouchily convalescent.

The schools re-opened; church bells pealed the Te Deum of thanksgiving that rang forth within every heart. Family upon family gathered themselves together, mourning the departed but grateful that so many had been spared. Were the sisters forgotten? No; for once deserved gratitude remained tangible in the loving smiles that greeted them on all sides. Newspapers throughout the State editorialized on their selfless service.

One of the first blessings received by the sisters was a visit paid by members of the City Council to Sister Mary Concepta Smith, Superior and Principal of Saint Mary's Cathedral School, asking her what reward the community would accept. At first nothing occurred to sister's mind. Then when the Commissioners continued their questioning, sister mentioned the Public Health Program then available to children in public schools, but not in parochial schools. "After all, gentlemen," she responded, "if we strengthen the health and correct early the physical defects of all our children in all our schools, public health in general will improve. There is nothing you can do for us, but this you can do for yourselves and for the future of your city. Make doctors, nurses, and dentists available to all children, including those taught in the Catholic school system."

The Commissioners left, thoughtfully considering the matter. Within two months the City Council had officially provided all the parochial schools with an interlocking system of free medical care for needy children, and medical inspection for all. City agencies followed suit in other localities large enough to make the move practical.

Did the sisters escape the dread contagion entirely? A few of the sisters, including Sister Mary Patrick McCallion who was dangerously ill and narrowly escaped death's early termination of her future brilliant career, contracted influenza, but all the nursing sisters were saved from its grasp. Sister Mary Patrick became one of New Jersey's greatest Mercy leaders.[15]

NEW YORK

Civil War

Patients, suffering from ghastly wounds, were brought straight from the battle-field in the most pitiable condition, the clothing glued to the wounds with clotted blood, the hair matted, the limbs hanging by a thread, as it were, to the body—mangled victims of that fratricidal war whose horrors sent a tremble through the bosom of Christendom. The soldiers were young and old, educated and ignorant, American, Irish, Creole, German—it was all the same to their kind nurses. Their hideous wounds were delicately touched and cleansed, and all that medical skill and the gentlest nursing could accomplish was done till the poor creatures, worn out with agony, excitement, and loss of blood, sank through sheer exhaustion on their pillows. The stricken had the best that could be procured of everything. The sisters were determined that nothing that they could procure should be wanting to their patients, and the local officers generally, but not always, seconded their zeal.

Once when what seemed chance brought some Sisters of Mercy into the presence of Jefferson Davis, "Will you allow me, ladies," said he, "to speak a moment with you? I am proud to see you once more. I can never forget your kindness to the sick and wounded during our darkest days. And I know not how to testify my gratitude and respect for every member of your noble Order."

A few years later ex-President Davis, now in his eighty-first year, expressed the same sentiments to the writer in much stronger language, when speaking of the stirring times of the Confederacy. The most distinguished men on both sides frequently expressed similar sentiments. On meeting the sisters on the train or elsewhere they loved to speak of bygone days, and tell how at the approach of the sisters the eye of the invalid would brighten. And yet so little could be done in proportion to the enormous pain and anguish spread out daily and nightly before their pitying gaze, that the sisters thought they had done nothing, certainly little in comparison with what they desired to do.

When their sad business came to an end, they were recalled to their convent homes. And here the sisters, aided by the rest of the community, busied themselves for many years in taking care of the widows and orphans of the brave fellows who fell on the battle-field or slept peacefully in God, soothed by their loving care in crowded hospitals.

There had been for years talk of erecting a monument of some sort to commemorate the work of the nuns of the Civil War, but until early in 1914, nothing actual had come of it. In the summer of that year, at a national convention of the Ancient Order of Hibernians, the members and the Ladies Auxiliary which met with them in Norfolk decided the time had come for active work.

Cardinal James Gibbons announced that he was heartily in favor of it and said he was glad that at last some recognition was to be given to the long file of sisters who had lessened in some degree the horrors of war for sick and wounded men by their "bright deeds of Christian charity."

The War Department had to have absolute proof of the nuns' services before permission could be given to erect a monument on government property. Immediately the data on the nursing nuns was sought.

It was indeed a labor of love, but it was to prove a very difficult matter. The names of the nurses when gathered were submitted to the various war secretaries. The work went on under three presidents, all of whom were cooperative and friendly. Many of the members of Congress helped too. Eventually, mainly due to the efforts of Speaker Champ Clark, one of the members was able to present the Nun's Monument Resolution to Congress. It had been buried in committee for almost two years. The bill was debated and passed on St. Patrick's Day, 1918, and was immediately signed by President Wilson.

Markers made of white American marble were sent as tokens of the nation's gratitude to be placed on the individual sisters' graves. Each was forwarded as soon as the record of any nun's name was verified. It was not, however, until September of 1924 that the monument was at last unveiled in Washington.

It was erected at the junction of Rhode Island and Connecticut Avenues, a handsome sculpture of marble and bronze. In the center at the top was carved a wreath which encircled a cross, and underneath it were the words, "They comforted the dying—nursed the wounded—carried hope to the imprisoned—gave in His name a drink of water to the thirsty."

Under the bronze figures of nursing nuns which formed the main part of the sculpture was the inscription, "To the memory and in honor of the various orders of sisters who gave their services as nurses on battlefields and in hospitals during the Civil War." The figures were of all the orders who had helped, and the central figure of the group was that of a Sister of Mercy.

Catherine McAuley combined the active and the contemplative life, the duties of Martha and of Mary both, just as in her own person the natural combined with the supernatural instead of superseding it. Cardinal Newmann, who had known her in the days when her Institute had just been established in England, and while he was still an Anglican, remarked in later years that from the very beginning the finger of God had been clearly manifest in the Order she had founded.[16]

Sanatorium Gabriels

In the 1890's, Bishop Gabriels of the Ogdensburg Diocese was greatly concerned over the number of Catholic tuberculous patients arriving daily in Saranac Lake, New York seeking a cure for their condition, and who were without the spiritual atmosphere and benefits of their Catholic faith. For this reason, he appealed to the then young and small community of Sisters of Mercy in New York to undertake the building and operation of a T.B. Sanatorium, similar in style and administration to the Trudeau Sanatorium in Saranac Lake. This institution was built under the direction of Dr. Edward L. Trudeau who had come from New York City to this area as a T.B. patient. He credited the improvement of his health to the wide open spaces and abundance of fresh air of the Adirondack Mountains. His cure became known throughout the country and this was the reason for the influx of ailing T.B. patients to the areas.

The initial start of Sanatorium Gabriels (named after Bishop Gabriels) was begun in 1895 when two sisters, Mother Mary Perpetual Help Kiernan, and a companion, Sister Mary McAuley Connelly, arrived in the middle of a wilderness with their only asset the sum of $15.00. The New York Central Railroad lent the sisters a small freight house which became their home for many months. Someone gave them a donkey named Dynamo to help them in their travels. Mother Mary, as the foundress and director, immediately began a life of travel seeking funds for buildings and the needs of an institution. Sister Mary McAuley remained at home and became the jack-of-all trades as housekeeper, bookkeeper, and supervisor during Mother Mary's absence. A small chicken farm was begun which provided fresh eggs, and a cow or two was obtained to supply fresh milk.

Through the influence of the President of the New York Central Railroad, the sisters were given about 100 acres of land by Paul Smith who owned and operated a hotel and a hunting lodge about three miles from Sanatorium Gabriels. The blueprints for the new buildings were drawn up by a New York State architect who became a staunch friend of the sisters. He gave all his services free and spent many months following through on the project.

Mother Mary's begging tours brought her often to the lumber camps which were erected in the deep woods many miles from the main roads. To arrive at these camps, Mother and her sister companion had to walk many miles over rough, rutted lumber roads. On arrival, the sisters always received warm welcomes from the lumberjacks, and when they left, carried with them many generous donations from all the men. On leaving the camp, again the sisters had to walk over the same rutted roads, a most exhausting journey.

Mother Mary also visited many well-to-do businessmen in their offices in the large cities. A number of these gentlemen would receive her with a warm welcome, and before she left would give her a generous donation. She also experienced a quite different reception from others. She was always a lady and expressed thanks for the visit.

On one occasion, Mother and her companion were kept waiting in an outer office for several hours. Finally, in the late afternoon, she was shown into the office of the gentleman she had come to see. She made known the motive for her visit. He listened courteously to her, but in a short time, signs were made that the visit was over. As the gentleman saw the sisters to the door, he slipped a fifty cent coin into Mother Mary's hand. She thanked him profusely. When out of distance from the office, the sister companion complained about the small donation, but Mother Mary hushed her up immediately. The sisters were extremely tired as they had been on the road all day and had had nothing to eat since early morning.

Many years later, there was a sequel to the story just told, a proof of Mother Mary's great trust in Providence. In the late 1930's Sanatorium Gabriels received a legacy of $57,000.00 given by a relative of the above mentioned gentleman. At this time, Mother Mary had died over 20 years previously.

The above gift could not have come at a better time. It was in the 1930's depression years, and Sanatorium Gabriels was experiencing great financial difficulties. The patient census was down to 16. This number could never support the Sanatorium. The depression did play a great part in the lack of patients, but not the whole part. In this same period of time, New York State politicians promoted free care to the State's tuberculous patients. This arrangement was a tremendous benefit to poor people, but many persons of means took advantage of the free care with the result that private institutions, which depended on the income from patients for the services rendered to them, soon found themselves with buildings and no patients. One by one the private institutions were obliged to close for lack of funds. Sanatorium Gabriels managed to carry on this special work until the early 1950's.[17,18]

OKLAHOMA

Indian Territory Missions

In 1857, at the request of Bishop John Augustine Verot, Sister Mary Ligouri and three sisters were sent from St. Xavier's Convent, Providence, Rhode Island, to open a school at St. Augustine, Florida. As the work of the sisters increased, Frances Warde sent new recruits to this southern mission. In 1862, the devastating effects of the Civil War caused Verot to transfer the sisters to Columbus, Georgia. Here they also suffered many trials, privations, and hardships. It was expedient to find another place of refuge. The community records show that in 1866 on June 23, Pentecost Sunday, Sister Mary Ligouri and her sister, Sister Mary Agnes Major, arrived at St. Joseph's Convent of Mercy, St. Louis, Missouri, and were admitted as members of this community.

In 1878, at the earnest request of Reverend John Powers and with the approval of the Reverend John L. Spalding, Bishop of Peoria, Sister Mary Ligouri opened a convent at Lacon, Illinois. From this community at Lacon came the first permanent religious order of women in Oklahoma.

The pastor at Sacred Heart Parish in Oklahoma was not contented with only a boys' school. So he built St. Mary's Academy for Indian girls. On September 5, 1880, six Sisters of Perpetual Adoration from New Orleans arrived to take charge. For four years they carried on the work under trying conditions. "The records of the convent . . . indicate that the great distances involved and the exceedingly trying character of the life in the Indian Territory convinced the Mother Superior that the task was too difficult." On July 2, 1884, the sisters were withdrawn. There was "difficulty in persuading the authorities of any convent to undertake the work." Father Robert of Sacred Heart Parish made an appeal to Mother de Sales of the Sisters of Mercy at Lacon, Illinois, in 1884 for needed help in the Indian Territory. The plea was not in vain. From among the volunteers were chosen five sisters who were willing to endure a life of real sacrifice and abnegation among the Indians.

The sisters and their followers came to stay even as the Benedictine Fathers had resolved to do. Both at Sacred Heart and at the many parishes and missions which the Benedictines were to found, these sisters opened schools and cooperated to the fullest extent, so that they must be accorded a large share in the honor due to those who brought the Catholic Church to the Oklahoma frontier.

The Sisters of Mercy met the Indians who had come to welcome them and also to assist them on the overland trip to Sacred Heart Church. Three days and two nights were required for this journey—a journey over prairies, through forests, and across troublesome streams. Four prairie covered wagons preceded by Father Robert in the missionary hack formed the procession.

"A tent was pitched . . . every night and like gypsies we entered our primitive quarters. Sleep no doubt would have been refreshing but for the thought of the rattlesnake, the hooting of the owl, the dog-like bark of the coyote, and the unpleasant buzzing of the mosquito." Thus wrote one of the travelers. Father Robert never thought of self. After seeing that everyone was cared for, he wrapped a blanket around him and slept on the ground. Indeed the trip was not without danger.

On the second day, early in the afternoon, the travelers reached the treacherous South Canadian River. At times it was no more than a streamlet, and then again, it became a raging torrent destroying everything in its path. On this particular afternoon it was a streamlet whose shifting white sands gleamed in the hot July sun. Since no bridge crossed it, a place for fording was selected. Brother Dominic, in the provision wagon, took the lead. All went well until the opposite bank was almost reached. One of the horses began to lag, and although urged on by the anxious lay-brother, the poor animal sank deeper and deeper into the quick-sand. With the help of the other drivers, the horse was pulled to safety. The rest of the group crossed the river at another point, not without hesitation and fear, but fortunately without another mishap. A few hours later they came in sight of Sacred Heart Monastery and St. Mary's Academy. The emotions of the sisters at the sight of their new home are well described in the following passage:

> Instead of a small cabin for a convent, a tent for a kitchen, wide prairies for a garden, the walks to which we had bid adieu, and the many little comforts so inseparable from ordinary life, which we had left behind with a good will, never expecting to see them again for years, lo! we suddenly came in view of the convent with its surrounding groves and field—the latter in waving grain; the monastery to the right—all presenting a grand surprise and delight to our longing eyes.

The news of the Mercy foundation spread rapidly. The New York *Freeman's Journal* carried the following account:

> . . . It was with great joy that they (the sisters) were received. Gladly had they left home, friends and relatives and cherished companions . . . to go whither obedience sent them, even to the little-befriended Indian. . . . They will be prepared by the fall of the year to receive and educate the children committed to their care.

Early in September, school opened with thirty names on the register. Originally a day school, St. Mary's gradually became a boarding school also, for the Indian girls. Later, at the request of white parents who had sons at the Benedictine monastery and college, white girls were admitted. Girls of the Pottawatomie Nation living near Sacred Heart, and daughters of prominent Chickasaw and Seminole Indians were enrolled. The Governor of Chickasaw Nation placed his daughter with the sisters, and a number of the officials whose families resided at the military post, as well as cattlemen of the plains, took advantage of the mission school.

The work at the mission was arduous and exhausting. In spite of sickness, scarcity of personnel, and the great amount of work to be done, other missions were opened by the sisters. On September 7, 1886, a small school was started at Krebs, a small mining town in the Indian Territory. The sisters not only taught school during the day, but after a month's time also opened a night school. In this way boys working in the mines were given an opportunity for instruction in religion and in certain secular branches. Later a commercial department was added. From this night school came the first converts.

"The ordinary conveniences of life were not available. Drinking water was brought by the barrel." For washing purposes, "water was carried from McGuire's and the sisters had to cross two stiles in doing so. A cold drink of water was unknown to them."

In those trying days, working conditions were far from ideal. Accidents were frequent in the mines. In 1892, a terrible explosion in Mine 11 took the lives of eighty men, and over 150 were severely burned. In disasters such as this, the sisters were not found wanting. The school was closed so that the sisters could minister to the injured in their homes. No hospitals existed at this time. A vivid account of this tragedy is found in the *Indian Advocate:*

> . . . On the evening of January 7th, as the miners were about to leave the mines after their day's work, a dreadful explosion took place causing the deaths of almost the entire corps of miners; only those near the next shaft escaped uninjured. Father B. Murphy, O.S.B., with his usual promptness and presence of mind, went immediately to the shaft and gave absolution to the poor dying miners, many of them members of his Congregation. For the next few days the scene at the mine was heart-rending in the extreme. Men, women, and children were seeking their loved ones and in many cases their only support. The Sisters of Mercy at once closed the school to devote themselves to the care of the wounded, with untiring charity going from one poor cottage to another, consoling the widows and orphans, and dressing the wounds of the poor suffering.

Before safety precautions were compulsory in the mines, the drug store kept vaseline in 500 pounds quantities, linseed oil (for burns) in fifty barrel lots, and antiseptics in gallon cans.

The mining industry was hazardous, yet prosperous. Many foreigners, especially the Italians, made their living working in the depths of the earth. Years later when fuel oil and gas were discovered, the mining industry declined. Krebs, the prosperous town, "became the unimportant suburb of South McAlester." In 1924, the Sisters of Mercy, no longer able to furnish teachers for the school, "withdrew from a field in which for thirty-eight years, they had sown the seeds of charity and truth, reaped a harvest of spiritual consolation, but which became a land of desolation, of ramshackled buildings and empty stores."[19]

IDAHO AND UTAH

Pioneering Sisters in Idaho and Utah

Historically concomitant with the "winning of the West" for these United States of America was the westward expansion of the apostolate of Mercy, at times challenged by a series of temporary locations before more permanent roots could be established for ministering to the needs of a regional citizenry. As evidenced by the complex origin of our Idaho sisters, this notable characteristic of frontier Merciana history prevailed even into the opening decades of the present century. Theirs is an inspiring story because in valiant, dedicated efforts to serve the shifting demands of a fast-developing western apostolate, these pioneer R.S.M.'s experienced traumatic wanderings reminiscent of the tribulations endured by God's chosen people delineated in scripture.

The seed of this Idaho saga was sown in Georgia at the 1878 religious profession of Sister Vincent de Paul Mahoney in Macon. After almost three decades of service in her native south, this remarkable woman, destined to become leader of a migrating community, began her long trek westward alone in 1904. Seeking relief for chronic asthma in the Rocky Mountains, she resided for a while with the Colorado Sisters of Mercy. While undergoing further treatment in Southern California, Sister learned of the need for a nursing facility in Bakersfield. Here in 1908 at St. Clair's Hospital was formed the nucleus of a new Mercy foundation. Two postulants received the habit in June 1909, one to become major superior of the Idaho community years later.

However, this west-coast locale proved but a brief sojourn for the fledgling group. When the Los Angeles Sisters of Mercy in 1910 were asked to assume charge of the Bakersfield Hospital, Sister Vincent accepted an offer from the Utah diocese to operate a retirement home for aged and ailing miners in Salt Lake City. Two novices accompanied her into Mormon territory. Within five years this venturesome trio multiplied to 20 members.

Despite the obvious blessing of numerous vocations, Judge Mercy Hospital, named for a local mining magnate, was an undertaking precarious from the start. In 1915 when a new diocesan prelate served sudden notice of the closing of the sisters' work, they became threatened with possible dispersion. The crisis undoubtedly aggravated Mother Vincent's delicate health. Nonetheless, her courageous trust in Providence enabled her to set about planning the orderly exodus of an intact community northward into Idaho where the sisters were assured welcome at Poca- tello, a booming railroad freight center. Like Moses of the Old Testament, the leader herself was never to reach that promised land. Anguish and anxiety hastened an untimely death at the age of 61 on September 9, 1916. A simple granite marker at Salt Lake City's Mt. Calvary Cemetery indicates the grave of the only sister of Mercy buried in the entire State of Utah.

Dauntlessly the new superior, Sister Ignatius Brady, soon led the first contingent into Pocatello, Idaho. Because their promised hospital was still under construction, for seventeen months the community rented a house where living was spartan and support came from taking in sewing and nursing in private homes of the parish. When the nation-wide influenza epidemic struck in 1917, doctors from Nampa appealed for volunteers to take charge of a small general hospital near the Oregon border. Four sisters responded, finding the frame structure so overflowing with patients that they themselves were forced to live in a tent which became their abode for the next two and one-half years. "As in a foreign land, dwelling in tents. . . ." How Biblical overtones highlight Idaho Mercy history!

Meanwhile in Pocatello three sisters were fatally stricken while min- istering to influenza victims. But slowly the apostolic seed, nurtured by suffering and sacrifice, took root and flourished at last in Idaho. St. An- thony's Hospital opened in Pocatello in 1918; two years later Mercy Hos- pital was dedicated in Nampa. After 59 years of ministry, in 1977 the Pocatello institution transferred ownership to the Intermountain Health Care Corporation, one sister continuing on the staff in pastoral care. In Nampa, 1968 witnessed erection of an entirely new Mercy Medical Center still thriving today. Through seven decades in Idaho an ecumeni- cal influence has characterized Mercy health care facilities which have always had a high percentage of patients and personnel affiliated with the Church of Jesus Christ Latter-day Saints.

Since the early 1960's, in various state locales Sisters of Mercy have also responded with zeal to apostolic needs as diversified as college cam- pus ministry, welfare work with teenage girls, and diocesan religious edu- cation programs.[20]

PHILADELPHIA, PENNSYLVANIA

Arrival in Philadelphia

The echoes of civil strife had for five months been molesting the peace of the City of Brotherly Love when Mother Patricia Waldron and the first Sisters of Mercy set foot on its cobbled streets. It was Thursday; August 22, 1861, and tradition has it that the intense heat which rose from Philadelphia's highways added much to the discomfort of the eleven pioneers. Nor was their peace enhanced by the lorries and horse-drawn trolleys that lumbered noisily over the cobblestones, shattering the quiet of their none-too-attractive dwelling. Their modern counterparts would have made note of such harassing—though perhaps no less heroically-borne—details. But no allusion to discomfort found its way into the journals of that early community. Tales of their hardships came from kind neighbors and friends, who observed their suffering and went charitably to its relief.

As they entered the house numbered 1135 Spring Garden Street, there was little to indicate that they were about to hang aloft a shield whose protecting influence was to reach across the American Continent and under whose aegis the natives of far-off India would one day know healing. Probably very few noticed the group of dark-clad figures wearing widows' bonnets and cloaks.

They were arriving from Manchester, New Hampshire, to open the first house of the Sisters of Mercy in the city of William Penn. They had come at the invitation of James Frederick Wood, Bishop of Philadelphia, and were to conduct a school in the parish of the Assumption, of which Charles I. H. Carter was pastor.

Conducting the group was the intrepid figure, Mother Frances Warde, who had already to her credit a network of schools, hospitals, and orphanages stretching north, east, and west from her original convent in Pittsburgh. It was she who, following an uprising of the Know-Nothings in Providence, Rhode Island, had said to the Mayor, "If I were Chief Executive of Municipal Affairs I would know how to control the populace," and who, with the help of a few Irishmen, had faced the mob about to attack her convent.

Her long and active life ended in 1884. Her revered remains rest in the cemetery of the Sisters of Mercy in Manchester, where she spent her last days.[21]

Classroom and Hospital

It is no small tribute to the zeal and efficiency of Mother Patricia Waldron, first Superior of the Philadelphia Sisters of Mercy, that within ten days after their arrival they had opened a day school, a night school, and an academy, with a curriculum including, among other subjects, foreign languages, literature, science, and art.

The process of conversion of the convent from parlor-bedroom to classroom involved the daily removal of straw mattresses, not to mention the triple function of refectory, community room, and infirmary provided by the adjoining room. Added to all this was Father Carter's exaction of complete and literal obedience even in matters far beyond his jurisdiction. Yet the harassing combination of hardships elicited no complaints. The visitation of prisoners and of the poor was begun and, writes Joseph L. Kirlin in his CATHOLICITY IN PHILADELPHIA, "the Sisters of Mercy . . . were summoned to act as nurses to the sick and wounded" in the hospitals established in Philadelphia to care for the veterans of the Civil War.

Lifted in blessing over the poor, the sick, and the little ones, the hands of Mercy, like the hands of Christ, must of necessity be nail-pierced. Like her valiant predecessor Catherine McAuley, Mother Patricia was to suffer the nails of misunderstanding. In less than two years after coming to Philadelphia, she and her sisters had to abandon the Spring Garden Street project and move to the basement of a house adjacent to St. Malachy Church, Eleventh and Master Streets. From the Philadelphia Superior in these trying circumstances came only the "fiat" which accompanied her acceptance of all vicissitudes during her long years of service. Not even among her intimates then or in later years did Mother Patricia ever cast the slightest aspersion on the exacting, if well-intentioned, clergyman, whose later friendship gave tacit admission to his errors in dealing with the heroic little community.

In the Sisters' new home there were no means of sustenance, and had it not been for the kindness of some parishioners, and in particular of a Mrs. Sweeney, whose three daughters later entered the Congregation, as well as of two Irish maids, subsequently members of the Community, the sisters might well have experienced hunger.

When Mother Patricia planned the erection of the first hospital conducted by the Philadelphia Sisters of Mercy in 1913, she was well aware that she was adding an indispensable element to the network of activities she had already initiated. Misericordia became the first in a chain of hospitals stretching as far as Jamshedpur, India, and ministering over the years to more than a million sick or injured.

Because they are denominational, Catholic hospitals receive no financial assistance from the state. Yet the Sisters' services are extended to rich and poor alike regardless of race or creed. Their Constitution states: "The sisters who have the special privilege of ministering to Jesus Christ in His suffering members should manifest the tender compassion of Christ." Especially in clinics and wards, where the sisters serve the sick poor, this spirit is evident, not only in Misericordia, but in the other Mercy hospitals as well. Diocesan administrators see to it that chaplains are provided to administer the sacraments daily to the patients. The visits of the sisters bring spiritual comfort.[22]

Influenza Epidemic

The Sisters of Mercy of Philadelphia, whose Motherhouse had moved to Merion, Pennsylvania, recorded the dread visitation of influenza in the fall of 1918.

Fear seized upon the bravest hearts as strong robust men, women in the bloom of life and strength, fell victims to the fatal epidemic. The populace, left to itself, fled from the haunts of suffering. The Church called forth her children and asked them to minister to the sick and dying; and throughout the whole time that the epidemic was raging, the sisters went in all directions to nurse: to their own Misericordia Hospital, to the Emergency Hospitals, and to private families, called sometimes by the attending physician, again by the families of the sick. They went about their work with Christian Charity, aiding and comforting the sick and suffering by day and by night, making no exception either for nationality or for creed. They cheerfully attended severe cases, and as soon as one patient was on a fair road to recovery, each sister transferred her sphere of usefulness to new scenes, wherever the need was greatest. The following experience was common.

Nestling among the green fields was a little Catholic homestead in St. Margaret's Parish. In one of the rooms, surrounded by pictures of God and his Saints, the young mother of the house lay critically ill. She was deserted by her friends and neighbors, through fear of the dread epidemic.

The young husband, fearful of losing the wife he so tenderly loved, asked for help of the Sisters of Mercy. Two were immediately sent, one for the day and one for the night duty. The traces of disorder, consequent upon the illness of the mother, were quickly removed from the little dwelling. Deft hands tenderly cared for the poor sufferer, leaving her refreshed for the doctor's visit. Knowing that a life hung in the balance, medicine was administered with scrupulous care and exactness, and the doctor's directions were faithfully carried out.

Feebly crying in his impoverished cot beside the mother's bed, lay a little babe a few days old. The little fellow depended on the sisters for his whole care. Like a time piece, he regularly reminded them that he was alive and waiting for attention.

Days and nights passed, during which the poor mother hovered between life and death. The dreadful fever which wasted her frame seemed to have gained the mastery. All through the silent hours of the night, the

sister watched, filling the ice cap, bathing the fevered brow, and quieting
with gentle words the wild visions of the patient's disordered brain. It was
pathetic to hear in broken sentences the quaint Irish prayers, grown as
second nature from constant use. When the day dawned, and the patient
lay exhausted among the pillows, each sister's heart sank with fear lest,
after all, the struggle was in vain. Prayers from all the sisters ascended
through the day to Jesus for the mother and her helpless little one. The
Divine Master heard their prayers, and slowly, like one rescued from the
grave, the patient recovered.

While nursing the above patient, one of the sisters contracted the
disease, and was replaced immediately by another member of the
community.[23]

PORTLAND, MAINE

Historic Account of Mercy Hospital in Portland, Maine

By the erection and operation of Mercy Hospital, the Sisters of Mercy
in Portland are carrying on a tradition established for them by their
foundress Catherine McAuley and those courageous ladies who, with her,
were the first members of their Order. Strange as it may seem to us, of this
generation, it is nevertheless an historical fact that the creation of this
tradition was accomplished in the face of tremendous obstacles. In our
day the care of the sick is looked upon as a noble profession. Within the
Catholic Church this has always been true because caring for the sick is
one of the corporal works of mercy. In the centuries which preceded the
Reformation, the spread of Christianity was accomplished by the erection
of hospitals. Their most common name was "Hotel Dieu"—God's Hos-
pice. St. Catherine of Siena, for example, typified the medieval nurse who,
whatever her lack of technical knowledge may have been, possessed the
first requisite of any nurse—that deep love which made the sick realize
that she suffered with them. We must know this truth of history if we are
to appreciate the fact that the credit for the reestablishment of nursing as a
respectable occupation among English speaking women is due to the religious orders of women in the Catholic Church. In this Mother McAuley
and the first Sisters of Mercy played a major part.

Three centuries separated the Reformation and the Crimean War.
What the Reformation had done to the attitude of non-Catholic English
women toward nursing is clear from the history of that conflict. A special
correspondent of the *London Times* in the Crimea wrote to that paper
about the bad nursing facilities arranged for the British soldiers and ex-

tolled the good fortune of the French in that respect because their nurses were the Sisters of Charity. This reaction among the people of England was intense. On everyone's lips and in every newspaper was the challenge: "Why have we no Sisters of Charity?" Everyone knows that it was because of her answer to that challenge that Florence Nightingale is credited with being the mother of modern nursing. What they do not know so well is the fact that she was ready for that hour because of her study and training with Catholic Sisters. Here are her own words:

> The Catholic Orders offered me work, training for that work, sympathy and help in it, such as I had in vain sought in the Church of England.

She volunteered to organize a corps of nurses, and in that first band of ten whom she took to the Crimea five were Sisters of Mercy from the convent of that Order in London. Mark this well. At that time the Sisters of Mercy were only in their infancy as a religious community. This convent in London was established by Mother McAuley herself shortly before her death and was the first in England since the Reformation. It was she who appointed Mother Clare as its superior, and it was this same Mother Clare who sent the Sisters of Mercy to the Crimea in answer to Florence Nightingale's summons. The hardships and privations these women suffered in the midst of all the horrors of war, the absence of so many necessary facilities and the crudity of those they did have, the death of two of their number on the battlefield—all this forms a saga of heroism.

With the inspiration of such a history and such a tradition in the care of the sick coming to them from their foundress, it is little wonder that the Sisters of Mercy have counted no sacrifice too great to be made in order to establish and maintain hospitals wherein they may carry on this part of their corporal works of mercy. Their contribution to the actual building of the Mercy Hospital in Portland, Maine was to assume the crushing burden of mortgaging all their material possessions to the limit permitted by law. As in the days of the cholera epidemic in Dublin, so today there are many who share with Catholics an almost natural instinct to entrust themselves to Catholic sisters in the moments of fear, anxiety, and suffering which accompany sickness. They agree wholeheartedly with these convictions of Florence Nightingale: "I do most entirely believe that the religious motive is essential for the highest kind of nurse. There are such disappointments, such sickenings of heart, that they can be borne only by the feeling that one is called to the work by God, that it is a part of His work, that one is a fellow worker with God." Sickness is a crisis whenever it comes. In it we depend with much of the appealing helplessness of a child on those who care for us. The Sister of Mercy by the very nature of her religious life is trained and equipped for the personal inconveniences, weariness, and exasperation of nerves which come from the exactions and often the unreasonableness of the sick. She does not measure her hours of service by a clock.

Nursing is a war against disease, but its methods do not consist in any rapid assault or a taking by storm. It means laying siege to sickness, camping before the enemy's wall and wearing him out by patient fidelity. This is the most wearisome and vexatious of procedures. For this too is the Sister of Mercy prepared by her daily religious life. The true religious spirit sees whatever is done to one of the suffering members of Christ's Body as done to Him. The religious knows the doctrine that our most ordinary actions merit an eternal reward if done out of love of God. Add to all this the acquisition of all the technical skills required by the most exacting standards of modern nursing, and you know the reason for the love and esteem with which the people of Portland, Catholic and non-Catholic alike, regard the Mercy Hospital and the Sisters of Mercy who labor therein.[24]

Education at All Levels in Portland, Maine

It is so true in life that what is easily won is cheaply held. The present crisis of our day with regard to our Catholic schools has arisen chiefly because there are not enough sisters to staff the schools we already have, to say nothing of staffing new schools which are so desperately needed. No one can know this more vividly than I. Before 1950 a pastor seldom needed to be concerned about whether or not there would be a sufficient number of sisters to staff each grade of his school. Then about 1950 enrollment began to increase to the extent that the usual late summer sermon to parents about their obligation to send their children to Catholic schools gave way to a plea for them to increase their church support in order to meet a new item of expense—the salary of lay teachers. It was no longer a question of commanding attendance. What was a more acute problem was obtaining the services of properly equipped teachers. Vocations to the Sisters of Mercy had not kept pace with the increased enrollment in our schools. With the added cost of lay teachers' salaries and the difficulty of obtaining them in the first place, we were made vividly conscious of the real truth in a tribute paid to the sisters so often in the past—the astonishing accomplishment of the parochial schools in the United States would never have been realized but for the dedicated service of our teaching sisters.

In these days when the march for civil rights for blacks has aroused our Christian conscience to a realization that we have been paying only lip service to our belief that every human being was made by God regardless of the color of his skin, the work of the Sisters of Mercy among the Indians awakens us to the fact that for all these years they have been laboring among people who, just like the black, have been deprived because of the color of their skin. Since 1878 they have persevered in their labors at the three Indian reservations in our diocese. Doubtlessly this work must have been discouraging at times. Like the black, the Indian has a sense of hopelessness of ever improving his status in society because of society's attitude toward him. How ironic it is that we condemn these people as unfit and unprepared to assume their status of equality in our democratic society, while all the time we have fostered the very system that has rendered it impossible for them to make themselves thus fit and prepared. While most people had little interest and cared less about these people, our Sisters of Mercy have remained faithful through all these years in laboring among the Indians to feed their souls with eternal truth and to develop their minds and talents. These labors form a glorious page of dedication in the history of these past years.

As we scan the chronological history of the development of the Sisters of Mercy in the diocese of Portland, we find not only establishment of schools and convents and work on the Indian reservations, but also works for the care of the sick and the needy: St. Elizabeth's Orphanage in Portland in 1873, St. Joseph's Home for Aged Women on the grounds of the present Motherhouse in Portland in 1881, Holy Innocents' Home for abandoned infants in Portland in 1907, St. Michael's Orphanage in Bangor in 1911, the Madigan Memorial Hospital in Houlton in 1915, and the Queens Hospital in Portland in 1918. In the light of their vow of "service of the poor, the sick, and the ignorant," emphasizing the special work distinguishing this Order from the others, and the work of the first members of the Order in the cholera epidemics in Dublin and in the Crimean War, we see now that the Sisters of Mercy in this Diocese in founding these institutions have been perpetuating the tradition established by their foundress.

Throughout these many years of development, the two projects which were outstanding, because of the courage and foresight involved, were the expansion of the Queens Hospital into the present Mercy Hospital, and St. Joseph's College, moved from its original location on the grounds of the Motherhouse to its present location in North Windham. Unlike schools and convents where the major burden of building and maintenance is borne by parishes, the Mercy Hospital and St. Joseph's College involved risks and burdens assumed by the sisters alone. A further cause for admiration and praise is the manner in which they have staffed both institutions with sisters possessing the required training and skills. Providing the years of graduate study necessary for acquiring these skills was an accomplishment for which they must be highly commended. That both institutions have met the requirements and maintained the standards of similar state and secular institutions in these same highly specialized fields, is for the diocese itself a reason for justifiable pride. The religious formation of the nine months of Postulancy, the two years of Novitiate, and five years of Juniorate might not surprise the critics of our Catholic schools, but I fear they do not know so well the academic studies, leading to a college degree, pursued by all the sisters, first at Mercy Institute, itself a department of St. Joseph's College, and completed at the college itself. Our Sisters of Mercy are prepared not only morally and spiritually, but intellectually, professionally, and culturally so that they may act courageously and creatively to meet the needs of our time.

"It is difficult to measure in words what the true accomplishment of these sisters has been. From a small beginning there is hardly a people or an area in the vast span of our State that has not been touched in some way by them. Not in institutions alone do their greatest contributions lie, but in the innumerable souls they have reached through their dedicated service to God." We have all witnessed their loyal performance of duty and because of it have felt strengthened in our own tasks. May God continue to shower his blessings on His devoted Sisters in Christ Jesus.[25]

PORTLAND, OREGON

Mercy Home for Business Women with Contemporary Theme

The Jeanne d'Arc Young Women's Residential Hall was opened by Mother Mary Agnes Boland on May 20, 1919.

The following tribute to Saint Joan of Arc was published on the twenty-fifth anniversary of the founding of the Jeanne d'Arc Residence Hall.

One of the first considerations in the opening of an institution is the selection of a suitable name. Catholic houses are usually given the name of a saint, with the idea that their residents may imitate his virtues and enjoy his protection. At the time of its opening, Portland's Catholic Residence for women invited its friends to send in their suggestions and recommendations in the choice of a house patron.

Probably because it was the year of the canonization of Joan of Arc, many persons asked that she be chosen. This house, then, is one of the first in the world to have been dedicated to the Maid of Orleans after her elevation to sainthood.

The choice of Joan of Arc as patron saint is in every way a happy one. Nearly everyone who reads her life becomes devoted to her. Even cynical old Mark Twain once set about to write a book ridiculing her, and ended by writing a heartfelt tribute to her. "She came with powers and with genius which should be the marvel of the whole world while the world stands." So wrote Andrew Lang in his book, "The Maid of France." Michelet, in his book, "Jeanne d'Arc," writes how "no ideal that man has conceived approached this most certain reality."

Joan of Arc is an inspiration to the Catholic who is determined to reproduce Christ in her life. Like Christ, Joan was "obedient unto death"; like Him she hated war and prayed for peace, whatever part she may have had to take in war. Joan could hate sin and still love the sinner; with all her meekness she knew how to wield authority. Like Christ she was betrayed by the very persons she sought to save; like Him she seemed to try her judges rather than be tried by them. Like Christ she experienced a most bitter dereliction and died with her cause written above her head.

The woman who works will see in Joan her own status raised to greatness. Joan was in every sense one of the people. Like all the people, she suffered for the sins of those in power, and with them she bore the penalty of war. Like any woman she grieved to leave her home and her family, and did so simply because God asked it. Like any devout Catholic she lamented the scandalous lives of other Catholics of her time, but was clear-sighted enough to keep her own faith as firm as ever.

Each year about the thirtieth of May, her feast day, the Jeanne d'Arc Residence does homage to its patron. The bishop of the diocese offers Mass in the chapel dedicated to her; residents are acquainted in a sermon with the life and virtues of the Maid. Thinking of her greatness and her lowliness, as well as her idealism, devotees of Joan of Arc are reminded of the words a modern poet wrote of her:

Omnipotence and impotence are one.
Saint Joan of Arc is riding to the Sun.

The first home for business women operated by the Sisters of Mercy in Portland, Oregon was opened in the year 1896 by Mother Mary Joseph Lynch and six companion Sisters of Mercy, coming from Morris, Minnesota, at the request of the Most Reverend William Gross, Archbishop of Oregon City, Oregon. The sisters took over the old dwelling at 31 N. Sixteenth Street, (old style) Portland, and it was known as Mercy Home. The building in 1918 could accommodate only twenty-five. At this time it was estimated that fully 5,000 young women were in Portland earning their livelihood away from their homes and without home influences. There was at all times a lengthy waiting list.

The Sisters of Mercy hoped to build a new Home to meet the rapidly increasing demands of young women applying for residence at Mercy Home. The permanent guests were most eager that the opportunities for home-like accommodations, such as they enjoyed, should be extended to the large number of young women applying daily at the Home, and whom the sisters had to refuse because of lack of rooms. The young women co-operated in every possible way and campaigned for funds. Within a short time five thousand ($5,000.00) was raised. This start by the forward looking young women resulted in a new organization under the leadership of Reverend Edwin V. O'Hara of St. Mary's Cathedral, Portland, Oregon. The campaign of these inspired workers raised by public subscription the sum of forty thousand ($40,000.00) dollars within three months.

Restrictions on building materials resulting from conditions relative to World War I, 1914–1918, rendered the erection of a new building impossible at that time. The Sisters of Mercy were therefore obliged to relinquish their plans to build. The Most Reverend Alexander Christie, Archbishop of Oregon City, Oregon, zealously advocating proper provision for young women, exercised his foremost efforts in the immediate solution with the successful result that on May 1, 1919, purchase was made of the building then known as the Virginia Hill Hotel. The Sisters of Mercy took possession of the one hundred thousand ($100,000.00) dollar hotel on May 20, 1919. The cost of furnishings and equipment added to the purchase price the sum of forty-five thousand ($45,000.00), making a total investment of one hundred forty-five thousand ($145,000.00) dollars. The Jeanne d'Arc Residence Hall was the culmination of a dream.[26]

PROVIDENCE, RHODE ISLAND

Founder of the Convent in Providence

Reading the life story of two remarkable women, Catherine McAuley and Frances Warde, we are brought face to face with a fact that must have been clearly apparent to their contemporaries. Intimately close friends as they were, joined together in a voiceless, spiritual covenant to bring to successful issue the work that each felt was the Creator's own ordaining, yet theirs were of so strongly contrasting temperaments that, in the reading, we stop and muse. The Foundress, sweet, gentle, even tempered; Frances Warde, ardent, impetuous, moved by a flaming spirit of fire in all that was for God. Nevertheless, although so dissimilar, they were as one heart and one soul in an all-absorbing love for God, and an over-mastering love for the neighbor. And as we become cognizant of their similarities and dissimilarities, we say: Why, here is the germ of the substantial life of the Sister of Mercy; an intimate blending of action and of contemplation.

When in 1830, Catherine McAuley, influenced by force of circumstances and advised by friends, undertook the organization of a Religious Institute, she and two others, Sister Anna Maria Doyle and Sister Elizabeth Harley, placed themselves under the direction of the Presentation Nuns, George's Hill, outside the city of Dublin, in order that they might be formed for what lay before them. Frances Warde, with eight others, remained behind to continue the administration of Baggot Street House. During this time, trials because of deaths, and trials because of other harassing difficulties, brought out in strong relief the power of control that was in her. A power that only those who are called in a signal manner to spread the Kingdom of Christ, seem to possess, and are able to bring forward when opportunity comes. Then in January, 1832, Frances Warde, with six other candidates received the religious habit of the new Order that had been founded December 12, 1831. And in 1838, she with three other novices pronounced their vows at a ceremony which was the initial Religious Profession in the Congregation of Mercy. Frances was the first to make such vows.

Mother Warde was an Apostolic woman in every sense of the word. Sufficient proof of this is given in the array of foundations created by her in Ireland, then indirectly in Australia and New Zealand, then in the United States, where innumerable convents were established under her special direction. It is believed that in the inauguration of these convents, she traversed more miles than St. Paul himself in his many journeyings. The magnificent, the inspired work of directing the spread of the Institute of Mercy was begun by her in Carlow. Its convent was the first of its kind built outside the Irish capital, and at the time of erection, it was considered the finest conventual structure in Ireland. From its very opening, St. Leo's, the Carlow house, prospered both in the spiritual and in the material sense. God's blessing seemed to rest upon it visibly. A happy omen as to the future.

Every one of Frances Warde's foundations, even Carlow itself, began in the poorest and smallest way. But, Mother Warde had a wonderful spirit of poverty. Her thoughts on this virtue served to bring home the truth, that the soul possessed of poverty of spirit must be imbued with charity, because as she said: "The truly poor in spirit have no ambitions, no personal interests, no clashing of the will with that of another. All these are buried in the Will of God." She illustrated in her daily life that saying

of Catherine McAuley: "We should cherish holy poverty as a Mother";
and remembering that He, the Divine Spouse, loved poverty and consecrated it in His own person, this brave follower of Catherine inspired her
sisters with actual courage in making the best of inconveniences entailed
by poverty. And the Lord Himself, not wishing to be outdone, blessed her
foundations with a success far beyond all that she hoped for.

Frances had a boundless attraction for those not of the Faith. There
was within her a yearning for all outside the Church; the same longing that
has animated the missionary in every age, a love that seeks to win all to
God. She reached forward to the other sheep; she felt for them, and in
feeling showed an affection that was truly remarkable. This particular
form of zeal, love for conversions, never left her; in her dealings with
converts she "was able to bring the vague aspirations of a groping soul into
a clearness which surprised even the seeker himself." On into her latest
years, with that wonderful power of touching the heart, she still continued
the instruction of her dear converts. And they on their part responded
with the ardor of the early ones, asking admittance to the Church. This
desire of bringing to God souls who had never known Him was associated
with the desire of a never-resting haste after those who had fallen away
from their religion. Only the day of judgment will reveal all that Frances
accomplished in leading to God souls who had not been of the Faith, and
in bringing back strayed ones to His feet.

In the government of her communities, Mother Warde availed herself of every means to train her daughters in solidly grounded principles of
the religious life. She constantly repeated to her Religious, "Keep your
thoughts buried in the Divinity, and busy yourselves in spreading God's
Kingdom in the hearts of men." Emphasizing Mother McAuley's saying,
"Anything savoring of sadness shortens God's arm," she urged upon
them to take up each difficult task as if it were the only hard thing that
would ever confront them. And in asking them to face the disagreeable,
the arduous, she herself was at all times the living example. She would
repeat, again and again, "Since God loves a cheerful giver, let us try to be
cheerful workers, taking nothing away from the glory of His service by
half-heartedness in our duties. We must be steeped in holy joy and eager-
ness to imitate our divine model in labor and prayer; in teaching and
instructing; in consoling the sick and the sorrowful."

A very beautiful quality in one governing was hers in a high degree:
she invariably saw noble traits in those she dealt with. She worked with
certain souls, defective in character or training, as if they needed but a
little more polishing, and she polished, carefully, tenderly, until the diamond, deeply hidden before, shone out in its brilliance. She had shown
these souls that the desire of human nature to be trusted was well under-

stood by her. She had shown them that all the while she had held a high estimate of their worth. Hence the result.[27]

The young and the fair came from all points to the old stone mansion which became the first Mercy Convent in Providence, Rhode Island. Harriet Kelly, an Irish girl for some years resident in New York, who might have posed as a professional beauty, and Eliza Bradley of Rochester, both ladies of no small intellectual ability, were the first Sisters of Mercy to make their vows in New England, and they made them in the dim old chapel in Providence. Others speedily followed. In six months twenty-one candidates were received. These young religious labored, under very adverse conditions, to spread the kingdom of God. In their daily walks to and from the parish schools, and on the visitation of the sick, insults and opprobrium were heaped on them by the fanatics who represented the religion and culture of the Providence of that day. The epithets which these refined exponents of liberty and equality bestowed on the Sisters will not bear repetition; it is sufficient to say that the religious never once appeared on the streets without exciting some one or other of the "natives" to anger.[28]

Bigotry in Providence

The threatened attack upon the convent, which occurred in the spring of 1855, culminated the series of insults toward Mother Frances Warde personally and officially, and toward the sisters in her convent from the first week of their arrival in Providence.

For about four years the Catholics of Providence had been suffering these annoyances—for whatever hurt the nuns afflicted their friends still more—when, one morning, they were astonished to see pasted on the walls and fences of Providence small bills—8 × 10 inches—worded as follows:

AMERICANS!
TO WHOM THESE PRESENTS MAY COME.
GREETINGS:
Whereas, certain rumors are afloat, of a certain transaction, of a certain ANTI-SAM party in the vicinity of the corner of Claverick and Broad streets, every true Native American Born Citizen is requested, one and all, to assemble there, Thursday Evening, March 22nd, 1855, at 8 o'clock, precisely. There with true regard to Law, and consulting the feelings and sympathies of SAM, proceedings of the most solemn and unquestionable nature will be transacted.

One and All to the Rescue!! The Password is "SHOW
THYSELF."

So great was the excitement that the heads of some of the leading
Protestant families went to Bishop Bernard O'Reilly and offered the protection of their homes for the sisters until danger would be over. Bishop
O'Reilly was both surprised and grateful for this evidence of their good-
will and sympathy, but while he sincerely thanked them for it, he said he
thought it better that the sisters would remain in their convent, and for
that reason could not accept the kind offer.

Fearing that a mischievous few might precipitate a riot, the Bishop
felt it his duty to call upon the aid of the State and municipal authorities
for military and police protection. A large body of police was stationed
around the convent, orphan asylum, and grounds, and continued there
for several successive nights, though in greatly diminished numbers. Several bodies of militia were ordered to report at their armories and hold
themselves in readiness to march to the defense at a given signal.

The convent—as that seemed the main point of attack—and
grounds were put in a state of defense. The cellar door opening on Claverick street was walled up with solid masonry; the strong wooden shutters
and iron bolts with which the windows had been provided when the house
was built, were now found most serviceable for protection. When evening
came, the cellar had its score of armed, courageous men, guns well
primed; the garden fence on Broad and Foster street had its complement;
the open space on Claverick street, where the excavation for the cellar of
the new orphan asylum had been commenced, was barricaded and a
strong posse of men stationed there with watchword, while the little orphan children had a double guard. On the first floor of the convent building that evening a few gentlemen—Protestant and Catholic—were
assembled.

The hours were passing. Everything was quiet outside. As far as the
eye could reach, up or down the streets, back into the lanes and alleys, was
a dense mass of heads. Even the windows of the houses around were filled
with anxious spectators, some being personal friends of the sisters then in
the convent. Sometimes a groan of derision would be heard, then a general laugh. A pleasant good-natured gathering it seemed, but the quiet
patience with which everyone remained on the spot, scarcely moving,
boded no good to those who would dare to begin hostilities. Of the two
thousand assembled all were friends—whatever their creed or nationality
—and the sisters' fears had long ceased to be for themselves or their helpless charges, but lest any harm should befall their defenders.

After the lapse of some hours, Bishop O'Reilly requested that the

Riot Act be read. The Mayor seemed very reluctant to do so, but a gentleman was present who had a mortgage on the estate, and insisted on his reading it. The Mayor, thus urged, complied; the Riot Act was read and the crowd dispersed. One policeman remarked that he had never before seen so good-natured a mob.

For the remainder of the night—or rather morning—the streets wore their usual deserted look.

The Catholic gentlemen who had so bravely come to the rescue were not satisfied, however, for they formed certain numbers of their comrades into companies that took turns for many a night afterward in watching over the safety of the convent, until assured there were no further grounds for alarm.[29]

The following editorial had appeared in the *Providence Journal,* March 22, 1855:

"Some mischievous fool has placarded in the streets an invitation for a mob to assemble in front of the Convent of Mercy this evening.

"The nearest way to the watch house is by College street, but if any rowdies prefer the more round about course of annoying and insulting defenseless women in their own house, they can accept the invitation offered. The placard would be most atrocious if there were any chance that its suggestions would be acted upon, but this we do not regard as possible.

"Should an attempt be made to violate the laws, the authorities lack neither the disposition nor the means to preserve the peace of the city, and they would have the support of all the friends of law and order of every Party."[30]

ROCHESTER

Travel in Care of the Sick, Service in Influenza Epidemic

With the division of the Diocese of Buffalo, an Episcopal See was established in Rochester, and Bernard J. McQuaid of Newark was consecrated Bishop in 1868. Upon his first visit to Auburn, the Bishop found affairs in such a sad condition that he immediately made such changes as he deemed necessary and beneficial for the Sisters of Mercy.

Among the many interesting happenings that occurred in Auburn, the following might serve to illustrate how much the modes of travel have improved since the early days there. In the fall of 1876, two of the sisters were sent to visit an invalid many miles from Auburn. They were driven to their destination in a lumber wagon. The patient thoroughly enjoyed their visit and assured them that they would have a conveyance to take them home. Imagine their chagrin when the "conveyance" proved to be a "hand car." There was no alternative: so the nuns were "pumped" home on the railroad tracks by two sturdy and honored men. Since those days many changes have occurred in Auburn! Holy Family Parish has now one of the finest churches and schools in the state. It has also added a high school to the grammar department.

In every city in the Diocese where the sisters labored, they offered their services in caring for the sick, especially during the "flu" epidemic of 1918. They spent weeks at the Epilepsy Colony at the Sonyea Hospital, while the sisters from Mount Carmel and St. John's worked with the Red Cross nurses in an improvised hospital on Davis Street. There many a heart-broken child poured the sad story of the loss of a loving father or mother into the ears of the willing sister listeners, who, at times, found it hard to repress their tears. The sisters went to the hospital at eight in the morning and did not return to the convent until eight at night. It was while they were there that the false news of the Signing of the Armistice was received, and not even one was able to describe the grateful faces of the poor, stricken "Flu" patients at this seemingly joyful news.

The sisters from St. Mary's and from other convents also did both day and night work with the black people of the city, and they were an object of the greatest interest to the black sufferers, as well as the recipients of every courtesy that it was in their power to bestow on the nuns. In Oswego the sisters were especially commended for their work among the "Flu" patients, for many of the social workers were too terrified to allow themselves to run the risk of contracting the dreaded disease. God certainly takes care of his own, and despite the fact that a great many of the sisters were in the midst of the sufferers from the beginning to the end of the epidemic, not one of them succumbed to it.

In 1917, eighteen acres of land on Blossom Road, a part of the estate of Patrick J. Tolan, was given to the Sisters of Mercy of the Rochester Diocese as a site for the new Mother House of the Sisters.[31]

ST. LOUIS

Foundation

The Sisters of Mercy of St. Louis, founded from New York in 1856, faced severe obstacles in their new foundation: hunger, poverty, and loneliness. Then came a day of dread decision. While the foundress, Sister M. de Pazzi Bentley, was seriously considering returning to New York from

St. Louis, one of the sisters approached her saying: "Mother, we have not a loaf of bread in the house to feed the sisters, and we have only one dollar to our names. What are we going to do?"

"Do," mused Mother M. de Pazzi. "I don't know. Wait a little and I shall go into the chapel and pray. The Lord will help me make up my mind." While she was still praying, a man rang the doorbell. The portress was handed an envelope and without a word the unidentified man left. Inside the envelope was one hundred dollars. The sisters never discovered whence the money came. From the day that Mother M. de Pazzi wrestled with the problem of survival as she knelt in supplication before the tabernacle, the sisters placed all their problems in their Master's hands. Their confidence was rewarded. God raised up others to assist them in their work.

Service in the Civil War

Motivated by compassion for the victims of the Civil War and by loyalty to Archbishop P. R. Kenrick, Mother M. de Pazzi, shortly after the capture of Camp Jackson, wrote to the Archbishop offering the Convent of Mercy as a temporary hospital for wounded soldiers should the need for more accommodations arise.

While the St. Louis Sisters of Mercy visited the wounded and the prisoners in the city, a contingent of Sisters of Mercy from Chicago came to St. Louis and later moved to take charge of Jefferson City hospitals. Southerners looked askance at the group; the sisters were unknown in that section of the country. It was not long, however, until suspense and prejudice were allayed and the sisters were believed to be heaven-sent.

When the army moved on in 1862, the Sisters of Mercy left Jefferson City to the accompaniment of serenades sung by the soldiers—Protestant and Catholic alike. The men in uniform, the civilians, and all who came in contact with the sisters had come to love and revere them.

The Sisters made many trips on the churning old boat going to Pittsburgh Landing, back to Shiloh, thence to St. Louis and to Louisville. The only joy in those weary months was their opportunity, during a landing, to attend Easter Sunday Mass and to receive the Sacraments. It was their privilege to bring peaceful resignation to numberless dying men who might otherwise have felt only despair. They effected many conversions. They listened to many deathbed confidences, and carried last messages to loved ones at home. Boys, in blue and gray alike, came to look upon the Sisters of Mercy as their only confidantes. What the Sisters of Mercy did in that great national crisis served to spread respect and understanding for the Catholic faith as nothing else could have done.

Pension School

By a graduate of the "select" school of the Sisters of Mercy in St. Louis, written in 1955:

"As far back as I can remember—1872—I entered the private school conducted by the Sisters of Mercy, located on Twenty-Third and Morgan Streets. This one room was to the back of the building. Sister M. Mercy Brennan conducted the classes from first to eighth grade. There was no kindergarten in those days. The tuition was twenty-five cents a week.

"The students started with a primer, learned their A.B.C.'s and then advanced probably to the fourth reader. More attention was paid to catechism, penmanship, and spelling than at present. The older girls were sometimes assigned to look after the younger girls. Mother M. de Pazzi, the Superior, was planning to build a new chapel, which was eventually built.

"As the sisters were contemplating the expansion of their hospital facilities, the original school room was taken for that purpose, and the classes were moved to a small house on Morgan Street, adjoining the convent. By that time the senior students were preparing for their first Holy Communion. This took place in the convent chapel. It was a big event."

Soup House

A report of the Immaculate Conception Conference of the Society of St. Vincent de Paul in St. Louis in 1861:

"We regard the spiritual works of mercy to be one of the most important works of the conference. Our operations in this respect have been under the care of our spiritual director, the Sisters of Mercy, Sisters of Charity, and the regularly appointed visitors of the conference.

"The St. Vincent de Paul Society established a store under the charge of the president of the conference to distribute food to the poor.

"In addition to the store they opened a 'Soup House' for the benefit of the poor residing outside of the parish which was under the charge of the Sisters of Mercy. The conference furnished them material for the Soup House; the sisters attended to the visiting of the poor applicants and to the distribution of articles among them.

"During the cholera epidemic of 1866, the sisters worked unceasingly with the sick in the plague-stricken districts of the city. The district nurse, so much heralded today, finds her early counterpart in these pioneer Sisters of Mercy who waited not for misery to come to them but sought it out in the homes of the poor."[32]

Prisoners

When prisoners were under sentence of death, the sisters of St. Louis visited them as frequently as possible, and made every effort to aid them spiritually and to turn their precious time to fullest profit.

The conviction that religion can be a powerful factor in the rehabilitation of prisoners led Sister Mercy Brennan to use her influence in having Mass celebrated in the city jail on Christmas Day, 1886.

On this occasion the jailer allowed all prisoners to attend the service. "The Catholic prisoners who had been to confession the previous day approached Holy Communion at this Mass, each bearing a card which read: 'AD COMMUNIONEM, Christmas, 1886,' and was subscribed with the confessor's name." The following day the event was recorded in the newspapers:

CHRISTMAS DAY
Jail Occupants Treated to a Religious Surprise
The First Mass Ever Celebrated Within the Four
Courts—Santa Claus and His Gifts
Among the Poor

Because prisoners given more than a two-year sentence were not permitted to remain in the city jail, constant departures and replacements occurred. This arrangement gave the sisters an opportunity to meet, though briefly, men and women of all races, nationalities, and creeds, persons sentenced for virtually every type of law violation.

It is clearly obvious that this field of mercy was so large that the sisters' influence was restricted by the time and means at their disposal. Though many flaunt their opinions about the absurdity of spending time and energy in endeavoring to rehabilitate those who have run afoul of the law, the sisters realized that many individuals appeared before the courts of justice more from lack of character in resisting evil than from malice in wrongdoing. The following letter, written by a prisoner to Sister M. Mercy Brennan, is proof that many resolutions made in jail are kept following release:

May 20, 1892

Dear Sister:

   I thank Reverend Mother and you for the consideration
which you show me. You marvel at my present condition. It is
the old story of a desire to get rich in a moment, lack of experience, and betrayal on the part of supposed friends. All three of
these things have contributed to place me where I now find myself. Experience is a dear teacher and my experience has not
been without benefit to me. In the future my guiding star will be
the old adage, "A shoemaker should stick to his last." Had I
stuck to my profession I would today not owe a dollar but besides would have money to my credit in the bank. . . . I ask no
compromise. All I want is time and I will pay every dollar I owe.

                                              Respectfully yours,
                                              E_____ G_____

   Another letter from a former prisoner, who later did very satisfactory
work in one of the institutions operated by the Sisters of Mercy, proves
that many prisoners profit from their experience and justify the confidence placed in them by employers:

   All my hopes for the future are wrapped up in this parole, because I know the last six years have worked a wonderful change
   in me. I am afraid even to think of what three or four more will
   do—or should I say what I shall do with them. I like to think that
   I have used the opportunities which God has given me. And
   used them well. Maybe I have earned another chance. God
   knows I've worked hard to be a better person than I was.

                                              _____ No. 85726

Night Refuge

   The Night Refuge opened by the Sisters, or Night Hospitality as it
was later called, offered shelter to poor women who could not be admitted
to the working girl's home, because they were accompanied by very young
children or for some other reason. "Many were cared for in this refuge
every year who, without money, could not secure lodging elsewhere, and
being strangers were ineligible for admission to the city institutions."

   The Night Refuge was also used by women from out of town who, for any reason, had to remain in the city overnight. On one occasion Mr. Alexander P. J. Garesche addressed the following letter to Mother M. de Pazzi on behalf of one of his clients:

> *St. Louis, Missouri*
> *26th November 1884*

Rev. Mother M. de Pazzi
St. Joseph's Convent of Mercy
Dear Rev. Mother:
    I ask of you if you will receive an old woman who came to town to consult me. She awaited my return to my apartment. But I never return until after dinner (7 P.M.). I know nothing of her, but honestly believe her to be a good woman. She owns property, so she says, and so I believe. But I can do nothing for her professionally. Let her have a lodging for the night and breakfast in the morning.
    The little boy who accompanies her is not her son, but one who, to oblige me, accompanies her to show her the way.
    With great respect—Your friend and obedt. servant,

> Alex P. J. Garesche

From the time the Night Refuge was opened in 1876 until it was discontinued in 1911, an average of 2,632 women received hospitality every year. Assisting Sister Magdalene Dowling in the administration of the Night Refuge were Sisters Angela Molloy and Martha Kettler. When these sisters discovered women in need of work, they referred them to the employment office in the Young Girl's Home.[33]

TENNESSEE

A Century of Service in Tennessee: The Spirit of Mercy in Nashville

    It is indeed a temptation to wax eloquent about the great part the Sisters of Mercy have played in helping the Church advance from the state of a struggling infant to its present respected and influential position in the state of Tennessee, but I have deliberately chosen another topic.
    Let me pursue the point of the spirit of the Sisters of Mercy. Since this spirit is made up of many intangible elements, I shall not try to define it. However, since all of us here today are friends of the sisters, I am confident that each one has a good idea of what I am trying to describe.
    I think that this spirit is the result of the sisters' concerted and untir-

ing search for the good, the true and the beautiful in all the things which God has made. Since the search leads them inevitably to God Himself, the sisters retrace their steps and show to others what they have found, the path that seems so clear to them. They find the search exciting and enriching, and somehow they manage to communicate this same excitement and enrichment to those whose footsteps they try to direct.

One cannot long be in the presence of a Sister of Mercy without realizing the closeness of God's presence to her. She seems to be so close to Him, that it makes His nearness more believable and understandable and, above all, more desirable to others. Those who have been deceived into believing that virtue is dull and uninteresting can profit much by spending time with the sisters.

Because any school boy is convinced that sister reverences truth, his most authoritative argument about any subject is, "Sister says." Because she plays so important a part in the development of his mind, the teacher places a stamp upon that youthful character that is well nigh indelible. Knowing full well the importance of a good education, she drills and challenges, corrects and inspires those confided to her care. They are her sacred trust. At the same time, she is at her best, perhaps, when she assists the troubled boy or girl who lacks confidence or outstanding natural ability. How many of us who are here today owe our positions in life to the hard work and inspirational qualities of some dedicated teacher who taught us to believe in ourselves. We were shown and made to believe that dreams can come true for those who are willing to work.

In one area we must say a word about the spirit of the Sisters of Mercy. Into a Southland that was devastated by the Civil War and its aftermath, these cultured ladies brought their love for and appreciation of the beautiful. A tradition established under such adverse conditions has been faithfully carried on by generations of the Sisters in good times and in bad. Thousands of lives have been made richer by a taste for good music and art and literature acquired under their guidance. The sisters have imparted by word and example a manner that has added immeasurably to the cultural standards of those whose lives they have influenced. Just as an example—those pleasant, inviting parlors, to be found in Mercy convents throughout the state, have shown many a housewife of limited means that good taste can quickly make up for the absence of costly furnishings.

One could go on and on in recounting the blessings the Diocese of Nashville has received through this past century of service from the Sisters of Mercy. Even though, since 1929, our Tennessee Sisters are no longer diocesan but through amalgamation have become a part of the Province of Cincinnati, they still cherish the key role they have played in the progress of this diocese. Those sisters who were not born here but who have come to work in Tennessee seem to have grasped and come to share the outstanding loyalty and pride in the Church's progress throughout the state.

From these schools have come many vocations to the priesthood and the religious life. Nashville is unique among Southern dioceses in the predominance of native sons among its priests. In my mind there is no doubt that such a happy condition stems largely from the early training and example of the sisters in our parish schools. More than 50 priests now serving in this diocese received at least a part of their early education under Mercy guidance. The older sisters always took great pride in the fact that the late Samuel Cardinal Stritch and our own metropolitan, the Archbishop of Louisville, were products of their training. More than 100 girls have joined the ranks of the Sisters of Mercy or other orders, who first learned about the religious life in Mercy schools. And who can count the pillars of the Church among the devoted laity, living and dead, who first learned to love and honor God under the direction and good example of the sisters whom we honor today?

It would be an impertinence for any one of us to say that he fully appreciates the extent of the sisters' influence for good. God alone knows how often and how extensively He has used these willing instruments to accomplish His miracles. It follows that only God can render them the kind of thanks and reward that is their due.

I wish I could convey to the sisters how happy and honored I am to be the spokesman for the clergy and the laity of this diocese in assuring them on this occasion that we appreciate and value the work and sacrifice that is their very life. We further assure them of our prayers and loyal support as they begin their second century of a "Return of Love." Ad multos annos!

By Francis R. Shea[34]

VICKSBURG

Civil War: A Unique Mercy Experience

On November 7, 1861, a charter of incorporation was approved under the title of "Sisters of Mercy" in the City of Vicksburg "for the purpose of establishing and maintaining an Academy and Free School in the City for the education of female children, and also maintaining a House of Protection for homeless and indigent females to qualify them by training and education for the discharge of domestic duties as well as to enable them to procure protection and support. Also for the purpose of establishing and maintaining an infirmary for sick people." Five young women, one of them a Vicksburg girl, Martha Newman, offered their services to the new foundations and sought admission to the Order.

The first two years were, however, filled with foreboding and suspense over the coming war. Although the sisters had received two liberal loans amounting to $2,000 with which they purchased lumber for building purposes, the uncertainties of the time warned them against completing such an undertaking.

Their fears were well justified, for in 1861, Civil War was declared. During the next twelve months the importance of Vicksburg to both sides became apparent to all. "All the inhabitants fled into the surrounding country; those who could not get houses camping in the woods, and living in caves which they dug in the sides of the hill." For the first time, and sad to say, not the last, in May, 1862, the sisters were forced to close their school. Father Leray, wholly aware of the imminent danger, sent them to Major Jared Reece Cook's plantation outside the city. But they offered themselves to the Confederate army to serve in the capacity of nurses. Three sisters returned to the convent in Vicksburg to care for the wounded, only to find that "sickness, terror, death reigned everywhere. Soldiers without shelter, or else lying on the bare floor, were scattered through the town." Finally, a makeshift government hospital was established at Monroe, Louisiana, and the sisters were solicited to operate it.

Thus was inaugurated a series of wanderings throughout war-torn areas; the sisters followed the stricken warriors while enduring almost unbelievable distress, adversities, and privations. Their work at the Monroe Hospital was such as is ordinarily required of men. Since, however, the sisters made no complaint concerning their strenuous occupations, it was not until their excessive labors were brought to the attention of a superior officer that they were relieved. Fortunately, this hospital was soon closed, and the sisters were transferred to Mississippi Springs. Hardly had they organized their work at Mississippi Springs, caring for as many as 700 soldiers at a time, when the hospital was abandoned by the government because of its remoteness from the battle fronts. The sisters were next invited to nurse at the Deaf and Dumb Institute in Jackson, which had been turned over to the use of the Confederacy for the duration of the war. Observing, however, that those already in charge had complete control and that their services were unneeded—or unwanted—the sisters withdrew within one week of their arrival. From Jackson the little band of Sister nurses moved to Oxford. Again their stay was short-lived, for at the end of a month's time word was received of the approach of the Federals toward that city. The hospital had to be evacuated immediately. Within three days all the wounded, except those too ill to be moved, departed in every available conveyance. The sisters found themselves once more in Jackson; now however, at the request of Doctor Warren Brickell. This second sojourn of the sisters in Jackson lasted from December, 1861, to July, 1863, when at last Vicksburg fell; and the Federals turned their cannons westward towards the capital.

Jackson, nevertheless, was able to hold the enemy at bay for a short period; at length it, too, was forced to succumb to a stronger arm. Towards the end of the siege of Jackson, when the sisters' particular situation became quite precarious, Father Leray, their constant companion, arranged to have them lodged in the capitol building itself. As central Mississippi was now almost entirely controlled by the Federals, the Confederacy, at Doctor Brickell's behest, moved its wounded completely outside the state across the border to Shelby Springs, Alabama, followed again by the faithful little group of nuns and Father Leray. Here they remained for almost two years until 1865 when peace was finally restored.

Constantly the sisters were faced with this uncertain, nomadic existence and continuous unsureness of their own security as well as the safety of the many helpless under their care. In addition they met with prejudice, dirt, lack of facilities, at times little or no personal privacy let alone comforts, and a want of man-power. Many of the soldiers, because of preconceived ideas concerning the sisters, refused their ministrations at first. On occasions when civilian help was rendered to the government hospitals, the sisters watched as other institutions received aid while they were offered none. If doctors or superior officers failed in their duty toward the wounded, the blame was often passed on to the sisters. They were even suspected of espionage.

The only hospital which was clean upon the sisters' arrival was the Deaf and Dumb Institute in Jackson. At every other place they were greeted with dirt, filth, and disorder. Furthermore, because of the poverty of the Confederate army and the confiscation by the union forces of the meager stores which the Confederates did possess, the work of the sisters was greatly hampered by insufficient facilities—Shelby Springs did not even boast cooking utensils—and worse still, by a shortage of food. Though the sisters "had refused all compensation from the beginning" of their employment by the government, it was mutually understood that their ordinary living needs would be provided. But a greater suffering to them, rather than their own deprivation, was to see the sick soldiers suffer from want.

When transferring from place to place, the sisters traveled in freight cars, slept sometimes on mattresses, but more often on the bare floor or leaning against their luggage. Once their train was derailed and the cars turned over. No one was injured; but when Sister M. Ignatius Sumner in her childlike confidence refers to this incident, she declares that "our dear Lord takes care of his own under all circumstances." Because of the scarcity of anything black, the sisters mended and re-mended their habits with white thread; while rabbit skins served as shoes.

Probably the greatest hardship which the sisters were asked to face was the lack of personnel. It is characteristic of new religious foundations that members are never wanting. Inspired by the self-sacrificing spirit of a particular religious group and attracted not only by the opportunity of giving their life to Christ, but also, possibly, by the novelty of a new and different Congregation, youthful subjects flock to the young Order and seek admission. Thus it was with the first Sisters of Mercy in Mississippi. Within two years, the group of six had almost doubled itself. But with the advent of the war, followed by reconstruction, the membership of the little band of nuns suffered great adversities.

Many reasons for this seeming paradox come to mind: the insecurity of the times, the sacrifices which the war put upon all, and the wanderings of the sisters which prevented their making permanent personal contacts. Sister M. Ignatius even goes so far as to make this comment concerning the consequent result of the civil conflict upon the people: "The demoralizing effect of the war was such that it was easier to die well than to live well." Whatever the cause, at the end of the war in 1865 the sisters numbered only ten, one less than when the war began. They had gained one postulant but lost two. Nor in the years of reconstruction did many volunteer; often those who did come were found unsuitable. Too, death claimed some quite suddenly. By October, 1870, when the young community celebrated its tenth birthday, its records showed the following; entered, 22; dismissed, 8; dead, 4, leaving a total of twenty. And yet, astonishing though it may seem—and certainly imprudent when viewed by the progressive moderns of the 1990's—by October, 1870, these twenty sisters had opened two branch houses in Pass Christian and Jackson.

With all its demand upon the patience and endurance of the sisters, the war was not wholly void of consolation, both human and spiritual.

Through the selfless God-like charity of their nurses, the very soldiers who had mistrusted them and felt revengeful towards them were won over to entire confidence. With total faith in the goodness of his nurse, one convalescent declared, "Sister, can it be that you are the people that I have been taught to hate?" The conversions among the Confederate soldiers and the Union prisoners, of Protestants as well as fallen-away Catholics, were numerous.[35]

YREKA - RIO VISTA - RED BLUFF

Service of Little Children

The Sisters of Mercy who traveled across America from Manchester, New Hampshire, to Yreka in Northern California to establish a Mercy mission suffered many trials in the early eighteen-seventies as they moved from Yreka to Rio Vista and to Red Bluff, and finally became a part of the San Francisco Congregation. All of these hardships are recorded, but a unique sad note remains in the letters of a little girl who was a boarding student at the Yreka Academy, lovingly urged by the Sisters to write to her father after her mother's death. The father did not answer the letters of his little girl. Following are four heart-breaking examples of the letters of the lonely child. They indicate how the sisters sought to make life more pleasant for their little boarding students.

> *St. Joseph's Academy*
> *Yreka, California*
> *February, 1872*

My dearest Papa

I hope you get this letter because it is the first one I ever wrote you. I am well and studying my lessons very hard. I hope you will come to see me very often. I would like to see you very much. I hope you are well. I wish you would please get me a comb and brush. Don't forget to send me some nuts this summer. Papa, did you get wet when you were going over to Humbug? Were you tired? I hope not. I have to go to supper in a little while so I will stop. Give my love to Mrs. Barton.

> Goodbye my dear papa
> This letter is from
> Annie

March 16, 1872

My dearest Papa

I hope you are well. I received your letter and answered it last Saturday week but received no answer. I suppose you are very busy or you would have written to me. Do you often see Mrs. Barton. When you do give her my love and also Katie McCann and tell Mrs. Barton that my eighth birthday will come on the first of April. Dear Papa goodbye now from your fond child

Annie

St. Joseph's Academy
Yreka, California
March 25, 1872

My dear Father

I have written to you twice but received no answer. I hope you will answer this or I don't know what I will do, perhaps fly off to Humbug and surprise you there some fine night.

We have such nice weather here. We went to the top of the mountain in front of the Convent and we had a picnic there. We were all tired when we returned and slept well that night.

Dear Papa when are you coming to see me. It seems so long since we were together.

Goodbye my own dearest Papa
from your fond child
Annie

(Annie's father remarried, so Annie now writes to both parents.)

St. Joseph's Academy
Yreka, California
Jan. 6, 1873

My dearest Papa and Mama

How have you been since I saw you last. I hope you enjoyed yourselves during the holidays. I was disappointed that you did not come over for New Year as you know I had a little piece to speak expressly for yourself. However I spoke it and substituted Father Farley for you. We had a very happy time during Christmas. I got a great many presents. Did Santa Claus pay you any visits in Humbug. I hope he did as he was very kind at the

Convent. How is Mrs. Barton and Mrs. McCann. Give them my love and accept the same from your fond child.

Annie[36]

Notes

1. *Alabama Heritage,* University of Alabama, Winter, 1989, pp. 12–13, 16–17.
2. Sister Mary Augustine Roth, *Written in His Hands,* Laurance Press Company, Cedar Rapids, Iowa, 1976, pp. 42–43, 193.
3. Sisters of Mercy, Chicago, *Reminiscences of Seventy Years,* 1846–1916, The Fred J. Ringley Co., Chicago, Illinois, 1916, pp. 27, 30, 51–52, 99–101.
4. Mary Lucille McGee Middleton, RSM and Marjorie Elizabeth Allan, RSM, *The Quality of Mercy,* Lincoln Press, Royal Oak, Michigan, 1980, pp. 185–87, 190. The following pages on the Civil War, while referring to Sisters of Mercy all over the States, are included here because they were researched and collected by the Detroit Sisters for their Archives.
5. Mary Lucille McGee Middleton, RSM, *Mercy on the Battlefield,* Detroit Province, 1980, pp. 10–13.
6. Archives, Detroit.
7. Single Page, Author Unknown, n.d. Archives, Detroit.
8. Mother Mary Frances Xavier (Leeson), *Sixty Years,* Magnificat Press, Manchester, N.H., 1929, pp. 32–37.
9. Sister M. Benigna Doherty, RSM, *The First Hundred Years of the Manchester Sisters of Mercy,* Privately Printed, Manchester, New Hampshire.
10. Sister M. Lucille McGee and Sister Marjorie Elizabeth Allan, *Quality of Mercy,* Lincoln Press, Royal Oaks, Michigan, 1980, pp. 161–63.
11. Mother M. Bernard McGuire, *The Story of the Sisters of Mercy in Mississippi (1860–1930),* New York, P.J. Kenedy and Sons, 1931, pp. 51–61.
12. Sister Mary Edmund Croghan, *Sisters of Mercy of Nebraska.* 1864–1910. Catholic University of America, 1942, pp. 56–96.
13. Sister Mary Ignatius Hogan, *Memoirs,* Archives, North Plainfield, New Jersey.
14. Sister Mary Ignatius Hogan, *Mercy Memoirs,* Written in 1920s and early 1930s.
15. "Light in the Valley—1918." Type-written Manuscript, Archives, North Plainfield, pp. 1–7.

16. Katherine Burton, *His Mercy Endureth Forever,* Sisters of Mercy, Tarrytown, New York, 1946, pp. 228–29.
17. Sister M. Consolata Kelly, *Heritage,* Archives, Dobbs Ferry, New York.
18. *Annals of the Sisters of Mercy, New York* (1846–1920), Archives, Dobbs Ferry.
19. Sister Mary Mercedes Morris, R.S.M., *The Sisters of Mercy of Oklahoma,* Catholic University of America, October, 1947, pp. 9–15. Archives, St. Louis.
20. *Commemorating Pioneer R.S.M. Spirit*—On to the Rockies, Bakersfield, Salt Lake City, Utah, Pocatello, Idaho, pp. 1–4. Archives, Silver Spring, Maryland.
21. *A Century of Mercy,* 1861–1961, Sisters of Mercy, Philadelphia, Pennsylvania, p. 10.
22. *Ibid.,* p. 15.
23. *Philadelphia Annals,* Book IV, pp. 1–2. Archives, Philadelphia.
24. William G. Cunneen, *The Sisters of Mercy Celebrate Diamond Jubilee,* 1873–1948, p. 12. Archives, Portland, Maine.
25. "The Sisters of Mercy Celebrate Jubilee of Foundation in Portland, Maine (1873–1948), "*The Church World, Portland,* May 28, 1948. Unsigned Article.
26. Twenty-Fifth Anniversary Celebration: Jeanne D'Arc Young Women's Residential Hall, Portland, Oregon (1919–44).
27. Carroll, *Annals,* III, 1888, p. 392.
28. *Ibid.,* pp. 393, 395–406.
29. Sister Catherine Morgan, *A Little Sketch of the Sisters of Mercy in Providence,* 1851–1893, T.A. and R.A. Reid, 893, pp. 25–27, 30–32, 40–41, 50, 74–75, 89.
30. Sister M. Josephine Gately, *Seventy-Five Years in the Passing, Providence Visitor Press,* Providence, Rhode Island, 1926, pp. 32–41, 82–83.
31. Sister M. Antonia Hyde, *Mercy,* George P. Burns Press, Inc., Rochester, New York, pp. 27, 53–54.
32. Sister M. Elizabeth Jean De Muth, RSM, *The Mercies Will I Sing, 1961,* Chapter, VI, pp. 15–22.
33. Sister Mary Isidore Lennon, *Milestones of Mercy,* Catholic Life Publications, Bruce Press, Milwaukee, 1956, pp. 18–31, 95, 101, 104, 105, 121.
34. Sister Mary Loyola Fox, *A Return of Love,* The Sisters of Mercy in Tennessee, 1866–1966, Bruce Publishing Company, pp. 16–17.

35. M.M. Bernard McGuire, *The Story of the Sisters of Mercy in Mississippi,* New York, P.J. Kennedy and Sons, 1931. pp. 56–101.
36. Annals of Sisters of Mercy in Yreka, Rio Vista, and Red Bluff. By Sister Agatha Marie, RSM, Mercy Academy, Red Bluff, California, pp. 6, 8, 9. Archives, Burlingame.

IV.

BIOGRAPHICAL SKETCHES

211

INTRODUCTION

If a student of Mercy spirituality in the late nineteenth century were to attempt to write of the personal characteristics of the great spiritual leaders of the Mercy Institute, several books would be required. To choose a few biographical sketches of a number of these women offers at least a hint of the holy lives they led. It would be foolish to refer to the "plaster saints" who were "canonized" by romantic writers of the last century. The following brief sketches in no sense "gild the lily." All of these Mercy leaders were human, with human faults. Others might just as easily be named as the ones chosen.

A Passionist priest companion of Frances Warde's friend, James Kent Stone, was once asked to write down his impressions of Father Fidelis Stone's heroism. He wrote:

"Since heroism in the evangelical virtues is the supreme test applied by Mother Church in calculating the merit of her saints, rather than the absence of human traits, Father Fidelis should rank high on this score. It could not be said of him, as Disraeli in fine sarcasm said of Gladstone, 'The man has not a single redeeming fault.' Father Fidelis was adorned with his full quota of faults. Like Liguori, Patrick, Augustine, Paul, he was intensely human in his faults. There are some persons so weak mentally or spiritually that they take offense at the human in God's servants. They cannot bear to know the whole truth about even an Apostle. But those who best know the human in Father Fidelis admired the heroic in him all the more. His heroic love of God, and of perishing souls, flamed forth more gloriously from the human setting of his faults. It was intensely real in an intense human being. We who have no experience and scarcely an understanding of his sacrifice, we must all bow to his heroism."

It is good to keep in mind thoughts such as these when we consider the spirituality of the Mercy Sisters of 1850–1900. There are historic and personal reasons for choosing the ones named in this chapter, but some of the least known Mercy Sisters can lay claim to a profound spirituality known to few. Only God knows the spirituality of his children. But now and then a human being receives the gift of putting a loved one's spirituality into words.

In the long run, perhaps the essay of the Sing Sing prisoner captures best the Mercy spirituality of the late nineteenth century. It has been suggested to the editor that no prisoner could write so magnificently of Mercy spirituality. Perhaps. If Prisoner No. 50,940 had a mentor who helped him, thank God for it.

213

*   ·   *   *

MOTHER FRANCES WARDE'S FAMOUS JOURNEY
FROM CHICAGO TO PITTSBURGH

When the Sisters of Mercy reached America in 1843, Father William Quarter, Bishop-Elect of Chicago, was the first to bid them welcome to the New World. After a few words of greeting, he begged Mother Warde, the founder, to give him a colony of Sisters of Mercy for his new diocese. She made a provisional promise.

Three years later, in 1846, Bishop Quarter renewed his request, and Bishop Michael O'Connor urged Frances Warde to redeem her promise by sending a foundation of sisters to Chicago. On the 18th of October, 1846, Mother Warde with five sisters, Agatha O'Brien, Vincent McGirr, Gertrude McGuire, Josephine Corbett, and Eva Schmidt, left Pittsburgh for the West. They were arrayed in secular garb, as the wearing of the religious dress would have exposed them to great danger in those "Know-Nothing" days.

Traveling was difficult at that time, and many perils beset the party on their journey. After six days of incredible hardship and fatigue, they reached their destination, but as it was thought they would travel by a different route, there was no one to meet them when they arrived in Chicago, on Mercy Day, September 24th. They made their way to the Episcopal Residence, a one-story frame building. The Bishop gave them a most cordial welcome and then accompanied them to the church to thank God for their safe arrival.

Mother Warde remained with the Sisters in Chicago until the end of November. Then, when they were well established in their new home and everything was in "working order," she left them to return to Pittsburgh. A heavy storm was raging on November 27, when she took her place in a wagon in courtesy called a coach.

To spare the young sisters the fatigue and danger of coming for her from Pittsburgh, she got permission from Bishop Michael O'Connor to travel alone. Bishop William Quarter wished to accompany her, but this she would not allow. An invalid priest, who was going to Allegheny to visit relatives, offered to look after her comfort, but was too ill during the journey to give attention to anyone but himself. The route seems to have been different from that taken in going to Chicago, as no such great inconveniences are mentioned on the first journey. In the grief of parting, all forgot the lunch basket, and so poor Mother Warde was two days and two nights without tasting food.

When Frances looked at the hardened faces of the men who surrounded the taverns where the stage stopped for meals, she chose to suffer hunger rather than partake with them of the coarse food of the taverns. Part of the journey was made in an ox cart that jolted and bounced until every bone in her body seemed to be dislocated. As Mother Austin Carroll remarked, "Traveling alone across the vast prairie was indeed terrifying. No sound could be heard at night but the snoring of the passengers, the howling of wild beasts in search of food, and the screeching of prairie chickens."

When the driver of the vehicle called out "Toledo," Mother Warde inquired if there was a Catholic Church in the town. Receiving an answer in the affirmative, she resolved to rise early the next morning that she might have the happiness of hearing Mass and receiving Holy Communion before continuing the journey. But the next morning, when she opened the door of the poor hotel where she stayed, she found the snow piled in great banks and the wind blowing a perfect hurricane. However, she ventured out in the snow. She called a coach, but the driver, after taking her a short distance, made her depart; he would not attempt to go farther. She was forced to make her way through heavy snowdrifts to the church where, to her great joy, she was able to receive her Lord in Holy Communion. The good priest, Father Louis de Goesbriand, showed her much kindness, and saw that she reached the hotel safely after the storm had abated.

The following morning she left Toledo in a rickety old stage coach, which broke down when it had gone about ten miles. It took the passengers two hours to procure logs from a nearby woods to raise the coach out of the mud. In the meantime, Mother Warde sat in the coach, fearing each moment that one of the wild beasts of the prairie would make its appearance and devour her. At last the passengers were on the road again, but before they had gone many miles the stage fell into a rut and two yoke of oxen gotten from a farmhouse were required to draw it out of the hole.

After leaving the prairie, the stage driver informed the passengers that they were now in a region where the hills were so steep that they would have to get out and hold back the coach to prevent its falling forward on the horses; otherwise, all would likely tumble into the deep ravines that bordered the road. In the jerking of the stage, an iron bar fell on Mother Warde's head, but her fellow-travelers made no more account of this accident than if she had been struck by a straw.

At Brownsville, the coach stopped at a clean-looking hotel, but as Mother Warde had tasted no food since she left Toledo, her stomach would retain nothing. After the passengers had taken their evening meal, they were ready for the steamer to Pittsburgh. The boat was connected with the river bank by an unsteady plank, covered with sleet which was falling heavily. However, all crossed safely, and at 3:30 a.m. the boat reached Pittsburgh.

Mother Warde found no one waiting for her at the wharf. Evidently the sisters had not received her letter sent from Chicago. So she went out into the dark morning, rain and sleet falling about her, to try to find the Penn Street Convent. When she reached the convent and succeeded in opening the outer gate, she rang the doorbell, but the bell did not awaken the sisters. It was fully a half-hour before the door was unlocked and poor Frances, her clothes saturated with rain and splashed with mud, was taken into a place of warmth and shelter.

There being no longer a necessity for exertion, she collapsed. She was at once hurried to bed, and Dr. William Addison was summoned. The doctor declared her condition was such that any movement, or an attempt at taking food might prove fatal. For ten days her recovery was considered doubtful, but her strong constitution and the assiduous care of the doctor and sisters at length brought her through the dreadful attack. It is said, however, that she never fully recovered from her terrible sufferings on the journey from Chicago.[1]

SISTER CAMILLUS BYRNE: CLASSIC EXAMPLE OF SERVICE

In 1844, Sister M. Camillus Byrne, godchild of Catherine McAuley, accompanied Mother Mary Agnes O'Connor to New York. In 1854, she joined Mother Frances Warde in Providence, R.I., and in 1856, she was sent by that Superior to assist Mother Catherine Wynne in Baltimore. Here she remained for the rest of her life, a period of twenty-nine years. Love for the poor was a passion with her. No matter how ungainly or even filthy a child might be, Sister Camillus would not repulse her; on the contrary, the greater the moral or physical needs, the greater her zeal for those she was called upon to succor.

But devotion to the sick was the grand feature of her life. For a quarter of a century at the convent on Poppleton Street, she had charge of the visitation of the sick. There was not an urchin in any lane or alley for miles around the convent, not a convict in the Penitentiary, or an outcast in the House of Correction, who did not know Sister Camillus. Her ability for imparting catechetical instruction was unsurpassed. She possessed a peculiar talent for reclaiming by her sympathy and her zealous words the most abandoned. The number of lives reformed through her instrumentality, of conversions effected by her zeal, and of souls led to embrace the faith by her instructions, is known only to God. The good she effected in penal institutions would suffice to render the life of any individual remarkable. Yet this was but one item in her career.

No one ever possessed a kinder, more tender, or more forgiving heart, and few Religious have been blessed with a more perfect community spirit. Even in old age, this venerable nun would go to the top of the house to oblige the youngest Sister in the convent. A tale of sorrow regarding any of God's people would draw from her tears of sympathy. From the officials of the State Prison, County Jail, and House of Correction—all non-Catholics—she received the greatest respect. After their first visit to the State Prison, contrary to the regulations, the Sisters' baskets were never searched. The prisoners crowded around her to hear her instructions, and she proved, under God, the means of bringing many of these poor men to the faith. One of the convicts who, through her instrumentality, was pardoned a little before his death by the governor and removed to the City Hospital, died in the faith.

In the sick-room her interest in every detail of the patients' troubles, and her impressive manner of praying, made her visits a consolation to the poor sufferers. For a few years before her death she moved to Mount Washington, Baltimore, where she gave instructions to externs. All the early members were of the community of Sisters celebrated for their skill in giving instructions. But Sister Camillus had a special gift in this way, and, like those among whom she had been reared, she was a brilliant conversationalist. A New York Monsignor used to say that he would willingly undertake the journey from New York to Baltimore for the pleasure of conversing with her, or of hearing her give instructions to her poor![2]

SISTERS OF MERCY IN SERVICE
THROUGHOUT CALIFORNIA AND ARIZONA

The story of Mercy in California dates back to the pioneer history of the State. Just five years after the discovery of gold, Mother Baptist Russell and her volunteer group of eight sisters arrived in the raw young City of San Francisco, December 8, 1854. In response to the plea of Archbishop Joseph Sadoc Alemany, they left their quiet convent home in Kinsale, Ireland, to do their work of mercy among the wretched poor and distressed of the seaport town.

There were, however, before the close of the century other groups of Mercy Sisters who contributed to the story of Mercy in the Golden West. Mother M. Camillus McGarr and three companions in 1876 opened a school called St. Gertrude's Academy in Rio Vista (half way between San

Francisco and Sacramento). These sisters had left the Manchester community in 1871 to work among the poor in the mining town of Yreka. Unfavorable conditions there forced them to seek another area for the exercise of their zeal. A very small group of sisters in Ukiah, California, was amalgamated with the Rio Vista sisters in 1903. These sisters had come from Eureka, California, where their Superior, Mother M. Josephine Cummings, had gone as a novice from the Convent of Mercy, New York, in 1871. For twenty years they had labored for the poor, especially the Indians, before asking to be incorporated into a larger community. The Rio Vista sisters became a part of the San Francisco community in May, 1917.

Two other pioneers in the works of Mercy in California were Mother M. Michael Cummings and Mother M. Bonaventure Fox. Both of them knew Mother Baptist Russell and were encouraged by her to undertake the works of mercy they pioneered in the southern part of the state. Mother Michael and her companion were from St. Louis and together they laid the foundation of the later flourishing community of San Diego. The Mercy Hospital in San Diego and St. John's in Oxnard, California were the fruit of the small beginnings made in San Diego in 1890. Mother Bonaventure and a companion from Grand Rapids, Michigan, in the same year offered their services to Bishop Francis Moran of Los Angeles. They opened homes for the working girl, the orphaned, and the aged. Schools were also staffed. Among them was St. John's Military Academy located in Chatsworth. In 1912, the Los Angeles sisters took over St. Clair Hospital in Bakersfield. And in 1913, a New Mercy Hospital opened there. Also, several schools were opened in Bakersfield—St. Francis (1912), Our Lady of Guadalupe (1920), St. Joseph's (1925).

The Arizona portion of the Mercy Sisters owes its beginnings to the sisters who came from St. Louis in 1878 to Mesilla, New Mexico. Mother M. Josephine Brennan and five companions, after laboring heroically in Mesilla, went to Silver City, New Mexico, where they had both hospitals and schools. Changes in the diocesan boundaries caused changes in the administration of the community: Mother M. Paul O'Grady, who was elected Superior in 1887, and five sisters went to Phoenix in 1892 where they opened a school. Later the motherhouse was moved from Silver City to Phoenix. Service in the schools was discontinued in 1903, and St. Joseph's Hospital which had opened in 1895 was the single apostolate in that city. Hospitals in other cities and towns of the area were operated by the sisters for as long as the need existed, but by 1940 St. Joseph's Hospital, which originally served miners and railroad workers, was the work of mercy that superseded and excelled the others in the quality and extent of its health care services.

The sisters in Arizona had long desired to be united with the Mercy Houses in California. The first step toward this union was effected in 1921 when the Arizona Sisters became one with the Los Angeles-San Diego community. Later in the same year, all the sisters voted to be amalgamated with the San Francisco communities. This goal was effected by a Rescript of the Holy See, March 27, 1922.

The California Motherhouse was transferred from San Francisco to Burlingame in 1924. By 1932, the new Burlingame Motherhouse was completed. This foundation in time required expansion, and in 1963 the novitiate-juniorate wing, McAuley Hall for the administration, and Russell Hall, the college, were added.

Today the Burlingame community continues to quest for the most effective way to witness to God's mercy in the modern world. Among its services are five large hospitals in California and Arizona, a School of Nursing in the University of San Francisco, sixteen elementary schools, six high schools (two community-owned), one home for the aged, and one foreign mission in Peru. The community has also pioneered in establishing much needed psychiatric clinics especially to help disturbed youth. The same openness of spirit and faith that inspired Mother Baptist Russell and her adventuresome followers to cross an ocean and a continent to meet the unknown needs of a strange land now motivate the untiring search for new ways to show God's mercy "from generation unto generation" in a rapidly changing universe.[3]

MOTHER MARY PATRICIA WALDRON: MODEL OF COMMUNITY SPIRIT, CHARITY, AND LOVE OF THE CHURCH

No one who came in personal contact with Mother Patricia Waldron could escape the impression that she was endowed with eminently high qualities of Christian womanhood. Her natural and deep sympathy was enhanced by a clear mind, calm temperament, never-failing tact, and a simplicity begotten of singleness of purpose, which made her solicitude for the welfare of others prompt and efficient. She was an admirable manager, and men of the world who had business with her were outspoken in their recognition of her sagacity, her high sense of integrity, and her unswerving justice in all transactions.

She possessed by nature a tenacity to duty which would absorb all her faculties for the time being. She was little concerned with rivalries and ambitions, and took no note of the doings of others, unless it were to speed their good work, or to learn from them how she might do her own more perfectly; native nobility of character placed her above the temptation to criticize.

This is the impression which she has left on those who knew her best in life. She belonged to the class of great religious superiors, women like Mother Seton, Madame Duchesne, Mother Warde, and Mother Austin Carroll who have blazed a spiritual trail through the secular underbrush of American life, by which thousands are enabled to reach the true faith and the joys of heaven.

A certain simplicity characterized Mother Patricia's devotions. She did not lean toward, nor encourage, a multiplicity of diverse exercises which might be but the intermittent vagaries of individual piety. Her principle was to attend and perform punctually, and well, the common exercises of prayer to which the *Rule* called the members of her order. She felt, rightly, that there was a special blessing on these exercises because they were done under obedience, prevented singularity, and stifled that self-elation which accompanies acts of ostensible virtue when they tend to separate us from the community.

In like manner, her exhortations and lectures were characterized by simplicity and attractions which made you conscious that the words were but the rhythm of the music that was being made in her heart by the accord of the spiritual truth which she uttered with her own desire to correspond to it in action.

Love of Church

She knew no distrust or doubt of the loving purpose of Divine Providence, though that purpose might strike ever so far from mere human calculations and destroy the present earthly paradise of imagined hopes. Hence the humors of disappointment were wholly alien to her disposition.

Yet it would be altogether mistaking her disposition to believe that this conformity to the Divine Will, without a trace of passive resignation to indicate that she was making any sacrifice, was due to the absence of temperament or purpose. She had very definite views of what she wanted to be accomplished, and with a strong tenacity strove to obtain results in harmony with the beneficent purposes of her institute. Whatever project she undertook, she first considered all its details and consequent responsibilities. Then she recommended it to God, urging the combined prayers of the Community to that end.

Moderation

The habit of religious moderation was manifest in her voice, her gestures, her walk. There were no traces in it of aloofness, or of that prudishness which suggests censure; yet it would have been impossible for any one to display in her presence levity or vulgarity without at once feeling humiliated.

Charity

Her charity to the poor was commensurate with her personal love of the virtue of poverty. She never hesitated an instant to relieve to the fullest extent of her ability the cases of distress that came to her. The writer knows instances in which she gave absolutely the last money she had in the house to some poor woman in need of her rent.

"We came here to serve the poor and the sick and the ignorant." With this obligation in mind, she insisted that the sisters should make it their business to visit the sick in the parishes wherein they taught school, or wherever they might be called. They were thus not only to relieve the miseries of the poor in the material order, but to comfort them, and if need be, prepare them for the sacraments and for death. Indeed, any case of distress called forth her spontaneous cooperation; and in these matters she never asked, by way of following a precedent, what others did. She simply consulted her own present resources and the sympathy that moved her to action.

Work and Recreation

In Mother Patricia's community there were no drones. They could not have lived in the atmosphere created by her own incessant example of activity. In truth the spirit of mutual helpfulness that has always characterized the sisters was one of the things that must have struck even the casual visitor to the Merion Mother House or its dependencies in the Archdiocese. If one nun was called away from some duty that required attention, another would quickly slip into her place, to take up the work, so that no one would suffer. Frequently, especially on feast days, there was music, hilarity, and fun that betrayed quite unsuspected funds of humor and natural capacity to amuse. This cheerful spirit made Mother Patricia very happy. Sometimes at these recreations she would read a letter of interest to the community, or a story, or some entertaining bit of information from a periodical. She was an excellent reader and could hold the attention of her hearers in a marked way.

She laid particular stress upon the duty of every member of the community's cooperating to maintain the spirit of family cheerfulness. She did not think the convent was the place for persons inclined to sulk or to nourish private grievances. Morbid sensitiveness was a thing she warned her daughters against as a subtle danger to the peace of community life. "We must avoid giving offense—that is the duty of common Christian charity."

A True Model

There was no sphere of the religious life in which she was not a model for the imitation of the sisters. She had early begun to give herself unreservedly to the guidance of those who sought to perpetuate the spirit of Mother McAuley by the observance of the duties imposed by the *Constitutions* of her Order. An aged sister who had known Mother Patricia as a novice wrote on the occasion of her death: "I had the good fortune in the first days of my religious life to be led on to the beauty of our holy state by her beautiful example."[4]

MOTHER CATHERINE SETON:
SERVANT OF THE POOR, THE SICK, AND THE PRISONERS

The first candidate for admission to the new New York community was *Josephine Seton,* youngest daughter of the celebrated Mrs. Eliza Ann Seton, foundress of the Sisters of Charity in the United States. Josephine Seton had been carefully brought up at Emmittsburg, and had improved her mind by foreign travel under the protection of her friends of the Carroll family, at whose home near Baltimore she had spent much of her time. Though blest with a religious vocation, she felt no attraction to the congregation established by her mother.

When she consulted Bishop John J. Hughes of New York as to her future course, he advised her to wait patiently a little longer. "I know of an order," said he, "that will satisfy all your aspirations, and I intend to introduce it into my diocese very soon." On her introduction to Mother M. Agnes of the Sisters of Mercy, all arrangements were made for her entrance. As to years, she was in her forties, but in disposition she was as young as the youngest member.

On April 16, 1847, she received the white veil from Bishop Hughes, who preached with his usual graceful but vigorous eloquence. Bishop

John McCloskey, his coadjutor, was present with a large number of the clergy; also, many of Miss Seton's friends and relatives, mostly Protestants. From the first, this Sister devoted herself in a special manner to the relief and instruction of the sick poor, and the inmates of hospitals and prisons. This service she continued until she was incapacitated by age. For many years, every Catholic prisoner executed in New York was prepared for death by her, and as late as 1888 she still took a lively interest in all the works of the Mercy Institute.

Mother Elizabeth Seton's granddaughter, Miss Helen Seton, followed the example of her aunt; she received the white veil from Cardinal John McCloskey, who was a personal friend of her family. Both ladies assumed the name Mary Catherine; as Catherine was the name of the venerated foundress, it was a favorite name with Mother M. Agnes. The New York Convent, like the parent-house in Dublin, is dedicated to St. Catherine. Mother M. Catherine Seton was professed as a Sister of Mercy April 17, 1849, on which occasion Bishop Hughes preached.[5]

MOTHER TERESA MAHER, FOUNDER OF SISTERS OF MERCY OF CINCINNATI: A REMEMBRANCE AND A EULOGY

In speaking of Mother Teresa Maher, founder of the Cincinnati Sisters of Mercy, one he knew so long and so well, Archbishop Purcell was several times overcome by the intensity of his feelings. For though he had been, God so permitting, the instrument of bitter grief to her, he had always esteemed and revered her. Mother Teresa was undoubtedly one of the great women of the Order of Mercy, and her works remain to praise her in the gate. Her children rise up to call her blessed. Her most salient characteristic was uprightness, and she was, in every relation of life, the soul of honor and sincerity. She certainly had nothing in her composition of the softness that leads to self-indulgence, or passes over as trifling, delinquencies that may have serious consequences. But no one made larger allowances for human frailty; often she would say of her Sisters: "They are doing the best they can; they mean well; we shall all be perfect when we go to heaven."

Large-hearted, generous, and trusting, she combined the simplicity of a child with mature wisdom. She loved the young with special tenderness, and her relations with them were marked with a genial warmth. She foresaw her death; the chief events of her life had taken place in November, and in the last summer of her life, she used to say that November would decide much for her. At her own request, she received the last sacraments several weeks before any one perceived immediate danger. Her life had been always marked with the cross. Nothing extraordinary came into her experience, as sometimes happens in lives consecrated to God in religion. Performing uncommonly well the common duties of every day, as the *Rule* recommends, she was a burning light to her associates, and her memory is held in benediction in the convent so long sanctified by her presence.[6]

MOTHER DE PAZZI BENTLEY:
HARDSHIPS OF EARLY NOVITIATE DAYS IN ST. LOUIS, MISSOURI

From 1856 until 1861 the novitiate was located at Morgan and Tenth Streets. When this convent became too small for the needs of the growing community and a new convent was erected on Morgan and Twenty-Second Streets, the novices moved to this location. The ensuing years saw a slow but steady increase of vocations to the community. This increase created a housing problem. Mother M. de Pazzi realized only too well that the spiritual formation of the Sisters depended upon the complete and solid concepts of the religious life learned in the novitiate. Under the crowded conditions existing in the convent at Morgan and Twenty-Second Streets, religious formation of the future community was seriously hampered.

Stories that have become part of the unwritten community history of the Sisters of Mercy, Normandy, indicate that the greater part of land on which the convent was located served as a vegetable garden for the entire community, and that a daily round of farm duties fell to the novices. In the absence of salaried employees, the Sisters were busy from morning until night planting vegetables, digging potatoes, milking cows, picking wild berries, and husking corn. Despite these back-breaking chores, their spiritual formation was not overlooked. That they advanced in wisdom, grace, and knowledge under the benign direction of Mother Ligouri is evident from the following petition addressed to Mother M. de Pazzi on Easter Sunday, 1876:

The Novices' Petition
We have come, dear Reverend Mother
To entreat a gift today,
One we long have wished and sighed for.
Oh! refuse us not we pray!

For our quiet little Convent
E're again we shall depart,
We would fain possess a statue
Of our Jesus' Sacred Heart.

Deep, deep in our souls' affections
We should have the Heart enshrined.
It should be the only object
That a place therein could find.

But alas, too oft it happens
That our wandering thoughts away
From the presence of Our Savior
To some earthly scene will stray.

And when thus our hearts are seeking
Pleasure in those phantoms vain,
What will help us to restrain them?
What will bring them back again?

Ah! We know what will recall them
What will bid vain thoughts depart,
'Tis the statue in your chapel
Of our Savior's Sacred Heart.

The property which the St. Louis Sisters purchased for $1,700 was practically a wilderness. The only shelter it offered was an old log cabin with four rooms and an attic. The cabin, supported by long pillars, was raised above the ground. To this convent Mother M. Ligouri and six novices moved early in 1879. The novices slept in the attic. Their capable and willing hands rapidly transformed the first floor into a community room and chapel.

The Eucharistic Presence inspired the novices with courage for the rugged life that was theirs. Not the least of their hardships during the first few years was the absence of a regular chaplain.

The early days of Josephville, as the Motherhouse was named, were characterized by hard work. Any longing the Sisters had for suffering was more than satisfied. They had even more hard work ahead of them than the Normandy group. They had to work in the fields, milk the cows, plant trees; they also had to carry building materials and help with the construction of the new novitiate building. In short, they had to bring into being an oasis in the barren land at Josephville.

Convent discipline, judging from interviews with veteran Sisters, was strict but not rigid. The frugal diet of the novices often consisted of black bread and coffee made from corn. There were no dishwashers, irons, or driers, and much of the work had to be done by hand. It was heavy at times, but sanctified under the inspiring guidance of Mother M. Ligouri and lightened by her cheerful smile and encouraging words.

The spirit of poverty was expressed in the furnishings of the house. A few stoves provided what little heat the Sisters had. For bathing purposes a small room was fitted with a washtub from the laundry. The tub was filled with water heated over log fires and carried in buckets up three flights of stairs. Through the chinks in the ceiling and the crevices in the dormitory walls the wind and frost found easy entrance. The novices, who at night-time carried basins of water to the dormitory for morning ablutions, frequently found the water frozen in the morning. Cornstalk mattresses and subzero weather were no incentives to luxury and ease.

The first decade of the nineteenth century was still a horse and buggy age, when automobiles were rarities. A black carriage with curtains drawn, hired for the day, carried Mother M. de Pazzi and her companions from the Motherhouse to Josephville. No such luxury was provided for the novices. In all sorts of weather they covered short distances on foot. To Sheve's store, a combination general store and post office located about two miles from the convent, they rode on horseback, observing the rule of companionship by riding two to a horse. For trips to the city a spring wagon, drawn by two farm horses, was used.

When in 1916 a tract of land in Webster Groves, Missouri, was donated by Mr. Joseph Sheets to the Sisters of Mercy, the Superior, Mother M. Gonzaga Sugrue, considered this a heaven-sent gift. With the consent of her Council, she decided to erect a new Motherhouse and novitiate on the property.

St. Joseph's Convent of Mercy and novitiate at Webster Groves, although little over a quarter of a century old, is full of tradition and steeped in history.[7]

FATHER WILLIAM MCDONALD OF MANCHESTER, NEW HAMPSHIRE

New Hampshire, the Switzerland of America, is a grandly beautiful region, full of picturesque streams, tall mountains, and dreamy lakes, and attracts more tourists than any other part of America, save Niagara. But I pass by its stern, rugged scenery to write of a man whose titles to our administration are chiefly of the supernatural order. Father William McDonald was for forty-one years the light of the manufacturing town of Manchester, and when I think of its looms, and spindles, and fire engines, and forests tall, red chimneys, and tens of thousands of operatives, Father McDonald is the figure that illumines for me the weird and grimy spectacle, and casts over it a halo of the supernatural. Little cared he for the sparkling rivers or bewitching lakes or romantic mountains of the Granite State; his whole interest centered in souls.

No ecclesiastic ever did more for the Sisters of Mercy than this holy man. The reader will therefore agree with the writer that he is entitled to a special chapter in these chronicles. Some sixty years ago, 1835, Irish immigrants began to come, timidly, and in small numbers, to the little manufacturing town of Manchester which rises on both sides of the laughing waters of the Merrimac. Bishop John Bernard Fitzpatrick, of Boston, learning that some hundreds of them were sighing for the ministrations of a priest, sent Father McDonald, July, 1844, to take charge of their spiritual interests.

Previous to Father McDonald's arrival, Father Daly, whose parish included all New Hampshire and Vermont, used to say mass in Manchester with unfailing regularity every three months. On these occasions he and his flock were hissed and hooted, and "blood-hounds of hell" was one of the "affectionate" epithets bestowed on them by the ubiquitous small boy. On one occasion the floor of the temporary chapel gave way, and priest, altar, and congregation were precipitated into the cellar. Providentially, beyond a few bruises and abrasions, no one was injured. The day before, the bigots, having heard that mass was to be said in the hall, had cut the supports from under the floor.

To these people the priest was an object of hatred and scorn whom they thought it would be a good work to kill, and William McDonald settled among them at the risk of his life. But in the face of duty he knew no fear. "The servant is not greater than his master," he would say. "If they have persecuted me, they will persecute you, also." To intimidate this dangerous papist, the natives used every means their perverse ingenuity suggested, but in vain. They soon began to admire his daring. In the end they liked him. Slowly but surely he won his way among them, and within a year of his arrival was able to hire the Granite Hall as a temporary chapel. In 1849 he built a church on a square purchased with his own patrimony, at the corner of Union and Merimac Streets. St. Joseph's and St. Augustine's churches followed. The success of the Sisters of Mercy was a great consolation to his zealous soul.

Though naturally somewhat abrupt, and entirely destitute of the sweet tongue so common among his countrymen, he was, with the sick and the aged, like a mother. He would make their fires, warm drinks for them, and see that they had sufficient covering. Though they all doted on "Father Mac" and made as bold with him as they pleased, they must not thank him, or even pretend they saw what he was doing for them, so well did they know that he worked only for Him who sees in secret.

Father McDonald was stricken with paralysis of the brain about six o'clock on Monday morning, August 24, 1885, and died two days later, while the Bishop and the Sisters of Mercy were praying beside his bed. In personal holiness, Father McDonald possessed the only power that makes the knee bend. Thirty years ago his sexton said to the writer: "I never opened the church in the morning that I did not find Father McDonald kneeling before the Blessed Sacrament. When he entered the church, no one knew."

A letter received after the good Father's death says:

> One night, at ten, the Sacristans, having forgotten something of importance about the altar, were obliged to step across into the vestry. On opening the sanctuary door, they saw, by the dim light of the lamp, a figure kneeling rapt in prayer, his eyes fixed immovably on the tabernacle, his arms folded across his breast. One of them raised the gas. Both were terrified till they saw it was Father McDonald. Lowering the light, they left the church. He may have remained there all night. We keep this holy priest in mind, whom Bishop Denis Bradley so justly styled, "the pioneer of Catholic education in New England." His people universally regarded him as a saint, and a great saint.

Saint and Spiritual Guide of Frances Warde

Father McDonald was Frances Warde's spiritual adviser in Manchester. No one knew her holiness better than he, and no one knew Father McDonald's holiness better than Frances. When each of these holy persons died, every business establishment in Manchester was closed to pay tribute to their greatness.[8]

TRIBUTES TO MOTHER CARMELITA MANNING AND MOTHER MARY RAYMOND O'LEARY: DETROIT, MICHIGAN

God has blessed the Detroit Province in numerous ways and is still blessing it. The going was difficult at first and everybody worked hard to make it a success. Young sisters will never know the hours of labor day and night that were spent to make their home a happy one.

Like the woman praised in Proverbs, "She rises while it is still night. . . . At night her lamp is undimmed. . . . She reaches out her hands to the poor" (Prov 31:15, 18, 20), Mother Mary Carmelita Manning exemplified the generous leader of her household.

Mary Manning was born in Lansing, Iowa, on December 24, 1888. She entered the Sisters of Mercy in Dubuque on February 2, 1909, where she was received on the feast of Our Lady of Mercy. Two years later she was professed on the same feast day.

Her first assignment was to the newly opened St. Joseph Mercy Hospital, Ann Arbor, Michigan. She worked there until 1927 and was administrator for the last five years of that period. Elected mother assistant to Mother Mary Daniel Gorman, new Reverend Mother of the Dubuque community, Sister Mary Carmelita returned to Iowa to serve from 1927 until the amalgamation in 1929. From 1930–1932 she was administrator of St. Joseph Mercy Hospital, Pontiac, Michigan, in the recently established Province of Cincinnati.

Widely known as an excellent administrator and a resourceful business woman, Sister Mary Carmelita was elected Mother Assistant Provincial of the Cincinnati Province in 1932. In 1936 she became Mother Provincial of the Province of Cincinnati. During the final year of her term in Cincinnati, the separation and establishment of the Province of Detroit took place. As Mother Mary Carmelita wrote to her superior, Mother Mary Grace, "I wonder how I ever traveled over three more states; and I am sure by now you realize that the work involved in three states is enough to keep any Mother Provincial busy." Indiana, part of Iowa, and Michigan now made up the Detroit Province, while Cincinnati Province embraced Kentucky, Ohio, and Tennessee.

The appointments for the new province were made on August 1, 1940. On August 16, temporary quarters for the new provincialate were established at St. Joseph Mercy Hospital, Ann Arbor.

Mother McAuley wrote in 1841 to Sister Mary Teresa White, "They say that the first separation from kindred was a joyful sorrow; but the separations in religion are bitter sorrows." There is a poignant little note from Mother Mary Carmelita to the Sisters of Cincinnati Province that echoes that sentiment nearly a century later:

> The simple little word "goodbye" never meant so much to me before. It seems that it is echoing out of every fiber of my body until I realize that I cannot say it in person.
> Because I have been so closely united with you for years, it

has created a bond of union making us one big family; it therefore makes the parting much more heartfelt.

Mother Mary Carmelita served three terms as Mother Provincial of Detroit Province (1940–43, 1943–46, 1952–55) and two as Assistant Provincial (1946–49, 1949–52). Under her administration Mount Carmel
Mercy Hospital (1939, Cincinnati Province), Mercy College of Detroit
(1941), Our Lady of Mercy High School (1945), St. Monica School
(1949), and Immaculate Heart of Mary School (1950) were founded in
Detroit. Within these same fifteen years new parish schools also opened in
Berkley (1943), Reese (1947), and Dearborn Heights (1955). The Sisters
of Mercy took over a parish school in Hazel Park (1943), replacing the
Sisters of Divine Charity. In 1948 St. Ann Hospital, Algona, Iowa was
established.

In 1942 Mother Mary Carmelita was awarded the Distinguished Service Cross of the National Catholic Hospital Association. The preceding
year she had won the key of the Tri-State Hospital Assembly for "distinguished service in the hospital and health field." She was given the Michigan Hospital Association Key Award for meritorious service in 1953. In
1955 she was honored as one of Detroit's Distinguished Women. Mother
Mary Carmelita was a vice president and trustee of the Michigan Hospital
Association, a Fellow of the American College of Hospital Administrators, and a member of the Social Security Advisory Committee, the Michigan Hospital Legislative Committee, and the Michigan National Defense
Council. All these honors Mother Mary Carmelita accepted as tribute not
to herself but to the Sisters of Mercy of whom she was a deeply spiritual
exemplar.

But it was none of these distinguished awards or honored positions
that made Mother Mary Carmelita Manning the great woman that she
was. Fifty-three years of selfless service to others as a Sister of Mercy until
her death on January 2, 1962 and her seventy-four years of life-long,
large-hearted charity, kindness and understanding made her great. Her
dynamic energy in directing and building hospitals, schools, and other
institutions to carry on the works of mercy was surpassed only by her
gentleness and her compassion for the sick, the stricken, and the broken.

MOTHER MARY RAYMOND O'LEARY

The Detroit Province was especially fortunate to have two great
women at the helm when it was launched. Mother Mary Raymond
O'Leary was Mother Assistant to Mother Mary Carmelita Manning from

1940 to 1946 and again from 1952 to 1955. She was Mother Provincial for two terms from 1946 to 1952. The wise man who compiled the book of Proverbs could have had Mother Mary Raymond in mind when he set down, "When she opens her mouth, she does so wisely; on her tongue is kindly instruction" (Prov 31:26).

Mother Raymond had two favorite verses of Scripture: "God so loved the world that he gave His only Son" (John 3:16) and "There is no greater love than this: to lay down one's life for one's friends" (John 15:13). This, she said, was supreme love. In order to repay this love, she tried to immerse herself, in her own way, in the multi-dimensional life of Jesus, the crucified Lord, thus—

His thorn-crowned head—she assisted as best she could in the
 physical, mental, and emotional ills of others.
His half-closed, bloodstained eyes—she fought pornographic mass-
 communication media untiringly.
His silent, cracked, swollen lips—she proclaimed the Good News,
 the Way, the Truth, the Life.
His nailed hands—she touched, blessed, soothed and healed in His
 name.
His pierced side—she made amends for the calloused, silent hearts
 that so wounded Him.
His torn, lacerated flesh—she prayed for the grave sins committed
 against the flesh daily.
His wounded feet—she helped as best she could all who trod a path
 to her door and disciplined herself for all those who lacked
 religious freedom or were imprisoned for matters of conscience.

One of Mercy's unforgettable women, Mother Mary Raymond O'Leary made the crucifix her autobiography.[9]

CHARACTER OF FRANCES WARDE AND TRAGEDY OF LOST LETTERS

It was, if not a virtue, a very pleasing weakness in Mother Warde that she always saw persons and things connected with herself at their best, or perhaps only while she held such views of them. The house she happens to govern for the time is actually or prospectively the best in the Institute, and her subjects the wisest, the brightest, the most holy and zealous in the world. She could see weak points in her children and surroundings with an Argus-like vision, but to no human being outside the walls would she admit this. Her letters to other members of her Institute, to ecclestiastics, relatives, and friends, covering the fifty-six years of her conventual life, are eloquent of this admirable trait.

The writer [Mother Austin Carroll] has hundreds of letters of Mother Warde which will, no doubt, yet illustrate the life of this remarkable woman.

The last letter ever written by her was to the writer [Mother Austin Carroll]. It is all the more prized because unfinished: death claimed her while she was in the act of writing. These letters, covering the period from her early days in Baggot Street to her death, nearly sixty years later, abound in sentiments of piety, zeal, friendship, and generosity, and unlike the letters of other remarkable personages recently published, are highly favorable to the character of the writer. (Many of these letters were unfortunately destroyed after Mother Austin Carroll's death.)[10]

MOTHER AUSTIN CARROLL: A WOMAN OF MERCY

[Sister Hermenia Muldrey, RSM, has done complete justice to one of the greatest American Mercy Sisters in her biography of Mother Austin Carroll, *Abounding in Mercy,* Habersham, New Orleans, 1988. It is difficult to choose a representative selection from this work, but the following pages are selected as beautifully representative of the spirit of Mother Austin.]

Often declaring that women and their accomplishments deserved much more recognition, Austin Carroll made this point forcibly in her second published work. This was the translation from the French of a life of Margaret Mary Alacoque, a book which seems to have been completed much earlier but not printed until 1867. To this biography by Father Charles Daniel, S.J., Austin added a forty-four page introduction, an exceptionally lengthy one even for the nineteenth century. This foreword gave quite a bit of space to women, for Austin explained: "God has often selected women for His greatest enterprises." Although she admired the humility of Margaret Mary, Austin's praise was showered upon the livelier gifts of other religious ladies, like the intellectual depth of Teresa of Avila, the energy of Jane Frances de Chantal, the enthusiasm of Catherine of Siena, and the affectionate heart and burning zeal of Catherine McAuley. Austin applauded Charles Daniel's use of the annals of the Visitation nuns, stating that convent chronicles are rich mines in which authors could locate veins of historical value in the interesting and detailed source material. After mentioning several memorable incidents from the records of religious women, Austin concluded that the chronicles showed not only gentleness and holiness associated with the nuns, but also that they had courage enough to face death calmly. Austin gave as an example the cloistered Carmelites of Paris, who sang as they moved toward the guillotine, the chorus becoming successively "a quintette, a quartette, a trio, a duet, and at last a solo."

Any reader who explored convent archives, Mary Austin believed, would be most agreeably surprised at the lovely courtesy and charming friendships pictured therein. "Sisters do not divest themselves of their human affections," she added, "they just regulate them." She wished to make it clear that a religious vocation was not a negative thing and made reference to an English minister who wanted Protestant sisters. Like the American Episcopalian, this man admired the work of the sisters on the Crimean battlefield, where the duties required not only love and patience but also "energy, foresight, economy, and the habit of working in concert and subordination." This minister assumed that all these qualities were the result of "the severe and methodical training of the Mercy novitiates." Austin wanted him to understand that a sister needed Catherine McAuley's spirit, her love of God and her zeal for His people. Otherwise, "all the discipline of the Prussian army would not avail. . . . All the heroism Protestants seek . . . comes from the fire that Christ came on earth to kindle, as Catherine McAuley often said." Unless a religious vocation was based on such positive reasons, Austin felt that it would not have the strength to overcome obstacles raised by the heart's affections. For this aspect of convent life she quoted the Mercy foundress on the pain of religious friends who are parted by their assignments.

This kind of heartache was that which Mary Austin knew well from personal experience because she had repeatedly had to leave close friends behind as she was sent down the road of Mercy service to her next appointment. Although she did not know it yet in 1867, Austin was to face that same pain again in 1869. For even as the reviews of *Margaret Mary* appeared in the press, the Redemptorist priests from New Orleans were searching for sisters to staff their parish schools. During the year and a half in which St. Louis refused the invitation, Austin found that the numerous sales of her biography of Catherine McAuley encouraged publishers to print her translation of the French works of Charles Daniel, SJ, and Jean Baptiste Saint-Jure, SJ. Translations such as *Margaret Mary* had been initiated long years before as "fillers for odd moments of time between other duties." For over ten years they had progressed steadily, but the St. Jure works were not yet complete in 1867 when arrangements for their publication were discussed. There would be six volumes in the entire series eventually, and the entire project took much longer than anticipated. The final volumes were published only after Austin was already down in New Orleans, for the books were published sporadically as she had time to complete the translations.

One might wonder if the material produced by the literary critics and book reviewers had any influence on Mary Austin. Even though there were occasional barbs about "a female writer," most of the critics were quite complimentary. Those who pleased Austin found some resemblance between the biographer and the biographee. One such stated "that a woman alone—and that woman a good and holy one, whose heart was in the great work of the foundress of her Order—could have done justice to the beautiful character" of the illustrious Catherine McAuley. That type of remark certainly pleased Austin Carroll, who had been seeking Catherine's spirit for sixteen years. The statement or one like it in 1869 might have caused her to analyze her years of Mercy service up to that point. If she did that, she would have noted a nice round dozen, twelve years, with the two Warde sisters. Austin's first three years in the Mercy Institute were under the tutelage of the gentle and generous Josephine Warde in St. Maries of the Isle in Cork. The ensuing nine years Austin spent serving wherever and however the zealous Xavier Warde assiduously assigned her in New England and New York and Nebraska. Then followed her transfer to St. Louis in the very heart of the country in 1865. Four years later in 1869, more than half her lifespan was still ahead of her, for she had forty full years left. During each and every one of these two score years Mary Austin Carroll was to give her loving concern and compassionate care to the people of God in New Orleans, Belize and along the Gulf Coast from southwest Louisiana to Apalachee Bay in Florida.[11]

MOTHER AUSTIN CARROLL, FROM HER BOOK,
GLIMPSES OF PLEASANT HOMES, A FEW TALES FOR YOUTH

Does not everyone know that good children are generally the children of good parents? And besides, as I write chiefly for boys and girls, why need I speak about parents at all? Well, the reason is this: the boys and girls of this generation will be the fathers and mothers of the next. To live in the world and to sanctify themselves therein, is the general vocation of all Christians. Now, in order to live well in the world, many things are necessary that cannot be acquired in a moment. I shall mention three as including all the rest: piety, intelligence, and industry. Now these must be cultivated in youth; if we have not commenced to practice them before our eighteenth or twentieth year, we shall hardly do so afterward. One of the three is not enough: piety without intelligence might enable parents to save their own souls, but it would not give them the necessary influence over their children; therefore young people must devote a few hours every day to study and reading, that when the graver duties of life devolve upon them they may be sufficiently intelligent to discharge them in the best manner possible. Industry without intelligence and piety would reduce parents to the condition of mere machines; while without industry, piety would be false, and intelligence useless.

I know it often happens that girls on leaving school think no more of improving their minds, while young men at that epoch sometimes begin to read most earnestly and steadily. Now, if education be necessary for the father of a family, it is still more necessary for the mother. In the moral and social order, the character of woman seems capable of attaining a higher degree of perfection than that of man; her sensitiveness is greater, so is her capability of bearing physical pain, though her actual strength is less; on occasions her generosity, her spirit of sacrifice is greater. . . . Her great mission is to make home happy and attractive, and it depends almost entirely on her to make it so. She should be able to educate her children physically, by inculcating the commoner laws of health, and those two things in which the prince of physicians said that all medical science, whether to preserve or restore, consisted: "Temperance and exercise." The moral and religious education of her children depends more on her than on any other human being, and the intellectual development of their faculties ought at least to be aided and superintended by her. Now, how can any woman who is not pious, industrious, and intelligent, fulfill efficiently the duties to her family which she is bound under pain of sin to perform? And how can any woman acquire these qualities except by daily prayer, daily effort, daily study, from girlhood, or rather from childhood, upward?

I have had another reason for setting down these remarks in the end of this little book: it is that, as many good parents adopt the sensible plan of reading, or at least looking over, everything they give their children to read, some, especially the mothers, who usually have more time to spare, may glance at this, and thereby be reminded of something that can never be too deeply impressed upon their minds; namely, that the formation of their children's character depends far more upon them than upon anyone else, and that teachers are only auxiliaries, whose success in giving or perfecting education depends in a great measure on the home training to which their pupils have been subjected from infancy. . . .

Sometimes children have the vices of adults with the stature of children; they are too independent to be polite, too proud to kneel in prayer, too rebellious to obey their natural guardians; they have too much arrogance to treat even the most respectable with respect, and just learning enough to excite them to jeer at the ignorance of their parents. Such children may have the knowledge that "puffeth up," but they want the "charity that edifieth." They have thought too much about their own rights, and have forgotten the rights of others, which ought to be respected as well as theirs. Too high an idea of our rights is apt to give us too low an idea of our duties, which nevertheless are immeasurably more important than our rights. . . .

But the good boys and girls must help the others to become good. See how our dear Lord helped sinners; sinners, too, for whom men would make no excuse. And how terribly severe he was with the Pharisees, whose greatest faults seem to have been want of mercy toward their weak, erring fellow-creatures! Oh! if we desire that God should compassionate us, we must be compassionate toward all. As we have been toward others, so will he be with us, and when in our last hour we lie utterly helpless before him, we shall have nothing to fear if only we have been kind to every one. The merciful are God's own children, and though a mother should forget her son, he will not forget them. . . .

Now, kindness is not half as much practiced, even among the good, as it should be. Neither is it sufficiently cultivated among the young. They have much to learn that parents and teachers often overlook, one of the most important lessons to be inculcated—the habitual exercise of kindness to everyone from childhood upward. . . .

Do not be ashamed, as some foolish children are, to honor and obey your parents and teachers. We should not be ashamed to observe the commandments of God. How sad it is to see, or even to read about, children that despise and neglect those whom they owe so much, that embitter their lives, and break their hearts. Who ever knew such children to be prosperous or happy? No one; because God is just. . . .

"My child," says the Holy Ghost, "honor thy father and never forget the groans of thy mother." "Listen, to the words of my mouth, and place them as a foundation on thy heart: Thou shalt have thy mother in honor all the days of thy life: for thou must never forget what she suffered for thee." "If thou honorest thy mother, it is as if thou wert heaping up treasures in thy heart. . . ."[12]

THE SISTERS OF MERCY

by Sing Sing Prisoner No. 50,940, New York

No human gets rid of "theories" as quickly as the chap who is "doing time."

His condition is made up of facts, and he arrays them before him the moment he gets inside the gates.

He ponders over them a bit, and here are his conclusions: "I came here for the doing of a pretty nasty piece of business; I deserve very severe punishment; I am getting it in big round doses; moreover, I've been a great fool, and am in receipt of a fool's reward."

Not very much sentiment in those reflections, is there? Not a bit of it. In fact we are surprisingly philosophical. We bend our backs, as do all the rest of this miserably unhappy world everywhere, to that angle which will bear our burden with the least possible discomfort, and we wear the proverbial "grin" so long as our nerve holds out. There is found here very little of that mawkish sentimentality, recently become very popular with people who have convinced themselves that they are philanthropists, which fastens the cause of our present distress upon any other quantity than our own weaknesses or viciousness. There may be some cases in the New York State Prisons which embrace the elements of Tolstoi's recent story of "The Awakening," but I don't believe any of them are in this particular establishment.

But while we accept for ourselves, with more or less stoicism, the inevitable rewards of our criminal acts, yet there are conditions connected with our situation that keep many of us awake o' nights.

Imagine a great, lusty, brawny six-footer going into his small private compartment here (7 × 3 are the exact dimensions) at 5 p.m. He throws himself on his cot, which may be soft or hard, so far as he cares a rap.

He opens the page of a magazine that is filled with attractive illustrations, but none of which his eyes can see. He throws it down and picks up a romance that ought to interest him, but upon which he cannot fix his mind to read. He looks through the squares made by the bars in his cell-door, and possibly counts them for the thousandth time (there are 42 of 'em, six rows up and seven across). Then he slowly raises his arm and watches the great muscles swell, muscles that have grown big and hard by work of which he never was afraid (for few come here from laziness; that sort of folk sink lower than we; they beg). Then old Six-Foot gives a vicious dab at his muscles, and glares at his immense legs as though he could tear them off. What ails the beggar?

Well, to tell the truth, he is all the same seeing a poor, frail, little woman, whose cheeks are pinched by actual hunger; he has just heard with agonizing distinctness the feeble cry of his mite of a daughter, who has always been ailing, and who is now worse because she can't have the proper care. And our friend on the cot curses in mighty and original oaths the ponderous muscles of his arm which could so easily provide for these dear ones had he not made his great strength useless by the weak, foolish or vicious act that culminated in a crime.

Now this picture does not contain a particle of sentiment; the whole business is actual fact. But the inmate does not know how to deal with it. It is an actuality that has become desperately real to his senses; he watches the woman's hopeless care of the babe through the entire night, sees plainly the fever flush grow brighter and brighter on the child's face hour by hour, and hears her every stir of restlessness; but he can't help either mother or child, and—he can't turn indifferently away from them and go to sleep.

If there is no possible help for this fellow, he will soon take a journey to the mad-house. Is there any relief for his distress? Sure there is.

And it is of this we want to write. How keen a pleasure it is to tell of it can only be estimated by those who have known the misery of the prisoners referred to above, and, like him, have been freed from their despair.

Once every month there come here two women who have made their monthly journey to us for many years. Their garb, their carriage, their manner, their faces declare their office—Sisters of Mercy.

They always come lugging with them a huge box of dainties for the poor chaps in the hospital, and this alone endears them to us when we reflect how beastly hard it must be to suffer physical pain in addition to imprisonment, and how far such ministrations must go towards alleviating the condition of these sick men. But then, EVERY thing the sisters do is of the practical sort.

Here are the questions they ask us:

"How long must you serve?" Never, "What crime did you commit?"

"Have you mother, sister, wife or children?"

"Are they destitute?"

"What can we do to help them?"

(Think of that poor lout on the cot being asked that last question).

You see, there is no more theorizing on their part than there is on ours. They have no doctrines to advance, no argument to make. They simply come to help us. And their work does not cease with their offer. Naturally, few of us know of their help to others than ourselves, for we don't like to speak of our difficulties to anybody except the sisters, and THEY never so much as whisper of the aid they render.

There are scores of prisoners' wives who have been helped by these women. The children who have been cared for, nursed back from death to life, fed, clothed, provided with educational facilities, are without number. That is the work of the sisters. That is what they come here for. There is no "fake" (excuse the gross word, but we are so very, very tired of "fakes") enterprise to be prosecuted. They have no ambition to be known to the public as the saviours of men who could be redeemed through the agency of nobody else.

They do not pose for portrayal in the yellow journals. They even lack the professional eloquence that "brings the tears to heretofore impenitent eyes." They only ask "how can we help you?" and when we tell them how, they immediately set about it. Their labor in our behalf embraces all that we ask for, so far as lies in their power.

There are living today men who have sat in our death cells awaiting execution for crimes they did not commit; men whose innocence was only established through the untiring energy of the Sisters of Mercy; freed men, whose lives are now a blessing to their families and friends. There are other men who walk our prison yard today who had been condemned to suffer the death penalty, but whose criminal act was afterward discovered, through the work of the sisters, to have been committed under such circumstances as entitled them legally and morally to a less severe punishment.

There will soon be liberated from here two young lads who were condemned to life imprisonment six years ago for a crime in which they had absolutely no part. The Sisters of Mercy collated the evidences in their case after extraordinary labor, and placed it before Governor Roosevelt, who was satisfied that the boys were innocent and commuted their sentences.

One could, of course, go on enumerating instance after instance where the sisters have brought happiness out of despair. But it is unnecessary. Each of us who knows them has his own experience with them to fondly dwell upon. Suffice it to say that they always have their memorandum book in hand and pencil with which to note our needs, and that their kindness is extended to all, absolutely irrespective of creed.

Above and beyond the reverence in which we hold the sisters, we love them; love them for their sweet charity, for the good-cheer they always bring to us, for the genuine affection they give us, and for their confidence in us. Unlike the rest of the world, they really believe that we still possess some sense of manhood; they are not at all of that mind which prompted the editor of a great Christian weekly in New York City to condemn certain of its own denominational preachers, a couple of years ago, because they advocated that a prisoner here should be kept upon the church roll, and because they went before the Governor to testify that the said prisoner had been a most helpful member of the community in which he had lived before coming to prison. The sisters believe that we are still capable of living good lives, and that we can attain to great success after we are discharged. Now THERE is a chance for theorizing, and here are the given quantities:

(A) Several thousand men of average natural intelligence.

(B) Their wits sharpened by adversity.

(C) Their bump of caution wonderfully developed by sad experience.

(D) Their hearts made brave and eager by the confidence and trust of two holy women, who unhesitatingly aided them after learning that they had committed a crime.

The undetermined quantity is:

Through how many generations will the effects of the sisters' influence spread? Through it, how many of the sons of men shall eventually have been delivered from evil deeds? In how many different ways of good will the benefits of the sisters' devotion be distributed? Perhaps one can estimate to an infinitesimal degree the extent of an evil action, since its power must diminish as the world grows wiser. But who shall measure the height and the depths and the might and the grace and the glory of good which shall spring from the kindnesses of the Sisters of Mercy to the forsaken, the forlorn, the despairing, as the ages are unfolded by our compassionate God?[13]

Notes

1. Archives, Manchester, New Hampshire.
2. Mother Austin Carroll, *Annals, IV,* 1895, pp. 107–108.
3. Archives, Burlingame, California.
4. *Mother Mary Patricia Waldron, First Superior of the Philadelphia Sisters of Mercy,* Archives, Philadelphia.
5. Carroll, *op. cit., III,* 1888, pp. 150–51.
6. Carroll, *op. cit., IV,* pp. 309–10.
7. Archives, St. Louis, Missouri.
8. Carroll, *op. cit., IV,* pp. 175–85.
9. Archives, Detroit, Michigan.
10. Carroll, *op. cit., III,* pp. 390–91.
11. Sister Mary Hermenia Muldrey, R.S.M., *Abounding in Mercy, Mother Austin Carroll,* Habersham, New Orleans, 1988, pp. 87–89.
12. Mother Austin Carroll, from her book, *Glimpses of Pleasant Homes, A Few Tales for Youth,* New York: The Catholic Publication Society, 9 Warren Street, 1869, pp. 227–236.
13. Extract from *The Star of Hope,* July 15, 1900, pp. 1–6. Archives, Silver Spring.

V.

REMINISCENCES

Mother de Sales Browne: From Pittsburgh to Natchez and the South

A Unique Experience: Sister de Sales as Wood Chopper for Soldiers: An Incident of the Civil War

Memories of Choctaw Indians in Neshoba County, Mississippi by Sister Alexis Corbett

INTRODUCTION

Reminiscences are preserved in Mercy Convent Archives for various reasons. Many of them center around Mercy leaders and their exciting, memorable contributions to Mercy service. Others are concerned with experiences as diverse as a rare day among prisoners about to die, or the everyday hardship or humor of a receptionist in a Mercy hospital.

Still other reminiscences go to the very heart of hardships beyond endurance: the actual sacrifice of Sisters' lives in plagues, wars, and natural disasters.

Even Sisters who had no time to write sometimes found time to record the rare and the uncommon, for example, a Sister's service as a lone wood chopper for sick Civil War soldiers. Or they preserved the letter or the magazine article written by an old man who could not forget a Sister who served in so unusual a manner as to make history.

Now and then an event bordering on the miraculous appears in Archives, like the account of Sister Martha's vision of Frances Warde's future service in Manchester, or the discovery "almost by accident" of a saint in the midst of the Sisters.

Though the tendency in Mercy reminiscences is more often to reveal the uncommon, it is amazing how everyday sacrifice of the Mercy Sisters always intrudes itself into the rarest accounts![1]

*   *   *

MOTHER AGNES O'CONNOR AND THE EARLY MERCY SISTERS IN NEW YORK

At the age of twenty-two Mother Mary Agnes O'Connor became a nun. She had visited several convents, but found none to suit her. "You ought to join our community," said one little novice to her; "you will find it very nice. But let me give you one piece of advice: Don't go near the Convent of Mercy; for if you meet Mother McAuley, and if you once speak with her, you will go nowhere else." The prophecy was fulfilled. The young applicant presented herself at Baggot Street, and had the happiness of being prepared and received by the holy foundress herself, who gave her the name of her recently deceased niece, Sister Mary Agnes.

She imbibed from the venerated foundress the true spirit of the Order of Mercy, evincing a particular devotion to the service of young girls. She was much loved by Mother McAuley, and received her last blessing and advice, and heard from her lips that God would allow her to do great things for His honor and glory.

In 1844 she went to Queen's Square, London, the fifth house of the Order of Mercy in England, with the understanding that as soon as it was fully established she should return. She came home, however, only to prepare for her departure for the New World. It was not without pain that Mother Agnes closed her connection with the London house; for she loved the sisters there, and to the close of her life used to recall their names.

But she was called upon to shoulder a new burden. When her mother learned of her intended departure for New York, she was heartbroken, and wrote at once to Bishop Murray of Dublin, begging him to interfere. This he refused to do. The mother's grief was intensified by the approaching death of her eldest daughter, Catherine. The community, pitying her grief, began a novena to St. Agnes to beg her intercession for the recovery of the eldest sister. Catherine was restored to perfect health. This favor, the persuasions of friends, and a letter Mrs. O'Connor received from the abbot of the Trappist Monastery, Melleray, partially reconciled the mother.

Mother Agnes' voluntary exile from home and friends found her head of an infant community in the New World, which had for its temporary headquarters West Washington Place, New York.

Though lively and gifted with fine conversational powers, the real attraction of Mother M. Agnes was for silence and solitude. All the time that could be spared from the duties of her office as superior was devoted to prayer and spiritual reading. She liked to take immigrant girls direct from the ship, train them to work in the ways of the country, and place them in good situations. Of these she saved thousands. One of the first things she did in her new home was to establish a circulating library, which attracted many young girls, who were found to be lamentably ignorant of the truths of their religion, but were quite willing to be instructed by their new friends.

As time went on, the amount of practical good these sisters accomplished under the leadership of Mother Agnes would be impossible to record.

While visiting one of the wards of Sing Sing prison, a sister once noticed a man who seemed very reticent, yet keenly observant of her every movement. Having reached his bedside, she asked if there was anything she could do for him. He replied with a courteous gesture that there was nothing he wanted, but that he remembered the Sisters of Mercy, who had been very kind to him many years earlier.

He had been at that time in prison in the Tombs in New York, and was now suffering for the crime of which he had been then proved guilty. The sister who visited the prison during the year he mentioned had given him a silver medal of St. Joseph, to which he had been strongly attached. Although not a Catholic, he said he always felt safe while wearing it. He was sentenced to a term of fifteen years in Sing Sing. He managed to effect his escape after a few months, and remained fourteen hours on the river with only a small piece of wood to cling to. He attributed his safety to St. Joseph's medal. He went to England, and after some years' residence there determined to come back to his native land. Although highly connected and well educated, he thought the ordinary way of making money was too slow and resorted to forgery. He was again arrested in the West, this time, however, on a false charge. The New York authorities, hearing of his return from Europe, sent an officer with requisition papers. He was brought back to New York and resentenced to serve his unexpired term of fifteen years.

From this same dread prison a man was given his freedom and honorably discharged who for years did the work of a missionary among his fellow convicts. Indicted for murder thirty years earlier, he lived in the Tombs, where the Sisters found him most untractable, unwilling to accept their proffered sympathy or to converse with them at all. After a lengthened trial he was found guilty and sentenced to imprisonment for life. It must be that in this terrible decree there was "a blessing in disguise," for by degrees he became most patient and penitent, and offered the years that lay before him in expiation of his crime. In his early days he had been a model altar-boy, was well brought up and thoroughly understood his obligations as a Catholic.

Now his better self was mercifully restored; his good conduct in Sing Sing soon won the confidence of keeper and prisoners alike, and he was given many privileges which he used to the best advantage, often lending most efficient aid to the sisters in their management of the cases that came under their care.

Letters from prisoners in Sing Sing and from Tombs Prison follow.

Sing Sing Prison

Dear Sister:

I write you these few lines to thank you in some way for your kindness to me in what you have done for myself and my soul. Sister, before you came to me, it was my intention to do something very bad. I was very much against the people who swore false against me; but your visits to me have made me a changed man, and your time with me was not lost. From the way you spoke to me and the way you told me of God I believed every word you said, and I have followed your advice. I am glad to tell you, if I have to die, I will go out like a man.

If I never saw you, I would not die with a priest or any one around me, nor would I forgive any one who had a hand in my conviction, but, sister, I will die with a priest, after receiving the rites of my Church, and from the bottom of my heart I forgive all who have injured me, and I ask pardon of all that I have injured.

I will ask our Blessed Mother to give you strength to be a good and holy sister, and long life to do your good work. Remember me to the other sisters, and may God bless you all.

Respectfully yours,

————————.

Tombs Prison

My Dear Sister:

My spiritual condition is improving daily under your guidance, and I can safely say I put my trust entirely in my God, and He is blessing me with His grace. I am now reading the sermons of the Paulist Fathers; also the little book called "Think Well On't," and the other, "The Voice of Jesus." The last two which you sent up last Saturday are very instructive and comforting to a wounded heart.

As I told you last Saturday, I have for the last two months learned and studied more upon the subject of religion than before in my whole life. I now very plainly see the truths and beauties of living a Christian life, and the peace and joy it gives; so I am determined to live such a life in the future, and also will take a step which will enable me to do so, the Lord willing. I will not take such a step for the sake of gain or notoriety, but because I am sincere and truly convinced of the good it will do me to inherit that eternal life where I can see Jesus face to face, and live forever with Him.

As I said, I will not take such a step as long as I am a prisoner, but, the Lord willing, I soon will be a free man. I am more and more convinced that He has brought this cross upon me so as to make me see myself as a sinner, and to bring me to Him through your kind advice and help.

May the Lord bless you, give you health and strength to fulfil your sacred duties, and make us meet in heaven above, where there are no sorrows, trials, or tribulations any more, is the prayer of

Yours respectfully,

———

Tombs Prison, New York City

My Dear Sister:

I am sorry that I give you so much trouble. How can I repay you for all this? The only way I know is this: That I henceforth live a good Christian life. The more I think upon it, my dear Sister, the more I am convinced that our acquaintance has been brought about by the good Lord, who wanted me to have this trouble so that I should come to see my sinful condition and come to him.

"The Lord be praised!" I can say from the depth of my soul, and I can say with St. Augustine, as I read this day, "And though I had not found out the truth, yet the faith of Thy Christ, our Lord and Savior in the Catholic Church, was strongly fixed in me." I say praise the Lord for such laborers in His vineyard! May He bless you in all your efforts and give you many souls. If only a man is willing, he cannot help seeing what a beautiful life the Christian life is.

Hoping everything comes all right very soon and hoping to hear from you, I remain thankfully,

Very respectfully yours,

———

MOTHER CATHERINE SETON, NEW YORK, SERVANT OF PRISONERS

Mother Catherine Seton was the youngest daughter of the saintly Elizabeth Seton, the Foundress of the Sisters of Charity in the United States. Strange to say, she had no attraction for her venerated mother's order, and when at length she decided on carrying out her religious vocation, she appealed to Archbishop Hughes to direct her choice. He had just completed arrangements for bringing the Sisters of Mercy to New York and advised her to wait their arrival.

She did so, and fascinated with the description of the works of Mercy given her by Mother Agnes O'Connor, she entered in West Washington Place on the 11th of October, 1846, being the first choir postulant admitted to the new community.

Before the sisters were ten months in the city, the Commissioners of Charity offered them free access to the prisons and hospitals. Here, Mother Catherine found her true vocation, and the visiting of the Tombs and Sing Sing was thoroughly organized by her at that remote period. Having spent many years abroad, she was thoroughly conversant with the French and Italian languages. As soon as she began the visitation of the Tombs, she set herself the task of learning German and Spanish, in order that her usefulness among the unhappy inmates might find no limit. She rejoiced in the title of the "Prison Sisters" and had a motherly way of speaking of the prisoners.

She certainly worked wonders among them and kept up her labor of love with advancing years until compelled to resign the actual work to younger though not less willing hands. Till the time of her last illness she held a general supervision over this cherished duty, and it was a matter of course for the sisters who had visited the prison to turn into Mother Catherine's room at evening recreation and give her an account of the day.

Some very laughable events occurred in her prison career. She was once sent a trunk from Philadelphia, supposed to contain books or clothing donated for the poor. Considerable curiosity was shown by the sisters regarding its opening, and genuine fun prevailed in the community when its lock was forced, and pistols, "jimmies," and a choice variety of burglar's tools were displayed to the astonished beholders. She made a shrewd guess at the sender, and not long afterward heard of his death. No doubt, he thought the convent the safest place for his strange legacy. On the occasion of Mother Catherine's Silver Jubilee, April 17, 1874, she was presented with several suits of men's clothing in the pockets of which twenty-five dollars in silver were deftly concealed. The gift of the prisoners was most gratefully received.[2] (This reminiscence was repeated frequently in Mercy Archives.)

MOTHER BAPTIST RUSSELL'S EXTRAORDINARY LOVE FOR THE POOR, BY A YOUNG SISTER IN SAN FRANCISCO

"After coming out here, I was very lonely, and I used to fret a great deal, but Rev. Mother would shake her finger at me with a sweet smile. When I would look at her working and scrubbing, I would feel ashamed of myself, and say, 'She is a fine lady and see what she does, so why should I complain?'

"We arrived here on December 8th, and went to stay with the Sisters of Charity. At the end of the year we made our Renovation Retreat, and Rev. Mother herself gathered a few sticks and made a sweet little crib for ourselves. We were as happy as it was possible to be.

"When we were really poor in the hospital, we did not have many fine beds, and Rev. Mother used to sleep in a little place at the head of the stairs. She waited one day until we were at recreation, and went and hauled the hair mattress which she had downstairs, and gave it to a poor man who had only a straw bed. She arranged his bed with her own mattress. I found that she did this, and I told Bridget Kennedy, and she went to Rev. Mother's cell, and found a piece of carpet stretched on the cot to take the place of the mattress. She then got her another mattress, and wrote 'Rev. Mother' in big letters, so that she could not give it away again.

"She was kindness itself in her visitations to the sick. One time she heard of a poor family, and when she went there she found the poor woman lying in bed in consumption. Her husband was away. When Rev. Mother saw the distress, she came back, and went over to the Home, and took all the dresses and shirts she could get and also went to the infirmary drawers and took sheets and tunics. She did this so often that they had to lock the Infirmary drawers on her. They used to tell her she would never make a poor man's wife as she would have him robbed, at which she always laughed. On the day I was speaking about, she went supplied with what was necessary, and when she got there, put on a tin of water to heat, washed the poor woman, and got her comfortably settled in bed. When this was done, she took the little children one by one and put them into the tub of water and washed them, and dressed them with new shirts. The last little one she had no shirt for, so she took a napkin and cut holes in it for sleeves, and fixed it around him and wrapped him in a comforter. She used to go and visit this family and help them nearly every day. She loved the poor. There used to be a crazy woman, who used to go the Mother's cell and say, 'I want to get into your bed,' and Mother would get up and put her in, not thinking that any one knew it, and would stay around her. She loved to make the poor woman happy even for a couple of minutes.

"We were always happy and united. It was like a heaven upon earth. Of course we suffered a great deal after coming here, but Mother would insist on doing all the drudgery. She would often stay at home and do the hard work, and send M. M. DeSales, Sr. M. Bernard, Sr. M. Gabriel and myself to the Hospital, from nine in the morning till six in the evening. She used to put her apron on, tuck up her habit, and do all the cooking, cleaning and scrubbing. She was a model of humility.

"After her visits to the Asylum, the penitents would say, 'Didn't Rev. Mother leave peace here after her? She made us happy.' She was very fond of them.

"One conversation I had with Mother some time previous to her death impressed me very much and serves to show her beautiful spirit of forebearance. I cannot remember her exact words, but the substance was as follows: Speaking of zeal, she said, if we remembered how patiently God waits for the repentance of sinners, we should be more patient with those who do wrong. We cannot force people to do right. God does not do so. How easily He could stop all the evil-doing in the world! But he chooses rather to suffer it and wait long for the good proceeding from man's free will."[3]

SISTER MARY JOSEPH LYNCH: BY HER FRUITS: GRAND RAPIDS; BIG RAPIDS; MORRIS, MINNESOTA; PORTLAND, OREGON

In the proposed rebonding of the Communities touched by Sister Mary Joseph Lynch, a monograph of her life and work must touch bud, blossom, and fruit. The project proposed by archivists, historians, and administrator at Brooklyn, on the occasion of the Congregation's 125th anniversary, set July–August of 1981 for printing and publication of that monograph, with a later date for distribution and a "Welcome Home" party in rebonding ties that had parted long before.

The value of the sowing and the merit of the sower are bound together in the fruit that comes from that seed. Mother Mary Joseph sowed according to her gifts in Mercy, from her entrance in Kinsale in 1844, to her death in Oregon in 1898. The fields in which she labored might render a harvest of thirty, sixty, or a hundred-fold as she traveled across the seas of water and of plains.

Brooklyn Community of Mercy revives the memory of Mother Mary Joseph for her twelve years of service as Mother Assistant and Bursar of the newly founded community in 1855. The links stretch from Brooklyn to join with further tasks in Rochester, New York, and in Michigan. In the former city, she had helped establish an industrial school. . . . In Michigan, at Grand Rapids, she had prepared the soil, and brought the seed to Big Rapids, where it was nurtured by her successors. What she sowed in Minnesota prospered, not without problems, but bore fruit for others to reap after she had gone. Her brief stay in Oregon prepared the fields for the harvest to come for her Community after her death.

When, in later years, the Sisters of Mercy began researching their own roots, and in particular the life of Mother Mary Joseph, they found some periods shrouded. In 1903, Sisters in Michigan celebrated the silver jubilee of their presence in Big Rapids; in 1923, the golden jubilee of their coming to that State. Because custom and circumstances of lines of communication between Communities at that time seem to have been less receptive to rebonding, it has remained for the present time, and the celebration of the one-hundred fiftieth anniversary of Mercy's first foundation in Dublin, Ireland, to revive Mother Mary Joseph's memory among us all, and to rejoice with her and with the many daughters of Mother McAuley throughout the world.

In the search carried out by Omaha's historian, Sister Cecelia Mary Barry, and by other researchers in Brooklyn and in Michigan, particularly by Sister Marjorie Elizabeth Allen, was revealed the fruit that ripened from Mother Mary Joseph's sowing wherever she went. Wherever she was, after she left Brooklyn, she began what she hoped would become a Motherhouse for a Community of Sisters of Mercy. That she herself moved on to other fields ripe for harvest did not keep what she began from coming to fruition.

In Michigan, the Community flourished and grew hardy under Mother M. Alphonsus Thilemann and her colleagues in Big Rapids, then blossomed anew in Grand Rapids, where Mercy had first come in 1873. Finally, that fruit is being harvested in the Sisters of Mercy—Province of Detroit, to which Michigan belongs in the Union of the Sisters of Mercy in the United States.

The sowing in Minnesota, where Mother Mary Joseph went from Michigan, was harvested in her own time, a span of seventeen years of loving labor for souls, the last year of which was to her a Way of the Cross in having to relinquish what she had thought would be her crowning work. Yet the harvest there brought other religious women to the task, and Sisters of many Congregations now carry on her work.

Oregon, almost at the ends of the earth, when Sisters of Mercy traveled across midwestern plains states, gave Mother Joseph only a year and a half to work at her apostolate before God in His Wisdom called her home. But there, as in each of the other sites, the Mercy Community grew and waxed strong in carrying on the works of Mercy. Now part of the Province of Omaha, the Community in Portland, and other Oregon cities continue to reap what Mother Mary Joseph Lynch had sown.

Brooklyn, to whose Convent of Mercy Mother Mary Joseph had come as a seasoned religious, could not claim her as founder, for Mother Mary Vincent Haire was that. It could and does revere and respect her for the great good that she accomplished while there, in her capacity as Bursar and Mother Assistant, and for the good she spread across the country when she left them. Hers was a share in the responsibility that brought the

Willoughby Avenue house into being, and hers the task of administering the industrial department there, the site of which can still be seen.

From the picture painted by Sister Mary Pius Teats, and displayed at the golden jubilee celebration arranged in her honor at Portland in 1896, we can conceive that Mother Mary Joseph had a genial and hearty personality, and that her smile was more often evident than not. The difficulties she experienced along her way to heaven may have been God's way of "writing straight with crooked lines."

Novices from Detroit Province, studying the history of their roots in Mercy, wrote of Mother Mary Joseph: "Judging from the photographs . . . she was a heavy-set person, with an expression of peace and happiness in her eyes. Her rare personality gained her not only success but the esteem of the whole community. From this it would be safe to assume that she was also a woman of frequent and fervent prayer, deep faith, and great generosity." Kinsale reminiscences also depict her as "capable, clever, charming—but a character apart."[4]

SISTER MARTHA'S VISION OF FRANCES WARDE
IN MANCHESTER, NEW HAMPSHIRE

Frances Warde stated:

"I was in a great hurry preparing to return to Providence when Sister Martha sent for me, saying she had something very important to tell me. I sent her word I did not intend leaving without seeing her. Shortly after, as I was packing a trunk, what was my surprise to see Sister Martha, like one risen from the dead, standing beside me. She said with great solemnity, 'Fearing I should not see you, Our Lord helped me to come to you. I hope and pray, dear Reverend Mother, that you will not remain in Providence. I am not in the habit of dreaming, but, last night, being wide awake, I was permitted to see you in a newly built convent, with a great number of Sisters around you. The house was large and handsome, with long corridors; it was on a rising ground, and built all for God, by a holy priest. You are to go there, and you will do more for God than ever you did before. Let nothing prevent your going on this mission.' Mother Warde said simply: 'I shall surely go wherever God appoints me to work for His glory.' "[5]

50TH ANNIVERSARY OF FOUNDING OF SISTERS OF MERCY
IN THE UNITED STATES (DECEMBER 21, 1893)

On the occasion of the splendid Jubilee celebration in Manchester, New Hampshire, December 21, 1893, Right Rev. Denis Bradley, himself a pupil of the Sisters of Mercy, preached a sermon worthy of the subject. "Fifty years ago," said the eloquent prelate, "they numbered seven. Today they number thousands, and are established in fifty-eight dioceses in the United States. We were favored in having as foundress one who drank in the spirit of the Order at its very source, one who governed this community for twenty-five years, the Reverend Mother Warde. She now rests among the hills of New Hampshire, in this land which was very dear to her. 'Rests,' did we say? We think she rests not, but is as near to each of her living children as to the dead by her side, reminding them of the blessedness of their high vocation, and of that reward exceeding great which awaits them in heaven."[6]

FRANCES WARDE'S LOVE FOR GARDENS

Mother Frances Warde always had beautiful gardens and loved flowers. ". . . In Manchester, the garden was simply beautiful; it reached from the little old chapel all the way over to the recreation hall. . . . A pretty rustic arbor covered with woodbine stood just a few yards from the steps of the convent piazza. The adjoining beds were filled with lilies of the valley. Those near the steps contained fuchsias, verbenas, and geraniums in profusion. All the little railing was covered with the lovely clinging vines, and a number of flowering bushes filled the space between the cedar hedge and the North wing. The site of the present chapel was a shrubbery containing numberless bushes, syringa, honeysuckle—and in the midst stood a tall pine tree, which was often called "The Sentinel.". . .

"Just half way between the convent and hall stood what was called 'St. Francis Xavier's Walk'—a path running across the garden, hedged on both sides by tall cedars; the hedge ended at the long walk on each side, and from the final cedar to the lattice on one end to the fence on the other was a little green vine-covered archway. The whole garden was beautifully laid out in flowerbeds, and one half of it contained all sorts of fruit trees—peaches, pears, cherries, and apples galore—beautiful apples, of every variety imaginable. . . ."[7]

A YOUNG SISTER'S LIFE IN PLAINFIELD, NEW JERSEY: MOTHER PATRICK MCCALLION (1916–1923)

I entered on October 2, 1916 and was assigned a desk class of fifth and sixth grade boys and girls at the Academy. I also taught Geography and History in seventh and eighth grades. I received the habit April 10, 1917. When we awoke that morning, the ground was covered with a light snow which disappeared later in the day.

In September I was assigned to Trenton Cathedral High School. The previous June Sr. Concilio, the superior and principal, had died. Changes in the staff of Cathedral convent were many. At this time I received the greatest shock of my religious life when the older nuns, mostly from Ireland, referred to the children who attended public school as the old "publickers." As I had been in public school through high school and did not consider that I was different from any other child, I could not understand their attitude.

We lived on the third floor of the school building. The lavatories in the middle of the third floor reminded me of the Liberty Street ferry boats. Several times a year when we went to the classrooms on the first and second floor, it was discovered that they had been burglarized during the night. We had a weird feeling, as Sr. Mauricius and I slept in the bedroom at the head of the stairs leading to the third floor with only a fragile door on the landing.

My second year in Trenton was the year of the flu epidemic and the armistice of 1918. Schools and churches were closed. One Sunday we attended an outdoor Mass in the yard of the cathedral. The coffins were piled up six feet high on the side walk outside Murphy's, waiting for burial. All the sisters went out to care for the victims of influenza. The city officials named the families, supplied brandy and transportation. Sr. Mauricius and I went to a family on Ferry Street where all the members were in bed, the men fully dressed even to overcoats. I went one night to an Italian family where the mother was dying with a new born baby and seven other children. We had to sit on each side of the bed to keep the woman from leaping out. In another room, the father had put five little black curly headed girls to bed in the one bed, three at the top and two at the foot. In still another room, two little boys were sleeping. The supper table was just as the father had left it after feeding the children. At four o'clock in the morning, I went out to the back porch to get the milk and hurried inside when I heard shots. The mother died and all the children were put in the Hopewell Orphanage.

Sister Mauricius and I became very sick with the flu. I felt ready to die, but Sister Concepta gave us good nursing care.

The day the armistice was declared everyone walked out of schools, stores, factories, and paraded through the streets. We watched the parade all day into the evening from the convent windows. The crowds were wild with rejoicing.

There were 11 sisters in the group for canonical year, two bands combined. The big question was where we would sleep, as the college was then at the Mount and growing fast. The novitiate on the third floor had been converted into a dormitory for Academy girls, so that the community room became our novitiate. The community sisters had nowhere to come together. Seven sisters slept in the room which is now the mother general's office and four slept in the bedroom with no screens between the beds, and a small old fashioned wash stand for clothing. Sr. Anicetus kept her clothes in a clothes basket and slept in any bed that was vacated by a girl in the dormitory. On Sunday nights Sister always waited to see what girl had not returned so she would have a bed.

My charge was to take the academy girls for a walk after school. We often walked up to the top of the mountain and into Plainfield. The year meant a great deal to me as I felt it was a great privilege to be released from teaching in order to prepare for profession. By the end of the year in retreat for profession, I was walking on air in the vestibule of heaven. We were professed on June 30, 1920.

I was assigned to South Amboy High School in September, where I taught Latin and Mathematics. The next September I was kept at the Mount to teach French in the Academy and the college. Jessica Dragonette was one of the students in my class. In January, Sr. Neri became ill in South Amboy and I was sent to replace her and a teacher hired at the Mount. I had to take some English classes then. In South Amboy we slept in a big dormitory of the old convent where we often used umbrellas for protection from leaks in the roof. There was one bathroom for about 14 sisters. The dining room was in the basement, and if we had a party at night, when we went down to replace the glasses and dishes, the floor was covered with silver fish and other crawling insects which disappeared during the day. I recall how revolting the act of stepping on or between these nightly visitors was to me.

In 1921 a new Convent was being planned to be built on the ground where the one we occupied stood. So we were told to go out and house hunt to find a building that would house 14 or 15 sisters while the new convent was being erected. We found a second floor flat over a butcher store on Broadway which appealed to us because it was new and clean and just rebuilt after a fire. Other places that we looked at did not appeal to our sense of cleanliness. So we selected that flat. Four of us slept in one little bedroom with one window. We kept our clothes in suitcases under the bed. Two slept in beds in the narrow corridor. One sister selected by choice to sleep on a porch which was enclosed but with no heat or light, just off the kitchen. There was one bathroom.

We moved to the flat in the Spring of 1921 and lived there until it was destroyed by fire in December, 1922. About seven o'clock in the evening

the sister who slept on the porch had left a candle burning while she went
to take a bath. Curtains blew into the candle flame, and before any of us
were aware, the firemen were dashing up the narrow stairs announcing
the fire. People from outside had seen the flames and turned in an alarm.
The fire crept to two other rooms at the back of the building. We all slept
in neighbors' houses that night. The next day we went into the building
and rescued our smoke-filled clothes. As it was within a few days of
Christmas vacation, school closed and we were scattered among the mission houses and motherhouse for vacation. We moved into the new convent when only the bedroom floor was ready for occupancy. The first
floor was still incomplete. After a few weeks, we were able to use the
kitchen and dining room. The date of moving in was a happy day for all,
February 23, 1923.[8]

MOTHER MARY AGNES BOLAND RETURNS TO GRAND RAPIDS FOR JUBILEE CELEBRATION, 1923

Mother Mary Agnes Boland of Portland, Oregon, one of the six sisters who established the Sisters of Mercy in Grand Rapids, was honor
guest yesterday at the ceremonies marking the 50th anniversary of the
founding of the Order.

Mother Agnes returned to relive the days of total hardships experi-
enced by those pioneer Sister nurses who came from [Brooklyn] New
York to carry out their missions of mercy in the lumber town of Grand
Rapids, Michigan.

Tears came to her eyes as Mother Agnes spoke of Mother Joseph
Lynch, who had charge of the five young sisters who sacrificed themselves
for the sick folk of the community. Mother Joseph served in the Crimean
War with Florence Nightingale. . . .

"We opened our hospital for the poor and sick in an old barn on
Canal Street, now Monroe Avenue," said Mother Agnes. "We had only
six beds, one chair, a pitcher and a washbowl, but we had strong hands
and faithful hearts, and we were anxious to serve the laboring people of
Grand Rapids.

"Our first real hospital was built in 1879, where St. Andrew's Cathedral now stands. The charity of the lumbermen kept it going. In 1891 St.
Mary's Hospital was put in our care, and is still operated by Sisters of
our Order.

"In 1879 a hospital was built in Big Rapids. . . . The work of the
Order grew steadily, and Mercy Hospitals were established in Manistee,
Bay City, Muskegon, Cadillac, and Grayling.

"Our greatest disaster was the fire in 1882 that totally destroyed our hospital in Big Rapids. . . . No hardship is great enough to destroy the courage of the Sisters of Mercy."[9]

SUFFERING AND MIRTH IN SPRINGFIELD, MISSOURI

In the early days of St. John's Hospital, Springfield, Missouri, there were no admission cards that might mystify the patient and fill him with vague dread. Instead of asking embarrassing questions, the Sisters satisfied themselves with the information revealed to a kindly glance. A Sister's sympathy shines through the faded pages of the admission book in underlined comments such as: "The little boy has *no home*," or "Poor old Lady, she is *very* nervous," "She has *no* friends." Censure is read in the shocked, "He was *dishonest. False Check* given."

The work of these pioneer Sisters was not lightened by the labor-saving devices we take for granted today. They had no elevator, no dumb-waiter, no gas stove, no nurses' aides, no nurses. Food was prepared and set on trays in the cellar, then carried up one or two flights of stairs by the Sisters. Equipment was meager in quality. The first stretcher had seen previous service as the door of a chicken house; the first sterilizer was an ordinary wash boiler. When the obstetrical department was added, new-born babies occupied a crib in the mother's room. This arrangement made it possible for the child to become acquainted with all the relatives and a few contagious diseases at the earliest possible date. Impetigo was as common as spring colds. In his spare time, the orderly performed a few higher tasks such as cleaning the stable or milking the cows. When Sister M. Stanislaus sought Sister M. Catherine's aid in taking out the body of a tall man who had just died, she cheerfully reminded Sister that the hall was narrow and if they wanted to carry him around the turn, it had better be done while they could still bend his knees.

To help provide food for the many poor and the sick patients, a large garden was cultivated near the hospital on Chestnut Avenue. A cow and one hundred chickens shared the barn. The inward peace of the Sisters' hearts seems reflected in the many tales told of their idyllic life in the early years. The flock of pigeons they had fed on Chestnut Street visited them on Main Street every morning at the same time for months after the removal. As the cow grew more fond of the Sisters, she became more gentle with them and more like a police dog to every one else. Sister M. Petronilla's cat knew he was expected to kill mice. Every time he performed his duty he laid the victim at her feet, receiving in reward an approving pat on the head. Sister M. Juliana gave two pet pigeons to a boy who lived far out in the country. He reported the disappearance of the pets the very day he brought them home; a week later Sister was amazed to see two exhausted birds with clipped wings walking down the road on bruised feet.

While they increased the resources of the Sisters, the garden, cow, and poultry added to the work which the Sisters had to do. Sister M. Martha gives an example of what one day might bring: "On Monday we began at three or four in the morning so that we could finish the washing on time. Twelve coal oil lamps had to be cleaned and filled, the wood supply carried in, ashes removed, the carpets in every room swept, chickens to be fed, the garden weeded, classes in German to be taught in the afternoon at St. Joseph's, a patient perhaps to be received, and usually a long journey made on foot to visit someone in distress.

Many are the stories extolling the wit, wisdom, and virtues of these pioneer Sisters. Sister M. Xavier once took the shoes off her own feet for a poor beggar, then continued her self-appointed task of shoveling snow from the path in worn house slippers. When Doctor Fulbright expostulated, she explained, adding: "And Doctor Fulbright, isn't it a wonderful thing, God gave me such big feet? That poor man and I take the same size shoes!" Sister M. Alacoque was one of the most beloved superiors the hospital ever had. A child remarked: "Even if she scolded me, I was happy because she was talking to me."

Not content with the manifold tasks of the hospital, the Sisters sought out the poor sick in their homes, often walking ten miles on such a mission of charity. People crossed the street rather than meet them in their strange religious dress and run the risk of being marked for life in some mysterious manner.

Did the Sisters have any compensations? One must have been the conviction that, with all sincerity, they could echo the sentiments of the peerless Catherine McAuley who once wrote:

> God knows that I would rather be cold and hungry than that His poor . . . should be deprived of any consolation in my power to bestow.

None of the trials they suffered ever disturbed their peace of soul. What others would regard as intolerable privations were made the subject of jokes and banter. They sent marvelous accounts to St. Louis concerning the steam heat, rare dishes, and rare food in the refectory. Sister M. Stanislaus ostentatiously removed the lid from the kettle of boiling water and gravely allowed the steam to escape for a few minutes into each corner of the refectory. That was the steam heat the St. Louis Sisters had been hearing about. One of the brightest hours in the day was the time these congenial spirits spent together at recreation exchanging hilarious experiences. When the bell rang for night prayers they entered the next room, into the peace of the chapel. What if every bone and muscle in a poor body goaded beyond human endurance was crying out for rest? New strength would come with the tasks on the morrow. The voice of the superior would begin the Litany, pleading with God, His Mother, the Angels and Saints for the needs of all.

And in the floor below were disillusioned, sad souls who had been observing these Sisters the long day. They had seen them toiling long hours and had felt sorry for them. They had heard such laughter ring out at their few minutes of relaxation, they envied them. And when they heard them at prayer—they wondered.[10]

FRANCES WARDE AND HER SISTERS: MIRACULOUS SERVICE OF POOR AND SICK; INDIAN MISSIONS; LABORS IN BRUNSWICK

Mother Frances Warde was always busy. "Every moment of her life seemed to be filled with some enterprise to such an extent as to appear almost miraculous."

But her confidence and trust were all in God . . . "I can do all things in Him who strengthens me" was her watchword. She frequently read the following extract to her community so as to stimulate them in the ordinary household duties of the convent:

"Humility, patience, and compassion for the poor are more easily cultivated among menial employments; the mistress, in imposing burdens which she has felt herself, is less likely to err against justice and charity; and the pride of intellect and condition is wonderfully subdued by submission to the yoke which is carried by the multitude. The reflections that naturally accompany manual labor are of an essentially wholesome and salutary character; for the indolent are reminded of the penance due to sin, and the haughty are confounded by the workshop of Nazareth. I know that the rich often excuse themselves from labor by urging as a duty of charity the employment of the poor; but the servant is not wronged by a share taken in her toils and occasionally one might employ others in light and easy work, and choose for one's own portion the drudgery of labor.

"It is astonishing how much time was at the command of the saints, and how little seems at the disposal of the generality of Christians!

"How eminently did the saints fulfill the duties of their state—union with God, devotion to the different offices their sphere of life called for,—

and still they did not fail to find time for those exercises of charity which only the few can compass at the present day.

"But even those whose fervor makes them visitors of the sick will often prove their hands to be but cowardly abettors, if they are not willing to insure themselves to the mortification of sense; and spiritual consolation will fall coldly from the lips of such as dare not relieve the sick at the expense of fastidiousnęss. Oh! what a powerful ally is the body of the soul who sees in it her servant, and accustoms it to serve; and under what a lamentable tyranny they groan who, because they will not triumph over some physical repugnances, are compelled to leave unsatisfied the best feelings of their hearts."

Frances Warde's many foundations while at Manchester entailed labor, fatigue, difficult journeys, privations, experience in trial, replete with Christian fortitude.

On September 14, 1878, Mother Frances Warde sent four sisters to Indian Island, Maine. Vast forests with aged pines, rugged oaks, swaying birch, and sugar-laden maple lined the Penobscot River. The four had a little temporary convent of four rooms, the dwelling place of Stockavesin Swassin, chief of the tribe, who vacated his hut for them. The Indians soon had enough money to erect a small convent. They were great protectors of the Sisters. Mother M. Austin Carroll records Mother Frances Warde's first visit to the Indian Missions in June, 1879.

"Indian Island, Pleasant Point, and Dana Point were the last missions established by Mother Xavier Warde in Maine, apart from St. Joseph's in Deering.

"On the feast of St. Aloysius, 1879, the band of Sisters of Mercy went to the Indian Reservation on Passamaquoddy Bay at Pleasant Point, opposite the North-Western shore of Deer Island.

"Three Sisters went—Sister M. Clare Leeson, Superior; her Mother, Sister M. De Chantal Leeson; and Sister M. Martha O'Brien, a lay Sister. They arrived in torrential rains. No fire awaited them in their little convent which was only a dreary hut. It was difficult to instruct Passamaquoddies, yet they clung tenaciously to the faith given them by the Jesuits over 200 years before.

"Passamaquoddy Bay had a summer loveliness. Curving banks of island shores, tinted skies above moving waters, white winged gulls, drifting clouds, far-off emerald crested hills, leave haunting memories."

In the first winter, the Sisters in the little house suffered from intense cold. They had only a small kitchen stove. The wood was often wet or covered with snow. There were wide cracks in the floor boards. Bear pelts from the Indians covered the floors. Mother Frances Warde had promised

Sister De Chantal to bring her back for the winter. Sister Stanislaus Griffin took her place. Sister De Chantal died in about a year.

The Sisters at Pleasant Point attended Dana Point four months each year, in the late summer and autumn season. Dana Point is a lovely spot on the Schoodic Lakes. The Sisters arrived in the glory of Indian Summer. Here the "murmuring pines and the hemlocks," grand old trees of Acadian Lore, slender birches, waving willows, tinted maple shade the lakes and cast reflections on calm waters.

The Sisters' convent at Peter Dana Point is on the brow of a hill overlooking the lakes, a modest church, and the school house. Beautiful dawn and sunlight prevail. In the distance is a picturesque mountain. Near are crystal lakes with tiny islands. Owing to disagreement over the election of the governor, the Indians had gone to Dana Point from Pleasant Point fifty years before. Dana Point was not as progressive as Pleasant Point. A missionary stated, "No matter what kind of life these Indians lead, in the Providence of God, they always die a good death."

At Dana Point, mosquitoes and large black flies were a torture until September. To get supplies at Princeton, a few miles away, the Sisters went in frail canoes. Often they were upset in the water. The Sisters left Dana Point each November and returned again in August. Often the previous good was undone! The mission was desolate in January, February, and March. The Indians retired to their huts.

Improvement came at the Indian Missions from about 1900 or 1910 on. There were not the early hardships. The Indians' religion had been preserved since the days of Sebastian Kale, S.J. At Morridgewock on the Kennebec, Bishop Fenwick in 1833 placed a rugged granite shaft to mark the spot where Kale shed his blood in defense of the Indians (1697–1724). Holy Mass was first offered on the shores of the Kennebec in 1611.

"But ended suddenly the dream of noble minds,
and over stream and wooded hill for many a
year a lovely silence fell."

The Sisters trained by Mother Xavier Warde learned at an early period and well, the meaning of the life of a faithful Sister of Mercy, and imbibed the true spirit of self-renunciation, devotedness to duty, prayerfulness, and uncomplaining acceptance of the cross. This wonderful teacher of religious instilled into the hearts and souls of her subjects that charity "is patient, is kind, is not puffed up, thinketh no evil," and "the peace which surpasseth all understanding" was theirs, as they worked for

God and souls with quiet cheerfulness, and loving loyalty to the Master whom they had promised to serve.

The Brunswick Mercy Convent opened in 1904. Brunswick is the seat of Bowdoin College. Beneath academic elms sat Hawthorne, Franklin Pierce, Longfellow. Here Harriet Beecher Stowe, wife of a Professor at Bowdoin, wrote *Uncle Tom's Cabin.* Just south in the Bay are Harpswell and Orr's Island. Whittier wrote of the locality in "Dead Ship of Harpswell":

> From grey fog, from icy drift,
>   From peril and from pain,
> The home-bound fisher greets the lights,
>   O hundred-harbored Maine.

Sometime in the nineties Bishop James Healy bought a tract of land on Little Diamond Island, with a large area of beach. Here he built a cottage for the Sisters and a pavilion for the children. Later he built a cottage for himself up on a pleasant knoll commanding a widely stretching view of Casco Bay.[11]

LEROY PERCY, REMINISCENCES OF
SISTER MARY EVANGELIST, VICKSBURG, MISSISSIPPI

Sister Mary Evangelist was born in the North and was an "adopted southerner." She will be remembered as an outstanding teacher and was especially partial to teaching the Catholic faith to young boys.

The first thing I learned there was the existence of evil. All the boys were herded together in the same classroom, presided over by Sister Evangelist, a midget of a nun with the valor and will-power of an Amazon, who taught every class, held prayers, cajoled, and beguiled us unflaggingly and devotedly. But there was one boy she was afraid of. The oldest and biggest boy in the school, was a monster of evil—cruel, nasty, bullying—with face and body so like Mansfield's Richard III that they published his qualities. All of us knew what he was and feared him.

Determination ranked high among Sister Evangelist's virtues, and among other things she determined that mine was a likely soul and she was going to save it. I gave up; there was no use resisting; into her hands I committed my spirit. She would have succeeded in her determination had not I incautiously remarked one day to Mother, who was bending over an ailing Cape jessamine at the moment, that I had decided to become a priest. I had anticipated dismay but not indignation. Mother rose from the flowerbed to her full height, the height, say, of Lady Macbeth or Clytemnestra; too late under the solemn fillet I saw the scorn. But her only observation was that there was no excuse for talking like a fool at my age. I must have been an unbearable little prig. I do hope I've outgrown it. If not, it wasn't Mother's fault. I shouldn't blame Sister Evangelist for my unbridled mystic fervor at this time; evidently my ground was plowed and harrowed waiting for her sowing.

I became intolerably religious, going to early mass at the slightest provocation, racking my brain to find something to confess once a month, praying inordinately, and fasting on the sly. It was infinitely trying to the family and so unexpected, so unlike anything in the case-history of any recorded member of the clan, French, English, or Scotch. I just couldn't help it, it was a violent attack, perhaps I've never fully recovered. Indeed, painful as it all was to the family, it was anguish and ecstasy, but mostly anguish, to me. I wanted so intensely to believe, to believe in God and miracles and the sacraments and the Church and everything. Also, I wanted to be completely and utterly a saint; heaven and hell didn't matter, but perfection did. Yet never, never for a moment, was my belief without doubt: the Satan of my disbelief was at my elbow scoffing, insinuating, arguing, day and night. I'm certain Shelley never sank upon the thorns of life nor bled nearly so often as I did between ten and sixteen. To be at once intellectually honest and religious is a rack on which many have perished and on which I writhed dumbly, for I knew even then there were certain things which, like overwhelming physical pain, you must fight out alone, at the bottom of your own dark well, beyond ministration of assuagement or word of advice, incommunicado and leper-lonely. If you die, it is natural; if you live, you have learned pity and the strength of silence.

I didn't die, and, curiously enough, neither did Sister Evangelist. Only last year I saw her, and she must be approximately a hundred. Sister Scholastica, my old music teacher and the only teacher I ever feared because she was absolutely impervious to my charm, telephoned me and announced that I was a godless, ungrateful, heartless monster (she always telephoned that way, never giving her name and knowing I would recognize her voice and style), that Sister Evangelist was on her deathbed in Vicksburg, that she loved me more than any of her thousand pupils, that in my baseness I ignored her and would not even take the trouble to visit her, dying, in fact barely this side of rigor mortis.

As usual I took Sister Scholastica's hint and dashed to Vicksburg. At the convent door a scared rabbit of a little nun asked my name and mission, suspiciously admitted me to the cool bare sitting-room, and left me there. There was a long pause during which I assumed they were propping up Sister Evangelist so that she could reach out feebly and blindly to give me her last blessing. It was pretty staggering, therefore, when Sister Evangelist came tripping in, unbent by her hundred years and vivacious as a cricket. She immediately loosed a diatribe of piety and invective, contrasting the promise of my past with the worm-eaten fruit of my present, and all with no more pause, punctuation, or capitalization than the last forty-six pages of *Ulysses*. At the first drop of a comma I got a word in edgewise: "Heavens, Sister! You talk as if God didn't have any sense of humor." She burst into gales of laughter, exclaiming: "Everybody forgets it; even I do sometimes," and the next two hours were chuckling gossip, singularly naïve. The incident helps me to understand better why St. Francis would drop over to visit Santa Clara when he was tired, and to appreciate Fra Angelico's versions of walking all over God's heaven. Those two old ladies with Machiavellian heroism and saintly mendacity had made one last try at saving my soul. Bless them, I wish they had succeeded![12]

MOTHER DE SALES BROWNE:
FROM PITTSBURGH TO NATCHEZ AND THE SOUTH

On the feast of the great St. John the Baptist, June 24th, our dear Fannie Browne left her home to enter the Convent of Mercy established in Pittsburgh, under the government of Mother Frances Warde, who had come to found the Order of Mercy in America. This noble woman, so truly great, was one of the first companions of the venerable foundress, and her long career in America was destined to prove how deeply she had imbibed the spirit of zeal and self-sacrifice from the fountain head.

The years of Fannie's novitiate fled swiftly and happily by, under the saintly mistress, Mother Xavier Tiernan, first American postulant. The sweetest and earliest recollections of Mother de Sales Browne, still cherished by members of her own community, are edifying stories of this saintly religious. When the memory of other old friends grew dim with the passing years, there always remained one bright spot that could enkindle the eye and make eloquent the tongue of our dear old Mother, and that was the story of those early days, spent under the guidance of Mother Xavier Warde who lived only to inspire her Novices with love for the poor of Jesus Christ, for whom she laid down her life.

Sister de Sales Browne continued her religious training, learning many lessons of heroic charity from the religious that made up that valiant band of Sisters that had come to found the Order of Mercy in America. As soon as Sister de Sales was professed, she was sent in charge of the Orphan Asylum in Pittsburgh, and continued to fill posts of responsibility, until the Infirmary at Washington was opened, when she was sent with three sisters to take charge of it, accomplishing much for suffering humanity.

Eventually, the Infirmary came under the direction of the Baltimore Sisters of Mercy, which will explain why our Mother de Sales was sent from the Baltimore foundation and not from Pittsburgh.

A singular instance occurs to us here, of the way in which God, even in this life, rewards the sacrifices of affection in His service. Mother de Sales had left her Pittsburgh home and her well beloved Sisters, and now, by a singular arrangement of Divine Providence, she finds herself in a community with her dear Sister Mary Regina, and Martha, later known as Sister Mary Vincent.

In the summer of 1860, the health of Sister de Sales began to fail, and Mother Catherine Wynne called her to Baltimore that she might rest and recuperate. It was just at this time that Mother Catherine, yielding to the solicitations of Archbishop Francis Kendrick, whose personal friendship for Bishop William Henry Elder made him an eloquent advocate for the Natchez diocese, resolved to furnish him with Sisters, and Mother de Sales was chosen to lead the little band of Sisters Southward.

Mother Mary Austin Carroll, the author of the *Annals,* speaks of the sorrow of this parting, in her unusually sympathetic way; for convent tradition told of the deep affection entertained by the Superior for the members of this new foundation, especially the two newly professed, Sister M. Ignatius Sumner and Sister M. Vincent Browne, whose religious childhood she had watched and trained.

Mother de Sales often spoke of the preparations for departure to the distant South, and when questioned by her own children in later years, she would say: "I tried to remain perfectly resigned to God's will, in spite of the feeling that with my ill health I was so unfit to establish our Order so far away; but because of the thought that I would have to bear this cross only a short time, since my frail body indicated a journey to Heaven rather than to Mississippi, I calmly waited until the burden of administration would be laid on abler shoulders."

This natural humility of Mother de Sales was united with a wonderful trust in Providence, and the last named characteristic enabled her to endure the interview with Father F. X. Leray, on the eve of departure, for those who remember this distinguished churchman, Leray, afterwards Archbishop of New Orleans, will readily understand how awe-inspiring he could be when he spoke of affairs connected with business matters, even when they referred to a subject as gentle as religious education.[13]

A UNIQUE EXPERIENCE: SISTER DE SALES AS WOOD CHOPPER
FOR SOLDIERS: AN INCIDENT OF THE CIVIL WAR

During the Civil War, when the convent school at Vicksburg, Mississippi, was closed, Father F. X. Leray, afterwards Archbishop of New Orleans, was made chaplain of the Vicksburg volunteers. He invited the Sisters of Mercy, seven in number, to take charge of the wounded soldiers. Under his guidance, they accompanied the hospital corps from one station to another.

The University of Mississippi at Oxford had been converted into a temporary hospital, and here the soldiers who were taken from the battlefields at Corinth experienced the sisters' ministrations. The services of the sisters had been enlisted for "Boys in Grey"; but wide arms of Mercy also took in the "Boys in Blue," and many a wounded one was nursed back to health through their gentle care.

It was at the end of a dreary November day, closing in with a grey sky that seemed to press upon the spirits of the sisters, whose hearts could not grow accustomed to the grim horrors of war, that news came that the flat car bringing in the wounded soldiers from Corinth had been derailed. There was immediate necessity for the surgeon, his limited staff, and the chaplain to go to the scene of the wreck so that these poor fellows, doubly disabled, might be rescued. Mother de Sales Browne was delegated to remain in charge and await the arrival of each new group of wounded soldiers. On account of the scarcity of mules and ambulances, the transfer consumed hours.

Evening deepened into night; and after Sister de Sales made those who had arrived comfortable with miraculous results, the scanty supply of bedding, clothing, and medicines was dwindling. The night was growing colder and the fuel very scarce. The heart of the sister in charge was filled with dismay at the thought of receiving these wounded ones out of the chilly night into a comfortless ward. What to do in this perplexity was the question. The little band of sisters had been scattered throughout the different apartments, and out of Mother de Sales own resourceful heart must come the answer.

She seized an ax and thus armed went quietly out into the night, alone and determined to supply the deficiency. This nocturnal scene has been described many times by her faithful companion, Sister M. Ignatius Sumner: she pictured an open space near the edge of the woodland where the gentle religious stood in her picturesque habit. Just in front of her was a growing pile of fire wood, made visible by the burning brush wood which she had kindled to frighten away the wild cats. As her frail body bent to the unaccustomed task of chopping wood, her beautiful eyes seemed to flow with the light of a new joy that out of her woman's heart and out of the straining of her woman's arm would come the comfort of warmth for many wounded soldiers.

The heroism of this deed lies in the fact that timidity was one of the characteristics of Mother de Sales. In this scene was enacted what would have chilled the life blood in many stronger hearts; but for the sake of mercy, she crushed her fears and went alone into the night where beasts growled and where perhaps human beings of a more vicious type were lurking.[14]

MEMORIES OF CHOCTAW INDIANS IN NESHOBA COUNTY, MISSISSIPPI, BY SISTER ALEXIS CORBETT

In August, 1896, Mother de Sales Browne, Superior of the Vicksburg, Mississippi Community, sent me to Tucker, Neshoba County, Mississippi, to teach in the Choctaw Indian School. I had a natural fear of Indians. As a small child, when numbers of them passed near my home, I would hide in fright.

At least sixty Indian boys and girls assembled under their new teacher. They gazed at me and then began to talk in their Choctaw language. By use of charts, signs, and pictures, the slow process of teaching began. After each instruction in Catechism or any other subject, I was greeted by one word "Hoo-Lah-Bee." On consulting an older Indian about the meaning of the word, I was told the meaning is "You tell a lie."

Some of the tragic happenings as well as those of a humorous nature occurred while I was with these children of nature. Two Indians had a fight, the cause of which no one could find out. One was sick and the other had imbibed too freely. Several Indians were spectators, but no one stopped the fight. When the sick Indian thought he had killed his opponent, he ran to the convent and said, "Sister, get priest, I think I killed him, Jim Jack." Father and two sisters went to the scene of conflict. We did what we could for the injured man, and when we returned to the convent we were greeted by the other Indian saying, "I stay here all night because the white men and Indians will kill me." A few hours later we tried to send him home, assuring him he would not be killed. He replied, "I no leave Father nor the Sisters for I must die soon and I want them with me until I go." No one arrested the Indians. The sick Indian died, and later his enemy moved to the Indian Territory.

Father Bekkers often took pictures of the Indians, but Polly, a woman of about 100 years, refused to pose for her likeness. Suddenly one

Saturday evening she appeared at the rectory and said "Me wash, take my picture."

The chief of these Choctaws was an old Indian named Tom Billy. No matter how far he had to go to work he returned on Saturday evening with his family to the Mission to be present at Mass Sunday morning. Often I saw him apparently asleep during the sermon, but after Mass he would mount the fence outside the church and translate Father's sermon into the Choctaw language. The important thing after Mass was the distribution of tobacco to all the men present.

Sister M. Ursula had trained one Indian girl to play the organ and other girls to sing the Mass. Louisa, Polly's great-grand-child, was a member of the choir. On Saturday mornings Louisa helped to sweep the Church. Before beginning her work, she would climb the highest tree near the Church and sing the entire Mass. Neither threat nor coaxing could move her from her perch until she finished her choir work.

One day while telling the class of the miracle of Our Lord's raising Lazarus from the dead, I wondered if they understood. I said, "Nettie Jacks, tell the story to me." This was her answer: "Lazarus, dead long time—four days—stink heap."

When Mother de Sales celebrated her Golden Jubilee, we sent two delegates to address the "White Mother." Nettie Jacks gave the address in Choctaw while Louisa translated it into English. These children of the forest were in the Jubilee Procession, and when they had to mount the steps going into St. Paul's Church, they went up on their hands and feet, much to the amusement of the spectators. Besides not being accustomed to stairs, these Indian girls of course never had the luxury of a bed. During their stay in Vicksburg, after Sister Bridget thought that she had "tucked them in" for the night, the sisters would find them perched on the highest outside part of the house.

Another pathetic incident occurred in the autumn of 1898. Arrangements had been made for our Catholic Indians to play a game of ball in New Orleans. The game was played. The white man took the gate receipts and left the poor Indians without food and means of transportation back to Tucker. In their dilemma, the poor creatures visited a kind priest who sent them as far as Meridian. They walked the forty miles back home. About ten days after their arrival home, one by one these Indians had a mysterious disease which took a toll of ten or more. I visited the poor sick ones every day and was the last to have this fever.

The Indians had a habit of entering a house without any ceremony. When I was convalescing, my superior, Sister Mary Rose, went to our kitchen to get some broth. She left the door unlocked. When she returned she found my cell crowded to the door with men, women, and children. I had had the presence of mind to throw a new quilt over my head and I looked like a sick squaw. I talked to them in their own tongue and comforted them in their grief over the deaths of their loved ones.

Polly, the oldest Indian, would bring in wood and do little things for the sisters in return for her board. One morning Sister said, "Polly, what will you have this morning, milk, tea, or coffee?" She replied, "I take 'em all."

Mantin Maley, the Indian Chief's step-daughter, married John Reese, an Indian. Father Augustine, a Carmelite, performed the ceremony. He thought it was a good time to speak about divorce. His remarks frightened the girl, so that she left the Church before the Mass was ended. One Indian was appointed to visit me and find out whether the marriage ceremony had been completed because they feared Father Augustine. I had a difficult interview, but they were married all right.

Did we have visitations? Yes, many times we followed a trail several miles through the woods, with an Indian for a guide.

One day we got a note like this, "John Billy she wife he got him a baby last night. Sister, come to see him." They came to the Sisters with every little ailment, toothache, earache, a splinter in the foot or finger. Even in the night they came. Once we had to set a broken leg. Well, our Guardian Angel must have assisted us as the boy became all right, and after a few months he was dancing, even though I paid him with a box of sardines to try to put his foot down the first time.

The worst case we ever had was a sick pig. An Indian led it to the convent. The poor animal was breathing as if it had croup. None of us had ever seen a sick pig. We fixed a good dose of lard and vaseline in some feed, and both medicine and food disappeared in a hurry. The man and his pig went home happy. We had a good laugh over the experiment. There was an Indian Medicine Man, but these Indians had no confidence in him.

Once we were called at 5:00 o'clock in the morning to an Indian child who had spasms. The man brought a horse and buggy he had borrowed. The horse had been accustomed to work in a double team and wanted to walk only on one side of the road. We made our six mile trip and found a severe case of worms. We used mustard bath for feet and legs. A flax seed poultice on the abdomen and a dose of squibs—and again our Guardian Angel came to the rescue and we left the patient sleeping quietly. We advised the Indians to send for a doctor, but the messenger said the sisters had done all there was to do, so he trotted back on his old horse, and we were glad to get home with our one-sided team.

We nearly always found the sick and even the dead lying on a quilt out under a tree. If a child was laid out, the mother always lay beside it, together with its little belongings. When we went to a ball game, we went supplied with bandages, or else we would go home minus handkerchiefs, having tied up heads, fingers, and toes hurt in the games. There were numberless cases like these, where we had to be both doctors and nurses.[15]

Notes

1. Helen M. Sweeney, *The Golden Milestone,* New York Benziger Brothers, 1896, pp. 24–27, 53–57.
2. Annals of Sisters of Mercy, New York, 1846–1920, p. 125.
3. Matthew Russell, S.J., *The Life of Mother Mary Baptist Russell,* New York, Apostleship of Prayer, 1902, pp. 56–58, 136.
4. Sister Mary Lucy McDonald, *By Her Fruits . . . Sister Mary Joseph Lynch—Sister of Mercy.* Sisters of Mercy, Farmington Hills, Michigan, 1981, pp. 91–92.
5. Carroll, *Annals, IV,* 1895, p. 159.
6. Carroll, *Annals, IV,* 1895, p. 282.
7. Sister M. Paul Xavier Warde, "A Backward Glance—II," *Mount Saint Mary Record,* VI (March, 1898), p. 109.
8. Mother Mary Patrick McCallion, *My Autobiography,* Archives, New Jersey (Revised, 1975).
9. *Grand Rapids Herald,* September 27, 1923. Archives, Detroit.
10. Sister Michaeline McAuliffe, *History of St. John's Hospital, Springfield, Missouri,* 1947, pp. 46–52. Archives, St. Louis.
11. Sister Mary Xaveria, *Memories of Mercy,* Manchester and Portland, 1931, pp. 15–18, 34, 42, 47–48. Archives, Portland, Maine.
12. Leroy Percy, *Lanterns on the Levy,* Louisiana State University Press, 1947, pp. 78–81.
13. *Annals,* Vicksburg, Mississippi. Archives, St. Louis, 1860.
14. Archives, St. Louis, 1860's.
15. Sister M. Alexis Corbett, *Memories of the Choctaw Indians, 1869.* Archives, St. Louis.

VI.

DIARIES

271

INTRODUCTION

Like all diaries, those found in Mercy Archives across the United States usually record personal experiences and observations. Because they concern daily Mercy life, they also reveal Mercy spirituality. Sometimes a Sister directs that her diary be destroyed, or that it not be made public. Personality seems to determine whether a Sister keeps a diary or not. Perhaps lack of time became a more decisive factor.

Spiritual counseling of the Sisters is occasionally heard indirectly, as in the amazing newspaper account of the death by hanging of "Tipperary Bill" in San Francisco in 1859. A happier note is found in the account of Sisters of Mercy serving the Choctaw Indians in the West.

One of the most striking diaries in Mercy Archives is Sister Nolasco McColin's loving, suffering, down-to-earth account of Sisters caring for the sick and wounded in the Spanish-American War. Yet the everyday, back-breaking service of the Sisters to the poor in early Brooklyn, New York, is, on the other hand, just as revealing of Mercy spirituality as the war diaries, even if the latter offer more striking and dramatic events for the reader. Spirituality is revealed in diaries in both simple and soul-searching ways.

*   *   *

SAN FRANCISCO

Death by Hanging of Convict "Tipperary Bill"

June 7, 1859: William Morris hanged in County Jail. We insert here a few observations on the subject of his death.

We found the poor fellow in a composed, and even cheerful frame of mind, yet little disposed to enter into any general conversation.

We told him we belonged to the press, saying it was very possible the newspapers might have done him some injustice in speaking of his former course of life, and in commenting on his character; and that if he felt such had been the case, we would gladly hear anything he might have to say in his own vindication and make amends so far as lay in our power. Without expressing any opinion as to whether he had been fairly dealt with or not, he declared himself satisfied with the result of his trial; that as far as

273

anyone might have injured him, he forgave them, as he hoped himself to be forgiven; that he cherished no animosity against any living being, but should die at peace with the whole world. This he said with a smiling countenance, indicative of entire resignation to the fate that awaited him.

The jailer told us, however, that he hardly enjoyed his usual serenity of mind yesterday morning, in consequence of the noise attending the erection of the scaffold, then going on in the jail yard. The pounding and sawing had disturbed his equanimity considerably, as well it might, since, although he could not see, he could distinctly hear, and well knew what these sounds portended. He looks pale and thoughtful, his naturally somewhat brutal countenance being subdued by the mental chastisement he has endured.

As seen now, he is by no means a bad looking man, and inspires a feeling of deep sorrow, that one so young, and so well fitted to have honorably fought the battle of life, should have been doomed to such an early and ignominious death. Several of the Catholic clergy, and also of the Sisters of Mercy, have been in constant attendance upon him, administering the consolations of religion and the holy rites of the Church.

The sentence of the law was carried into execution today, between the hours of 12 and 1 o'clock p.m., in the case of William Morris, alias Tipperary Bill, convicted of the murder of Richard Drake. The scaffold was erected in the north end of the yard, on the west side of the jail.

At half past 11 o'clock the Sisters of Mercy, who had been in the cell with the prisoner, rendering him the last few words of earthly comfort and consolation which his ears should hear, departed, and were succeeded by Fathers Maganotti and Morris who remained with the prisoner till his death, administering to him the last sacred rites of the Holy Catholic Church. At twenty-eight minutes before 1 o'clock the door of the northern end of the jail was opened, and Sheriff Doane and his deputies having the prisoner in their charge, and accompanied by the Fathers of the Church, entered the yard and ascended the steps of the scaffold.

Not a word was spoken by the crowd, who looked on with terrible impressive silence. Deputy Sheriff Ellis then read in a clear and distinct voice the sentence of Court, which directed the Sheriff to execute the death penalty upon the prisoner. The prisoner listened with respectful attention, and when the reading was concluded, he bowed his head as if assenting to its justice. He then advanced towards the front of the scaffold and, kneeling down, pressed the crucifix, which he held in his hand, to his lips, and said in a low, but distinct voice: "For all the sins that I have ever committed I pray God to forgive me; I forgive all who have wronged me; God be with you all, and pray God bless you all. Goodbye."

He then arose and stepped back beneath the beam, around which the rope was wound; his arms and limbs were then bound; the fatal noose was adjusted; the last few words of religious hope were uttered by the Reverend Father; the sable cap which was to shut out the world from the convict's view forever was drawn over his face; the rope was cut at 19 minutes before 1 o'clock; the trap-door fell, and in another instant the soul of W. Morris had departed, and the clay tenement it had once animated was left swinging to and fro beneath the scaffold, writhing in the spasmodic contraction of the muscles.

> St. Mary's Hospital
> San Francisco, July 4th, 1859[1]

CHICAGO

On the Efforts of Mother Genevieve of Chicago To Pay for the Property of the Sisters (1871–1880)

The following impressions of an old friend of Mother Genevieve speak for themselves:

No Date

I wish that I had the gift of eloquence that I might put into fitting words all I feel of admiration for my dear benefactress—noble and magnanimous Mother Genevieve. Of the many consoling talks I had with her, the following will give but a faint idea of her gracious spirit in a great emergency:

It was during those perilous years of panic and distress after the great fire of '71, when Mother Genevieve was chosen to steer the bark of the *then* new St. Xavier Academy through troubled waters, that her dauntless spirit, her wonderful ability to conquer apparently unsurmountable obstacles, made themselves heroically manifest.

After the death of Right Reverend Bishop Foley . . . she related to me something of her patient and untiring efforts to raise money to meet the payments on the debt of the Convent.

"It was almost in despair," she said, "that Sister Raphael and I set out early each morning to beg the assistance of the merchants and business men of the city. We would travel all day and return at six o'clock in the evening, weary and often discouraged. Frequently we met with rebuff and scant courtesy, but among those who treated us most generously were Mr. Marshall Field and Mr. John R. Walsh, who met us with unfailing kindness. The Community prayed continuously for our success, and God was with us then as always."

Notwithstanding her burden of care and anxiety, she found time to look after the poor who came to her gates. By her orders, during the panic year of '79, men unable to find work who stood in line at the basement door of Mercy Hospital, sometimes to the number of seventy, were daily fed and given clothing. When I questioned her as to why no publicity was given this charity, she replied, with that wondrous faith of hers, "Does not God know it? That alone is necessary."

At one time she told me of a visit to Mr. Walsh. It was for the purpose of obtaining an extension of time on the interest due on the loan which she had made to meet the payments on the new building, and for which the property on which the present Academy stands was given as security. She said, "We were in terrible fear that we would lose the property, as we had no money and did not know where to turn for help. Mr. Walsh had already extended the time more than once, so that it was with sinking hearts that Sister Mary Baptist and I started on our way to his office." "Mr. Walsh," she explained, "was no longer a man to be easily approached as formerly. He had a suite of offices—you sent in your card, or your name was announced by one or more clerks, and if the *great man* was not in the humor to receive you, there was no alternative but to depart as you came. But this time we were fortunate enough to be received, and while he had little to say on the subject, he was very respectful and granted all we asked." . . .[2]

MISSISSIPPI

Address to His Holiness Leo XIII from the Catholic Choctaw Indians of Neshoba County, Mississippi, United States of America, on the Occasion of His Jubilee

Most Holy Father, in the far off wilds of our native land, we your Indian children have caught the whisper of rejoicing that has stirred the souls of all Catholic peoples at the dawning of your Jubilee. Though but infants in the truth which we learned through the zealous labors of our loved Mingo Chito and Black Gown, we have learned to love our Great Father so far away.

We mingle our greetings with those of the pale face and pray that the

Great Spirit may bless with choicest blessings the Great Father under whose pontificate we have learned the truths of that Holy Faith which shall bring us to that eternal home, where the Red Man and Pale Face shall be as one household.

We kneel and beg your blessing on your neophytes in the Faith.

The Choctaws of Mississippi
Neshoba County, Mississippi,
United States of America, 1887.

The Bishop of Natchez sent the following letter to the Rector of the American College in Rome, asking a blessing for the Sisters of Mercy in Neshoba, Mississippi:

Tucher, Neshoba Co., Miss.
October 28, 1887
Holy Rosary Mission

Dear Friend,

Enclosed find an address in English and Choctaw or Chata of the Choctaw Indians' children who attend the school at the above mission.

The Mission is under the care of a priest and three Sisters of mercy. The Holy Father, no doubt, will be congratulated in most every known language, but we feared that no one would undertake this agreeable and filial task in the Choctaw tongue.

The Indians, who number about 3000 souls, are scattered through our Diocese, one of the first numerous tribes of the Southern Indians. They boast they never stained their hands in war with blood of the white man. In 1834 by treaty they sold their lands, and were removed to the Indian Territory. Some remained behind, concealed in the swamps; others returned to their native homes years later.

In 1883 I sent a priest among them, who after much disappointment and great privation, secured their confidence. In 1884 I dedicated the Church of the Indian Mission of the Holy Rosary, and in 1885 three Sisters of Mercy came to open the school. The Blessed Lady under whose protecting care this mission is placed has blessed the zealous labors of the priest and Sisters, about 150 of the Choctaws have been baptized, and the number is daily increasing.

Do me the favor in person to present this address to the Holy Father, and to make known to him the sentiments of filial love and devotion of his Choctaw children. You will also request of him a special blessing for me, for Father B. J. Bekkers, and for the three Sisters, Mary Agnes, Mar-

celline, and Gertrude, who with so much zeal and self-sacrifice have devoted themselves to this noble work.

> Believe me as ever,
> Your devoted friend,
> ✝ F. Janssens
> Bhp. of Natchez[3]

CINCINNATI

Newspaper Diary, Spanish American War, 1898: Sisters of Mercy Serve Sick Soldiers

The soldiers are going home—at least what is left of them. Almost daily the long train of cars passes through the city carrying up from Camp Thomas and elsewhere the boys—and they are scarcely more than boys—fever-smitten, wasted, the remnant of their former selves. Few looking at the weakened emaciated forms, the pinched ashen faces, would believe that these are the same fellows who three short months ago passed through this city, splendid in new uniforms, with a song on their lips, and hearts running over with soldierly enthusiasm, the idols of the hour: they return, not able to lift their heads from their pillows, with scarcely enough life remaining to murmur their gratitude for the ministrations of strange hands.

There is no exaggeration in the reports of the unspeakable state of affairs in Camp Thomas, and anyone who wishes to convince himself has only to visit at the Cincinnati depot. If these were men returning from a three months' campaign in the enemy's country, if their lost health were the result of the enemy's bullets, then hearts would be touched by their suffering, for it would be but reasonable to expect to thus see our heroes; but indignation is an inadequate term for the sentiment awakened when one remembers that the men here never left their camp, that this state of affairs, this loss of health and too often life, is due to the inhumanity of officers and the mismanagement of those in high authority. . . .

The Army and Navy nurses have acted nobly in their service, but the work grows beyond them. So last week the assistance of the Sisters of Mercy was solicited, and it is needless to say, with the record these holy women have in the history of this city or wherever they are established, the call was not made in vain. Last Friday the train bearing 280 soldiers stopped at Central Union Station long enough to allow the Sisters to supply them with breakfast, if we can call that a cup of milk or a little beef tea and toast—now the diet for Uncle Sam's boys.

On Monday morning the Sisters ministered to 256 more soldiers—New Yorkers these, and perhaps in the most pitable condition of any. They were all, or nearly all, young—mere boys—and numbers of them seemed to be in a dying condition. Yet the kind offer to send them to a hospital in the city would meet with prompt refusal on the victims' part. Home, home they all wanted to go. The Sisters supplied them with what light food they felt men in such condition should receive; and with what was done for these hearts sick for home and loved ones, they cheered them also with kind words. "That, Sister, is the only kind word I have heard since I left home," more than one grateful voice said as the nun offered consolation for the sad heart, as she poured the hot milk or tea for the famished lips.

One young fellow was noticed by a Sister who had ministered to other soldiers in '61. "Boy," asked she, "don't you want some coffee? Couldn't you drink some?" "Yes ma'am," said he faintly, "I could, but I have no money to pay for it." Very gently the nun told him she was not there to sell to him, but this incident spoke volumes concerning the neglect the volunteer soldier had endured in every way. . . .[4]

GEORGIA, TENNESSEE

Spanish-American War Diary: Sister M. Nolasco McColin

Sister M. Nolasco McColin, R.S.M. of Mount St. Agnes, Baltimore, Maryland, who served as a nurse in Detention Camps at Chickamauga Park, Georgia; Knoxville, Tennessee; and Columbus, Georgia during the Spanish-American War, kept a diary of her experiences from August 20 until December 22, 1898. She dedicated her personal diary, which included newspaper accounts and photographs concerning the war, to "my Sister Companions who served with me." The diary, written in long hand, was bound with a piece of canvas from a tent of the Third Kentucky Regiment. It is a tremendous actual account of the service of the Sisters of Mercy and of other Congregations during the Spanish-American conflict.

The willing service of the Sisters in life-demanding situations was recorded by Sister M. Nolasco in matter-of-fact fashion, without apparent fear. The following diary entries are chosen at random:

August 20, 1898

About noon, August 20, Saturday, came a telegram for Sisters to proceed at once to Chickamauga, Georgia. At that time the newspapers were teeming with the horrors of Chickamauga, and it seemed like going to certain death to go there. Yet no one hesitated. About five p.m. the Sisters arrived at the City Hospital. I was out buying beds to refurnish a ward for the Maryland troops on Sunday, August 21, when we volunteered to nurse. . . . At last, shortly before 9 p.m. we drove to Union Station in hacks decorated with flags. We could secure only ten berths, and the train was in two sections. We drew out of Washington at 1 a.m. All day long we traveled across North Carolina. . . . At 8 p.m. we reached Knoxville. We had only coffee, and it was vile stuff, but something hot. . . . At midnight we reached our destination, after twenty hours on the cars. We found one waiting room in the depot—filled with sick soldiers on cots and stretchers, attended by members of the Hospital Corps. . . . The poor sick men had traveled for twelve miles, had been waiting for a hospital train for six hours, and had had no nourishment. With much difficulty we persuaded the nurses (all men) to get them some milk. At 8 a.m. we again boarded the train, the dingiest, dirtiest I have ever been in. Our tickets were marked "Battlefield," which meant Chickamauga Station.

August 22, 1898

We reached Sternberg Hospital at 10 a.m. . . . It was decided we were more needed in another hospital than here, and that we would drive over after lunch to see it. Lunch consisted of dry bread and black coffee. Those who were sick were scarcely able to touch it.

August 23

When we arrived at the hospital, nothing was ready for us. We were crowded into one end of a hospital tent. This hospital contained between four and five hundred sick, most of them typhoid fever cases.

August 27

Each man had a tin cup. Into it was poured water, milk, beef tea, broth, oat meal, whatever was served at the time. It was never washed. . . . It must be borne in mind that the members of the Hospital Corps were for the most part rude, rough, ignorant men. . . . A great deal of the spread of typhoid we attributed to open sinks, for the flies carried the disease to the various kitchens.

August 31

We were mustered into the service of the U.S. Army today. The ceremony consisted in our standing in a line in front of "the Major" who was in full regimentals, sword, white gloves and all. He was totally unconscious of a broken suspender hanging down his back beneath his coat.

September 21

. . . I must go back to the first week to relate a circumstance of sufficient interest not to be omitted. Sister M. Celestine and I had charge of Ward G, containing 32 patients, the majority ill of typhoid. Out of this number we lost only J. R. McBride, No. 14, Company B., 21st Kansas, and he was in dying condition when brought in. . . . It happened that the chaplain of the 21st Kansas Regiment and his wife were staying somewhere near the hospital, and so took an active interest in McBride, since they were from the same town. One or the other, chaplain or wife, were with McBride nearly all the time. So I had to watch my chance to question him, as I felt sure he was not baptized. His mind was remarkably clear, and he was able to answer all my questions and express his belief in the chief mysteries of religion, sorrow for sins, and desire for baptism, as he had never been baptized. I had just finished going over all the preliminaries to baptism when the wife of the chaplain returned and asked if the patient would like her to sing for him, and then in a sweet, low voice she sang "Rock of Ages." The gorgeous sunset could just be seen through the open tent, the warm summer breeze playing over the form of the dying man. In a few minutes she went over to the hospital to see another man, and I felt that now was my chance. I baptized him. In less than five minutes both chaplain and wife returned, and McBride promptly related the whole transaction. Neither of them expressed resentment. In fact, I think they regarded it as a matter of indifference. McBride died within an hour.

The reason for the expected resentment is clear. A *newspaper account* published about the same time and placed in Sister Nolasco's diary states the following:

In a long recollection of sufferings caused by departmental bungling and incompetency, we search in vain for any parallel to the horrors imposed upon our men from Chickamauga to Santiago in this memorable summer. It is a perfectly disgraceful episode, almost incredible even if related of the prettiest State in the universe. . . . Our sick list of Chickamauga and elsewhere is out of all proportion to what it ought to be under businesslike management. It is fortunate for the administration that it is not dependent on army nurses and those of the Red Cross alone, else the strain must have proved fatal to many more.

The Sisters of Mercy (Sisters of Mercy is inclusive of other congregations) are now found to be of priceless value in the work of nursing the poor sufferers from the grasp of typhoid fever and water poisoning. When we remember that if the wretched bigots of this country had their way, these noble women would be driven away and their services rejected wherever proffered, we have every reason to feel grateful that malice toward them is understood and discounted by the better sense of the country.[5]

BROOKLYN

Sweet Charity: Sisters of Mercy Serve in Brooklyn, New York, 1855–1903

. . . The Sisters of Mercy came to Brooklyn in September, 1856. Like the beginnings of all work of divine inspiration, their entrance upon a new sphere of labor was humble and unassuming. Their first convent was a small house on Jay Street, and here they passed the first seven years of their existence as a distinct foundation. They had the zeal, fervor and devotedness of pioneers; and from their little convent, as from a luminous center, emanated, in the direction of the sick and suffering poor, the bright rays of consolation and good cheer. During these seven years privations and blessings came to the Sisters hand in hand. For a long time, deaths in the little community were so frequent that one might almost say that the first branch from the mother house was the small colony sent to heaven, there to help the work on earth as only the saints can do. There were no idle moments in the Jay Street convent; for, besides the unflagging energy of their labors among the poor, the Sisters taught the parish school under circumstances so inconvenient that there was ample scope for the practice of mortification.

At length the time came when the community had outgrown its surroundings, and in December of 1862 the Sisters moved into the new convent on Willoughby avenue. Without delay they inaugurated the work which had all along been the earnest wish of the Superior, Mother M. Vincent. Fully realizing and dreading for young girls the often corrupting influence of factories, she had longed for the establishment of an industrial school, in which they could be taught a trade, and thus rendered self-supporting. It grew and prospered, and the industrial school became an important feature of the services of the Sisters.

But now, almost imperceptibly and without any preconceived intention, the Sisters found themselves caring for orphans and destitute, homeless children. They themselves could hardly tell how this departure from their proposed work came about, but the fact stands. For many years, the Sisters were unaided by city or State; depending solely on their own strenuous exertions, they cared for from 100 to 150 orphan children. They resorted to every expedient; they left no stone unturned to obtain the means to support their little charges. It is true, the hand of charity was occasionally extended to assist them, and the help offered was most gratefully received, but it was not to be counted upon, and the labor of the Sisters was unceasing.

In 1876 the institution received the first children committed by the city, adding to, not substituting for, their former works. Six little girls formed the nucleus, around which are gathered now almost as many hundreds. This move necessitated additions to the property and additions to the building, the inevitable outcome being additions to indebtedness.

Let us span by thought the intervening period and see how the Sisters of Mercy stand at the close of 1902. As the first quality of a divinely inspired work is a small beginning, so the second quality is expansion under the combined influences of trials and difficulties and the sunshine of God's special blessings. Besides the large institution on Willoughby avenue, the Sisters have now a country house and farm at Syosset, L.I. This for the past year has been devoted to the care of little boys. The Angel Guardian Home, on Twelfth Avenue, Brooklyn, receives little girls in the number of 200. The Sisters have charge of parochial schools, Sunday schools, and sodalities. The Sisters in Syosset direct the Sunday schools at Oyster Bay and Huntington.

Meanwhile the works of mercy, the service of the poor, sick and ignorant receive the same attention and devotedness as of old. Last and least as regards its tiny objects, but far from least in importance and responsibility, the Sisters have a Home for Infants, and it is in aid of this latest work that the present appeal is made to the charitable public. About three years ago a number of ladies, earnest in the cause of charity, organized themselves into a guild for the Convent of Mercy. Their zeal is especially in touch with the helplessness of homeless infants, and under their auspices a benefit was undertaken to meet in part the expenses attending the preparation of a home for the little ones.

Sevenfold are the works of mercy, and sevenfold the gifts of the Holy Spirit, through Whom alone they can be successfully conducted. The animating principle of the Sisters of Mercy is found in these words of our divine Lord: "As long as you did it to one of these my least brethren, you did it to Me."[6]

BIG RAPIDS, MICHIGAN

An Unusual Vocation in Big Rapids, Michigan, 1906–1907

Miss Anna Panthers next applied for admission to the Sisters of Mercy and was to be on hand the eighth of December, 1906. Anna thought she would have no difficulty—until she made known her intention. Her father stormed and fumed and refused to let her leave her home. Nor would he buy her any clothes. He seemed to be willing to have her enter the convent if she would remain in Grand Rapids where she could live in the beautiful stone structure of the Dominican Sisters and wear a white habit. Anna's heart was not there, however, and she only waited an opportunity of running away from home. She smuggled a few of her belongings over to a friend's house and on July 4, 1906, took an excursion train that carried her to Big Rapids.

The Mercy Mother Superior had given up all hope of ever hearing from Anna when her surprise suddenly knew no bounds to see Anna walk in one Sunday morning while the Sisters were in retreat. Anna felt like a bird that had been caged but regained its freedom. She was as happy as a lark. Her father was wild when he heard the real state of affairs, but Anna did not fear. His paternal love got the best of him and he came to see Anna on Thanksgiving Day.

But Anna was not destined to wear the habit of a Sister of Mercy, for God called her to Himself before her reception. She was getting ready to mangle some clothes in the convent laundry on a February morning when, through carelessness on her part, she accidentally caught her arm in the mangle. Medical assistance was hastily summoned. Everything was done to relieve the intense pain caused by her badly crushed arm. After futile efforts to save the arm, it had to be amputated on March 16, 1907. She calmly breathed her last. Her short religious life was edifying and her death most beautiful.

Twenty minutes before she died she turned to her Superior and said, "I am waiting to receive Our Lord." The priest was waiting in the parlor and was hastily summoned. He was a little fearful that she would not be able to swallow the host, but Anna convinced him she could. He gave her Holy Communion and returned to make a thanksgiving for Anna. As soon as he had finished the prayers, she calmly closed her eyes and gave up her spirit.

Anna was laid out in the clothes that had been prepared for her reception. She was buried from her home in Grand Rapids. Her vocation is a strange one, but God is wonderful in all his ways.[7]

KENTUCKY

From "No Man's Land"—A Running Account of Cincinnati Sisters of Mercy Serving Kentucky Miners During Influenza Epidemic of 1918

Nov. 5, 1918

On train:

Dearest Rev. Mother,

Our joint letter written by Sister Mary Pancratius yesterday gave an account of our journey. The eight of us started this morning.

Sisters M. Lorenzo (Higgins) and Leo (O'Brien) for Hazard; Sisters M. James Conwell and Pius Foster for West Liberty; Sister Mary Antonio Cassidy and Monica Maher to Grahm (?). This place is not on the map.

Sister M. Monica and I had the happiness of receiving Holy Communion as our train did not leave until 7 a.m. Words cannot tell the kindness of the dear Sisters in St. Catherine's—slept on *feather* beds—Sr. Constance, the Superior, has a big Irish heart. We are now in the mountains, air clear and cold. All in fine spirits and good health. Sister M. Felicitas and seven Sisters are at the Hospital—did not get their appointments yet—I think all eight are going to open a Hospital.

The conductor tells us there is much flu in Grahm—Pray for us—I cannot write—train is too rapid.

Love to all—

Sisters M. Monica and Antonio

Mrs. King, our Mayor Galvin's Sister, has been most kind—met us at train and brought us to train today—We are now at Winchester—please excuse writing as the train moves so fast. I will post this when we reach our place—"No Man's Land."

Grahm 6 p.m. Nov. 5

Dearest Mother,

I wrote you a letter on the train this morning—arrived here at 11 a.m. Dr. Collins met us at the train—told us two Sisters from Loretto were here for part of the week—it was a mistake of Major McMullen to send us. The doctor left this afternoon—said he would telegram this evening after he saw Major McMullen—so we may move to another place tomorrow. Our first work began this noon after lunch—Sr. M. Monica and I went in a mule team part of the way up the mountain, then we walked the rest of the way—to where the Sisters were working in a camp of 200—about 50 died. We started right in to work—oh *dirt dirt* without end.

S. M. Monica and I cleaned and worked until the Sisters had us come down the Mt.—going up was hard—but coming down—slipping and oh —the Sisters of Loretto have done wonderful work here—baptized 5 before death—there is work for 4 of us here if we are to remain. I will hear tomorrow.

One house the father and little brother died and the mother and three children in bed—I washed and cleaned without fear—God has taken away fear when we are doing duty for God—I telephoned Lexington— asked where to go—I do not know how to reach Sr. M. Pancratius or any others. The camp is on the mountain above the *mine*—it is all so wonderful, 3 camps around here—all built over the mines, no race suicide here— 10 or more children in each family and all down sick at the same time, some 7 in one bed, 3 or 4 in another. We and the Loretto Sisters are in one house. Not one Catholic within 40 miles of this place—S. M. Monica and I have a room—the other Sisters have a room—we are only in our room at night, work all day.

This card shows how the homes are built, only much higher—I will write to you when there is a change—we may be home this week if we are not sent some place else—We are in splendid health—very heavy frost this morning. Nov. 6. Have not yet heard of a change—I am glad you made us bring warm clothes, we need them.

Love from S. Monica and S. Antonio

Grahm Nov. 6–10 a.m.

Dearest Mother,

Major McMullen ordered us to take the 11-02 train for Ashland where we would meet 6 other Sisters, then change for Big Sandy to go where?—I do not know, only God knows, away up in the mountains. We work here, now work there—S. M. Monica and I are fine, and a good night's sleep in *one* bed—said our rosary and prayers—worked all morning, now are leaving. We had the worst cases here—so we are not afraid. I hope our Sisters will be with us.

The two Sisters here are Srs. M. Ivo and Teresa from Loretto—they go home tomorrow—they have been real sisters to us. Nothing but friends and kindness since we left home. I will write when I know where I am *at*. Pray for us.

Love from both of us,
S. M. Antonio

Van Lear, Ky. Nov. 7

Dear Mother,

Left Grahm yesterday for Ashland, met by Father Cusack who brought us to his home for dinner—met our six Sisters, all came on the train for here—Fr. Cusack came with us to say Mass this morning for us, distance of 85 miles—In this camp (Van Lear) there are eleven Sisters of 3 orders, Black cap Charity from Cin., Notre Dame, Dominicans; 3 Sisters are very sick here—one is very low. Four of our Sisters stay at this camp and four of us go to Camp Jenkins 75 miles from here. S. M. Martina and Comp., S. Margaret Mary and Comp. stay here.[8]

Notes

1. Mother Baptist Russell, *Transcript Annals, I,* 1859. Newspaper Account by Person Present at Hanging.
2. Author Not Named, c. 1880. Archives, Chicago.
3. Indian Author Unknown. *Cincinnati Annals, II,* 1882–1916. Archives, Cincinnati.
4. *Cincinnati Annals, II.* Archives, Silver Spring, Maryland.
5. Archives, Silver Spring, Maryland.
6. Newspaper Article Published in Massachusetts, 1903, and Preserved in Brooklyn Scrapbook by Sisters.
7. *Big Rapids Scrapbook,* Big Rapids, Michigan, 1906–1907. Archives, Detroit.
8. Archives, Cincinnati, November 5–7, 1918.

VII.

VERSE AND POETRY

289

Jubilee," January 24, 1883, from St. Patrick's Convent of Mercy, down-Patrick, Ireland

"The Granite Cross, In Memoriam," by Mercedes, 1885

"An Order for a Picture," by Alice E. Shannon, 1893

"Sisters of Mercy in St. Louis (1856–1906)," by Sister Mary Constance Smith, St. Louis

Before and After the Armistice
"Why?" (Before the Armistice),
"Peace" (Armistice Day, November 11, 1918)
    by Sister M. Agnes, Rio Vista, California

"A Tribute to Mother M. Raymond Donahue on Her Golden Jubilee," by Mother M. Joseph O'Donahoe (1849–1924), Plainfield, New Jersey, 1921

"Sonnet Tribute to Mother Mary Frances Xavier Warde" (January 24, 1833–January 24, 1933), by Sister Mary of the Angels, St. Xavier Convent, Chicago, 1933

"The Sister of Mercy," 1873–1948, Portland, Maine

"Lines in Honor of the Golden Jubilee, Burlington, Vermont, 1872–1922," by Mercedes

"The St. Xavier Hymn to Our Lady of Mercy" (A Typical Nineteenth Century Mercy Hymn), Chicago, Illinois

Sister Mary Augustine McKenna, *Three Poems for Catholics and Converts:*
    "Lines Composed Before Writing a Petition for Means To Aid in Erecting a Home for Homeless Children";
    "To the Children of the Rich for the Children of the Poor";
    Benedicamus Domino"

INTRODUCTION

Catherine McAuley in Ireland initiated a trend among Mercy Sisters of writing their thoughts in very simple verse. This custom continued in America, often to the delight of the Sisters. It would be a mistake, however, to call the metrical verse that the Sisters wrote—especially for celebrations and jubilees—by the name of poetry. Now and then a real poem did appear because of the special gift of the writer.

Most of what follows is verse, often delightful verse. Perhaps it illustrates better than the vast majority of prose writings in this collection certain characteristics of American writing during the second half of the nineteenth century. Here we find an exaggerated romantic strain; a transcendental suggestion or two in the religious verse; unabashed sentimentalism now and then; a humanitarian tempo often; and an occasional readable ballad.

"The Old Soldier's Story" is a typical late nineteenth century romantic ballad. "Conquered at Last," a powerful tribute to the service of the Sisters of Mercy in the Civil War, goes far beyond the typical "romantic" in its beautiful simplicity. "Sister Veronica" reveals a warmth that conquers sentimentality.

Two poems by Sister Agnes, one written before the Armistice of 1918 and the other on the day of the Armistice, surpass most of the poems printed here in their simple honesty. The lovely Sonnet Tribute to Mother Frances Warde by Sister Mary of the Angels (1933) was written too late to be compared with the late nineteenth century poems considered here.

Perhaps the best poet among those printed here is Sister Mary Augustine McKenna of New York. And perhaps the best single poem in the collection is "The Sister of Mercy," which comes from Portland, Oregon, written around 1890. Its author is unknown. It appears at the beginning of this book.

*   *   *

POEMS FROM NOTEBOOK OF FRANCES WARDE, DATED BEFORE 1837

Lines on a Much Lamented Friend

Ah why hast thou left me,
Sweet spirit of meekness,
Ah why hast thou flown

Thus untimely away?
Ah! Could not thy flight have been
Stopped in its fleetness
Or a parent's fond prayers
Have prevailed?
Ah no, thou art called by a voice
So commanding
To a world more befitting thy virtues
Than this,
For the bud of thy youth whilst
In sorrow unflinching
Was destined to blossom in regions of bliss.
Then away with the tears which the fond recollection
Of thy seraph. . . . . [Incomplete]
(In Frances Warde's Handwriting)

Heart's Ease

I need not token flowers to tell
How deeply dear thou art.
Still music as thy accents swell
Thy witness in my heart,
Thy beauty floats before my eyes
In soft celestial light.
I liken day's repose
And pensive eye of light.
Farewell, thou shalt not be forgot,
My brother and my own.
O may thy sorrow of our lot
Bow down thy heart alone.
And this sweet flower when given to thee
Was moist with morning rain,
Shall breathe for thee
And live for thee until we meet again.
                    Sometimes think of me,
          (In Frances Warde's Handwriting)

Mary, Queen of Stars

I looked far back into the years
Laid, lo, in bright array.

I saw as in a dream
The forms of ages pass away.
It was a stately convent with its old and lofty walls
And gardens with their broad green walks
Where soft the footstep falls.
Fresh all around the antique heights
The creeping shadow graced,
And all around the noonday sun
A dreamy radiance cast.
No sound of busy life was heard
From out the cloister's shrine,
The tinkling of the silver bell
Or the Sisters' holy hymn.

And there five noble maidens sat
Beneath the orchard trees,
In that first bursting spring of youth
When all its prospects please.

(In Frances Warde's Handwriting)

To a Beloved Brother

When we parted, my Brother, in youth's ardour of gladness,
Oh! then our young hearts never dreamed they should mourn,
But alas in the lone dreary moments of sadness
Each feeling of friendship bound round them is flown.
When we part we may wander the wide world over,
Deluded by dreams of affection or truth,
But alas, in this waste, can we ever discover
One friend half as true as the brother of youth?
My brother, the sun
At even shall set mid our sorrows pure dew,
But alas when tomorrow from each scene returning,
Ah far, far divided those friends shall we view.
But alas, since together our young hearts were blended,
Let's cherish the memory wherever we roam.
And Oh, let us think when life's journey is ended,
That then we shall meet in a far better land.

(In Frances Warde's Handwriting)[1]

THE OLD SOLDIER'S STORY

He was a soldier old and gray; he'd been on fields of glory;
We children gathered round one day, and asked him for a "story."
"A story of the war," said we, "some deed both great and glorious."
Said he, "I'll tell of victory, where woman was victorious.
Methinks (he gravely shook his head) no heart that warms a true man
Can calmly beat when words are said ungraciously of woman.

"And yet, from infancy, I knew no mother's sweet caressing,
A lone and luckless lad I grew, uncheered by homestead blessing.
But little recked I, even then for love nor virtue caring,
I lived with rude and lawless men, their sinful pastimes sharing,
And thus for years, till o'er the land the storm of battles lowered,
'Twas then I joined the warrior band, and fell where bullets
    showered.

"And when I woke to life and pain, a woman's form was near me,
A woman's hand and voice were then upraised to soothe and cheer
    me.
The gentle hand seemed dropping balm, my shattered body healing,
That voice had words my soul to calm, faith, hope and love revealing.
She was not young, nor was her face with winsome beauty beaming,
But ah! a flood of wondrous grace was all around her streaming.

"I asked her what her name might be, as blundering I addressed her;
She, smiling my surprise to see, said gently, Call me 'Sister'.
I marveled at the strange sweet name (and was I, then, her brother?)
But soon I found that all who came ne'er called her by another.
She saved my life, her skillful care with ghastly death contending;
She saved my soul by fervent prayer, and gentlest reprehending.

"When I arose, with health endowed, to go where honor brought me,
I knelt, and to my God I vowed to live as she had taught me.
And that most solemn, sacred vow, each day of life renewing,
I've kept with grace, from then till now, and this has been her doing."
He paused. My gentle Sister May (no seraph could be sweeter)
Said timidly, "And since then, pray Sir, did you never meet her?"

"Athwart the old man's silvered head a ray of light came stealing;
He looked to Heaven, and then he said with sad and tender feeling,
"A month had passed when I returned; I looked for her and missed
    her;
I wept with those from whom I learned that death had struck the
    Sister.
And yet, 'twas well, her work was done, 'twas time for Heaven to
    win her;
The angels surely longed for one who saved so foul a sinner."

Then spoke sweet May, the story gave her heart's deep fountains
    stirring:
"Mine be the task to serve and save the suffering and the erring."
"And so 'twill be," he said, and smiled, prophetic utterance giving;
He's now at rest, and May, dear child, sweet Mercy's life is living.
*   A Pupil of St. Xavier's Academy, Chicago, 1859*[2]

YOU SILENT DEAD
SISTER IGNATIUS SUMMER, C. 1870's

The silent dead! The silent dead!
I've lingered where they sleep in peace,
Where care, and want, or thought of dread
There anguished vigils cease.

Our silent dead! Our silent dead!
They lure me to their mossy rest.
Where roses, snowy petals shed,
And birds sing requiems in their nest.

O silent dead! O silent dead!
Thus dreams my soul of deathless lands.
For in the limit of your bed
Time and eternity clasp hands.

You silent dead! You silent dead!
For me to come, for you 'tis passed,
And while the heavens bend o'er your bed
Your lessons wise and holy last.

Then silent dead! O silent dead!
Why should my restless spirit moan?
Your footsteps have to Calvary led,
And thither must my soul be borne.

The peace you breathe even now must come
When the night of time has fled,
When the Bridegroom calls me home,
And I, too, sleep with the silent dead.[3]

Civil War, c. 1870's

ON THE GOLDEN JUBILEE OF MOTHER M. JOSEPH O'DONOHUE
FIRST SUPERIOR AT BORDENTOWN, 1873
SISTER MARY IGNATIUS HOGAN

There's a vision that leads through flowers and weeds
To the place where youth's longings did start,
The memories of which so hauntingly please
When sunshine still dwells in your heart.

If sunshine still lives in the depths of your heart,
Oh, keep it there cozy and warm.
Suppress not the sigh nor the smile in the eye
That gave to your youth a true charm.

And since the great One through life like the sun
Has brushed all life's shadows apart,
To Him still unfold all your love still untold
While sunshine still lives in your heart.[4]

YELLOW FEVER EPIDEMIC IN VICKSBURG, MISSISSIPPI
ELLEN K. HEBRON, 1878

By a grandly sweeping river
  With broad, majestic waves
Whose ceaseless music—murmurs
  Beguile the land it laves,

Where floating palace steamers
   Go bounding to the sea,
There stands a stately City,
   Well known to you and me.

When war had flashed its banners
   This Southern land all o'er,
And foeman's mighty cannons
   Were belching from each shore,
Begirt with loyal heroes,
   The city nobly stood
With bulwarks firm which still defied
   All woes of fire or flood.

But in an hour unguarded
   a foreman crept within
Whose haggard, stony visage
   Rose over the city's din;
'Till men forgot their business,
   And women fled to prayer
To escape the deadly monster
   So swiftly rising there.

One single note of warning
   From a far-off inland town
Whose dwellers all, from old to young,
   Beneath his wrath go down,
Had scarcely reached your sentinels
   Before that form is seen
To quickly rise within your midst
   With Death's terrific mien!

O! then your faithful body-guard,
   Fair city near the sea!
Your bravest, noblest, truest, best,
   Still true were found to be!
While panic-stricken thousands fled
   From out the monster's grasp
Your moral heroes snatch his prey
   From out his stony clasp!

But a host of pitying Angels
   Are camped around the town,
Their busy wings are flitting by
   When daylight goeth down,
On thousand Mercy-errands
   All through the lonely night
To sick and weary still they go
   Upon their mission bright.

O! you who tend the afflicted
   With your doubly grateful care;
O! you who cheer the dying
   With your ministry of prayer;
O! you who stand beside them
   With patient, willing hand,
You all shall be rewarded
   In the far off better land![5]

FRANCES WARDE'S SMILE
FATHER EDMUND, C.P.

Our Lady of Mercy may well look down
   With tender glance upon this wide land.
Many a hamlet and many a town
   Can boast her daughters, a faithful band,
Shrinking like her, from the world's renown.
   Yet sharing her glory in heart and hand.

But of all the homes of our sisterhood,
   Is any so favored, so dear as this?
The least and poorest is rich in good,
   Better than best of earthly bliss:
But something more readily understood
   Gives ours a blessing the others miss.

For *we* have a mother who left the side
   Of *her* first children, to found and frame:
Came with *her* spirit to call and guide,
   Brought us the sisters in Mary's name.
We have the mother, our joy, our pride,
   More and more ours with each year's fresh claim.

Then take, dear mother, our simple lay,
  Warm as the hearts of your native Isle,
Take it, on this your festal day,
  In pledge that we lovingly pray the while
To be spared long, long, the golden ray,
  The peerless light of our mother's smile.[6]
St. Xavier's Day, December 3, 1878

CONQUERED AT LAST, MARIA L. EVE

"A prize was offered by the *Mobile News,* Alabama, for the most meritorious poem by a Southern author, descriptive of the gratitude of the people of that section of the country for the spontaneous benevolence of their Northern brothers and sisters in the days of the terrible cholera scourge following the Civil War. . . . The committee selected the following verses by Miss Maria L. Eve of Augusta, Georgia as most worthy of the prize." The speaker is a Southerner.

You came to us once, O brother, in wrath,
And rude desolation followed your path.

You conquered us then, but only in part,
For a stubborn thing is the human heart.

And the mad wind blows in his might and main,
And the forests bend to his breath like grain.

Their heads in dust and their branches broke,
But how shall he soften their hearts of oak?

You swept o'er our land like the whirlwind's wing,
But the human heart is a stubborn thing.

We laid down our arms, we yielded our will,
But our heart of hearts was unconquered still.

"We are vanquished," we said, "but our wounds must heal."
We gave up our swords, but our hearts were steel.

"We are conquered," we said, "but our hearts were sore,
With "woe to the conquered" on every door.

But the cholera came and he would not spare;
The angel that walks in the darkness was there.

He walked through the valley, walked through the streets,
And he left the print of his fiery feet

In the dead, dead, dead that were everywhere,
And were buried away with never a prayer.

From the desolate land, from its very heart,
There went up a cry to the uttermost parts.

You heard it, O brothers! With never a measure
You opened your hearts and poured out your treasure.

But Sisters of Mercy, you gave more than these!
You helped, as we know, on your bended knees.

Your part was human, but Oh! it was more,
When you shared our cross and our burden bore.

Your lives in your hands, you stood by our side,
Your lives for our lives you laid down, and died.

And no greater love has a woman to give
Than to lay down her life that her friends may live.

You poured in our wounds the oil and the wine
That you brought to us from a Hand Divine.

You conquered us, brothers; our *swords* we gave,
But we yield now our *hearts*—they are all we have.

Our last stand was here, and it held out long,
It is yours, O Sisters, you'll find it strong.

But your love had magic diviner than art,
And "conquered by kindness" we'll write on our hearts.[7]

TO SISTER VERONICA COLLINS ON HER GOLDEN JUBILEE
SISTER M. ANNUNCIATA LAWLESS

God knows her heart was heavy and the sad tears fell,
When to the little hills of Erin she said farewell;
But Jesus stilled her weeping and Mary held her hand,
And, guided by this wisdom, she found our southern land.
As ever in her heart she loved the ways the saints have trod,
Soon within her convent home she gave her all to God.
She gave her service to the King in sweet humility—
Her heart and soul and toiling hand—a noble trinity.
Through long, long years she labored; the linens, in her care
Lost the stains of living and ever seemed more fair.
The incense of her iron went up, the clothes became redeemed,
The shadow of a sacrament divine it almost seemed.
And for the fifty years she served so well her King,
Her sisters gather round her now and loving tribute bring.
We'd have her heart as happy as dancing Irish rills;
We'd have her thoughts as tender as mist on Irish hills.
And we wish our dear old sister to know how much we care
For the blessings she still brings us through ceaseless prayer.
One favor we would ask her—in the years that yet remain,
That of her daily "Aves" she'd weave a golden chain—
To draw our hearts together in bonds of love,
And bind them all forever to Jesus' heart above.[8]

GREETINGS TO MOTHER MARY FRANCES XAVIER WARDE
ON HER GOLDEN JUBILEE

"With the accompanying bunch of shamrocks from St. Patrick's grave, Rev. Mother and community of St. Patrick, Downpatrick, Ireland send their congratulations and affectionate wishes to Dear Mother Mary Frances Xavier Warde on the celebration of her Golden Jubilee, 24th January, 1883."

We send you the leaf
Of bard and chief,
The shamrock never old
To bear on its verdant page though brief,
Our wish for your Day of Gold.

May its hours be blest
In your home of the West,
As your dear little shamrock when given
By St. Patrick's hand
To our own loved land
'Neath the smile benign of heaven.

No care it knew
As it drank the dew,
This stem 'neath the trees that wave.
Their branches wide
On the green hill side
O'er St. Patrick's hallowed grave.

No brilliant dye
To charm your eye,
No fragrance to impart
Has our shamrock got,
Yet shall it not
Be dear to your Irish heart.

A type of the love
Of our *Mother* above
For the child of her cherish'd "*First Seven*,"
As green as our spray
For your Jubilee Day
With her smile and her blessing from heaven.[9]

THE GRANITE CROSS
IN MEMORIAM
ST. XAVIER'S CEMETERY, LATROBE, PENNSYLVANIA

There's a quiet peaceful City, not many miles away,
Where flowers bloom all summer and robins chirp all day.

Each house holds a single inmate, no more admitted there;
Man, or woman, or infant, each has a single share.

All day long come the people through the archways of the trees,
In the spring-time, in the summer, winter snows, or autumn breeze.

And the muffled footsteps falter as they leave new inmates there,
With aching hearts and mourning, with sobs half stifling prayer.

Under the moss and daisies, under the waving grass,
Silent, and cold, and pulseless, the dead lie as they pass.

The people turn in sorrow, and back to the living go,
And many forget their mourning, and a few live on in woe.

The missing are soon forgotten, the sorrow passes away,
While out in the Silent City the robin chirps away,

Now and then a mourner wanders along alone,
To kneel by a grave fresh sodded or a monumental stone.

Were I in the quiet City, where the shadows fall on the moss,
I would only kneel and linger by the side of a Granite Cross.[10]

Mercedes

AN ORDER FOR A PICTURE
ALICE E. SHANNON, 1893

Will you paint me a picture, my artist friend?
A picture sweeter than all the rest,
The dearest spot in the wide, wide world
To my heart, and yours perhaps. Ah! you have guessed—
The Convent Chapel. Well, listen to me,
And hear how I want this picture to be.

You know the Chapel! Yes, many a time
Have you knelt in it; many a time you have brought
Your burden of grief to its hallowed steps.
There were some days, I believe, when you thought
That the burden was greater than you could bear,
And that it could only be lifted there.

And so you can well understand the thought
That moves me to speak as I speak to you now.
I need not describe how the altar must look—
You know it—its carved fair beauty, and how
The white angels watch on the left and the right,
Where the Holy of Holies rests day and night.

And you know the rows of quiet straight stalls
That line the Chapel on either side;
And the windows above, where the sunlight streams through
In a purple and yellow and crimson tide—
You will picture them well, for you understand,
And the touch of Love will be guiding your hand.

But, Oh! What artist can paint the quiet,
The holy peace of this calm retreat?
Far off from the world and its strife and din,
In the dusk of the evening still and sweet,
When only the altar-lamp's rosy-hued glow
Shines out through the darkness. You cannot, ah no?[11]

SISTERS OF MERCY IN ST. LOUIS (1856–1906)
SISTER MARY CONSTANCE SMITH, 1906

What shall we of St. Louis say
From that time to the present day?
How count the golden deeds here wrought?
Poor are relieved and children taught;
The erring soul to Jesus brought;
The innocent preserved from sin;
The homeless stranger taken in;
Captives in dreary cells consoled,
Faith taught to those outside the fold;
The sick made happy in their pain,
The worldling turned from pleasures vain;
New branches of the Order sent
To cheer the poor where'er they went,
And lift them from despair.

Louisville and New Orleans may,
With San Diego bless the day
That brought her daughters there.
Where Springfield reigns the Ozark's queen
Sisters of Mercy now are seen,
Whose gentle words impart
To God's dear little ones His lore
While their blest works of love restore
Peace to the stricken soul once more,
And soothe the aching heart.

These works we see, but God alone
Knows all the good seed they have sown,
And He alone can tell
The increase that may yet appear
From what they cultivated here
So wisely and so well.

That seed once cast on earth so cold
Is yielding now a thousandfold;
'Twas planted amidst toils and fears,
Watered by fructifying tears,
Cultured by faith in One above,
Warmed by the surplus of His love
Enclosed by Mercy's watchful care
And vivified by ceaseless prayer.

O, may the harvest be
Abundant, Lord, when Thou shalt come.
To bear its garnered treasures home.[12]

BEFORE AND AFTER THE ARMISTICE
SISTER M. AGNES, RIO VISTA

Why? (Before the Armistice)

Some puzzles we find in life's pages.
    To read them we are at a loss.
In fact, to render them perfectly clear,
    We must solve them beneath Christ's Cross.

O, why do the innocent suffer,
    While the wicked, rejoicing, go by?
Why does the poor man meet failure,
    While the rich find success ever nigh?

"Might is right" with the man and the nation.
    The slave feeds his lord, without pay.
Oh, why is not justice the standard
    In the civilized world today?

O Mary, our Lady of Sorrows,
   At the foot of the cross tell us why
Did they scourge our Savior, and mock Him,
    And torture, and shout "crucify"? . . .

Peace (Armistice Day, November 11, 1918)

"Glory be to God on High," sang out the choirs of old.
Today glad anthems pierce the sky as swift the news is told.
From East to West, from pole to pole, rolls on the joyous sound;
And still the mighty word rolls on this globe of ours around.

The glorious news has come at last, and angels sing once more,
Peace, peace on earth! Oh, sheathe the sword.
The world's great war is o'er—Around the world, for friendship's
   clasp,
All Nations stretch their hands
And stand in brotherhood once more—Ne'er severed be those bands!

Rejoice! Rejoice! through land and sea, throughout this world of
   ours.
Sound loud the trumpet of the free and strew
the good-will flowers.
Sound the signal, loud and clear,
that summons war to cease.
Ring out you bells of freedom, ring the golden chimes of Peace.[13]

A TRIBUTE TO MOTHER M. RAYMOND DONAHUE
ON HER GOLDEN JUBILEE
BY MOTHER M. JOSEPH O'DONAHOE

There are many today, Mother Raymond,
   Who are crowning your head with gold,
And saying fine things of the records
   Your fifty long years have told.

And I too come with the others,
   My offering before you to cast;
But thinking of youth in its fullness,
   Makes my thoughts all run in the past.

We worked and we taught and we labored,
   Like those in the "Field-Afar,"
Our comforts never increasing,
   Our luxuries always rare.

We had then no fine stately buildings,
   No college on mountain so high,
But our dwelling was that of our Master
   The God of earth, air, and sky.

And now, my dear Mother Raymond,
   God has blest us and spared us to see
The mustard seed sown on the "HILL TOP"
   Grown up to the wide spreading tree.

Pardon, if long I have spoken,
   Of "Bygones" on this your own day,
But we are going so fast—we old young Sisters,
   And with us are passing away

So many traditions and memories,
   That precious and sacred we hold,
I feel that their beauty and radiance,
   Make all the brighter—this gold![14]

SONNET TRIBUTE TO
MOTHER MARY FRANCES XAVIER WARDE
BY SISTER MARY OF THE ANGELS

Bearing a lighted candle in her hand,
In comeliness and beauty she proceeds,
To sail the seas or girdle her bright land
Wherever Mercy calls or pity needs.
One step today—with strong, undaunted grace
The vows are made! Heroic parchment scroll
The name of Frances bears upon its face;
And Xavier's spirit overflows her soul.
Across the years that candle sends its beams
Symbolic of her faith, all nature stilled;

Across the seas she carries it—her dreams
Of missionary sainthood all fulfilled!
America gave welcome small and faint:
Today she brings her tribute to a saint.[15]

THE SISTER OF MERCY

She shares in the hopes of those who sow,
In the gladness of those who reap;
She smiles for the joys that the joyful know,
And she weeps with those who weep.

She prays for the living—she prays for the dead;
She joins in the children's fun;
And grief-worn hearts have been comforted
By the words of the gentle nun.

And a queen might envy her peaceful smile
Of radiant and deep content,
That tells how duty and love the while
In her life and heart are blent.

She walks in the path she chose in youth,
With never a thought for earth;
Bright in her holiness—grand in her truth;
Light in her innocent mirth.

In her Master's vineyard with willing hand
She toils from dawn to gray,
And well for her when she shall stand
At His right on judgment day.[16]

(Author Unknown)

LINES IN HONOR OF THE GOLDEN JUBILEE
BURLINGTON, VERMONT 1872–1922
BY MERCEDES

June—the month of fragrant roses; June—the month of birds and
    flowers,
With her sky of radiant sapphire, with her scenes from floral bowers,
Comes to us with rarest blessings—blessings even we not see,
Clustered 'round a glorious Fiesta—'round a Golden Jubilee.

Not within the halls of princes, swept with hangings rich in gold,
Not within the world's great mansions, glittering with wealth untold.
But within a convent's precincts, where the brides of heaven stay,
Are these fifty years recorded, have these decades slipped away.

Fifty years of gentle labor in the gardens of the Lord,
Fifty years of toil that seeks not earthly glory or reward;
Fifty years of sowing, broadcast, Mercy's ever fruitful seed,
'Til the harvest, in abundance, serves this queenly city's need.[17]

THE SAINT XAVIER HYMN
TO OUR LADY OF MERCY
A TYPICAL NINETEENTH CENTURY MERCY HYMN

Our Lady of Mercy, sweet and pure,
   We gather round thy shrine,
As near to thee we feel secure,
   From danger and from crime.
Our garlands at our Mother's feet
   We place with loving care,
And raise our voices loud to greet
   Our Queen and Lady fair.

Chorus

Our Lady of Mercy sweet and pure,
In thy blest care we are secure;
In mercy now thine aid bestow,
On us, thy children, here below.

Thy titles form a coronet
   Of gems both rich and rare;
The one we truly love the best
   Is Queen of Mercy fair.

That name so sweet has made thee ours
   By every right divine,
And thou wilt plead with Mother Love
   That we be always thine.[18]

THREE POEMS BY SISTER MARY AUGUSTINE MCKENNA,
NEW YORK

Lines Composed Before Writing a Petition for Means To Aid in Erecting a Home for Homeless Children

Sacred Heart of Jesus! fill my mind with light,
Give me words of wisdom, guide my pen aright;
For Thy homeless children, Jesus, I appeal,
Make we wisely utter what I warmly feel.

Once before, Lord Jesus, I essayed to aid
Homeless little children, to Thine image made;
Then I failed, unworthy and unfit and weak;
More unfit, less worthy now, yet must I speak.

Speak to men, Lord Jesus, men of wealth and pride,
Seek to turn their interest from the world aside,
Reach their hearts and win them to expend their gold
On the lambs that shiver in the wind and cold.

Use me for this service, send me love divine,
Jesus, Jesus, Jesus, make these children Thine;
Shelter them, Sweet Jesus, to Thy robe they hold,
Shelter them and save them, to Thy heart enfold.

Suffer little children close to Thee to come,
Help us to provide them shelter, comfort, home;
They are Thine, Lord Jesus, bless the words I say,
Draw them to Thy service, guide them on their way.

To the Children of the Rich for the Children of the Poor

Dear little friends, whose eyes bespeak the gladness,
　That in your hearts like God's bright sunshine dwells;
Whose eyes are filled with rays of home-affection,
　Twining o'er all such blissful, fairy spells.

List ye, and know, that hearts like yours are flowing
　With bitter sorrow,—and that bare, cold feet
Travel the city's walks, while ye are sleeping—
　Seeking for warmth and shelter, in the street.

That little childish heads are bowed in anguish,
  That tiny fingers toil and know not play;
That crouching figures fear their home's reception,
  And shrink e'en from that sweet word, "home," away.

To them it echoes not in love,—they know not
  The cherished tenderness with which you hail
Each eve's unbroken circle—joys and pleasures,
  No! they but see life's weary, darksome veil.

No gentle mother's smile to crown their labor—
  Perchance her soul hath winged its flight above;
Or if remaining—'tis the earth's cold bosom
  That speaks to her of future peace and love.

Sadly she folds her dear and suffering children
  Unto her heart, that would their comfort be;
But it is broken, and its songs are silent:
  Sorrow is very sad in infancy.

So, for the love of Jesus in His childhood,
  If to His Infant-Heart you would be dear,
Cherish and keep the legacy He leaves you:
  His own afflicted little ones to cheer.

Think of your happy homes,—deal out a portion
  Of kindly comfort to your sadder friends;

Believe their prayers will reach the Heart of Jesus,
  Deepening the love, which on you now He spends.

Benedicamus Domino

Let us bless the Lord, dear Sisters,
  Let us bless our gracious Lord,
Let us praise Him, let us bless Him,
  Let us love his holy word.

Let us bless Him for the woodlands,
  For the sun and for the shade,
For the myriad joyous creatures
  That for us His mercy made.

Let us bless Him for St. Xavier's,
　Where the city's ceaseless cry
Is unheard, and we are gazing
　On the pure, unshadowed sky—

Where in strangers we meet sisters,
　Sisters in affection true,
Sisters, linked in love of Jesus,
　Sisters, with one goal in view.

Let us bless Him that He brought us
　Here together at His feet,
Let us pray that each may serve Him,
　Till in heavenly bliss we meet.

Let us bless Him,—He hath called us
　By the bonds of love and grace,
And by vow and veil and promise,
　Till we see Him face to face.

Let us hasten—He has called us
　To pursue His chosen path;
Deeds of mercy, love and meekness,
　Are the milestones that it hath.

Let us hasten, O Lord Jesus!
　Calvary may not be far,
When the darkness comes, my Saviour,
　Oh, be Thou our polar star![19]

(Stanza three refers to meeting of New York Sisters with Pittsburgh Sisters of Mercy at St. Xavier's Convent, Latrobe, Pennsylvania.)

Notes

1. Poems from Private Notebook of Frances Warde. Archives, Pittsburgh.
2. Archives, Chicago. Printed in unidentified newspaper, c. 1870's.
3. Archives, St. Louis.
4. *Mercy Memoirs,* Bordentown. Archives, Plainfield.
5. Poem written August 25, 1878. Printed October 4, 1878, *Weekly Herald,* Vicksburg, Mississippi. Archives, St. Louis.

6. From *Precept Diary,* 1881, Compiled by Margaret F. Gell. Archives, Sisters of Mercy, New Jersey.
7. Date not known. Archives, Silver Spring, Maryland.
8. Archives, St. Louis.
9. Archives, Manchester, New Hampshire.
10. From *Wild Flowers from the Mountain-Side,* by Mercedes, J. B. Lippincott and Company, Philadelphia, 1885. Poem written at St. Xavier Cemetery, Latrobe, Pennsylvania. Archives, Sisters of Mercy, New Orleans.
11. Archives, Sisters of Mercy, Chicago.
12. Sister Mary Constance Smith, *A Sheaf of Golden Years* (1856–1906), New York, Benziger Brothers, 1906.
13. Sister M. Agnes, *Poems,* St. Gertrude's Academy, Rio Vista, California, 1925, pp. 9 and 30.
14. Sister Mary Ignatius Hogan, *Mercy Memoirs,* New Jersey. Archives, Sisters of Mercy, New Jersey.
15. Archives, St. Xavier Convent, Chicago, January 24, 1933.
16. "The Sisters of Mercy Celebrate Diamond Jubilee" (1873–1948), Portland, Maine. Author unknown. Archives, Portland.
17. *Mount Saint Mary Journal,* Burlington, Vermont (1872–1922), Jubilee Number, p. 1.
18. Archives, Sisters of Mercy, Chicago.
19. *Poems and Plays* by Sisters of Mercy, St. Catherine's Convent, New York City, New York Catholic Protectory, West Chester, New York, 1873. (Sister M. Augustine McKenna, Author.) Rare Book. Archives, Sisters of Mercy, New Orleans.

VIII.

NEWSPAPER AND PERIODICAL ACCOUNTS

OUTLINE

315

Tribute to Mother M. Fidelis of Manchester on Golden Jubilee (August 17, 1880—August 17, 1930)

Semi-Centennial Celebration in Pittsburgh of the Founding of the Sisters of Mercy in Ireland (1831–1881)

Sermon by Bishop James Augustine Healy at Funeral Liturgy of Mother Frances Warde (1884)

Early Days in Big Rapids, Michigan (1891)

Editorial on the Sisters of Mercy in America, Reviewing Their Tremendous Growth and Service Over Fifty Years (1843–1893)

Indian Legend Concerning Murder and Prophecy of Indian Maid at St. Xavier Cemetery, Latrobe, Pennsylvania (1900)

On the Golden Jubilee of the Hartford, Connecticut Congregation: Praise of Founder (1902)

On the Golden Jubilee of Mother Gonzaga, a Retrospective Glance at the Manchester Foundation (1906)

Description of Services of Sisters of Mercy, St. Alphonsus Convent, New Orleans (1907)

Story of Unusual Life Revealed in the Death of Sister Augustine Saniewska, Portland, Maine, c. 1914

Letter of Paul L. Blakely, S.J., of *America,* to Reverend Mother, Manchester, New Hampshire, January 24, 1921.

Editorial, *America,* on the Centenary of the Sisters of Mercy

A School Exclusively for Indians, Taught by Sisters of Mercy, Pleasant Point Indian Reservation, Perry, Maine (1878)

Pioneer Woman of Oklahoma, Mother Aloysius (1884)

Centennial Celebration of Sisters of Mercy, Loretto, Pennsylvania (1848–1948)

Sisters of Mercy in the Diocese of Brooklyn (1855)

Religious Communities Who Offered Their All in Civil War Service (1861–64)

Labor of Sisters on Three Indian Reservations in Maine Compared with Service of Black People (1878)

Tribute to Mercy Sisters in Manchester and Maine on Their Centenaries

The Impact of Mother de Pazzi Bentley, Founder of the Sisters of Mercy in St. Louis, Missouri

Five Sisters of Mercy To Found First Convent of Mercy in Canada (1957)

INTRODUCTION

Newspaper and periodical accounts ordinarily emphasize the extraordinary in everyday life rather than the usual. It is not surprising, then, that newspaper stories Sisters of Mercy thought worthy to place in their various archives throughout America tend toward the unusual. For this reason, these accounts are worth treasuring.

We discover through well-worn newspaper stories, for example: that all of the Sisters of the small Mercy Hospital staff in Pittsburgh died within a month in service of typhoid victims in 1848; that four Sisters of Mercy in Chicago died within one weekend in the service of Asiatic Cholera patients in 1854; that fifty-nine Sisters of Mercy died in the service of yellow fever victims in New Orleans, Mobile, Natchez, and Nashville in 1878; that service in the Small Pox Pest House in San Francisco was taken over completely by the San Francisco Sisters in 1869 (number of deaths of Sisters not recorded).

Pioneer work of Sisters of Mercy in such unsettled areas as Jackson, Mississippi (1870), Big Rapids, Michigan (1879), Oklahoma (1884), and Indian Reservations in Indian Island, Maine, are remembered in newspaper accounts. The numbers of Sisters who died serving the soldiers of North and South in the Civil War were tallied insofar as possible so that their graves might be marked with emblems.

One of the most touching accounts in periodicals is that of Orestes Brownson, who writes a review of Mother Austin Carroll's *Life of Catherine McAuley* in 1873. He declares:

"The Institute founded by that noble lady and true woman, Catherine McAuley, exactly serves the evils of our time. The specialty of the Sisters of Mercy is a mission to the poor, and the principle of life for the Order is love of the poor. We wrote many years ago, when we were a Radical and no Christian, 'Give the starving beggar a meal before you preach him a sermon.' Mother Catherine relieves physical distress . . . before commencing the spiritual works of mercy. She feeds the hungry, clothes the naked, and warms the freezing, as the first step [in love of the poor]."

The reader will note in the following accounts certain repetitions, in special newspaper contexts, of accounts given in earlier chapters borrowed from Annals and Archives. The local newspaper accounts have their own special flavors!

317

*   *   *

ALL OF SMALL MERCY HOSPITAL STAFF IN PITTSBURGH DIE WITHIN A MONTH IN SERVICE OF TYPHOID VICTIMS (1848)

All of the small Mercy hospital staff of Sisters, with the exception of Sister Isidore Fisher, Administrator, were wiped out in service of those suffering from typhoid epidemic. Following deaths are listed:

February 11, 1848: Sister Anne Rigney, Novice, died at Mercy hospital.

March 3, 1848: Kate Lawler, a postulant, died after short illness.

March 5, 1848: Sister Magdalen Reinbolt, Novice, died close to profession date.

March 9, 1848: Sister Xavier Tiernan, first American Sister of Mercy, died.[1]

THE MYSTERY, AN ABOLITION NEWSPAPER, PRAISES SISTERS OF MERCY HOSPITAL, PITTSBURGH FOR MAKING NO DISTINCTION IN SERVICE OF BLACKS AND WHITES (1848)

The last number of *The Mystery,* a very talented abolition paper, conducted by persons of colour, among whom we believe it principally circulates, contains a just and deserved tribute of praise to the principles and the manner in which this benevolent institution, Mercy Hospital, is conducted. The managers of the Hospital, from the very beginning, "avowed their determination to make no distinction of creed or colour. . . ." Protestants or Catholics, coloured and white, are treated with the same charitable solicitude. When the "new and splendid Mercy Hospital" is opened, the same Christian principles will prevail.[2]

BISHOP ANDREW BYRNE OF LITTLE ROCK, ARKANSAS, TO ARRIVE WITH SISTERS OF MERCY FROM NAAS, IRELAND AND ABOUT 600 FARMERS FROM WEXFORD TO SETTLE AN IRISH COLONY IN LITTLE ROCK (1850)

Rt. Rev. Andrew Byrne, Bishop of Little Rock, will come from Dublin with a clergyman, Sisters of Mercy from Naas, and about 600 farmers from Wexford to settle an Irish Colony between Little Rock and Van Buren, Arkansas. The land is abounding with fruit and corn.[3]

TRIBUTE TO CHICAGO SISTERS OF MERCY OVER SIX YEARS (1846–1852)

In the Chicago *Western Tablet* of August 21, 1852, we read of a reception in the Convent: "Since the first establishment of a branch of the Order of Mercy in this city, some six years have now elapsed, and during this short period vast and incalculable is the amount of good that has been, and is daily being effected by the members. Like the devoted daughters of St. Vincent, they shelter in their asylums and train with a mother's tenderness and vigilance a large number of male and female orphans who else would now be homeless little wanderers in the crowded thoroughfares of our city, and deeply contaminated, perhaps, with its corruption and vices. In their hospital, too, which, with the asylums, has been recently incorporated by an Act of the Legislature, the Sisters are assiduous in their ministrations by the bedside of the sick and dying; soothing with kind and gentle words their afflictions and binding up, like compassionate Samaritans, their bruised and sorrowing hearts. Whilst in their academies and schools there is imparted a healthy, solid, and refined education.

"The invaluable services, rendered daily by this devoted Sisterhood to the Catholics of Chicago, give them many strong claims upon gratitude and support."[4]

FOUR CHICAGO SISTERS OF MERCY DIE WITHIN ONE WEEKEND IN SERVICE OF VICTIMS OF ASIATIC CHOLERA (1854); TRIBUTE TO MOTHER AGATHA O'BRIEN

Died, at the Convent of Mercy, Chicago, Illinois, July 8, Mother Mary Agatha, (Margaret O'Brien), and Sister Mary Bertrand Hughes; on the 9th, Sister Mary Louisa Connors, and on the eleventh, Sister Mary Veronica Hickey (at the Mercy Hospital). These excellent religious have fallen victim in the service of the Asiatic Cholera epidemic—four Sisters meeting death in one week end.

The Western Tablet, Chicago, wrote of Mother Agatha:
"This most excellent religious entered the Order of Mercy in Ireland

in May, 1843, and soon after emigrated with Mother Frances Warde and five other Sisters to form the first establishment of the Mercy Order in the United States. In 1846, the year of her religious profession, she moved from Pittsburgh to Chicago with four other Sisters. Her community and schools have flourished. She and those Sisters who died with her will be imitated by those who lament her memory. 'Lovely and comely in their lives, even in death they were not divided.' "[5]

LETTER FROM COMMANDER OF STEAMER CORTES REFUTING ATTACK UPON SISTERS OF MERCY FROM BIGOTS (1855)

The letter which follows is the spontaneous reply of Captain Thomas B. Cropper to a communication sent to one of the city papers by one of the passengers, the purport of which may be learned from the Captain's reply.—

The Sisters of Mercy on Board the
Steamer "Cortes"

Editor of the *Herald:*—Owing to ill health, I have been absent from this city for several weeks, and it was only today that my attention was directed to an article signed "Observer," which appeared in the *Christian Advocate* of December 15*th*. Said article charges certain Reverend Fathers and Sisters of Mercy (who were my passengers from San Juan on the Steamer Cortes) with a neglect of a proper observance of the Sabbath, and with a disposition to indulge too freely in the use of intoxicating drinks. My position as the commander of a passenger steamer makes me a servant of the public in general, and especially so to those who come under my care and protection as wayfarers; and I feel myself called upon to notice the article alluded to, and to pronounce it the most disgusting, detestable calumny I have ever known or heard of. The Fathers and Sisters in question are Catholics, and on board the Cortes their seats at table were next to me, and I may say that at all times they were constantly under my eye and observation.

Their religious exercises were performed not only on Sunday, but every day by themselves, without intruding on others; and in regard to "hard drinking," I cannot imagine how any person could be so very base a slanderer as to prefer such a charge against them. The extreme propriety of their deportment, their unobtrusiveness, and the gentle manners of the Sisters, and perfect correctness of the Fathers, should have shielded them from so gross an outrage.

Thomas B. Cropper,
Commander of Steamer Cortes.

San Francisco, January 18*th.*, 1855.[6]

SAN FRANCISCO SISTERS OF MERCY SERVE VICTIMS OF FATAL CHOLERA IN STATE MARINE HOSPITAL (1855)

"Uncle Sam" arrives bringing in the fatal Cholera. The Sisters remain almost entirely in the Hospital, doing all in their power for the poor sufferers. *The Daily Times* notices their labors on this occasion as follows:

"We visited yesterday the patients in the State Marine Hospital, and a more horrible and ghastly sight we have seldom witnessed. In the midst of this scene of sorrow, pain, anguish, and danger, were some four or five ministering angels, who disregarded everything to render aid to their distressed fellow creatures. The Sisters of Mercy (rightly named), whose convent is immediately opposite the Hospital, as soon as they learned the state of things, hurried to offer their services. They did not stop to enquire whether the poor sufferers were Protestant or Catholic, Americans or Foreigners, but with the noblest devotion applied themselves to their relief. One Sister would be seen bathing the limbs of a sufferer, another chafing the extremities, and a third applying the usual remedies for the disease, while others with pitying face were calming the fears of those who were dying. The idea of danger never seemed to occur to these noble women. In the performance of the vows of their Order they heeded nothing of the kind. If any of the lives of the unfortunate are saved, they will in a great measure owe their preservation to these ladies."[7]

MERCY SISTERS FROM BUFFALO AND PROVIDENCE OPEN SCHOOLS AND VISIT THE SICK IN BUFFALO AND ROCHESTER, NEW YORK (1857)

Bishop John Timon, first Bishop of Buffalo, in 1854 attended the Plenary Council in New York, where heavy stress was laid on proper education of the young. He became anxious about affairs in his diocese and appealed to the new Mercy Community in Providence.

His appeal was answered by Mother Frances Warde and five Sisters in June, 1857. Bishop Timon negotiated with Father Thomas McAvoy, Pastor of St. Mary's, South Street, to receive the Sisters' plans to occupy a convent recently vacated by Bridgetine Sisters.

The Mercy Sisters in 1857 opened a "select boarding school" in their convent; a parochial school in St. Mary's Parish Church basement; and an industrial school for poor girls. They visited the sick daily. In 1862 they opened schools in Batavia, and in 1867 opened free and select schools in Auburn. Only in 1868 was the Rochester Diocese itself established.[8]

TREMENDOUS WORK OF ELEVEN SISTERS IN CINCINNATI, OHIO (1858)

. . . The special mission of the Sisters of Mercy in this city is to give gratuitous instruction to young girls in all the ordinary useful branches of education, to teach them lace work and other branches of industry by which they may be enabled to make a respectable living; to take care of very young children while their mothers are out at work; to receive into their house orphan children who have left the Asylum at Cumminsville, until they learn trades and are competent to provide for themselves; to harbor young girls while out of employment; to visit the jails and hospitals, sick and destitute, in every part of the city, and to do all in their power to reclaim the intemperate females, of whom, unfortunately, too many in the lanes and alleys of Cincinnati scandalize their neighbors and give bad example to their children. We do not disguise the fact that the Sisters of Mercy have a good deal to do. And the prayer of the friends of society must be, "May God who pronounced the Beatitude on the Merciful, enable them to accomplish it."[9]

MERCY SISTERS OF CINCINNATI FOLLOW ST. PAUL'S RULE: THEY SHOW THEIR FAITH BY THEIR WORKS (1858)

. . . Eminently practical in all their operations, the Sisters of Mercy seem disposed to follow St. Paul's rule, and show their faith by their works. . . . As their charity is bestowed alike upon Jew and Gentile, orthodox and heterodox, so they have equal claims upon all denominations of Christians and those of no denomination at all. . . .

They maintain a Sunday school of two-hundred youths; a week-day school with a nearly equal number; married women's classes Sunday afternoon, and on weekday evenings, classes in religious instruction for more than a thousand females; similar classes for two-hundred girls on Sunday afternoon; a laundry in which they employ destitute women and pay them current rates for their work; a sewing room "in which those able and willing to work with the needles are employed," and which so many attend that "they can execute almost any amount of sewing." The Sisters contemplate also "a free lodging for women and children in which they may be sheltered from the weather and influences of the Station House lodgings." In fine, if these various charitable objects do not furnish work enough to fill the time of twelve benevolent women, then we are at a loss to understand their capacity for labor.[10]

MERCY SISTERS AT SMALL POX HOSPITAL (PEST HOUSE) IN SAN FRANCISCO (1869)

"Permit me through the medium of your paper to express my opinion with regard to the Small Pox Hospital. I was an inmate of that institution for many weeks, and I thank the Supreme Being that I am one of the fortunates who walked instead of being carried out of it. . . . What shall I say to express my sentiments regarding those Ladies (so heroic), those angels of mercy! There were three, and the work they did for their suffering fellow creatures, no words can describe.

"I shall begin with the youngest. There she might be seen from six o'clock in the morning till a late hour at night, going around the wards carrying a tray laden with medicine or beef tea, wine or eggnog, always with a kind look and smile that did more good than anything the doctor could order for our health.

"The next, a Spanish Lady, whose kind interest in the poor sufferers was manifested by her untiring attention, going her rounds, morning, noon, and night with her pot of oil in one of her hands and a little brush in the other.

"The third, an old lady, a real lady in the best sense of the word; here words would fail to describe her goodness and kindness to all and everyone, no matter who they were. At midnight I have seen her kneeling beside the bed of the dying. . . . I have seen her perform blessed actions for the bodies of the poor sufferers. I could tell a great many more works of these holy ladies that made the Pest House a place of happiness even though it was a place of suffering. I hear that that most worthy and kind lady, the Reverend Mother of St. Mary's Hospital, is now at the Pest

House in place of one of the three I knew there. May God protect them all. They are real Sisters of Mercy and mothers to the afflicted."[11]

MERCY SISTERS AS PIONEERS IN JACKSON, MISSISSIPPI (1870)

Editor's Note—At a meeting of the Pioneers' club, held at Jackson, Miss., recently during which tribute was paid to pioneer teachers, Catholic and non-Catholic, the following paper was read by Mrs. Josie Fransioli, sketching the life of a Sister of Mercy, who, like so many others of the same great order, has been but too little known, as is true also of other great works of education they have carried in this section for so many years.

"The Sisters of Mercy, who came to Jackson in 1870 were women cast in heroic mould. They came to a city that was painfully recovering from the ravages of the War Between the States, where pestilence lurked, where resources were slender, and educational facilities few; but this band of religious women possessed the spirit of enthusiasm, the courage, the confidence, and the power of persuasion that make up the character of the pioneer. And in them was fulfilled the prophecy: "You shall bring forth fruit and your fruit shall remain."

"Outstanding among these brave women was the late Sister Mary Rose Stevens, who died November 1, 1937, and who, had she been spared a few months longer, would have attained her hundredth birthday on March 12, 1938.

"Laura Stevens was born in Benton, Mississippi, and reared in the fascinating atmosphere of the ante-bellum South. When she was sixteen years of age, application was made for her admission into one of the fashionable 'finishing schools' of the day; but because accommodations in the institution were limited, the late applicant met with refusal, and Laura found herself enrolled in a convent school, conducted by the Sisters of Charity in Nazareth, Kentucky. Here she became familiar with the doctrines of Catholicity, but it was not until she had finished school and returned home that, after an intelligent consideration of its claims, she was received into the Church at the age of twenty-one.

"In the year 1868 Laura Stevens, eager to do great things for God, entered the Convent of Mercy in Vicksburg, Mississippi, and was given the religious name of Sister Mary Rose. Two years later she was among the group of four who laid the foundation of St. Joseph's school in Jackson. This was in 1870, and with the exception of five years' service on the Indian mission, the greater part of Sister Mary Rose's life was spent in Jackson, dedicated to the all-important work of education; a work for which by talent and experience she was eminently fitted, and to which she gave herself with zeal and unwearied love."[12]

CATHERINE MCAULEY UNIQUE AMONG RELIGIOUS FOUNDERS IN SERVICE OF THE POOR (1871)

Nothing can be done to settle the terrible labor-question, now convulsing society, and already beginning to paralyze the industry of nations, so long as poverty is held to be a crime or a misfortune. So long as the poor are held to be the less favored class, and poverty an evil to be avoided, the evils which now afflict society, and which statesmen, legislators, political economists, sociologists, philanthropists of all hues only aggravate by their proposed or attempted remedies, will remain. We shall be utterly unable to see society in a normal state, and true social well-being secured, so long as we hold our present views of riches and poverty. We must begin, if we really wish to remedy the social evils we deplore, by consecrating poverty and honoring the poor. The church in her religious orders gives the true method, and the only practical method of resisting and overcoming these social evils. This method is in the three vows which the religious take—the vow of chastity, the vow of poverty, and the vow of obedience, which oppose to the world the practice, in an heroic degree, of the three virtues on which all true society depends. These virtues directly oppose the three great dangers to which at all times, and more especially in our times, society is exposed—licentiousness, covetousness, and insubordination.

These three vows are common to all religious orders, and we do not claim for the Sisters of Mercy a merit above or different in kind from that of other orders that combine the active with the contemplative life. We only say, in its specialty it combats the special evil of modern society, by cultivating and practicing the virtue of loving and serving the poor, and of honoring poverty.

The Institute founded by that noble lady and true woman, Catherine McAuley, exactly meets the evil. The specialty of the Sisters of Mercy is a mission to the poor, and the principle of life for the order is love of the poor. We wrote many years ago, when we were a Radical and no Christian, "Give the starving beggar a meal before you preach him a sermon." We find Mother Catherine recognizes the principle, relieves the physical distress, and performs one of the corporal works of mercy, before commencing to perform the spiritual works of mercy. She feeds the hungry, clothes the naked, and warms the freezing, as the first step. Then commences the work of education.[13]

TRIBUTE BY FORMER STUDENT TO SISTER PHILOMENA,
FOUNDING MEMBER OF SISTERS OF MERCY, VICKSBURG,
MISSISSIPPI (1876)

Sister Philomena was a native of Baltimore. Seventeen long and happy years were spent in divine service—years of beautiful labor. Visiting the sick and afflicted and administering to their wants, were her chief occupation and delight. During the late war she exposed herself to many dangers in attending the sick and wounded and, regardless of her own welfare, she was mindful of promoting the happiness of others.

For several years she was engaged in teaching, and many of the young men of Vicksburg received their first lessons from her. Before death claimed her, she had the happiness of seeing "her boys," as she familiarly called them, engaged in honorable pursuits in life, true Christians, and reaping the fruits of her early instructions.

The writer knew her for years, and to her he is indebted for many of the happiest moments of his life. Her gentle and amiable disposition won the hearts of all who knew her, and left impressions too endearing to be forgotten soon.

A solemn Mass of Requiem was said on Monday, at 8 o'clock, and afterwards her remains were born, by her former students, to their final resting place.

May your slumbers be quiet and peaceful, may the angels and bright choirs of heaven be your companions! And may your soul enjoy the sweet embrace of Him whom you have served so long, is the fervent prayer of an old pupil.[14]

SISTERS OF MERCY WHO DIED IN SERVICE OF YELLOW FEVER
VICTIMS IN VICKSBURG, MISSISSIPPI (1878)

To the Necrology of Religious who died of yellow fever during the recent epidemic, which was published in our issue of December 15, 1878, we have to add the following Sisters of Mercy who died in Vicksburg, Mississippi:

September 7—Sister Mary Regis Grant, native of Copiah County, Mississippi, age 23

September 7—Sister Mary Bernardine Murray, native of Pittsburgh, Pennsylvania, age 30

September 10—Sister Mary Columba McGrath, native of Queen's County, Ireland, age 22

September 13—Sister Mary Gonzaga Daly, native of Ale Kalb, Mississippi, age 23

Recapitulation now stands:

Archdiocese of New Orleans	-------------	23 Sisters
Diocese of Mobile	-------------	1
Diocese of Natchez	-------------	15
Diocese of Nashville	-------------	20
	Total ------	59 Sisters

These additions alter our recapitulation:

	Priests	Seminarians	Brothers	Sisters
Archdiocese of New Orleans	11	3	4	23
Diocese of Mobile	1	—	—	1
Diocese of Natchez	6	—	—	15
Diocese of Nashville	12	—	2	20
Total—30		3	6	59 [15]

TRIBUTE TO MOTHER M. FIDELIS OF MANCHESTER ON GOLDEN JUBILEE (AUGUST 17, 1880—AUGUST 17, 1930)

Mother M. Fidelis was received under Mother Frances Warde at Manchester August 17, 1880. The sermon of Msgr. Jeremiah S. Buckley, Pastor, St. John Evangelist Church, Vicar General of the Diocese of Manchester, on her Golden Jubilee follows:

"In the designs of Divine Providence, it may have been a prophetic assurance of the grace in store for the Institute of Our Lady of Mercy . . . that at the first ceremony of reception held at the motherhouse of the new Institute in Baggott Street, Dublin, there were *seven* sisters who received the holy habit. . . .

"One of the most precious gifts of Ireland to the new world was a band of Sisters of Mercy, numbering *seven,* who, on December 21, 1843, under the leadership of *The Flower of the Flock, Mother Frances Warde,* the first novice to pronounce her vows in the new Institute, established at Pittsburgh, Pennsylvania, the first community of the Sisters of Mercy in this country. . . ."

Mother M. Fidelis was the first superior in Concord, Massachusetts, where tribute this day was given.

"Thou shalt number to the *seven* weeks of years, that is to say *seven* times seven, which together makes 49 years, and thou shalt sanctify the 50th year, for it is the year of Jubilee." Tributes were offered in Manchester, Portland, and Concord.[16]

SEMI-CENTENNIAL CELEBRATION IN PITTSBURGH OF THE FOUNDING OF THE SISTERS OF MERCY IN IRELAND (1831–1881)

One mid-winter day 38 years ago there arrived in this city a little band of seven women. Strangers in a strange land, yet holding allegiance alone to God, they began a work whose scope was measured by their sublime faith in the truth of the words, "But the greatest of these is charity," and whose name, Sisters of Mercy, has been associated for a half century with deeds of self-sacrificing devotion unsurpassed in the history of religious zeal. Yesterday, the Golden Jubilee, the semi-centennial of the foundation of this order, was celebrated on a scale of magnificence fully comporting with the occasion, and as Pittsburgh was the first city in the United States where the sisterhood established themselves, it was but fitting that here the celebration should be endowed with especial interest.

At the Mother House, or convent, corner of Webster avenue and Chatham street, the exercises began yesterday morning at 9:30 with the celebration of Haydn's Imperial High Mass, and at 9:40 the resident and visiting clergy to the number of 40 or more filed into the chapel.

The event of the afternoon was the unveiling in the presence of all of a portrait of the foundress of the Order of Sisters of Mercy, Mother Catherine McAuley. This gem of art, the work of one of the sisters, was unveiled during the singing of a Hymn of Gratitude, written expressly for the celebration.

Of the original seven who almost four decades ago arrived from Ireland in Pittsburgh, but two survive, Mother Elizabeth Strange of the Convent of Mercy, this city, and Mother Frances Warde, of Manchester, N.H. From the little band has gone forth the power that has built the order and with it churches and schools and hospitals. They have labored in hovel and hamlet, crowded court and stifling lazaretto; oft time with no reward but a thankful look from eyes fast glazing in death. Upon the plains of Mexico at Buena Vista and Cerro Gordo, and upon the sodden soil of our Southern battle fields, their tender care and ministrations have been felt! Blue and gray, friend and foe know and bless them.

In the history of the Order in Pittsburgh they have removed but three times. From 1843 to 1848 they occupied buildings upon Penn avenue, but in the latter year they removed to their present site, corner Webster and Chatham streets. From seven sisters and one establishment in this city alone, they have increased to 200 sisters and nine establishments all under the charge of the Mother Superior at the Webster avenue convent. They are as follows: The Mother House, Webster avenue; St. Xavier's Academy, Latrobe; Mercy Hospital, city; Orphan Asylum, Tannehill street; Lawrenceville Convent, Forty-sixth street; St. Patrick's, Seventeenth street; Allegheny, McKeesport, and Braddock. The growth of the Order in the United States from this small beginning, the seed sown 38 years ago, has resulted in the establishment of over 200 convents and the conformation of over 10,000 sisters.

The reporter had a short talk with Mother Elizabeth Strange, one of the two living survivors of the band of seven. She is a bright-eyed old lady who talks rapidly but in a wonderfully entertaining way. Time, though he has traced wrinkles on the kindly, cheerful face, has left no imprint upon her remarkable memory, and she recalls dates and incidents with surprising facility. Eight years ago, after an absence of 30 years, she revisited the home of her girlhood, but returned to this, her adopted country, at the termination of her visit.[17]

SERMON BY BISHOP JAMES AUGUSTINE HEALY AT FUNERAL OF MOTHER FRANCES WARDE (1884)

. . . While warmth and devotion and strength of heart are by no means rare in women, there was in this woman's life a sacrifice and a fortitude which man can never fathom. Mother Xavier Warde was eminently strong of heart. One could never enter her presence without feeling the dignity, the almost majesty, which was inseparable from her. . . . Yet there was about her a gentle charm which rarely failed to attract. . . . Rise up and testify, you who have been associated with her. Testify to her spirit of sacrifice, her courage, her strength. As Mother M. Frances Xavier, she established herself and her Order, convent after convent, in Ireland and then in our United States. She was always and everywhere the same; she left one home after another, whenever God called, as though home were not home. . . . One who was admired, one who was everywhere respected, and one who won the affection of all who knew her. Her character was beautiful and her fidelity was never surpassed. She was always the religous seeking seclusion. Yet her works and she were known, I might say, almost from the Atlantic to the Pacific Ocean and from our northern frontier to the shores of the Gulf of Mexico. . . .

Mother Warde's praises can be properly sung only by the hundreds of the poor whom she has helped; the children to whom she has sent teachers of both earthly and heavenly wisdom; the sick she has comforted; the souls she has rescued by her own fervent words or those of her daughters. . . .

Mother Xavier has passed away from her devoted Sisters, who will miss each day her experience, her kind advice, her wise government. The never-wearying care, the love, the grand religious presence can never come back, but she is living in the true life. She will continue to be the guide and protector of this Community, whose glory she will be in that heaven which, by God's grace, her life of prayer and good works have merited for her.[18]

EARLY DAYS IN BIG RAPIDS, MICHIGAN (1891)

. . . The principal public institution of Big Rapids is Mercy Hospital. . . . The Order of Mercy, one of the religious foundations of the Roman Catholic Church, is modern in its establishment. It began in Ireland in 1827. . . . The founder was Catherine Elizabeth McAuley. Her work, at first local in its inception, has in sixty years spread nearly to the four quarters of the globe. . . . The visitor to Mercy Hospital at Big Rapids will see a spacious brick building two stories high, with mansard roof, which practically gives it another story, and a lofty and well lighted basement which affords room for the culinary and domestic operations. The interior is finished in the natural wood, and with hardwood floors. . . . All the sisters are indefatigable in pursuing duty. It is with them a constant season of self-sacrifice and toil. No one can behold them caring for the sick, providing for their comfort, nor observe them in their daily walk without a feeling of gratitude for their devotion and of respect for those who make such care their life work.

. . . The dormitory of the Sisters is in the upper portion of the hospital —four or five rooms, each with half a dozen single iron bed-steads, furnished neatly. White curtains may be drawn about a portion of the bed-steads, but there are no carpets on the floor. The walls are without ornament, save for an occasional picture of a saint, or the memento of vows of those who are professed nuns. These vows are written out and framed, duly signed and sealed, with the name in religion and the former name of the sister, and the obligation of charity, poverty, celibacy, piety and obedience, to which the individual subscribes. A certificate of devotion to a life of chastity and toil from which there is no divorcement.

. . . The hospital was opened in 1879, and to date has treated 7,366 patients. The list of diseases makes a formidable showing, running through the alphabet of the medical dictionary with a woeful number of injuries, fractures and other misfortunes that call for the surgeons' skill. . . . The main support of the institution comes from the sale of certificates of admission, which are good for one year, and are furnished to workingmen in lumber regions and in the towns for the price of $5.00. This sum gives medical attendance, a bed, board, care, and washing for one year. Mother Alphonsus says the hospital differs from a hotel; the latter is earning most when it is full; the hospital when it is empty![19]

EDITORIAL ON THE SISTERS OF MERCY IN AMERICA, REVIEWING THEIR TREMENDOUS GROWTH AND SERVICE OVER FIFTY YEARS (1843–1893)

The Sisterhood of Mercy had to bear its share of persecution in Know-Nothing times in New England. It grew up in California with the gold seekers. It went to war on the application of Stanton, the Secretary of War, for nurses, and served till the awful struggle was over, caring for the wounded of both sides. It suffered with the Chicagoans in their historic fire; and grew up to splendid proportions in the reguilded city. . . .

It has shared in the instruction of the country's youth; the relieving of its poor and sick; and the reformation of its criminals. It is now one of the most widespread, strong in number, and popular of Catholic religious Orders in America, having drawn to its ranks a multitude of able and accomplished women of every ancestry known among us—including converts of the older American stock.[20]

INDIAN LEGEND CONCERNING MURDER AND PROPHECY OF INDIAN MAID AT ST. XAVIER CEMETERY, LATROBE, PENNSYLVANIA (1900)

. . . The road to the little cemetery where the nuns' graves are clustered leads through a long tree-bordered lane, and the cemetery is enclosed by a thick hedge of evergreen. A particularly touching and beautiful legend is attached to this quiet burial spot, relating that long before Pennsylvania was settled by white pioneers, a band of Indians, converted through the efforts of missionaries, embraced Christianity on the very hills now occupied by St. Xavier's. The daughter of the chief, who was given the name Agnes in baptism, vowed her life to the God she had just learned to know and refused all offers of marriage.

The chieftain of the neighboring tribe, incensed at her refusal, mur-

dered her one day while she was praying, and as she died she pointed to
the hill nearby and breathed a prophecy that in future years a band of
virgins would build a convent on that hill, doing the work of God's charity, and their graves would be clustered round her own.

In the middle of the cemetery a marble cross is erected to the memory
of the Indian martyr, and Mother Elizabeth Strange was laid this morning
in the very shadow of this cross, around which the mounds of the dead
nuns are gathered, each marked by a slender cross of iron. Mother Elizabeth's grave will be planted thickly with laurel and at its head a cross will
be placed bearing only her name, beloved by all who knew it, and the
dates of her birth and death. The long record of years will be written only
in the hearts and memories of the thousand poor and sorrowful who have
reason to bless Mother Elizabeth Strange.[21]

ON THE GOLDEN JUBILEE OF THE HARTFORD, CONNECTICUT CONGREGATION: PRAISE OF FOUNDER (1902)

Such postulants [as Elizabeth Jane Tiernan] often fell to the lot of
Mother Warde in the convent founded by her, and surely no woman was
better fitted to emulate the tact of Catherine McAuley in winning accomplished young ladies to the service of God than this foundress of Pittsburgh, Providence, and Hartford. Mother Warde received from nature a
benign character which was sweetened and sanctified by her religious life
of 54 years. Attracted by the beauty of Mother McAuley's charity, she
entered religion when a mere school girl. Even then Fannie Warde was a
dignified personage. This elegance of deportment she never lost, while she
taught it, in some measure, to all whom she trained in the religious life.

The American foundress was not a calculating woman. On this account she was sometimes deceived, but more frequently she was rewarded
for her liberal estimate of others. She had the good fortune not to be
critical towards the weaknesses of her kind. If she did see the faults of
others, she was never known to give her thoughts expression on that subject. Therefore her universal charity, her special characteristic, covered
like a mantle, from the eyes of her companions, all her own little defects.

Mother Warde was a general favorite with those outside the faith and
perhaps no woman ever made so many converts. She excelled in the art of
conversation; and as she was well read in the Sacred Scriptures and thoroughly versed in religious controversy, she never lost an opportunity of
showing the beauties of the true Church to non-Catholics. Like St. Paul,
she could make herself all things to all men. She was as zealous instructing
the rough river men on the Ohio, and the factory hands of the Iron City, as

she was successful in explaining away the fallacies of the Greek schism to a Russian princess whom she converted at Newport.

The Indians of Maine well named Mother Xavier Warde when they called her "The Great Mother," and great maternal blessings she brought to them when she established a convent of her Order at Oldtown, a settlement of the ancient Abnaki tribe, now known as Penobscots and Passamaquoddies. For many years these children of the forest retained nothing of civilization taught them by the early missionaries except a treasured remembrance of the faith.

At the request of Bishop James Healy, Mother Warde sent her sisters among them. They commenced the instruction of the young Indians in the schools, and extended it to the squaws in their rude homes, where they impressed on their swarthy sisters the dignity of Christian womanhood. Soon there was a transformation in their mode of living. . . . Mother Warde went once a year to this settlement.[22]

ON THE GOLDEN JUBILEE OF MOTHER GONZAGA, A RETROSPECTIVE GLANCE AT THE MANCHESTER FOUNDATION (1906)

The little band of five who came to Manchester July 16, 1858 were gratefully welcomed by the few, contemptuously regarded by the many.

The tales of the effects of the bigotry which it was the sisters' first task to overcome are like romances to us of a younger generation. The two survivors of the brave band relate, in addition to the stories of the night watches of the zealous fathers of the present generation lest their convent should be burned over their heads, amusing anecdotes of how the visitors whom it was their task to conduct through the house that each might make personal search for dungeons, oubliettes, and such places of torture as only imagination could conjure up, invited them to effect an escape, promising them any assistance they needed. Open doors were not a convincing argument that no compulsion was being exerted to retain the sisters.

There are touching stories, too, of the faith and love which made the coming of the sisters and their work for the people a possibility—stories that cause glad tears to spring unbidden and make the heart thrill with joyous pride in Manchester's first Catholics. The spirit of the working girls of Manchester, whose sacrifices had enabled their venerated pastor to build the convent, was the spirit of the religious, the missionary, the martyr—the flower of our glorious faith. These devoted women had, after a hard day's work in the mills, given their evenings for months to scrubbing, cleaning, making bed clothing, and preparing for the sisters' coming. Well might an institution be blessed that was the fruit of so many sacrifices. Nothing less could have rendered it so sacred.

The prejudice with which the religious were regarded was vigorously combated by the intelligent portion of their non-Catholic towns-people. When the Sisters offered to give private lessons, the wife of the Mayor of Manchester was the first to make application, and there were many to follow her example. An academy was immediately opened as a means for the sisters' support and several young protestant ladies were admitted as boarders. They were permitted to spend their Sundays at home and were the loyal champions of their teachers among their friends. A much valued permission was that of bringing relatives to the convent chapel on Sunday. Thus a better understanding of the sisters' lives and aims was soon brought about with mutual profit.

The first parochial school for girls was in the convent. Later it was transferred to what is now St. Martha's Home—the first parochial school building in the city. The first parochial school for boys was in the basement of St. Anne's, under the principleship of Mr. Thomas Corcoran. . . .

Now about 250 sisters educate 200 children in Maine alone. Branches exist at Concord, Dover, Franklin Falls, Claremont, Laconia, Nashua, Portsmouth, Rochester, East Boston, and Gloucester. There are also orphan asylums, hospitals, home for aged women, night refuge, infant asylum, and home for working girls.[23]

DESCRIPTION OF SERVICES OF SISTERS OF MERCY, ST. ALPHONSUS CONVENT, NEW ORLEANS (1907)

The large institution on St. Andrew street, between Magazine and Constance streets, known as St. Alphonsus Convent of Mercy, was founded in New Orleans, on Easter Sunday, March 28, 1869. It is the Mother House of many convents, like St. Alphonsus' Orphan Asylum, the Newsboys' Home, St. Michaels' Convent of Mercy in this city, Biloxi, Jeanerette, La., St. Martinsville, La., Belize, British Honduras, and several others. The Sisters of Mercy were founded in Dublin, on the feast day of Our Lady of Mercy, September 24, 1827, for the education of youth and the relief of the poor and sick, and in the hundreds of establishments under their care in all parts of the world, the Sisters of Mercy, who number many thousands, are zealously engaged in their work of mercy.

In St. Andrew's street is a House of Mercy which has often afforded a home to young girls out of a situation. There is also an Academy of high grade, known as "St. Catherine's Academy," in which pupils who have completed their respective course in the junior schools are afforded every facility for pursuing higher studies, under a corps of teachers who, as to efficiency, have nothing to be desired.

It is the aim of these teachers to bring up their pupils, of whatever grade, in the fear and love of God, and train them to practice the gentle manner which conduces to the happiness of home, and adds a nameless charm to life whether within or outside of the domestic circle.

Besides these salutary works, the Sisters visit the sick in their homes and in the public institutions to relieve and console them in their misery and fill them with the hope which lessens their suffering. There is no class excluded from the benevolence of these ladies. Their lives are devoted to the practice of the spiritual and corporal works of mercy on which depend our blessed title to heaven.[24]

STORY OF UNUSUAL LIFE REVEALED IN THE DEATH OF SISTER AUGUSTINE SANIEWSKA, PORTLAND, MAINE, C. 1914

The story of a romantic life, of wealth possessed and lost, of a Parisian woman who at one time conducted a fashionable boarding school in Paris and who later was driven out during the time of the siege of 1870, was revealed in the death of Sister Mary Augustine Saniewska late Monday night at St. Joseph's Convent.

Few details of her life were available but enough to weave together the interesting career of Sister Augustine who was 84 years of age, 50 years of which had been spent in the work of the church.

Sister Augustine, as she was known at St. Joseph's, was born in Paris, one of five daughters of a Polish Count who had been banished from Poland on account of publishing a paper which was considered detrimental to the welfare of the nation. She was educated in the schools of Paris and later with her sisters conducted a private boarding school until the war of 1870.

At the time of the siege, Sister Augustine, driven out with her family, came to Paris with two sisters. Landing in the United States with but little means, she established a boarding school at Boston which she conducted a short time.

Stories once told to friends are that she then returned to Paris and did much to relieve the suffering and poverty of the people who were once wealthy and then were without homes or food. On one occasion, it was said, a relative in a convent was behind the German lines and in peril. Sister Augustine, on horseback, broke through the lines, rescued her relative and returned safely to Paris.

In her work at St. Joseph's Convent, Sister Augustine was considered a woman of refined character and devotion to the church. She continued her teaching in French and gave many private lessons up to a few years ago when her health began to fail and, crippled by rheumatism, she was unable to do so. She seldom spoke of her former life, many details of which will remain unknown to the world.[25]

LETTER OF PAUL L. BLAKELY, S.J., OF AMERICA, TO REVEREND MOTHER, MANCHESTER, NEW HAMPSHIRE, JANUARY 24, 1921

... I am sure you will be interested in knowing that my two copies of the Life of Mother Warde are in constant demand in this house and among several contestants for the historical prize. It is somewhat curious that a woman who did so much for the Church and for social and educational progress should be so little known in this part of the world. But perhaps we of New York are so blinded by our own greatness that we have no eyes for the work of others. ...

EDITORIAL, AMERICA, ON THE CENTENARY OF THE SISTERS OF MERCY

The original foundation of the congregation of Mercy in the United States was made in Pittsburgh in 1843 by Mother Xavier Warde, one of the first companions of the foundress. In reviewing the marvelous story of the Sisters in this country, it becomes apparent that from the beginning this little group was blessed by Divine Providence with wise counselors. Their first retreat was conducted by a holy Redemptorist Father, soon to be raised, we may piously hope, to the altars as Blessed John Neumann, who ended a long life of labor as Bishop of Philadelphia. Their immediate ecclesiastical superior was the saintly and learned Dr. Michael O'Connor, who after repeated solicitations was permitted by the Holy See seventeen years later, to resign the miter and enter the Society of Jesus. But the first of their blessings was their American Foundress, Mother Xavier Warde.

Preserved for nearly forty-one years of labor in this country, Mother Warde was one of the most extraordinary women in all the long list of foundresses. To unusual gifts of mind and character, she added a zeal for God's glory, and a burning desire to help the unfortunate which made failure impossible. At the time of her death on September 17, 1884, the group of seven who came to Pittsburgh forty years before were represented by thousands of consecrated women laboring in every part of the United States as worthy daughters of noble mothers.

Today the sisters number nearly ten thousand . . . distributed in more than sixty dioceses. . . . Their growth has been steady and solid, for the spirit which animated the little group in Baggot Street one hundred years ago has never flagged or grown weary. . . .[26]

A SCHOOL EXCLUSIVELY FOR INDIANS, TAUGHT BY SISTERS
OF MERCY, PLEASANT POINT INDIAN RESERVATION,
PERRY, MAINE (1878)

High on a Maine promontory, overlooking Passamaquoddy Bay where it joins Canadian waters, stands the eastern-most Indian reservation of the United States granted to the Passamaquoddy tribe by the General Court of Massachusetts in 1794. The Red man truly has an unfailing eye for locations. Across the blue expanse of the splendid bay of their name rise the purple headlands outlining the St. Croix River, dividing Maine from New Brunswick; to the east lies the noble stretch of the fog-famed Bay of Fundy.

Prominent on the peninsula stands a large brick and stone church, recently given to the Indians by the Maine Catholic diocese plus the Indians' gift and insurance, to replace a wooden church destroyed by fire in 1927. The modern edifice is fireproof (costing $67,000), fine and imposing without and within; the neighboring church at Eastport contributing the inside furnishings. Before it, a lovely statue of the Virgin rises from a brilliant circle of geraniums. Beside it, a small convent is occupied by four Sisters of Mercy, one a nurse who has a dispensary and clinic besides visiting the sick. These Sisters are paid by the State.

Nearby is the State school building, presided over by Sister Beatrice, with twenty brown-faced pupils doing good work in free-hand drawing. The majority of the children are of modified types, but a few show the strong, high-featured, aboriginal face. Seven of last year's pupils graduated into the high school at Eastport. In another room were younger grades; forty alert children taught by a young Sister, who commandeers a lusty school chorus in descriptive songs.

The Catholics, from the earliest days of the Franciscan Fathers with Champlain in 1605, have been most successful and understanding in their work among the Indians; partly perhaps by appeal of the church ritual to their innate Indian sense of beauty.

Beyond the school grounds, along a curving road, live the villagers, numbering about 250. Some homes are little more than cabins, others fairly commodious. The tribe numbers about 500, a portion of it living inland at Princeton. Their occupations are fishing, basket-and-moccasin making, and road repairing; not large paying industries, yet the people survive the severe winters and love their ancestral homes. There is an excellent Indian band which is in demand for fairs and festivals. A medicine woman dispensing herbs represents the aboriginal trend. Although Indians were not drafted in World War I, seventeen young men enlisted from this small village. Eight were killed, several incapacitated, but the uninjured are eager to serve again. It is said that when the Indians were asked why they enlisted so much faster than the whites, they replied, "We have been here longer."[27]

PIONEER WOMAN OF OKLAHOMA, MOTHER ALOYSIUS (1884)

Word comes tonight that Oklahoma's pioneer woman, Mother Aloysius, has breathed her last prayer and her great heart has come to rest.

No symbol in bronze with jaunty step and Bible in hand: this pioneer woman lived to bring Christ into the lives of men, to light the fires of zeal, to struggle and toil and spend, to seek stray sheep and Christianize as dawn came over an empire.

Death, the supreme crisis, put the final stamp on her character. Confronted by the inexorable hour, Mother Aloysius awaited it with Christian fortitude and patient resignation, smiling a benediction on those around her, an inspiring model of the fervent Faith to which she devoted her golden span of life.

Mother Aloysius never changed with the years. As she faced the setting sun, she was just as gracious, tender and tolerant as when she bade goodbye to friends and loved ones 55 years ago to come to an unchartered land to give her all to place the name of Christ on the cornerstone of Oklahoma.

God alone knows how far-reaching was the influence of this beloved Sister of Mercy from the era when Oklahoma was yet unborn down to the last day of Mary's month of May when she went to final rest. The tired body, spent through sacrificial years, will rest in the land of her devotion; her soul rises tonight above banks of clouds that float over these, her beloved plains.

Why call the roll of the years? Why speak of the thousands she has befriended? Why recite the litany of her joys and sorrows, her trials and her accomplishments, when God has taken careful note of her half-century of stewardship? All over Oklahoma tonight memories will return, memories of pioneer times and wagon trails, of crusts of bread and dimly-lighted cabins, of murmured prayers in miners' shacks and rosaries under the stars, of a valiant nun who came in 1884 to minister and not to be ministered to, of a soul whose every heart beat was for the glory of God and for the eternal welfare of people, red and white, in Oklahoma.[28]

CENTENNIAL CELEBRATION OF SISTERS OF MERCY, LORETTO, PENNSYLVANIA (1848–1948)

Amid difficulty and hardship Frances Warde persevered in making foundations in this country. Twice her life was despaired of; once after her return from Chicago, where she had suffered so greatly from exposure and accident that she was more dead than alive; again in 1848, when the cholera carried off five of her finest sisters in the space of three months, and her physical strength collapsed from grief and anxiety. . . . One of her favorite sayings was "let all be lost, provided God be not lost."

An old sister recalled early days at Loretto, Pennsylvania. The sisters were removed from the primitive wilderness. The call bell rang at five. Then came meditation and office, and Communion four days a week. On these days, spiritual reading was done before Mass. The sisters walked through the snow with one carrying a lantern. The kitchen stove was a relic of the Civil War. Ovens were enclosed in brick. Water was cold, and had to be boiled for cooking and cleaning. Washing was done on washboards with homemade lye soap. The young sisters milked the cows every morning and evening, then returned back through the snow to spiritual reading and Mass. After supper, everyone got hot gruel and went to bed. Coal had to be carried upstairs to keep the fire in the stoves during the day. Oil lamps had to be collected on three floors every morning for refilling, cleaning, and trimming wicks. The sisters carried water to fill pitchers which often froze overnight. Water was pumped from an artesian well by an old wind mill. The community was isolated.[29]

SISTERS OF MERCY IN THE DIOCESE OF BROOKLYN (1855)

On September 12, 1855, a small group of Sisters of Mercy crossed the East River and the Brooklyn foundation was made. Sister Mary Vincent Haire was the Mother Superior.

The first Brooklyn home of the Sisters of Mercy, which they called the Convent of St. Francis of Assisi, was a small brick house on the corner of Jay and Chapel Streets, close to the Bishop's residence. They began at once to teach the girls of St. James parish and continued to do so until 1869, when they relinquished the school.

A few months after their arrival, the Sisters of Mercy were happy to hold their first reception ceremony in Brooklyn when Julia McKenna received the white veil and also the name in religion of Sister Mary Francis.

It is a significant fact that the first Convent of Mercy and the first religious name bestowed in Brooklyn should be so closely related, maybe by coincidence, but more likely it would seem probable that the Mother foundress wished to instill into this young community a deep spirit of poverty and an ardent desire to emulate one another in performing the numerous works of charity awaiting them. It is not surprising, therefore, that their little convent was overflowing with orphans.

Before long Mother Mary Vincent realized that the small building on Jay St. would not be adequate if they were to assist all who claimed their help. With Bishop Loughlin's assistance, they were able to have built a new Convent of Mercy which stands on the present Motherhouse site at 273 Willoughby Ave., Brooklyn, and into which they moved Dec. 3, 1862.

A few years later, March 8, 1865, Mother Vincent was able to announce to her zealous community that a Charter of Corporation had been granted to the Convent of Mercy authorizing it to care for neglected and dependent children.

Here at the Convent of Mercy the Sisters conducted the St. Francis Industrial School, where girls were taught useful trades such as needlework, artificial flower making, family sewing, making of wreaths, banners, vestments and many other arts.

This training served a twofold purpose. Besides the actual service given to the girls themselves, it proved to be a means of revenue for maintaining the home. The work of the girls was advertised and their services were sought by private families as well as by manufacturers.

Thirty cents for a dozen linen shirt fronts was a mere pittance but pennies earned this way helped to feed and clothe. It was not until 1875 that the first monetary assistance was offered by New York City.

When the Sisters relinquished the St. James school at Jay St. in 1869, they undertook opening what was known as a "select" school in the motherhouse at Willoughby Ave. The aim for this establishment was to provide for the education and religious instruction of girls in St. Patrick's parish. The Sisters also found time to visit the sick poor in their own homes and in hospitals, bringing spiritual and temporal comforts to them. The prisoners in the city jails were instructed and various Sunday schools were attended to provide religious instruction.

On the day Mother Mary Vincent Haire took her religious vows she received a motto "Father, into Thy Hands, I commend My Spirit," which was to be an encouragement to her in the years ahead. When, on March 29, 1883, the first Superior of the Brooklyn Sisters of Mercy commended her spirit to the Heavenly Father for the last time, it was to close the chapter on a life spent laboring and encouraging others to labor that more would know and serve him better.[30]

RELIGIOUS COMMUNITIES WHO OFFERED THEIR ALL IN CIVIL WAR SERVICE (1861–64)

The Sisters of Mercy of Pittsburgh turned over their own hospital, the first in Western Pennsylvania, and one of the finest of the nation, for the war wounded. It became known as the Western Pennsylvania Military Hospital. They likewise served at the vast Stanton Hospital in Washington, housed in its long row of frame blocs.

Lincoln, even in the darkest days of the war, never failed to visit the Military Hospitals. The chronicles of the Sisters of Mercy at Stanton Hospital tell of the tall, slender man, with drooping shoulders silhouetted against the crimson sunset, who would come in the evenings to comfort the sick and suffering.

He encouraged the nuns in their work and went from ward to ward, chatting with Union and Confederate patients alike. Many times after these visits, with the President's drawn face haunting her thoughts, Mother Rose Hostetter, superior of the nuns at Stanton, would ask the Sisters to pray for the man whose shoulders the woes of the nation pressed upon so heavily.[31]

LABOR OF SISTERS ON THREE INDIAN RESERVATIONS IN MAINE COMPARED WITH SERVICE OF BLACK PEOPLE (1878)

The work of the Sisters of Mercy among the Indians awakens us to the fact that for all these years they have been laboring among people who, just like the negro, have been deprived because of the color of their skin. Since 1878 the Sisters have persevered in their labors at the three Indian reservations in this diocese. . . .

While most people had little interest in and cared less about these people, our Sisters of Mercy have remained faithful . . . in laboring among the Indians. . . .[32]

TRIBUTE TO MERCY SISTERS IN MANCHESTER AND MAINE
ON THEIR CENTENARIES

The tremendous acclaim accorded the Manchester Sisters of Mercy on the occasion of their centenary celebration is proof of the warm affection felt by citizens of New Hampshire for these holy women. It also was a vote of appreciation for their outstanding contribution to education in New Hampshire.

From a strictly financial standpoint, it is hard to estimate the millions of tax dollars that would be required to duplicate the education being given by the Sisters of Mercy at no cost to the community.

The steady growth of the Sisters of Mercy after an extremely hostile reception back in the 1850's is a tribute both to the splendid way in which they have carried out their responsibilities and to the efforts of those who have worked so hard to foster interfaith cooperation.[33a]

The value of the contribution of the Sisters of Mercy in Maine is not measured, however, by the staggering statistics of the numbers educated in Mercy-staffed schools and academies, or by the great number cared for in their hospitals and orphanages, or by the cumulative years of missionary service given by successive generations of Mercy Sisters in various parts of the diocese, particularly among our Indian people. God alone can measure the impact of these Sisters upon the souls of those whose lives have been touched by these women in religion the length and breadth of the diocese over the course of one hundred long years. We are truly in their debt. May they have many glorious years in the service of the Church.[33b]

THE IMPACT OF MOTHER DE PAZZI BENTLEY, FOUNDER OF THE
SISTERS OF MERCY IN ST. LOUIS, MISSOURI

When Anna Marie Bentley was born in 1832 into a well-to-do family in Dublin, Ireland, no one suspected the impact her spiritual leadership would have in the far-off city of St. Louis, Missouri.

As foundress of what is now known as the St. Louis Province, Mother Mary de Pazzi Bentley watched the Sisters of Mercy grow in number as new foundations were established throughout Missouri and its surrounding states to continue the mission of social service begun in Ireland in 1831.

In describing Mother de Pazzi's life, Sister Mary Isidore Lennon, RSM, once wrote, "It is difficult to describe a Superior of Mother M. de

Pazzi's calibre. Such characters are rare today when the principles acted upon seem to be the lines of least resistance.

"Mother M. de Pazzi Bentley was a woman animated by high ideals which were related to the concrete material of life.

"This attitude, together with her spartan self-control, her dogged adherence to the Holy Rule, and the quality of her persistence in spiritual things enabled her to lay a strong foundation for the Mercy foundation in St. Louis."[34]

FIVE SISTERS OF MERCY TO FOUND FIRST CONVENT OF MERCY IN CANADA (1957)

Five Irish Sisters of Mercy from Callan, County Kilkenny, left for Prince Rupert in the Columbia Territory of West Canada to open the first house of the Order ever in Canada.

That has always been the way with the Sisters of Mercy. They have never been able to resist an appeal from any part of the world. . . . The lovely district on the far west coast of Canada now called them.

It is likely that in the years to come there will be many Canadian postulants for the Order and that communities of the Sisters of Mercy will spring up all over Canada as they have done with almost miraculous frequency in so many other countries.

The growth of the Sisters of Mercy is one of the most extraordinary events in the history of the Church. . . .

Two years after the death of Catherine McAuley, the first Sisters of Mercy were on their way to the United States from Carlow to establish a community in Pittsburgh. . . . From the outset, their efforts in the States met with phenomenal success so that, up to 1950, 861 convents had been founded, the greatest number in any one country in the world.

Eight Sisters went from Callan to Australia in 1874.[35]

Notes

1. *Pittsburgh Catholic,* March 11, 1848.
2. *Pittsburgh Catholic,* March 4, 1848.
3. *Pittsburgh Catholic,* October 19, 1850.
4. *Western Tablet,* Chicago, August 21, 1852.
5. *The Metropolitan,* Chicago, September, 1854.
   Western Tablet, Chicago, September, 1854.
6. *The Herald,* San Francisco, January 18, 1855.
7. *The Daily Times,* San Francisco, October 5, 1855.

8. *Catholic Courier–Journal,* Rochester, New York, September 23, 1857.
9. *Cincinnati Catholic Telegraph and Advocate,* August 28, 1858.
10. *Cincinnati Daily Commercial,* October 25, 1858.
11. *Morning Call,* San Francisco, May, 1869.
12. *Jackson Pioneer,* Jackson, Mississippi, November, 1938 (Account of 1870).
13. Orestes Brownson, Review of *Life of Catherine McAuley* by Mother Austin Carroll, New York, 1871, in *Brownson's Quarterly Review,* I, July, 1873, pp. 399–409.
14. *Weekly Herald,* Vicksburg, Mississippi, December 18, 1876.
15. Vicksburg, Mississippi, Newspaper Clipping, December 15, 1878. Newspaper not identified. Archives, New Orleans.
16. Unidentified Newspaper Clipping, Manchester, New Hampshire, August 17, 1930. (Account of August 17, 1880.) Archives, Portland, Maine.
17. Unidentified Pittsburgh Newspaper Clipping, December, 1881. Archives, New Orleans.
18. *Manchester Mirror and Guardian,* September 19, 1884. Archives, Manchester.
19. *Detroit Free Press,* January 2, 1891. Archives, Detroit.
20. Unidentified Hartford Newspaper Clipping, December 21, 1893.
21. Unidentified Latrobe Newspaper Clipping, February 9, 1900.
22. *Hartford Catholic Transcript,* by Sister M. Cecelia O'R., 1902.
23. *Mount St. Mary Record,* XI, May, 1906, 3–8.
24. Catholic Newspaper, New Orleans, April 24, 1907. Archives, New Orleans.
25. Portland, Maine, Newspaper Clipping. Paper Unidentified, c. 1914.
26. (1) *America,* January 24, 1921.
    (2) *America,* December 12, 1931.
27. *Boston Evening Transcript,* November 1, 1930, (1878).
28. Oklahoma Newspaper Clipping, Not Identified (1884). Archives, St. Louis.
29. *The Call of India,* IX, 1948, pp. 12–20 (1848–1948). Archives, Cresson.
30. *The Brooklyn Tablet,* September 3, 1955, p. 13 (1855–1955).
31. John Bebel, "Sisters in Civil War," *Denver Register,* January, 1958.
32. William C. Cunneen, *Portland Press Herald,* Maine, June 1, 1965 (1865–1965).
33. (a) Editorial, *Union Leader,* Manchester, May 10, 1958.
    (b) Editorial, *The Church World,* Portland, Maine, June 4, 1965.

34. Unidentified St. Louis Newspaper Clipping, "The Impact of Mother de Pazzi, St. Louis Mercy Founder."

35. Michael Mills, "Five Sisters of Mercy to Found First House of Order in Canada," Providence Newspaper Clipping, (Unidentified), September, 1957.

IX.

LETTERS

Letter from Sister Mary Augustine Power, Cork, to Frances Warde on Death of Her Sister, Mother Josephine Warde, Cork

Advice of Mother Frances Bridgeman, Kinsale, Ireland to Superior of Cincinnati Congregation of Mercy, Concerning the Holy Rule, 1879

Sister Mary Evangelist, San Francisco, to Mother Mary Emmanuel Russell, on the Character of Mother Baptist Russell

Letter of Newsboys of New Orleans to Mother Austin Carroll on the Occasion of Her Silver Jubilee, July 11, 1881

Letter of Gratitude to Mother Baptist Russell, California, for Pictures of Catherine McAuley Sent Through Mother Austin Carroll, from Savannah, Georgia, August 15, 1893. Mother Austin had visited and instructed the religious order founded by Bishop John England of Charleston, South Carolina. After the death of Bishop England, Rome had directed the religious order he founded to affiliate with the Sisters of Mercy

Humorous Letter of Advice to a Novice from Her Irish Priest Cousin

Statement on Death of Sister M. Vincent Haire, Superior, Brooklyn, New York, First Sister of Mercy Professed in New York

Letter of Mother Baptist Russell to a Sister in Charge of a Branch House on How To Handle a Difficult Sister, c. 1883

Letter to Frances Warde on Her Golden Jubilee from Isaac Hecker, C.S.P., Founder of the Paulists, and Father A. Young, C.S.P.

Letter to Frances Warde on Her Golden Jubilee from Father Edmond, C.S.P. Father Kent Stone, whom Frances aided so significantly, had been both Paulist and Passionist.

Letter from Chicago Sisters of Mercy to Frances Warde on Her Golden Jubilee, Chicago, 1883

Letter on the Spirituality of Sister Juliana Purcell, Providence, Rhode Island, 1888

Sister Elizabeth Strange, One of the First Seven Sisters of Mercy in the United States, Makes Surprising Suggestion That Intending Sisters Should Wait To Enter Community Until They Are Out of Their Teens, 1890

Description of St. Xavier's Academy, Beatty, Pennsylvania, to Chicago Sisters, 1893

Service of Sisters in Spanish-American War, San Francisco, 1898: Tribute by United States Army Officer, W. S. Matthews, Major and Brigade Surgeon, 1898

A Christmas Letter from a Younger Sister to an Older One, Grand Rapids, Michigan, 1903

Letter from Cook County Jail, Chicago, Written to a Sister of Mercy by a Young Man Involved in a Murder, 1904

Letter Full of Memories from Mother Patricia Waldron, Merion, Philadelphia, to Mother Clare Leeson, Portland, Maine, on the latter's Golden Jubilee, 1913

Mother Patricia Waldron Records International Novena Petitioning That Catherine McAuley Be Declared "Venerable," 1914

Letter of Gratitude to Sisters of Mercy of Grand Rapids, Michigan, for Their Services in Terrifying Epidemic of Influenza and Pneumonia, 1918

Letter from American Red Cross, Louisville, Kentucky, to Sister M. Hilda, Superior, Sisters of Mercy, Cincinnati, Concerning Service of Sisters During Epidemic of World War I, 1918

On Happy Memories and Sad Parting in Ireland, from Thomas Leahy, Loughrea, Ireland, to Sister Columba Marie Leahy, His Sister, in Cincinnati, 1919

Mother Genevieve, Dubuque, Iowa, to Miss Helen O'Connor, Janesville, Wisconsin, later Sister Mary Virginia, on the Meaning of Religious Life, 1926

George C. Ryan, Lawyer, to Sister Edwardine, on Mother Alphonsus Thielman as a Wonderful Subject for a Book, Saginaw, Michigan, 1928

On the Quality of the First Mercy Boarding School in the United States, by Sister M. Xavier Reilly of the Monastery of the Visitation, Parkersburg, West Virginia, 1931

Chief Louis Nicholas, Governor of Indian Reservation, Old Town, Maine, Protesting Attempt of Governmental Officials To Remove Sisters of Mercy from the Schools

Letter to a Friend on the Death of Mother Baptist Russell, Founder and First Superior of San Francisco Congregation

Bishop Matthew F. Brady, Manchester, to the People of Manchester on the Golden Jubilee of Sisters of Mercy in New Hampshire, 1958

A Letter on Love from a Mercy Sister to a Friend, Big Rapids, Michigan. Author and Date Unknown

INTRODUCTION

The letters found in Mercy Archives throughout the United States, especially those written before 1900, are surprising in their revelation of spirituality through content, style, and diversity. After 1900 or 1910, the letters tend to become more business-like, but earlier letters offer fascinating reading.

A suggestion in 1851 that the Sisters of Mercy have a motherhouse for the entire United States anticipates the Mercy Institute today. Also, a letter written in 1890 expressing the opinion that young women should not enter the Sisters of Mercy until they are out of their teens anticipates a judgment on qualifications for religious life today.

Heartwarming letters offer a style found in no other chapters of the present collection of writings: a letter from a non-believing, unhappy guardian of a beloved young woman desiring baptism; Kent Stone to Frances Warde on the death of his baby girl; a letter from Ireland to Frances Warde on the death of her sister, Mother Josephine Warde; a message from newsboys of New Orleans to Mother Austin Carroll on her silver jubilee; a golden jubilee letter to Frances Warde from Isaac Hecker, founder of the Paulists.

Humorous letters appear too: advice of a priest cousin to a young novice, and the response of a novice to a Superior who asks a young woman why she entered the convent.

A most unusual letter on death from Mother Baptist Russell to her brother Arthur is startling. So are letters from convicts in Sing Sing and other prisons to Sisters of Mercy.

Surprising to the general reader is an announcement by Mother Patricia Waldron of Philadelphia in 1914 of an international novena petitioning that Catherine McAuley be declared Venerable.

Letters from families in Ireland; from Indians in Maine; letters on the meaning of religious vocation and on the meaning of love—the variety of Mercy letters is both startling and fascinating. Their spirituality is unquestionable.

*　　　*　　　*

PITTSBURGH NOVICE REPORTS BACK TO CARLOW
AFTER SIX MONTHS IN AMERICA, 1844

June, 1844
Pittsburgh

To Sister M. Catherine,

Although I know not if I shall have time to write as I would desire most sincerely, to all the Sisters, I was at least resolved that Dear Dear Sister Catherine, my former docile pupil, should not be forgotten.

How delightful to us were all your letters so full of interesting intelligence. Many and many a tear was dropped in the perusal of each loved and well known handwriting. They even came to the eyes of our sweet Sister M. Xavier, who was then a postulant—so much did she seem to feel the affection of those we had left behind, and whom she already knows perfectly by name and character, so often do we dwell on a subject so near to our hearts.

And tell me now, how are you all going on, and dear Sister M. Catherine, yourself especially, for whom I have ever and shall always feel the warmest affection. I am so glad that Sister Anne Butler, whom I conclude is by this time a novice, is your Mistress at French. How pleased I shall be to hear of your proficiency. . . .

As for Sister M. Josephine Cullen, of whom you say we did not speak, I will tell you something of her that will make you laugh. She has become almost more droll than Sisters M. Paul and Juliana; on shipboard, from morning till night, she was the life of us all. Sometimes she would say, "Oh, what shall we do when we go to Pittsburgh? We will then have no excuse not to be good. Here we can say, 'Oh, passengers on sea can't be expected to be everything they ought.' " We told the bishop and he was much amused. Another time I reminded her that it was Monday, we had to pray for the souls in Purgatory, but it being at night, and she feeling very sick and sleepy, replied, "Oh, let them stay there for tonight. It will give me a deal to do to mind my own soul at present." But I must add, at the same time she gave them a double portion next day. I only mention this as a sample of her continual merriment—her zeal is more ardent than ever.

I must not forget to tell you of the "doing up" I got before my profession, which took place in the immense Cathedral on St. Leo's day. I had a most holy German priest, a Liguorist, as extra-ordinary, to whom I made a general confession. He spoke broken English, but I believe he understood it very well, at least I hope so. I must tell you that I retained the "angelical youth" Aloysius for my patron. This I was induced to do the more readily, as dear Reverend Mother has had the pleasure of giving her patron's name to a far more deserving client than I, one indeed who for a long time had a great devotion to that great apostle of the Indies. Was it not a very remarkable coincidence that for a length of time, before she had ever heard of Sisters of Mercy coming to the States, she had wished to join them from the account she read of them in *Geraldine?* She commenced a novena for that purpose to St. Francis Xavier. When, on the day it was concluded, happening to take up the newspaper, she read that, at that time, Rt. Rev. Dr. O'Connor was on his way to America with seven Sisters of Mercy. Now does it not seem quite evident that the hand of Providence was in it all, sending us to her and her to us?

But now, dearest Sister M. Catherine, it is time to bid farewell. I write in great haste. Believe me your fondly attached in Christ,

Sister M. Aloysia[1]

MOTHER AGATHA O'BRIEN SUGGESTS A GENERAL MOTHERHOUSE FOR SISTERS OF MERCY IN THE UNITED STATES, 1851

Convent of Our Lady of Mercy
St. Francis Xavier's
Chicago - June 28th, 1851

My ever dear Sister Mary Elizabeth,

The day after I posted my last letter, the copy book containing the little plays arrived. I am grateful for them, dear Sister. They will be very useful, and especially the little poems which I think quite appropriate.

And now I must thank you for your long, kind welcome epistle which reached me a few days since. Indeed I was delighted to receive it as it contained so much good news of our dear Order as also the restoration of our dear Mother Josephine's health which is most consoling. I hope sincerely she will not return to the city until the warm weather will have passed lest the heat should cause a relapse. Sisters Vincent and Aloysia are very much pleased with their little notes; they will answer them if possible. The former is at the hospital, which succeeds very well and is making many kind and interested friends for our dear Order amongst our Protestant neighbors. We hope soon to have a new hospital erected which will be much more convenient; the present one was built for a hotel and does not suit so well for hospital purposes.

It seems to me that the Order of Mercy is destined to do immense good in the United States, but I think there is one thing that is a great drawback to it and that is our not having a *Mother house* such as Emmittsburg is to the Sisters of Charity, where the young might be trained for the different missions and brought up according to the Spirit of our holy Institute. You know, dear Sister, that our dear Order is liable *in time* to be governed by Superiors of different nations whose views and ideas on matters and things will be widely different from ours. Therefore, they can and will make innumerable changes without exactly impinging on our Holy Rule. For instance, my sister told me that in Ireland they say the Office in Latin, and she has actually sent me out a Latin Office book, and here we say it in English; then again, I am told that in New York, they don't receive Holy Communion as often thru the week as we do; also, their street dress in summer is different from ours, and even when I went down to Pittsburgh last time I found there a change, which was, that they never spoke on recreation days until after dinner, and this quite surprised me as I had never heard one word of it before. Here there has been no change in the *smallest degree,* everything is done just as it was when I was in Pittsburgh.

These reflections, dear Sister, sometimes afflict me much; not on my own account, of course, do I speak, but because I am fearful for the time to come. Now if our Order had a parent house where all could be trained alike how much better would it be, and besides it would soon become independent as the surplus moneys from the different houses could be all sent there. But I suppose my dear Sister Elizabeth will laugh at my foolish remarks and think me very simple, but nevertheless it is quite an ease to speak of our troubles to an old dear friend. You must not think, dear Sister, that there is anything wrong here. No indeed, thank God, everything is doing admirably, far better than I deserve, and not only that but the clergymen from the various missions throughout the State are continually crying out for the Sisters to form new missions in their districts. I fear we shall have to send out a Colony this fall to Borbonnois Grove, a French Settlement about 60 miles from here. . . .

My fond love to all and believe me forever your devoted in our Lord,

Sister Mary Agatha[2]

LETTER FROM SISTER M. FRANCIS BENSON, SAN FRANCISCO,
TO ROSCOMMON, DESCRIBING EARLY
NINETEENTH CENTURY MISSION, 1859

Within the precincts of our Hospital are included Convent, House of Mercy, Orphanage, Magdalen Asylum, and an office for procuring situations for servants, here called "help." To describe the multitudes that have found shelter under St. Mary's roof would be a difficult task. We have had members of all religions. I do not know any country unrepresented. We have had perpetrators of every crime, under advice, instruction, or care; in truth, the hospital is a world in itself. Within it goes on the administration of every sacrament except Holy Orders—baptisms of infants and adults; confirmation of children, grown people and converts; first and last Communions; confessions, anointings, and marriages of parties brought to repentance during sickness or on a death-bed.

Add to these pledge-taking, investing with scapulars, churchings, professions of faith, last indulgences; the reconciling of quarreling husbands and wives; rescuing unfortunate creatures from self-destruction; snatching others from the verge of degradation, and exciting to contrition those already fallen.

It is quite common here for American Spaniards to adopt Irish children and bring them up as their own. Hence there are thousands of Irish bearing Spanish names, some of whom are ignorant of their origins.

In a short space, the House of Mercy, for destitute women of good character, received and provided for 600 young women. The Widows' Home too is quite populous.

In the office for procuring situations for women, 9,448 were provided for in a few years. Twenty-one women of evil life who came to the hospital for treatment in its early days were converted.

Pray a great deal, please, for us and our mission. Bear in mind, beloved Sister, that in your quiet convent home you may convert thousands in America.[3]

LETTER FROM A GUARDIAN TO A YOUNG WOMAN STUDENT CONVERTED TO THE CATHOLIC FAITH BY FRANCES WARDE, MANCHESTER, 1865

My Darling Child:

I hardly know how I feel about your Roman Catholic conviction, looking at it from a mere worldly and selfish point of view. But when I remember how my heart and hope and prayer for you have always been burningly eager that you might become a truly heavenly-minded person, I simply say to myself: "Well, this is God's work, and it must be right."

What seems to have most affected your mind is the death of the convent Sister, and death is God's best lesson and teacher. I don't know whether it is best for you to join the Roman Catholic Church. I can only pray that God who has begun your spiritual schooling will complete the work, as seemeth to Him good. I only know this, that not all the felicity of earth would make me so happy as to know that you are steadily tending upward toward the pure, sweet heaven, where my mother is. You know you always reminded me of her. She was angelic in character, and in love for me, her son. She died divinely happy.

If you really feel deeply in your very soul that the Catholic religion is the only true one, and realize how trivial and little life is, and how magnificent and unlimited eternity is, then follow the heavenly impulses of your lovely nature.

I think you have a most pure and charming nature, too lovely and delicate for this bad, black, bitter earth's rough contact. I want you to be sheltered in your remaining progress through it by a holy consciousness and strengthened by a daily dependence on Almighty God. I feel that my own life is passing rapidly away, and the thought that you are going forward toward heaven (I care not by what route) will comfort me in every remaining day of my totally unsatisfied existence.

Observe, then, my darling child, that I advise nothing on a subject so awful as religion. I say, follow God's leading, wherever it goes.[4]

FRANCES WARDE TO A FORMER STUDENT SHE HAD INSTRUCTED IN THE CATHOLIC FAITH

As you were not aware of my absence from home, you must wonder at my seeming negligence, so pray excuse me this time; you know what a faithful correspondent I have been of yours. I was obliged to go on business to Hartford, and the Providence Sisters said if I failed to call on them they would take it as an everlasting slight. I was sorry to find by your last letter that your health is not good. I often wish you were here, as the weather is delightful.

I regret you had so much trouble, dearest, about a place in the Church, but you know that in country towns the Catholic churches are always crowded and the sextons are not always very polite. But I am sure that, on reflection, you were glad to make this little sacrifice to Him who has done such great things for you.

You must soon come back to your convent home and that quiet holy chapel where you so often prayed and received so many graces and blessings. Plain as it is at present, I see nothing anywhere I love half so well. Mary B—writes that she must come back to us, and, better still, that she is now eighteen and will be a Catholic. Pray for her and for us all. Thanksgiving will be the Feast of St. Andrew, a great day with us, and the following Monday, dearest Hattie Xavier will be the first of our dear Saints. Of course, you will be, please God, prepared to approach the Sacraments with all our children.

With unchanged affection, believe me, ever yours, devotedly,[5]

ON SERVICE OF BLACK SMALLPOX VICTIMS IN SAN FRANCISCO, BY MOTHER BAPTIST RUSSELL, 1868

In the summer of 1868, smallpox, a more terrible visitor than earthquake, came to the Queen City of the Pacific. The first case appeared in March. In June there were twenty; in July, forty-eight. The authorities obliged all to go to the Hospital, hoping thereby to stay the plague. But such reports were circulated of the horrible treatment of the poor sufferers that to be sent there was considered dooming a patient to death, or worse. Coming to the ears of the community, this report so stirred the zeal of the senior member, Sister M. Francis Benson, that, with permission of the Superior, she asked the Archbishop to allow the Sisters to offer their services to the managers of the smallpox Hospital. He lost not a moment in sending his cordial approbation. As the necessity was urgent, the Superior interrupted her retreat to write the following note:

Sir: It is one of the privileges of our Order of Mercy that we attend our poor fellow-creatures in whatever form of disease it is the Divine will to afflict them. Therefore, if the city authorities are willing to accept our services, our Sisters will, D. V., go to the pest-house and take up their residence there until the Almighty wills to deliver the city from this terrible malady. If the authorities are willing we shall go on Monday, August 17. One small room is all we shall require. You know the accommodations of a Sister of Mercy are very simple.

Wishing you every success in your work,

Sister M. B. Russell
Superior of the Sisters of Mercy[6]

KENT STONE TO FRANCES WARDE ON THE DEATH OF HIS SMALL DAUGHTER, ETHEL, AT THE CONVENT IN MANCHESTER, 1870

Cambridge, Mass.
Dec. 16, 1870

Dear Reverend Mother,

My heart is full tonight (ah! *more* than full) of gratitude to Almighty God for the tender mercies which he has showered upon one, who, if you only knew it, am so unworthy of them. He has given me more than a hundred fold in this life in showing me how he has raised up in you and your kind Sisters at Manchester so many sweet mothers for my little children. Believe me, I have been most observant, and most profoundly touched by the self-forgetful devotion and the delicate, exquisite sympathy which have been silently shown during the past two days. Should I live to be a century old, the freshness of these scenes will not grow dim in my memory. And if unworthy prayers are heard, then additional blessings will be called down upon you from God, who, I know, would bless you even if no prayers of mine were offered. I will pray for you all in general, and also, so far as I know the names, in particular.

I could not but fear, as we stood by the little grave this morning, and the icy wind blew over the wintry hills, that some of you, and perhaps some of the little children, would be chilled, and perhaps made very ill. May God prevent it.

Won't you tell the dear children of the school, whom it gave me such sweet pleasure to see in the chapel and by my baby's grave, that I said for *them* this evening the five glorious mysteries of the rosary, with the following intentions for the several mysteries:

1. Conversion of heart;
2. The desire of heaven;
3. Purity of soul, and meditation on divine things;
4. The grace of a happy death;
5. Confidence in the Blessed Mother of God.

I do not think that the gracious little life which has been so soon closed on earth has been wholly without its lesson. And now that tender soul is surely already made radiant by the vision of God. May we all be soon brought into our Lord's own presence as peaceful and unsullied as she. Meanwhile, as Cornelia said this morning when she left the tiny open grave, "Goodbye, little Ethel, and pray for papa and me"—yes! and for us all.

Your servant in Jesus Christ,
J. K. Stone[7]

TWO LETTERS BY SISTER AUGUSTINE MCKENNA, NEW YORK
TO A YOUNG NOVICE, 1872–1873

I have begun a novena of Communions for you (January 28, 1872), and am asking our Lord to grant you the special graces you need. Be heroic in corresponding with them. God did not call you here to withdraw His aid: there are some principles you must determine to act on; the first is Faith. View all things in the light of faith. "Not a hair of your head can fall to the ground without my Father's will." If this is true, can things be said or done without His will to affect our souls? Take all as coming from Him. If you are blamed or misunderstood, be sure He knows it, and means it to do some work of purgation in your heart. God sees all, knows all, directs all.

Second principle: Recollection—the habit of entertaining ourselves with God, making aspirations, keeping fast hold of God's hand, as it were. Then we are ready at any moment to fight with evil.

Third principle: Generosity with God—courage in His service; self-sacrifice. Make these the watchwords of your novitiate days. Paradise is not for cowards. The easy way is the hard way, paradox though it seem. When we don't spare ourselves, when at any cost we do right, God helps us sensibly; we revel in grace and, consequently, in spiritual happiness.

I pray God that your heart and soul may be devoted to the poor, sick, and ignorant. And that serving the Lord in His poor, He may make you rich in graces and blessings, but above all in the spirit of prayer and self-sacrifice.

The old live in the past, the young in the future. It is only in the present and future we can serve God, and to serve Him is to reign. . . .

*

On this wondrous eve of your holy profession (April 16, 1873), my heart will not rest unless it speaks some of its thoughts. . . . In God's name, let this one grand act of your life be complete. You have made that astounding meditation on the sacrifice of the soul. It has to be made piecemeal, though offered entire. Inch by inch this sacrifice is exacted by little trials, more galling than great ones. To say nothing when we should naturally say something sharp; to do simply as we are told, without objection or remonstrance, for the sake of the sacrifice obedience involves; to seem cheerful when the heart aches; to be kind in return for unkindness; to save others all the pain and trouble possible, to bear and forbear—these efforts will be sacrifices, endorse our vows, and combine into one glorious holocaust. Take up your cross and follow Me. Yes, take it up. Whatever is contrary to inclination or habit forms a real cross. Yet it is one thing to take it up and another to carry it after Jesus.[8]

FEAST DAY GREETINGS FROM FRANCES WARDE, MANCHESTER, TO MOTHER PATRICIA WALDRON, PHILADELPHIA, 1876

Mount St. Mary's
Manchester

My Dear Mother M. Patricia,

Your feast day this time has stolen over me before I was aware that it was so near, although I have been saying every evening in Choir as usual the Novena to our dear Saint to whom we are indebted under God for divine Faith. I made a special intention for you at the commencement of the Novena and I thought of you so often during the Novena. The sisters were so very busy getting up a little Concert for the Orphans this evening that I forgot I should have written to you two days since, but you will kindly excuse me. I assure you that I made special petitions for you before and after Holy Communion at Mass. Accept them, my dear Sister, my affectionate congratulations on the return of your feast day. I trust that it will be a blessed and happy feast for you and that you will receive through the intercession of our Glorious Patron and Father a great increase of divine love and all the graces that will enable you to become a most "Perfect Religious."

   With much love and blessings for all the dear Mothers and Sisters,

I am yours most faithfully in Ct,
M. M. Frances Xavier Teresa,
Convent of Our Lady of Mercy,
Feast of Saint Patrick, 1876[9]

SISTER AUGUSTINE MCKENNA, NEW YORK, TO A FRIEND ON ST. PATRICK'S DAY, 1878

   I hope the mail (March 15, 1878) will be quick, that you may receive my poor congratulations on St. Patrick's Day. I trust our blessed patron will obtain for you many graces and blessings, especially his peculiar spirit of prayer, for if we pray we shall all do well. A French priest, whose English is not the best, said that the most remarkable thing about St. Patrick was "his awful faith." Thank God, he secured the same "awful faith" to his children, and it will always be the most remarkable thing about them. . . . He must feel bound to help you by his powerful intercession, devoted as you are to the children of his poor exiles. It grieves me when children we bring up know little about him and about St. Brigid, the glory of Irish women; not little, but nothing, I might say, about Ireland itself; ignorant of the land to whose martyr courage they owe their faith. . . . Two hundred Irish girls landed together lately to work in the New-England factories.[10]

LETTER FROM SISTER MARY AUGUSTINE POWER, CORK, TO FRANCES WARDE ON THE DEATH OF HER SISTER, MOTHER JOSEPHINE WARDE, CORK

Cork

Dearest Mother M. Frances,

   How shall I express in words the heartfelt desolation we are in for the loss of your gentle, loving, devoted sister. It was all so sudden. Our darling Mother held Chapter on the last Wednesday of November and gave a beautiful exhortation on the Chapter of *Charity!* She spoke in her own beautiful mild spirit, and related how Mother McAuley had only that Chapter to instruct her community while the copy of the Holy Rule was at Rome for approbation. She poured out her beautiful spirit and had no lack of words to entreat and exhort each one of us to practice that great virtue at home, that its over-flowing may be given abroad.

After Chapter, as was her custom, she saw the locals [Sisters living at the Convent].

When your welcome likeness was sent us, it was I who opened the case and took the picture into the room. Tho' I was at a great distance from Mother Josephine and she had not yet looked at it, she turned quite pale with emotion.

I often saw her looking at that picture which she had hung up in the Community Room, and I know that all the love of that warm, tender heart was for you, *her dearly loved and valued sister.*

I have not words to console you, but I pray that the tender and compassionate heart of Jesus will soften the heavy blow to both you and us, her deeply afflicted children.

Dearest Mother Frances, I enclose a favorite soliloquy of Gerald Griffin that our Mother loved, and this one was printed for her by me years ago.

With love and sympathy from our Mothers and Sisters, ever believe, dearest Mother Frances, your devoted child in J.C.,

Sr. M. Augustine Power

Dearest Mother, our loved Mother received Holy Communion at $9\frac{1}{4}$ o'clock in the morning and breathed forth her pure soul at about $1\frac{1}{2}$ o'clock p.m. that day. I enclose Mother M. Anastasia Becket's note of sympathy.

Your devoted child,
Sr. M. Augustine[11]

ADVICE OF MOTHER FRANCES BRIDGEMAN, KINSALE, IRELAND
TO SUPERIOR OF CINCINNATI CONGREGATION OF MERCY
CONCERNING THE HOLY RULE, 1879

. . . No general remedy can be applied to the matters you mention. The Rule is as binding as any other code could be, and more so. I see no use in further legislation where its prescriptions are set aside.

Let us pray, and be doubly careful to allow nothing that could be twisted into a precedent for irregularity at some future time. That is all we can do. Considering the extent of the Order, its numerous members, and various duties, it is to a special providence we owe it that matters are as straight as they are. Untoward events occur in Orders less exposed, generalates included. If a house of ours strays away for a time, it generally steadies down and comes right at last by means of the good example and advice it receives from the other houses. Let it be our privilege to always breathe forth the good odor that will attract others to walk in the right way. I don't know of any Irish house going wrong.

I believe the only way of keeping others right is to keep right ourselves, allowing no expediency to draw us from the straight path. When others see this course succeed they will follow in it. . . . The faithful standing by community and superiors is a capital good point in the character of any member. You cannot allow any one to suppose you sanction faults, or are blind to them, even though fear of worse should oblige you to tolerate them. You should admonish strongly and approach to this goal.[12]

SISTER MARY EVANGELIST, SAN FRANCISCO, TO MOTHER MARY EMMANUEL RUSSELL, ON THE CHARACTER OF MOTHER BAPTIST RUSSELL

You can, no doubt, give some interesting details of the generosity shown by your mother and dear Sister Mary Aquin, when your good mother hesitated, for a time, about Mother Baptist's going to San Francisco. Sister M. Magdalen says you were here at the time, and did your part bravely, too. I asked Sister M. Magdalen's own opinion of dear Mother Baptist, and she said, with tears in her eyes, "All I have to say of her is that she was the most perfect being, in every sense of the word, that in my judgment I ever came across."

She was so calm, so perfect in fact, in every way, that she was held up as a model to young Sisters. What I admired most in her was her cordial, affectionate manner in the Community, and her great love for the poor. She could never see a Sister in any difficulty without trying to help her out of it, even at her own great inconvenience, so that many times she got herself into difficulties in her effort to get others out of them.

As for the poor, it used to be one of my greatest ambitions to be with her on visitation, especially at the workhouse. You know the state of misery they were in there at the time, and it would touch any heart to see her trying to console them and to help them to bear their sufferings. However calm she was under her own trials, I have known her to shed bitter tears on our way home from the workhouse, at the thought of the wretchedness she had witnessed and the little she could do to relieve it. Any little extra time of freedom she might chance to have, was always devoted to helping or relieving the poor in some way or other. She did many things in this way that others would not venture, and that were not always approved of, but she did them with so much simplicity and good faith that no one could blame her. She was one of the most loving and generous souls I ever met.[13]

LETTER OF NEWSBOYS OF NEW ORLEANS TO MOTHER AUSTIN CARROLL ON THE OCCASION OF HER SILVER JUBILEE, JULY 11, 1881

Newsboys' Home, New Orleans, July 11th, 1881

Dear Honored, Reverend Mother:

We would like to express our feelings on the occasion of your Jubilee. We would like to give you three Cheers and a Tiger! We would like to take the roof off with a "Hip, hip, hurrah!" But we rather think we would enjoy this better than you would, so we will draw it mild this time, and just take it out in wishing you the jolliest kind of Jubilee.

This is the kind of wedding we like, the first and only one, in fact, in which we boys have been remembered when the good things come around. There are weddings every day, rich ones, too, but we have never had a bid from any of them yet.

We would like your jubilee to come around oftener, and we hope you will have twenty-five more regular EDITIONS of this day besides a whole lot of EXTRAS, and that there will be some of us around to cry them out for you. We wish we could yell out today, "Here's your twenty-fifth edition! Full account of Reverend Mother's Jubilee." But to come down to business, we would like to express our feelings on this occasion in the proper kind of words. We would like to thank you for all you have done for us boys. Why, if you could, we know, you would give us everything a boy needs to be comfortable in this world, and yet that is nothing compared to all you have done to help to make us comfortable in the next world.

Perhaps some day when we are men, our lives will praise and bless you louder than any tongue can do. It almost seems at times as if Saint Elizabeth, Saint Cecilia and a lot of other saints had come back to earth to work for our benefit, and when we see you in our Night School teaching us fellows, and at our Sunday Mass helping us to sing God's praises, we don't think there is a very great difference between the saints on earth and those in heaven.

We are not great hands at making wishes, but we would like to make some strong ones for you. We wish you good luck, long life, and much happiness. But as we, Newsboys, represent many newspapers, we will conclude our remarks with an earnest prayer, that the TIMES here in this world may be always prosperous and bright for you, without a single unpleasant ITEM to disturb your peace of mind. May every PICAYUNE of a boy here grow up to be a true man such as you wish him to be; and although our different STATES of life may lie far apart, may we always follow out the pathway traced by you, so that whether we be DEMOCRAT or REPUBLICAN here below, we may every one of us shine like a MORNING STAR in the fadeless crown of immortal glory, reserved for your eternal Jubilee.

From your friends,
THE NEWSBOYS[14]

LETTER OF GRATITUDE TO MOTHER BAPTIST RUSSELL,
CALIFORNIA, FOR PICTURES OF
CATHERINE MCAULEY SENT THROUGH MOTHER AUSTIN
CARROLL, FROM SAVANNAH,
GEORGIA, AUGUST 15, 1893. MOTHER AUSTIN HAD VISITED
AND INSTRUCTED
THE RELIGIOUS ORDER FOUNDED BY BISHOP JOHN
ENGLAND OF CHARLESTON,
SOUTH CAROLINA. AFTER THE DEATH OF BISHOP ENGLAND,
ROME HAD DIRECTED THE
RELIGIOUS ORDER HE FOUNDED TO AFFILIATE WITH THE
SISTERS OF MERCY

Convent of Mercy
Savannah, Georgia
August 15, 1893

Dear Reverend Mother,

Please accept the thanks of your Sisters in Savannah for the pictures sent through dear Mother Austin Carroll. I assure you, we appreciate lsz

deeply such a favor, but more, the kind and generous recognition of us as members of your great Community, who have been up to now, strangers to you. Two things we have to be especially grateful for in this great happiness. First, of course, the goodness of God, who by His mercy has smoothed all difficulties we anticipated; second, in having opened the way for us, through dear Mother Austin, to whom our lifelong gratitude is due. We reverence her as a dear, good mother, who by her broadminded liberality and consideration made the transition as easy and pleasant as possible for us, and then her charity has influenced you all favorably toward us, for which we are more grateful than I can well express.

May God bless you all and make us worthy members. Reverend Mother begs your prayers for herself and Community, also for the Bishop who is a good friend and Father to us. He and Mother Austin have a mutual admiration society between them. With Mother's love and that of the Sisters,

Yours in the S. H.,
Sister M. Ignatius[15]

HUMOROUS LETTER OF ADVICE TO A NOVICE
FROM HER IRISH PRIEST COUSIN

My Dear Cousin:

I cannot tell you how glad I am that you have become a Sister of Mercy. I like the Order of Mercy very much, and I think it will suit you well. I am only afraid you are not wild enough. It requires considerable life and fun to bear up against hard work, and, especially, if you have to take care of the sick and poor you will have to be very cheerful, or your duties will be only half done. You must stir yourself and be always joyful and cut up as many pranks as you can, provided you do not break your rules (or your neck).

These are strange virtues to be recommended to you; in fact they are partially of my own invention, but I know they are useful in preventing old age, gray hair, and bad temper. I would also remind you never to sleep more than two-thirds of the time of your morning meditation—you might find the position rather uncomfortable. Besides, quietism, ecstasies, visions, and such horrible mortifications as sleeping on one's knees are not in accordance with the spirit of your state.

It is also a very good thing to give your Mother Superior or novice-mistress a good long talking—a piece of your mind, once in a while, without getting angry. It is bad for digestion to keep everything hatching on one's mind; and by telling it to the Superior, you strike at the root of the evil; because, as a matter of course, when anything goes against you, it is always her fault. If you have any autobiographies to relate to your director, try to bring them out in a very abridged pocket edition. These holy people are very thick-headed, and cannot remember long stories. For any further direction, consult Rodriguez, St. Francis de Sales, or their agents in your convent.

If your entrance into religion has given you any influence with the one that makes throats in heaven, I wish you would try hard to get me a new one. The old one, which was never much good, is completely worn out shouting at sinners. I expect some hard fighting with asthma this winter. I will pray Our Lord to make you a fervent, loving, devoted Sister of Mercy. I will not feel satisfied till I hear you are bound by the sweet, strong bonds of the holy vows.[16]

STATEMENT ON DEATH OF SISTER M. VINCENT HAIRE, SUPERIOR, BROOKLYN, NEW YORK, FIRST SISTER OF MERCY PROFESSED IN NEW YORK

I knew her well for many years, and never perceived in her the slightest motion of jealousy, or the least infraction of the law of heavenly charity. . . . The constant smile on her peaceful face ever expressed her blessed union with the will of her Lord in all things. We can never forget the light of her bright example—a beacon leading us on to all that is holy, pure, and loving, in religion. We shall never cease to thank God that He has given us in this weary world such a vision of peace.

If there was any expression more than another written on her face it was, "Jesus, my God, I love Thee above all things." And her last word was the invocation of the Holy Name of her Heavenly Spouse. Her directors have realized this union of her soul with God, and have a sincere veneration for her memory. . . . She had always looked for a sudden death.[17]

LETTER OF MOTHER BAPTIST RUSSELL TO A SISTER IN CHARGE OF A BRANCH HOUSE ON HOW TO HANDLE A DIFFICULT SISTER, C. 1883

Part of Mother Baptist's secret of calmness, peace, and self-possession she reveals in the counsel given to a Sister whom she had placed in charge of a branch house and who was evidently tried a good deal by one of her subjects:

"Don't on any account let her shortcomings or anything of that kind bother or disturb you in the least, like a good child. God leaves each one of us our free will, and we are accountable for ourselves. See how even the immediate presence and personal meetings with our Lord did not keep the unhappy Judas right. So do what you can, but keep your mind not alone peaceful but joyous, and the more joyous, the better for yourself and all."

She ends this letter with the following very commonplace advice: "See that all the Sisters have heavy, good shoes, and everything necessary to keep them warm and dry, and keep a good fire. Call for a little music occasionally, or play yourself."[18]

LETTER TO FRANCES WARDE ON HER GOLDEN JUBILEE FROM ISAAC HECKER, C.S.P., FOUNDER OF THE PAULISTS, AND FATHER A. YOUNG, C.S.P.

As Father Hecker and I have been promoted to the rank of General Invalid, it will be quite impossible for either of us to make the journey to Manchester at this season in order to be present at the great occasion of your golden Jubilee.

We are going therefore to make an act of virtue out of this unwelcome necessity, and do that which costs us the most while this joyous festivity is being celebrated—which is to stay at home.

Indeed we would both rejoice, dear Reverend Mother, to show you, as you are most worthy to receive, our fraternal respect and heartfelt congratulations, and in what I am saying to interpret the directions of Father Hecker, and as the expression of my own feelings, I am repeating as well the sentiments entertained by all our Community.

I add for myself—(and no doubt with willing assent of everybody)— that, if we of the clergy do not stay you up and strengthen your soul by prayers at God's Holy Altar, then we are little deserving of having had such a woman and such a religious as you have been in our day and generation. It is to be hoped that in fifty years' time of service to the servants of God you have managed to acquire enough humility to bear just a little praise to your face.

May Our Lord bless you, love you, and give you joy and divine peace here and hereafter.[19]

LETTER TO FRANCES WARDE ON HER GOLDEN JUBILEE FROM FATHER EDMOND, C.S.P., FATHER KENT STONE, WHOM FRANCES AIDED SO SIGNIFICANTLY, HAD BEEN BOTH PAULIST AND PASSIONIST

It is certainly a grand thing to have been in religion fifty years. . . . Ah, what a pledge of your own perseverance, dear Mother, you already have! And what a consolation it must be to your heart, to look back over

such a vista of years and see the many vocations which have begun, continued, and ended, under your fostering rule!

Do you not feel like holy Simeon when he sang his Nunc Dimittis?
Could you not use his beautiful words as you look back on the past, so
thickly strewn with mercies? Ah, how good God is! How true the Sacred
Heart of Jesus. How faithful the heart of Mary. To God be all praise for
what you and your Sisterhood have accomplished in this great land. God
bless and keep you always, my very dear friend.[20]

LETTER FROM CHICAGO SISTERS OF MERCY TO FRANCES WARDE ON HER GOLDEN JUBILEE, CHICAGO, 1883

Glancing back on the precious years that have flown, you will think
of our small convent on the lake shore. The seed you cast on this prairie
has been blessed by God, and produced fruit for eternity—a hundredfold.
Grateful memories of you, dear Mother, still linger here. In union with the
good Sisters who greet you in person to-day, we pray our dear Lord to
grant that you may be spared many years to promote His glory. The gentle
spirit of our Holy Foundress will rejoice in your joy, and obtain special
blessings, not only for the companion of her early trials, but also for those
who have the honor and happiness of being numbered among her
children.[21]

LETTER ON THE SPIRITUALITY OF SISTER JULIANA PURCELL, PROVIDENCE, RHODE ISLAND, 1888

In the *Providence Visitor* is a letter published on the death of Sister
Juliana Purcell (1883–1888) concerning the friendship between Sister Juliana and the writer of the letter. Sister had once asked the latter: "Why are
you not a Catholic?" The reply was: "I like them too well. There is not
hatred enough to work on for a conversion."

The writer continues: "From that time she never gave me over, and
her prayers and efforts were unceasing until she saw their result. There
were other causes remotely at work, but the threads were gathered up by
her hands, and there were cries which to human judgment would certainly
have put an end to progress but for her zeal and faith. Once I wished I had
never seen her, so resolutely did she work, so cruel seemed the ordeal; but
in proportion to the struggle was the reward, and when the moment of

mutual holy joy came, my sense of obligation was deep and has never since diminished. If my soul ever approaches her own hereafter, or those of members of my family are given her to rejoice over, I believe it will be the legitimate harvest with which Almighty God has crowned her faithful exertions.

"Wherever she was at ease the most prominent trait of her character was a joyousness born of innocence. I can never read of St. Filippo Neri, 'Saint of the merry heart,' without filling out the picture of Sister Juliana. But this mirth was never excessive or trivial. The face that was always smiling, rarely laughed, and in moments of the greatest freedom she never for a moment lost dignity.

"The hearty sympathy she extended to all brought her a larger circle of friends than is given to most. Friends multiplied about her wherever she was placed, and well do I remember the reproach of a school-girl who thought that friendship meant exclusiveness. 'Sister Juliana has so many friends.' To my thought her love for great numbers was like concentric circles. The more they extended, the more room they gave to those of the inner space, and those with her were holy ones. It was at one time my privilege to see her sorely grieved, and for a continuous time. From this I learned one of the best lessons of my own life, and one of my strongest consolations at this bitter moment is the firm ejaculation of her hour of trial: 'Now I am sure of heaven,' and she repeated the assertion.

"If, in ordinary life, she showed solicitude, the greatest I ever saw was for pupils for whom she feared she had failed to accomplish what she strove for. I have sometimes felt a reflection from the cross in its infinite sacrifice for all mankind, as I have seen her face grow weary and the brow contract with pain over some stolid, indifferent scholar, yet blaming only her own want of skill. Small wonder that her pupils loved her.

"With her admirable organization, the capacity for every enjoyment was marked, and in the latter years of our acquaintance I did not fear to allude to her sacrifices. Her responses would have satisfied the most rigid. Never for a moment had she known a regret, though she keenly appreciated the cost of her devotion. Her religious life was her choice, and would have been had it to have been made again at any day or hour.

"The single word which I have heard in endless repetition from both religious and secular, as applied to her life, was "unselfish." I think we have a clue here to the most that we saw. . . .

"A fine, high nature has gone where, for the moment, we may not follow; but if ever I saw a being that God might delight to place in heaven, it was this holy woman."[22]

SISTER ELIZABETH STRANGE, ONE OF THE FIRST SEVEN SISTERS
OF MERCY IN THE UNITED STATES, MAKES SURPRISING
SUGGESTION THAT INTENDING SISTERS SHOULD
WAIT TO ENTER COMMUNITY UNTIL THEY
ARE OUT OF THEIR TEENS, 1890

> *St. Mary's Convent of Mercy*
> *Webster Avenue*
> *Pittsburgh, Pa.*
> *St. Lawr 'Toole 1890*

Accept, my dear Mother M. Gertrude, the affectionate congratulations of your old Sister of long ago, on the return of your *patronal day.* May it bring you every grace and blessing you may need or wish for, whatever they may be. I'm certain it will bring a prayer from this community, my dear, such as they are. As you know, the Forty Hours are being held here since Wednesday. They close this evening, and I did not neglect to pray for the welfare and prosperity of every community in our holy Order, and to make a special intention for dear old Loretto, where I at one time spent a couple of quiet, happy years. There we considered the height of prosperity to mean *twenty-two* pupils, and with justice, for to accommodate that number was the extent of S. Aloysius's capacity in those far-off days. I sometimes am surprised when I think of what a *happy family* those children formed and how well they applied to their studies. *Now-a-days* the schools make everything easy—*Progress* everywhere. I'm glad all your schools at *home* and abroad are going so nicely.

The dear Sisters, your daughters, were over here so recently they no doubt have told you all that is worth telling. Were you not glad to hear of the fine painting of which thro' the Bishop's generosity your community has become possessed? And I congratulate you on the accession—which shows my generosity, for 'tis far more valuable as a work of art than the one he brought us. But ours is rich in indulgence, counterbalancing the worth of the offering.

Our poor little S. M. Mercedes is still sinking—and a good many others—chiefly the young are complaining. I almost think that in Communities like ours and yours where there is so much labor, 'twould be well to let intending subjects wait till out of their teens when the constitution is formed and the mind matured. But this could not be an invariable rule.

I'm taking up too much of your time, I know. Your day will bring plenty to see to as well as to enjoy, but before closing I must tell you how little we liked the sudden departure of dear M. Justina and Sister M. Joseph. When I saw them at supper in cloak and bonnet, I thought they had just come in, but when I beheld them ready to take leave, I was, as dear S. Isidore used to say, struck with *awe*. I hope they got to Homestead without accident. Our streets are so dangerous. Since the accessing of the electric Cables, one is afraid for her life even in broad day light. What must it be at night! My love to dear M. de Sales and all. Many would send love if they knew of my writing. But every one is here and there.

As ever, dear M. M. Gertrude,
Yours affectionately in Christ,
S. M. Elizabeth (Strange)[23]

DESCRIPTION OF ST. XAVIER'S ACADEMY, BEATTY, PENNSYLVANIA TO CHICAGO SISTERS, 1893

St. Xavier's Academy
Beatty, Pa.
Oct. 20, 1893

My Very Reverend Sister Mary Thomas:

Your very kind letter was duly received, but I could not get time to answer it until now. Yesterday morning we took a walk to the grave yard; it is surrounded by a beautiful hedge of Arbor Vita about twelve feet high. We also walked to the barn and the pasture ground, where the cattle were grazing. They have a pretty little donkey, which a priest bought in Mexico for $1.50, but it cost $25.00 for freight to bring it here. When it is two years old, they will get a little cart and the children can ride around the Academy grounds. It is really a pretty little animal. Sister Pius was quite taken with it. Its hair is mouse color, but it has a cross of black hair on its back.

After dinner Mother Mary Neri, Mother Mary Mechtildis, Sister Mary Pius and I had a ride in the Sisters' carriage over to Latrobe. I do not know what the distance is, but we were no less than an hour on the way. We passed by the Benedictine Monastery. It was a delightful ride over hill and dale, and the weather was charming, as it is also today—the air so balmy, it is quite invigorating.

I am very grateful for the prayers said for our safe return. Tell dear Sister Mary Alexis to persevere in praying until we get home.

Sister Mary Pius unites with me in love to all the dear Sisters.

Your devoted in our Lord,

Sister Mary Genevieve[24]

SERVICE OF SISTERS IN SPANISH-AMERICAN WAR,
SAN FRANCISCO, 1898:
TRIBUTE BY UNITED STATES ARMY OFFICER, W. S. MATTHEWS,
MAJOR AND BRIGADE SURGEON, 1898

Fateful 1898 has another entry in the community ANNALS, a final gleam of the spirit that animated Mother Baptist, "Mercy hath set up a throne, and opened wide the door of her heart."

April 21, 1898. The Spanish-American War was formally declared today.

Our dear Mother wept on seeing the boys embarking for the war. San Francisco was in the grip of a new excitement. For the first time in its history it became a base for military operations on a large scale. One of the most important military objectives was the occupation of the Philippine Islands. As the chief port of the Pacific, San Francisco became the concentration point for the men and materials required for the prosecution of this phase of the war. The military facilities of the city were entirely inadequate to handle the many thousands of men funneled through, and when typhoid and pneumonia broke out in alarming epidemics, the Division Hospital at the Presidio simply could not cope with the situation. In the tradition of Mother Baptist, who could not turn away from a call of distress, four Sisters from the many volunteers were sent to nurse the stricken men. During the two and a half months that they lived in cramped quarters on the military reservations, the Sisters were on duty twenty-four hours, nursing, counseling, and writing letters for the men. The commanding officer of the Presidio Hospital, Major W. S. Matthews, wrote to the Sisters in appreciation:

On September 26th I had the occasion to make an official report to the Surgeon General, Washington, D.C., which will more clearly express my estimate of the services than anything that I can write. After detailing the forces and help we had in the Hospital, I stated, "In addition to this force we are blessed with the services of the Sisters of Mercy who are receiving no compensation for they will accept none, exhibiting a most self-sacrificing and patriotic spirit. Their work is as good as could possibly be desired. The patients have all been delighted and have been benefited by their services.

Assuring you that their services will long be remembered and always desired by those who have been connected with this Hospital in an official way, and again thanking you for myself, my staff, and the soldiers who have received their care, I am

> Most sincerely yours,
> W. S. Matthews
> Major and Brigade Surgeon
> United States Army[25]

A CHRISTMAS LETTER FROM A YOUNGER SISTER TO AN OLDER ONE, GRAND RAPIDS, MICHIGAN, 1903

Merry Christmas, 1903

My dear God Mother, (Mother Mary Philomena)

You locked the Community room door and took the key away, so I am obliged to cut a sheet out of the Prescription Book to scribble on. You know I could not let this beautiful festival pass without telling you how happy I have been with you during our little time together, how much I appreciate your kindness—not only to my poor miserable self but to everyone I know. I am often very trying, but that will be an incentive for you to pray more for me that God may permit me to acquire a little humility which I sorely need. Your great spirit of charity to excuse everyone, which often provokes me, will obtain pardon for my *misdemeanors* (is that spelled right?) which are certainly numerous. Hoping our *Holy Abbot* will be able to give us plenty of spirituals, and praying the Sweet Infant Jesus to obtain for you many favors both spiritual and temporal and a long life filled with good works, I am as ever, Your devoted God child in the Sacred Heart.

> Sister M. Paul Quigley[26]

LETTER FROM COOK COUNTY JAIL, CHICAGO, WRITTEN TO A SISTER OF MERCY BY A YOUNG MAN INVOLVED IN A MURDER, 1904

Chicago, Sept. 15, 1904

Dear Sister:

I was up to trial today and was sentenced to eighteen years in the penitentiary.

It is more than I had expected, but I suppose I may consider myself very lucky that it is no worse, when you take into account the happenings in the city for the past two weeks.

Well, dear Sister, I haven't lost confidence in St. Anthony and the Blessed Virgin. I am sure that they will yet open up a way for me to get out. I am afraid that I may not see you any more for a while, as I expect to be taken away about Monday.

I want to thank yourself and the other kind Sisters out there, who have taken such a kindly interest in me since I have been here. I will say good-bye and ask you to remember me in your prayers.

Will you kindly send me two pairs of scapulars? Father O'Callahan said Mass Sunday, and also delivered another of his real good sermons. He certainly reached the hearts of some of the men, as two of them asked me to get scapulars for them. Yours respectfully,

S.J.Q.
Cook County Jail

It may seem from this letter that the prisoner was well educated and had a very good position doing clerical work, but evil communications corrupt good morals.

His prayers were answered, as his behavior was so admirable and his former friends so numerous that he was released at the end of five years. Long after, he called on the Sisters who used to visit the jail, and he was accompanied by his two little sons, of whom he was proud, as he was giving them the right training.[27]

LETTER FULL OF MEMORIES FROM MOTHER PATRICIA WALDRON, MERION, PHILADELPHIA, TO MOTHER CLARE LEESON, PORTLAND, MAINE, ON THE LATTER'S GOLDEN JUBILEE, 1913

May 27, 1913

My dear Mother M. Clare, (Leeson)

Your old friend who was the agent of whom God made use, to bring you from Ballinrobe in dear Ireland, to the Convent of Mercy, Manchester, in 1860 or perhaps 1861. Your old friend, then known as Sister Mary Patrick, now wishes to offer you her sincere congratulations on the coming happy anniversary of the 50th year of your holy Profession. I recall your entrance in the Novitiate there, when I was Mistress of Novices. As dear Rev. Mother Xavier Warde would not use the masculine form of the name, I was called Patricia. You remember, therefore, that she brought me to Philadelphia which has been my happy Convent home since 1861. This address of this house means the same Diocese of Philadelphia. It is the Mother House and is the center of about 30 acres of ground and is therefore more adapted for a Novitiate than the one occupied by the

Sisters in the City. Sister M. Agnes Patricia writes to me sometimes, and it was from a letter of hers that I learned of your Jubilee in June, and I send you my word of loving remembrance and good wishes now, for I think it will take some time to reach you, as I have no idea of your location but through Portland. I hope it will arrive by the 11th. I was sorry to hear Sr. Agnes Patricia and your youngest sister, M. Camilla, were both very ill, but I am glad to hear that both are better, and were staying on a visit to recruit, in the Mother House of Manchester, Hookset Heights, which, I hear, is a very beautiful place.

My dear Mother M. Clare, I hear you are bright and strong and at all the exercises of the Community and that you are in your 76th year, and otherwise active, thank God. I am, also, first in the Chapel every morning, and at all the exercises, and I am in my 80th year; but I take a rest, every day, and my Assistant attends to the active duties of a Superior for me, for I walk but slowly, and stairs would be difficult to me more than once a day. Our Chapel is on the same floor (the 2nd.) as the Community room. We are both grateful to God, and I hope we will meet in Heaven for God has blessed us on earth, my dear M. Clare.

Your old Sister in J.C.,
M. M. Patricia

(M. Patricia Waldron came from Ballinrobe, Ireland, to Manchester with Sr. Mary Philomena Hughes and Sr. M. de Sales Geraghty.)[28]

MOTHER PATRICIA WALDRON RECORDS INTERNATIONAL NOVENA PETITIONING THAT CATHERINE MCAULEY BE DECLARED "VENERABLE," 1914

February 2, 1914

First holy Mass of the Novena humbly offered in union with all the members of the Order throughout the world to make petition that our revered Foundress, Mother McAuley, be declared "Venerable" by the Church on earth.

My dear Sisters, we hope to show ourselves as her worthy daughters in this holy Institute of Our Lady of Mercy.

Ash Wednesday: Last Day of Novena

The Novena petitioning God for the Beatification of our revered Foundress ends February 10, but the true Daughters of the Order of Mercy will continue to show in their daily lives the faithful observance of our holy rule.

Humility, charity, and obedience will not fail to draw down the blessings we earnestly desire.

Amen[29]

LETTER OF GRATITUDE TO SISTERS OF MERCY OF GRAND RAPIDS, MICHIGAN, FOR THEIR SERVICES IN TERRIFYING EPIDEMIC OF INFLUENZA AND PNEUMONIA, 1918

A. M. D. G.
Knights of Columbus
War Activities
Camp Grant, Illinois

October 7, 1918

My dear Mother Thomas:—We are in the midst of a very terrifying epidemic of influenza and pneumonia. Over ten thousand have had a touch of the disease. The base-hospital is filled to overflowing. We chaplains have all but lived there. I have just returned from there and have grasped this free moment to write you a few lines in commendation of the nurses who came at the end of the week from St. Mary's Hospital, Grand Rapids. They are doing heroic work. Besides their strictly nursing duties, they have been of unexceptional aid to us priests in finding our Catholic men. In one long ward, one of them had a list of all Catholics awaiting me. She said, in the most matter of fact way: "We always find out their religion first thing." Another had baptized a patient who was unconscious when I reached his side. I gave the other sacraments.

Many a poor soul has had his way opened up in heaven because of the judicious care of the nurses trained under your Sisters and I want to let you know of it. We of Grand Rapids can all be proud of them. A careless nurse would have neglected the spiritual side when it was evident that the material life was slipping away. Despite the most careful nursing, many are dying. We had 116 deaths yesterday, and 47 up to noon today.

Please tell Mother Gertrude of the Hospital how proud I am of her nurses.

I have office to say, and then I must return to the base-hospital; hence I can write no more.

Asking your prayers for all of us, I am,

Yours very sincerely,
A. A. Fitzpatrick

1st Prov. Reg. Hd.,
161st Depot Brigade,
Camp Grant, Illinois[30]

LETTER FROM AMERICAN RED CROSS, LOUISVILLE, KENTUCKY, TO
SISTER M. HILDA, SUPERIOR, SISTERS OF MERCY, CINCINNATI,
CONCERNING SERVICE OF SISTERS DURING EPIDEMIC
OF WORLD WAR I, 1918

THE AMERICAN RED CROSS
Lake Division
Columbia Building
Louisville, KY

November 30, 1918

Our Lady of Mercy Academy,
Cincinnati, Ohio
Attention: Sister M. Hilda, Mother Superior

Dear Madam,

Your letter of the 27th was received yesterday together with your expense account. In that you will find you have made a mistake of $1.00, the charge for thermometers—10 at $1.12 $\frac{1}{2}$ should be $11.25 instead of $10.25, and therefore the check enclosed is for $302.98. Also enclosed find the Field Voucher made out in triplicate. Will you please sign these where checked and return for our files.

I am so distressed to hear that one of your number paid "the supreme sacrifice" after her heroic work in helping others. She no less gave her life for her country than did our brave boys; for this Flu epidemic threatened our country most seriously, and nowhere was the suffering more than in our mountain section. I know that you did everything to save her, but that her life went as she wanted it to go in doing for others.

Hoping most sincerely that the others who answered this call are well, I am,

Gratefully,
R. C. Banard Thurston
Asst. Manager, Lake Division for KY

Enclosure[31]

ON HAPPY MEMORIES AND SAD PARTING IN IRELAND,
FROM THOMAS LEAHY, LOUGHREA, IRELAND,
TO SISTER COLUMBIA MARIE LEAHY,
HIS SISTER, IN CINCINNATI, 1919

Grallagh
Loughrea
8th. June '19

My Dear Sister,

John and I are just back after a fortnight's visit home together. We had quite a splendid time. . . . Our old home is somewhat neglected and nothing of Shiel's now remains—only some old walls. . . . I know that no one of us cried so much as you did when you were leaving. I was up at the school and at the bog, and the day was summer-like. I could easily picture the old times. They were happy ones. . . . How I enjoyed the ramble over the old hills and listened to the well remembered ripple of every stream, saw the sun glisten on the rocks; met the children coming from school. They are nearly all strangers to me and would be to you too. They are ruddy-cheeked, happy, very happy dearlings. The whole scene was a treat to me. The sun was shining. Did you ever notice that in your dreams of home, it is spring? There was a dreary hum of flies, the skylarks were singing, the swallows were flying around as only they can. One of the Kellys was whistling at a dog which was driving the cattle too fast. Pat was sowing cabbage. We had a long chat about Mike, R.I.P. They all expect a fellow to have tea and it is hard to get away.

I sat on the hill where we so often played. Every nook and rock unchanged. I thought of you very much then. Those hills and the old school where today the teacher tells the story of your life and holds you up as an example to the students. A magpie has built her nest again in one of the Scotch firs in our garden. There are no youngsters to climb up there to disturb her now. I suppose she doesn't regret the change anyway. I went up across the hill and had a chat with John Shawn Kelly. He told me that people are glad to pay a pound for a load of turf. He used to sell it one time for 4 or 5 shillings. Our old house is in good repair. Of course, I explored it too. There was no one around—so I had plenty of time to daydream. . . . Home and happiness are now in Grallagh. . . .

My dear Mary Kathleen, as we all still call you, we all hope you are well and happy. We often think and speak of you, and you are in our prayers. . . . I will now close by sending you from all of us our very best love and wishes for your happiness.

From your ever loving brother,
Thomas[32]

MOTHER GENEVIEVE, DUBUQUE, IOWA, TO MISS HELEN O'CONNOR,
JANESVILLE, WISCONSIN, LATER SISTER MARY VIRGINIA,
ON THE MEANING OF RELIGIOUS LIFE, 1926

Mount Saint Agnes
Dubuque. Feb. 27

Miss Helen O'Connor
306 Lincoln Street
Janesville, Wis.

My dear Helen:
After reading your letter, I set about looking up something that would throw light upon a subject that seems to be interesting you very much just now. You have the booklets before this, and in them you will find an answer to many of your questions.

What is the religious life? It is a special call from our Lord to leave all to follow Him, and the young soul says whole-heartedly, if not in words, in act, "Lord, here I am." Is it easy to leave home and friends and sometimes country to follow the call? Oh, no. But the Master has promised a hundredfold in this life and heaven in the next to those who follow the call. Speaking for myself, the call was so strong that I never doubted it, either before or after entering the convent, and I am wearing the habit since February 7, 1872—figure the time for yourself. Trials and difficulties there are, of course, but a look at the cross shows how our Lord loves and we are always under the roof with Him in the Blessed Sacrament.

Now, does this satisfy you? If not, ask some more questions.

One word to yourself. If you feel grace calling you, pray hard and consult your confessor. I would be pleased if you had a vocation to the higher life. Being a Sister of Mercy, naturally, you know where I would like to see you, but I would not say a word to dissuade you from joining any Order to which you felt called. All are beautiful, but to *me* the Mercies are the finest in the world.

The Novitiate is a model Convent; it is a training school for religious life. The postulants are kept about six months before they receive the veil, then they are novices. For a period of two years their time is given to prayer, instruction, study and work. They are taught to observe the rule, and are instructed in the knowledge and practice of the vows they will make at the end of that time. They have two ends in view: their own sanctification, which is first and most important, and the service of the neighbor. To an outsider the days seem monotonous, but if you heard them laughing at their free time, you would think them the happiest people in the world—and they are.

I hope your dear Father is feeling better again. I am sure you all enjoy having John with you for a few days. That reminds me that I'd like to be on very good terms with him, too, as I expect to attend the Eucharistic Congress. [Chicago, 1926. We did.] He might like to do something for me that I'd like to have him do. Please send me his address sometime.

Love to everyone at home, and a special love for you, dear.

Ever yours in our Lord,
Sister Mary
Genevieve[33]

GEORGE C. RYAN, LAWYER, TO SISTER EDWARDINE, ON MOTHER ALPHONSUS AS A WONDERFUL SUBJECT FOR A BOOK, SAGINAW, MICHIGAN, 1928

Law Office of
George C. Ryan
Miller Block
Court and Hamilton Sts.
Saginaw, N.S., Mich.

December 13, 1928

Dear Sister Edwardine:

I have your favor of the 7th in reference to the Thielman family: also the card and the book for which I thank you.

As I promised you, I took upon myself an investigation of the history of the Thielman family intending to run it down through the New York City directory. With this in view I called on the Polk Co. in Detroit, but was unable to get anything for you. If, however, you will write to R. L. Polk & Co., 524 Broadway, N.Y., you can get the names and residences of this family, for years, and you may also use this information in running down other facts and circumstances.

If you like to write and I know you do, in Mother Alphonsus you have a wonderful subject. You are privileged to tell the story of a builder, a general, and a heroine. As a builder, her foundations will wear longer than the universe; as a general, she met daily in mortal combat the combined powers and principalities of darkness and, unarmed like David of Old with her beads in hand, she was victorious; as a heroine, her life will include one of the greatest romances ever written. All you have to do is review her early struggle; tell of her hazards; picture her in the lumber camps and her care of the lumber jacks, how she met poverty and difficulty, and you have written that book.

Respectfully yours,
George C. Ryan[34]

ON THE QUALITY OF THE FIRST MERCY BOARDING SCHOOL
IN THE UNITED STATES, BY SISTER M. XAVIER REILLY
OF THE MONASTERY OF THE VISITATION,
PARKERSBURG, WEST VIRGINIA, 1931

Dear Sister Josephine (Gately),
    . . . . I am an Alumna of your very first boarding school, St. Xavier's, Latrobe, and knew well some of the Sisters who in childhood were acquainted with the Foundress. Among them was dear Mother Ligouri McCaffrey who will ever live in my memory as the personification of gentleness, firmness, religious reserve, affability, and everything else that beautifies the feminine character. She was for many years the idolized directress of the Academy. . . . Most of the faculty had been St. Xavier's girls and knew the old traditions. It would be difficult to find anywhere a cloister that harmonizes so perfectly as St. Xavier's. The example of these Sisters has been my guiding star. . . . The impressions . . . made are indelible. I can never thank God enough for having known so well the daughters of Catherine McAuley. Mother Elizabeth Strange, one of the founders of your Order in the United States, I knew well. . . . I may say I knew the Sisters of Mercy from infancy. . . . I never can say enough in favor of the Sisters of Mercy. They are the most perfect picture of the stainless woman of Nazareth that I ever met, during my childhood and youth. To think of them is a prayer. They knew the human heart and could fertilize the barren soil, producing fruit when . . . all seemed hopeless. . . .[35]

CHIEF LOUIS NICHOLAS, GOVERNOR OF INDIAN RESERVATION,
OLD TOWN, MAINE, PROTESTING ATTEMPT OF GOVERNMENTAL
OFFICIALS TO REMOVE SISTERS OF MERCY FROM THE SCHOOLS

Indian Island
Old Town, Maine
November 16, 1932

Reverend Mother Eugenia:
    We the undersigned, residents of the Penobscot Indian Reservation, in appreciation of their considerate and consistent work, do hereby apply to you not to remove the Sisters of Mercy from our Reservation. We promise to give them our support, consideration and respect.
    For fifty years the Sisters of Mercy, who know no home but the Heart of Our Lord, have labored untiringly among the Penobscot Indians. Many sacrifices were made by them for the education of our children.

From the first, the Sisters' work was not confined to secular studies, but many weary hours were spent visiting the sick and the dying.

Since 1881, State Officials appointed by the Government to investigate the conditions of the Maine Indians have been unanimous in their high praise and appreciation of the labors of the Sisters among the Indians. As late as 1930, that praise was heard through a statement issued by Mr. W. O. Chase, Superintendent of the Old Town and Orono School Department concerning the Indian children who came from the Island to the Old Town Schools:

"I have carefully examined the records of every Indian child attending the Old Town Junior and Senior High Schools. I find that in their work they have maintained standards somewhat above the average of the schools as a whole. I also have carefully examined the records which they made during the first year after their transfer to the Old Town schools. Not one of the pupils now in school failed in his work during the first year."

Considering the facts stated herein, we hope you will grant us our request.[36]

LETTER TO A FRIEND ON THE DEATH OF MOTHER BAPTIST RUSSELL, FOUNDER AND FIRST SUPERIOR OF SAN FRANCISCO CONGREGATION

What sympathy has been poured out by the whole city for the loss of the great, good Mother of the Poor, Mother Baptist Russell, whom God has taken to heaven. Was there ever another like her, so gentle, so tender, so sympathetic, so big-hearted? And that rich contralto voice, and those beautiful grey eyes; 'tis sure we shall never look on her like again. And now she has left you all, sorrowing and lonesome. But, ah! if we were good Christians, 'tis singing canticles we ought to be that the bride is enjoying the happiness of heaven. Little did she have to atone for. Possibly she may have had to say, "Lord, I loved the poor too much"; and inasmuch as He Himself became a fool through love, He will not have found it hard to forgive her.[37]

BISHOP MATTHEW F. BRADY, MANCHESTER, TO THE PEOPLE OF MANCHESTER ON THE GOLDEN JUBILEE OF SISTERS OF MERCY IN NEW HAMPSHIRE, 1958

September 7, 1958

To the Clergy and Laity:

The State of New Hampshire, whether it realizes it or not, owes a tremendous debt to the Sisters of Mercy. They came here over a hundred years ago, a small valiant group of devoted women, to teach not only the works of Christian charity and eternal truth, but also the rudiments of what we now call secular education. . . . The then ruling fathers of our community hired their services for a pittance in the public school system. There were no other teachers available. . . . The expanding Mercy Community eventually was able to replace them, but their initial services to the community did not cease during one hundred years, but broadened out into the parochial school system that now saves taxpayers more than $\frac{3}{4}$ million dollars annually. . . . The Sisters of Mercy are the largest as well as the longest contributors to this happy eventuality. . . . What would the Church have done without them? They are the outstanding factors in the strength of the faith today as well as in the past generations. . . .[38]

A LETTER ON LOVE FROM A MERCY SISTER TO A FRIEND, BIG RAPIDS, MICHIGAN. AUTHOR AND DATE UNKNOWN

My very dear _____ :

Do not imagine that the love of God is a bar to all that is tenderest and deepest in human affection. Has it not, on the contrary, been proved over and over again that no earthly love is permanent and secure that is not built on the foundation of this higher love? When we love without reference to God, we set up an idol in His place, and sooner or later we discover its insufficiency to satisfy us. The bright painting and guilding wears off after a while, and nothing remains but the bare void.

Our hearts are made for the Infinite. Is it any wonder the finite should always come just short of filling them? It is an ideal that we worship; we expect perfection, perfect sympathy, perfect love. Can we be surprised that, perhaps through no fault of those on whom we set our hearts, these hearts are turned back upon themselves with a nameless, aching disappointment?

The only love that endures on earth, the only love that passes into heaven, is the love that is founded on God. When God is enthroned in his proper place in the heart, all is order, all is peace, all is happiness. We love as tenderly, perhaps more tenderly than others, the dear friends He gives us, but we do not look for perfection in them. We know where alone that is to be found. For the rest, we bear and forebear, sometimes meeting with slight disappointments, but receiving again with compensations more than we could have expected or hoped for; and at the most, we always have that first, best, changeless, satisfying love to fall back upon.

When creatures are loved with God, for God, in God, that love is not based on fleeting personal charms or natural endowments, but on the little way of God's beauty, the little spark of His goodness that has touched and transfigured their souls. Time's icy breath can never chill such love: it will grow and strengthen with years, and only reach its full perfection in our Father's eternal home.[39]

Notes

1. Annals, Carlow, Ireland, June, 1844.
2. *Ibid.,* 1851.
3. Mother Austin Carroll, *Annals, IV,* 1895, pp. 23–24.
4. E.G.P. to Hattie Dix, Manchester, New Hampshire, March 13, 1865. *Ibid.,* pp. 203–04.
5. *Ibid.,* pp. 284–85. No Date.
6. Mother M. Baptist Russell, August 10, 1868. Archives, San Francisco.
7. Kent Stone, Cambridge, Massachusetts, to Frances Warde, Manchester, New Hampshire, December 16, 1870. Archives, Manchester, New Hampshire.
8. Carroll, *Annals, III,* pp. 214–15, January 28, 1872 and April 15, 1873.
9. Archives, Philadelphia, March 17, 1876.
10. Carroll, *Annals, III,* p. 216, March 15, 1878.
11. An original, undated letter. Archives, Silver Spring, Maryland.
12. Carroll, *Annals, IV,* pp. 317–18.
13. Sister Mary Aurelia McArdle, *op. cit.,* pp. 40–41.
14. Archives, New Orleans.
15. Sister M. Ignatius, Savannah, Georgia, to Mother Baptist Russell, San Francisco, August 15, 1893. Archives, San Francisco.
16. Archives, New Orleans. Author Unknown. No Date. Carroll, *Annals, IV,* pp. 528–29.
17. *Ibid, III,* pp. 152–54; *IV,* 540.
18. McArdle, *op. cit.,* 92–93.
19. January 20, 1883. Archives, Manchester.
20. Archives, Manchester.

21. *Ibid.,* January 24, 1883.
22. Carroll, *Annals,* III, pp. 439–41.
23. Sister Elizabeth Strange, St. Lawrence O'Toole, Pittsburgh to Sister M. Gertrude, Loretto and Cresson, Pennsylvania, 1890. Archives, Pittsburgh and Silver Spring.
24. Sister Mary Genevieve, Chicago, from St. Xavier's Academy, Beatty, Pennsylvania, to Sister Mary Thomas, St. Xavier's Academy, Chicago, October 20, 1893. Archives, Chicago.
25. McArdle, *op. cit.,* pp. 156–57, September 26, 1898.
26. Sister M. Paul Quigley to Sister Mary Philomena, Grand Rapids, Michigan, Christmas, 1903. Archives, Detroit.
27. From S.J.Q., Cook County Jail, Chicago, to a Sister of Mercy, September 15, 1904. Archives, Chicago.
28. Archives, Portland, Maine. May 27, 1913.
29. Archives, Philadelphia. February 2, 1914.
30. Camp Grant, Illinois, October 7, 1918. Archives, Detroit.
31. R. C. Banard Thurston, Assistant Manager, American Red Cross, Louisville, Kentucky, to Sister M. Hilda, Superior, Cincinnati, Ohio, November 13, 1918. Archives, Cincinnati.
32. June 8, 1919. Archives, Cincinnati.
33. February 28, 1926. Archives, Detroit.
34. Big Rapids Convent, December 13, 1928. Archives, Detroit.
35. To Sister Josephine Gately, St. Mary's, Pittsburgh, August, 1931. Archives, Pittsburgh.
36. Old Town, Maine, November 16, 1932. Archives, Portland, Maine.
37. Sister Arurelia McArdle, *op. cit.,* pp. 184–85. No Date. Author Unknown.
38. September 7, 1958. Archives, Manchester.
39. Archives, Detroit.

INDEX

Other Volumes in This Series